Shakespeare in Hollywood, Asia, and Cyberspace

Comparative Cultural Studies,
Steven Tötösy de Zepetnek, Series Editor

The Purdue University Press monograph series of Books in Comparative Cultural Studies publishes single-authored and thematic collected volumes of new scholarship. Manuscripts are invited for publication in the series in fields of the study of culture, literature, the arts, media studies, communication studies, the history of ideas, etc., and related disciplines of the humanities and social sciences to the series editor via email at <clcweb@purdue.edu>. Comparative cultural studies is a contextual approach in the study of culture in a global and intercultural context and work with a plurality of methods and approaches; the theoretical and methodological framework of comparative cultural studies is built on tenets borrowed from the disciplines of cultural studies and comparative literature and from a range of thought including literary and culture theory, (radical) constructivism, communication theories, and systems theories; in comparative cultural studies focus is on theory and method as well as application. For a detailed description of the aims and scope of the series including the style guide of the series link to <http://docs.lib.purdue.edu/clcweblibrary/seriespurdueccs>. Manuscripts submitted to the series are peer reviewed followed by the usual standards of editing, copy editing, marketing, and distribution. The series is affiliated with *CLCWeb: Comparative Literature and Culture* (ISSN 1481-4374), the peer-reviewed, full-text, and open-access quarterly published by Purdue University Press at <http://docs.lib.purdue.edu/clcweb>.

Volumes in the Purdue series of Books in Comparative Cultural Studies
<http://www.thepress.purdue.edu/comparativeculturalstudies.html>

Shakespeare in Hollywood, Asia, and Cyberspace, Ed. Alexander C.Y. Huang and Charles S. Ross

Comparative Central European Holocaust Studies, Ed. Louise O. Vasvári and Steven Tötösy de Zepetnek

Marko Juvan, *History and Poetics of Intertextuality*

Thomas O. Beebee, *Nation and Region in Modern American and European Fiction*

Paolo Bartoloni, *On the Cultures of Exile, Translation, and Writing*

Justyna Sempruch, *Fantasies of Gender and the Witch in Feminist Theory and Literature*

Kimberly Chabot Davis, *Postmodern Texts and Emotional Audiences*

Philippe Codde, *The Jewish American Novel*

Deborah Streifford Reisinger, *Crime and Media in Contemporary France*

Imre Kertész and Holocaust Literature, Ed. Louise O. Vasvári and Steven Tötösy de Zepetnek

Camilla Fojas, *Cosmopolitanism in the Americas*

Comparative Cultural Studies and Michael Ondaatje's Writing, Ed. Steven Tötösy de Zepetnek

Jin Feng, *The New Woman in Early Twentieth-century Chinese Fiction*

Comparative Cultural Studies and Latin America, Ed. Sophia A. McClennen and Earl E. Fitz

Sophia A. McClennen, *The Dialectics of Exile*

Comparative Literature and Comparative Cultural Studies, Ed. Steven Tötösy de Zepetnek

Comparative Central European Culture, Ed. Steven Tötösy de Zepetnek

Shakespeare in Hollywood, Asia, and Cyberspace

Edited by

Alexander C.Y. Huang and Charles S. Ross

Purdue University Press
West Lafayette, Indiana

Printed in the United States of America.

Library of Congress Cataloging-in-Publication Data

Shakespeare in Hollywood, Asia, and Cyberspace / edited by Alexander C.Y. Huang and Charles S. Ross.
p. cm. -- (Comparative cultural studies)
Includes index.
ISBN 978-1-55753-529-0
1. Shakespeare, William, 1564-1616--Influence. 2. Shakespeare, William, 1564-1616--Adaptations--History and criticism. 3. Shakespeare, William, 1564-1616--Appreciation--Asia. 4. Shakespeare, William, 1564-1616--Film and video adaptations. I. Huang, Alexander C. Y. (Alexander Cheng-Yuan) II. Ross, Charles Stanley.
PR2880.A1S575 2009
822.3'3--dc22

2009007092

Contents

List of Illustrations

Introduction to *Shakespeare in Hollywood, Asia, and Cyberspace*

Alexander C.Y. Huang and Charles S. Ross

With the rise of Asian economic power, new possibilities of creation ushered by Web 2.0, and an unparalleled global interest in Shakespeare, the present time is especially propitious for studying the complex relations between Shakespeare, Hollywood, Asia, and cyberspace. What is entailed in the cultural practice of screening, in both senses of the verb, Shakespeare in transnational audio-visual idioms in modern times? The past decades have witnessed diverse incarnations and bold sequences of screen and stage Shakespeares that gave rise to productive encounters between the ideas of Asia and of Shakespeare. Kurosawa's *Throne of Blood* (*Macbeth*, 1957) and *Ran* (*Lear*, 1985) are far from the earliest or the only Shakespeare films from Asia; around the time Asta Nielsen's cross-dressed *Hamlet* (1921) was filmed, gender-bender silent film adaptations of *The Merchant of Venice* and *Two Gentlemen of Verona* were being made in Shanghai. In 2006, mainland China director Feng Xiaogang adapted *Hamlet*, Hollywood visual language, and the martial arts genre in his feature film *The Banquet*. Hollywood films such as Baz Luhrmann's *William Shakespeare's Romeo+Juliet* and John Madden's *Shakespeare in Love* have inspired creative re-interpretations of these films and of *Romeo and Juliet* in Anthony (Yau) Chan's Hong Kong film *One Husband Too Many* and Cheah Chee Kong's Singaporean film *Chicken Rice War*.

In the other direction, Hollywood and the global economy in general have brought Asian cultures forcefully into the Western cultural register, as evidenced by the mediation and reception of Shakespeare and world cultures on screens big and small, including silent film, television, feature film, documentary, and such media as online games, anime, and YouTube. Two prominent examples are Kenneth Branagh's *As You Like It* (2006), set in Japan, and the appropriation of eastern spirituality in Thich Nah Hanh's scene in Michael Almereyda's *Hamlet* (2000). In both directions of the intercultural traffic, Asian audio-visual idioms have been appropriated along with Shakespeare's text on stage and on screen. Therefore, we need to ask: On what terms do transnational Shakespeares animate and redirect the traffic between different geo-cultural or virtual localities? In turn, how do the collaborative processes of signification operate as local stagings of Shakespeare and global locales?

These are some of the questions that have inspired the present collection of articles on a truly global array of appropriative strategies. The proliferation of re-interpretations of Shakespeare in the present time calls for sophisticated models of theorization. At stake is how to reinvent the interpretive energy by destabilizing conventionalized interpretations of "Shakespeare" and its Others—past, present, and to come. Fully attuned to the intricate dynamics between different localities and between the ideology of print and other media, such a theory will help us to understand how and when Shakespeare becomes a necessary signifier against which popular and world cultures define themselves on screen, how the ideas of Asia operate in such a film as Branagh's *As You Like It*, what ideological understanding of Shakespeare informs a computer game such as *Arden: The World of Shakespeare*, a MMOG (massively multiplayer online game), and many other new questions. This collection of essays represents a collaborative effort to bring into productive dialogue studies of Shakespeare in Asian and Western forms of cultural production that range from theater to cinema to cyberspace.

The cultural translation of Shakespeare into Hollywood may be regarded as a commercial enterprise in the same way that the presence of his plays in Asia may be thought of as a colonial legacy. One may bemoan the loss of the language or the vision or the "essence" of Shakespeare and imagine what further horrors the translation to cyberspace has in store. Or one may think of the glass as half full. That is, one may accept the obvious limitations of film as a visual rather than a verbal medium; regard the problems of translation into a language like Chinese as an opportunity to perhaps bring Asian culture to the attention of Americans and vice versa; and look forward to the development of cyberspace as a place that might just make it possible to restore the old-fashioned pleasures of textual reading and creative performance of more than just the few scenes of Shakespeare that linger in the popular imagination, a place that fosters an enabling relation between Shakespeare in print and in other media.

There are, after all, at least thirty-six Shakespeare plays, many waiting their turn for renewal. Each has an uncanny ability to appeal to a generation or a culture: the hesitating Hamlet dominated the European imagination after the fall of Napoleon, as Isaiah Berlin has argued, just as *King Lear* and *Macbeth* struck a chord in twentieth-century Japanese and Chinese cultures. *Troilus and Cressida* was a cult play for the antiwar generation's experience in Vietnam. As shown by some of the essays collected in this volume, Shakespeare's other plays have been used to comment on politics in China. But Shakespeare is about more than political resonance. For Mozart, every key had an associated emotion—one key for seduction, another for anger. Similarly, Shakespeare's plays strike chords often difficult to hear because our experience is limited. At a lecture at Tatung University in Taipei a student asked what prevented *Pericles*, that mystical Mediterranean voyage of discovery, from being performed or filmed or read with sympathy in Taiwan. He wondered if there was a way to bring its subtle religious themes and brooding sense of morality into the Asian experience; or rather, he wondered why it had not been done. Similarly, one may be surprised that comedies such as *The Taming of the Shrew* and *A Midsummer Night's Dream* are a staple of student productions in Asia, since one generally thinks of comedy as more culturally bound than tragedy. It may be that it takes a different culture, perhaps a local city or island or language, to remind us of some aspect of Shakespeare that has a claim on our attention.

This volume is about how Shakespeare has played out in film, performance, and scholarly projects that connect Asia and English-speaking America. About half of this volume derives from a thematic issue of *CLCWeb: Comparative Leterature and Culture 6.1* (2004) <http://docs.lib.purdue.edu/clcweb/vol6/iss1/> entitled *Shakespeare in Asia and Hollywood*, edited by Charles S. Ross (the volume at hand is Annual 4 of the journal in the Purdue monograph series of Books in Comparative Cultural Studies). The other half of this volume derives from selected and peer-reviewed papers presented at symposia or conference panels Alexander C.Y. Huang organized, as well as articles by the editors' invitation. The editors are proud to present the work in the volume on the multifaceted relationships between Shakespeare and Hollywood, China, Indonesia, Cambodia, Japan, Taiwan, Malaya, Korea, and Hong Kong to complement the articles on film, which naturally focus on Akira Kurosawa, one of the key Shakespeare filmmakers, as they provide a rich cultural background for his work. The result is a volume in three interconnected sections, each of which questions the products of cultural translation while also recognizing the value of finding ways to connect Asian and Anglo-European modes of representation. Further, the volume includes a fourth section with a chronology of Shakespeare in Hollywood, Asia, and Cyberspace and a selected bibliography on the same topic.

Localization and appropriation

Despite the significance of textual and performative appropriations, critical ideologies and biases have, for a long time, relegated them to the periphery and limited the interpretive possibilities. As late as 1988, "localization" was still viewed as "intolerable, imprisoning," according to Leah Marcus, who traced the attitude back to 1623, suggesting that

> Even though every interpreter of Shakespeare depends on the work of previous 'localizers' for such basic things as determining the order of the plays' composition and establishing the texts in which we read them, we have tended to set such work apart from the mainstream, as though by assigning the localizers to a fenced-in preserve we can minimize their impact on something we are willing to perceive only as universal and without limits. The tendency is not new. Even though the word *localization* dates only from the nineteenth century, resistance to the activity it names goes back, in the case of Shakespeare, at least as far as 1623. More than any other English writer, Shakespeare has been made the bearer of high claims for the universality of art. (*Puzzling Shakespeare* 1-2)

If textual and performative reconfigurations can be broadly categorized as acts of appropriation, the subjects of appropriation are certainly not only Shakespeare's texts as presented during his lifetime but also local politics (in temporal and spatial terms). As productions like Heiner Müller's *Hamletmachine* (1978), Ariane Mnouchkine's *kabuki*- and *noh*-inflected *Richard II* in Paris in 1981, David McRuvie and Annette Leday's *Kathakali King Lear* at the Globe in London in 2000, Yukio Ninagawa's multiple Shakespeare productions for European festivals, and Ong Keng Sen's *Search: Hamlet* with a multinational cast that appropriated European and Asian performance idioms (2002) have shown, staging a Shakespearean play is a process not simply of representing that play itself but rather of negotiating the dynamics between the locality Shakespeare represents and the locality of the performers and the audience.

Further, some appropriations have themselves become subjects to be appropriated; historically, the works that constitute Shakespeare's afterlife do not always remain secondary. Many productions have had afterlives of their own (Huang; Gallimore). The Restoration and eighteenth century produced some of most perplexing cases. Nahum Tate's *King Lear* dominated the English stage until 1836, and David Garrick's *Catherine and Petruchio* was regularly staged until 1887. Goethe's *Hamlet*-inspired *Bildungsroman*, *Wilhelm Meisters Lehrjahre* (1796), has an extended presence in Novalis's *Heinrich von Ofterdingen* (1802) and Penelope Fitzgerald's *The Blue Flower* (1995). Beyond Europe, Tsubouchi Shōyō's translations have had a lasting legacy in Japan, while Shu Lin's rendition of Charles and Mary Lamb's *Tales from Shakespeare* has defined the first generation of Shakespearean performances in China and inspired a new project in 2001 to retranslate Shakespeare's plays in prose narratives—following the footsteps of the Lambs and Lin.

Although worldwide appropriation of Shakespeare is hardly a new phenomenon, this cultural practice did not become a subject of scholarly analysis until the early 1990s with the emergence of a handful of works on related topics, such as Michael Bristol's *Shakespeare's America, America's Shakespeare* (1991). When Jean I. Marsden published the landmark study, *The Appropriation of Shakespeare* (1991), she lamented the lack of scholarly attention to "Shakespeare after the Renaissance" and pointed out that "it is this void that [her collection] address[ed]" (5). Recognizing that "what we think of 'Shakespeare' is . . . culturally determined," Marsden contends, Shakespearean appropriations "present a view of Shakespeare embedded not only in his own culture but in ours, forcing us to consider both the impact we have on the plays and the impact they have on us" (8). Dennis Kennedy's groundbreaking works, *Foreign Shakespeare* (1993) and *Looking at Shakespeare* (1993)—although with an Anglo-European focus similar to Marsden's volume—made "foreign" Shakespearean appropriations important subjects of further scholarly inquiry. The 1991 World Shakespeare Congress in Tokyo fueled the interest in the subject and led to the publication of *Shakespeare and Cultural Traditions* (1994), a collection of essays that examine the traffic between Shakespeare and world cultures (see Kishi). A decade of theoretical reflection and historical studies culminated in the launch in 2005 of a new peer-reviewed journal, *Borrowers and Lenders*, edited by Christy Desmet and Sujata Iyengar, that is devoted exclusively to the study of Shakespeare and appropriation.

Studies in the field broadly conceived as reception and audience studies (performance, film, popular culture) can be categorized into three related but different lines of work. The first mode of research brings critical theory to bear on various modes of representation (on and beyond the stage), as has been pursued by Michael Bristol, James Bulman, John Joughin, Barbara Hodgdon, Christy Desmet, and W.B. Worthen, among other key critics. The second mode of research draws upon case studies or specific stage histories. Some studies draw upon more personal experiences, such as John Russell Brown's *New Sites for Shakespeare: Theatre, the Audience and Asia*, while other studies concentrate on practices in specific cultures and their theoretical implications (see Dessen, Shaughnessy, Hoenselaars). Still others focus on less familiar appropriations in Europe, Africa, Asia, and other locations, and provide analyses of important materials from these sites that contrast those sites that have been privileged by Anglo-American criticism. This line of work has broadened the horizon of Shakespeare studies (see Chaudhuri and Lim; Makaryk, Orkin, Hoenselaars, *Shakespeare's History Plays*; Esche). A third mode of research engages the histories and reception of Shakespeare's images, biographies, and reputation. One of the best-known works in this category is Gary Taylor's *Reinventing Shakespeare* (1989). A new contribution is *Shakespeares after Shakespeare*, edited by Richard Burt, a two-volume encyclopedia chronicling bits of Shakespeariana in mass media and popular culture. The present collection is the first book to consider Shakespeare across a spectrum of media, including cyberspace, and to examine, side by side, the cultural production of Shakespeare in Asia and in Hollywood.

While textual variations and editorial interventions raise similar issues and share general avenues of approach, textual permutations have not been widely recognized in terms of their appropriation of Shakespeare. A few works, however, do begin to treat textual strategies as acts of appropriation (see, e.g., Erickson's *Rewriting*, which examines Shakespeare's representation of women along with contemporary women's rewriting of Shakespeare; see also Erne and Kidnie). It is also worth mentioning that as appropriation received more critical attention in Shakespeare studies, other relevant fields were also affected by a renewed interest in the theoretical implications of adaptation as a genre. Film studies, in particular, witnessed the emergence of new works that revisit the question of authorship and representation (see Griffith; Cartmell and Whelehan; Naremore).

Reception studies that reassess historical circumstances have shown that the concepts of afterlife and appropriation can be paradoxical. If, as the critical language of our time suggests, literary works could not contain meanings in and by themselves, the notions of appropriation and the original would be redundant, for the "text" is constituted of nothing other than these permutations. This tendency is reflected in critical positions held by the reader-response theorists, by Julia Kristeva's notion of intertextuality, by Jacques Derrida's conception of the "iterability" as the nature of all texts, as well as by some Shakespeareans who subscribe to presentism, such as

Terence Hawkes and Graham Holderness. For example, Hawkes argues that texts cannot provide self-contained meanings; rather, "we mean by the text we choose" (*Meaning by Shakespeare* 3). On the other hand, if meanings are defined by nothing but the literary artifact, appropriation—in the sense of making something one's own—would not be possible. These issues form the core of critical debates not only in Shakespeare studies but also in fiction, film adaptations, and performance studies, prompting recent works to revisit the very problem with naming. In her 2006 book, *A Theory of Adaptation*, Linda Hutcheon devotes the preface and entire sections in section 1 of the book to discuss these problems. Daniel Fischlin and Mark Fortier, co-editors of the latest critical anthology of Shakespearean adaptations, devote similarly a section in their introduction to the problem of naming (which considers the inadequacies of terms such as adaptation, appropriation, parody, offshoot, alteration, spinoff) and a section to the relationship between adaptation and contemporary culture theory, emphasizing that adaptation is "not a simple rejection" of the notions of the author and the canon. Fischlin and Fortier argue that "to understand the cultural politics of adaptation, we must also examine how adaptation takes place within a certain structured relationship to . . . a broadly accepted group of works that is a consensual (though not uncontested) site of foregrounded study within the academy" (6).

Asian voices

The articles in the first section of the volume, Shakespeare in Hollywood, differ somewhat from those collected by Lynda Boose and Richard Burt, who argue in the introduction to their first edited collection of essays, *Shakespeare: The Movie*, that it is impossible to make comparisons between modern products and an original because the original referent is "no longer there." It is true enough that few people have the sensibilities of an Elizabethan or can know for sure what those sensibilities are, but there are a few problems with insisting that the original is no longer there. The phrase is self-contradictory, implying some magic moment of disappearance, but by the same token also suggesting some previous moment when Shakespeare's original had not yet disappeared. That is, the statement implies the existence of a time when the original was "there," before it gradually disappeared either over the centuries or in our personal development because our investment in the original takes on less meaning as our critical consciousness grows. Our assumption, instead, is that moment of origin never disappears, because directors have always had access to the text, more or less, and always will have. We challenge the presumption that Shakespeare is disappearing because such thinking blurs the difference between knowing what Shakespeare intended or what his audience understood with the presumption that Shakespeare did not mean anything and his audience did not read anything into his plays, which seems unlikely. The articles in the section on Shakespeare in Hollywood look at both text and film, and at how the directors look at text and film, for however sophisticated we may become in the ways of the cinema and the cultures for which these films are produced, Shakespeare on Film as a pedagogy can always find something to say about what directors put into a film and what they leave out. The young scholars of comparative literature, many from China and Taiwan, whose voices are heard in the opening section of the volume, generally start with the basic text and then develop reasons for the changes made in the transition from text and theater to film. They look for the ways in which Shakespeare has been culturally translated, either by modifications of the text or by the way directors substitute visual images for words as they search for cinematic equivalents to what they perceive to be the meaning of Shakespeare's texts.

Mei Zhu, in "Shakespeare's *Taming of the Shrew* and the Tradition of Screwball Comedy," analyzes Franco Zeffirelli's *Taming of the Shrew* as an example of the Hollywood genre of screwball comedy. Zhu helps us see the universal appeal of comedy in cultural terms by noting the influence of screwball comedy on Chinese film as well. Although Su Peirui, who contributes an essay titled "Shakespeare and Al Pacino's *Looking for Richard*," grew up in northern China, she developed a fascination with Al Pacino that in turn should fascinate American readers by providing a Chinese perspective on Pacino's film about producing Shakespeare's play *Richard III.* Pacino's film suits this cultural perspective because its theme in turn is Pacino's fascination with Shakespeare's play and what it meant to him as an actor famous for his role as Michael Corleone in *The Godfather.* We are all in a sense amateurs before Shakespeare. As Harry Levin once said, the goals of comparative literature are impossible. He could read and keep up in English, French, and German, but he had to draw the line at Korean. The conventions and sometimes disappointing formulas of Hollywood film, which remind us of our own cultural limitations, are the subject of Charles S. Ross's "Underwater Women in Shakespeare Films," which looks at the literary and film history of the underwater woman as an image of social oppression. Examples can be found in Chinese fiction, in Kate Chopin's *The Awakening*, and in various Hollywood films from the 1990s, including Luhrmann's *Romeo+Juliet*, Branagh's *Hamlet*, and Taymor's *Titus.* As the trope of the underwater woman indicates, cross-cultural relations are nowhere more strongly contested today than in the relation of women to power, the subject of Xianfeng Mou's "Cultural Anxiety and the Female Body in Zeffirelli's *Hamlet*." Using the insights of her own reading in feminist theory, Mou explains how the way Franco Zeffirelli films Gertrude and Ophelia in his version of *Hamlet* expresses a certain view of women and power. She also argues, in part, that the film techniques of Hollywood often disappoint us politically and as effective readings of Shakespeare.

Shakespeare and Asia, the remix

Gender and politics intertwine in the discourse on culture that characterizes many of the articles in the section on Asia in the volume. The first is David Bevington's article, "Imagining the East and Shakespeare's Asia," first presented at a Shakespeare seminar at National Taiwan University. Although as Bevington reminds us, Shakespeare's text always bears renewed scrutiny, the studies in the volume invite us to see anew something that has become familiarly known—Shakespeare's plays—and to contemplate the possibility that what seems an untroubled part of ourselves, as Stephen Greenblatt puts it, might not be something from a different time and place. Next, Yuwen Hsiung looks at Kurosawa's influence on two versions of *Macbeth* that were staged in China and Taiwan during the 1980s. The central issue is how to translate Shakespeare, and the solution comes in the form of Asian theatrical conventions that allow different perspectives on individuality while also introducing readers to the problem of literal Chinese translations of Shakespeare. Asian alterations of Shakespeare are also the subject of Lei Jin's essay, "Silence and Sound in Kurosawa's *Throne of Blood*." The thesis of the article is that Kurosawa uses silence, sound, and *noh* music as cinematic equivalents to Shakespeare's text, playing on the emotions of the audience in scenes such as Kurosawa's version of Macbeth's murder of King Duncan. In a related study, "The Visualization of Metaphor in Two Chinese Versions of *Macbeth*," Alexander Huang establishes the central importance of Shakespeare's language as the basis for the stage's audio-visual idiom, as it is for visualization in films and as it will be for whatever form the internet manages to provide: video games, searches, interactive websites. One would hope that language, dialogue, metrical stresses, the play of pauses, and every aspect of rhetoric would come alive in cyberspace, but we can only wait and see. Huang's essay leads into a series of essays on Shakespeare in performance in various locations throughout Asia.

Daniel Gallimore's article, "Shakespeare in Contemporary Japan," helps explain the primacy of Japan in this field by arguing that a lack of a dominant tradition has allowed the kind of creativity Western audiences find in Kurosawa's adaptations. As Gallimore says, "Shakespeare production in Japan is arguably as ephemeral as cyberspace in its detachment from any integrative tradition." The independent production companies whose work in recent years Gallimore surveys and a rich tradition should bring Japan to the attention of serious Shakespeareans. Part of that tradition centered around one of the several replicas in the world of the Globe Theater. In "The Tokyo Globe Years 1988-2002" Michiko Suematsu provides a detailed account of a company that experimented with various blends of Shakespeare, local tradition, and creativity. The goal was to find what worked in performance, as it was in Korea, Malaya, Okinawa, Cambodia, Indonesia, China, and Hong Kong, the geographical subjects of the next set of articles. As Meewon Lee shows in "Hamlet in Korea," Shakespeare came to Korea under the influence of Japan and through the surprising intermediary of Charles Lamb. British rather than Japanese colonial influence produced some humorous results but also drew on local culture in Malaya, as Nurul Farhana Low bt Abdulla shows in "Bangsawan Shakespeare in Colonial Malaya." Masae Suzuki provides historical detail to what in this volume becomes a familiar account of localization in her article "Shakespeare, *Noh*, *Kyōgen*, and Okinawa Shibai." Next, Evan Darwin Winet reviews the evidence for a seventeenth-century *Hamlet* in his article "Spectres of *Hamlet* in Colonial and Postcolonial Indonesia."

After these historical and geographical surveys the Asian section closes with two articles on contemporary performance. In "Remembering the Past in the Shanghai Jingju Company's *King Lear*" Elizabeth Wichmann-Walczak gives a fascinating, first-person account of the political environment and artistic decisions involved in a production of *King Lear* characterized by an intense interpretation of the play and traditional Chinese opera forms. Adele Lee then surveys the problem of postcolonialism where it may not be a problem in "*One Husband Too Many* and the Problem of Postcolonial Hong Kong." Here the educational system has to meet expectations that perhaps do not hinder performance.

Cyberspace, game space, and media

With the advent of new technologies of knowledge transmission, Shakespeare has become ubiquitous, available in print, theater, cinema, video game, online in various forms, and now as full text <http://www.playshakespeare.com/news/3668-shakespeare-on-iphone-update> and animated quotes on iPhone. In addition to asking what "Shakespeare" has become, we now have to ask: where is Shakespeare? Presumably if one wishes to look at *Hamlet* as one does the *Mona Lisa,* one can turn to the three editions printed between 1603 and 1623. Until recently, Shakespeare's plays have been firmly located within the bounds of the pages of the folios, quartos, editorially mediated modern editions, and to some extent performances. Digital media and the Internet have complicated the question of where *Hamlet* is. In some instances, new technologies challenge the ideological insistence in particular ways of reading Shakespeare. In other cases, these new technologies of knowing reify rather than deconstruct the idea of the printed text. Cyberspace (archives and interactive theater websites), game space in video and online games, and media illustrate the assumptions and problems of mediation in Shakespeare as a virtual event. Cyber Shakespeares may lead us to expect revolutionary new forms of engagement. And yet the ultimate goal of many online projects is to redirect the audiences to identifiable, palpable sites of the real.

Despite the radical virtualization of events, online games so far have been the staunchest guardians of the currency of the text, foregrounding squarely traditional values of the text and established interpretations of Shakespearean characters. One of the most ambitious games is *Arden: The World of Shakespeare*, a one-of-its-kind MMOG (massively multiplayer online game) currently being developed by Edward Castronova of Indiana University, with Linda Charnes as the consultant for contents related to Shakespeare's plays in *Arden: The World of William Shakespeare*. The game is built around Shakespeare's plays, beginning with *Richard III* in the first phase. Players walk around a virtual Elizabethan playground, with seventeenth-century regalia, London taverns, and characters from Shakespeare's works.

The mediation in *Arden* occurs on at least two levels. On the level of the virtual world, Castronova argues that *Richard III* fits easily into the MMOG conventions because of such elements as battles, "knights in shining armor, and peasants and woodworkers" (qtd. in Terdiman 1) in the play. On the pedagogic level, the game setting is designed to promote learning of Shakespeare, and the Shakespearean environment is used as a smoke screen for a virtual laboratory for research on macro-level social phenomena. On both levels, Shakespeare's texts, and not just Shakespeare's status as a canonical author, are emphasized repeatedly. In fact, soliloquies and speeches become collectible artifacts in the game. Both Castronova and Charnes believe that the unique element of Arden is Shakespearean texts, "many of which will be the most valuable treasure players can find" and Castronova explains: "If you collect the 'To be or not be' speech and then take it to a lore master or to a skilled bard, he can then apply the magic to your broad sword or you [could] utilize the magic in a battle situation to give you this massive [advantage]" (qtd. in Terdiman 2). This design initiates intensive competition for the best speeches of Shakespeare in the player's play book. *Arden* is by far the most innovative online project with the highest degree of user participation at the core of its design, going beyond the self-contained and controlled approach of most so-called interactive theater websites that promote specific productions. *Arden* envisions new audiences of Shakespeare who make conscious decisions in the process of collecting these texts, interact with other characters and players, and plot their movements. And yet *Arden*'s overwhelming emphasis of the text reveals a lot about the ethos of the designers and the fetishization of Shakespeare in contemporary culture. The *Arden* project turns out to be less radical than it may seem in the first instance. The project valorizes the aura of the texts, with a strong influence of the publishing history of Shakespeare, turning players into collectors of texts. A similar assumption informs the design of online games on the Royal Shakespeare Company's *Exploring Shakespeare* project website . In one of the "interpretation games" the user is asked to match excerpts from theater reviews with photos of particular productions from different time periods. Both the Royal Shakespeare Company's website and the *Arden* project prioritize commentary on historical interpretations rather than tools for users to create their own interpretations.

One hopes that performance and creative readings will always revive Shakespeare's text. Lucian Ghita, in his article "Fragmentation in Julie Taymor's *Titus*," starts with the opening scene that Peter Donaldson analyzed in terms of the revolving angles of a video game in order to give coherence to how Taymor's ritual vision takes the past and pushes it somehow into the future. Simone Caroti's article on "Science Fiction, *Forbidden Planet*, and Shakespeare's *Tempest*" is similarly a pre-vision of how Shakespeare can be accommodated to strange or at least different places, a process that connects all the essays in the volume. Richard Burt, in his article "Mobilizing Foreign Shakespeares in Media," takes a long view of the problem of postcolonial interpretation, setting Europe against Asia and stage against screen while suggesting numerous possibilities for future work in world of rapidly changing technology.

For now the challenge is that the places will not be "strange" enough, creativity not creative enough. Cyberspace is a search engine, as Christy Desmet and Sujata Iyengar show in their review of Shakespeare studies online in their article "Appropriation and the Design of an Online Shakespeare Journal." Cyberspace must not reify the past, enshrine interpretations, or close off creative outlets, as Peter Holland argues in the closing article of the section, "Performing Shakespeare for the Web Community." He suggests that this exciting cultural landscape calls for a careful critical reassessment of various assumptions. Internet Shakespeare does not supersede stage creativity or live nonvirtual performance. Rather, it creates a space between the backstage and the box office, between various virtual worlds, in which new communities can be formed. It is worth pointing out that although the volume concludes with articles on cyberspace, it should not be taken as a sign of de riguer celebration of new forms of expression as necessarily more liberating, desirable, or promising. What seems to be "social and intellectual advances in digital living" today (Lavagnino 194) may quickly give way to new technologies of reading and writing that will create and inhabit new cultural spaces (see Landow). One hopes that language itself will come alive, and that US-America can adopt transcultural Shakespeares—perhaps learn a little Chinese in the process—by means of the new technologies and that these articles provide an informative introduction on this important cultural exchange.

Critical apparatus and media

This being a book about Shakespeare performance and pedagogy in various media including cyberspace, it would be ironic not to put theory into practice. The critical apparatus of this collection is presented in two parts for two kinds of readers. Readers curious about the long history of the global travels of Shakespeare's texts can consult the chronology at the end of the book. Key historical events and media events (such as the release of a major Shakespeare film or the staging of a major production) are listed along with the most significant Asian-themed performances of Shakespeare. Each article can only necessarily focus on selected historical moments, but the chronology can help to contextualize the larger cultural contexts. The first chronology of its kind, it is both a useful pedagogic tool and an index for cross-referencing.

Scholars in the field and bona-fide Shakespeare fans will find the online *Shakespeare Performance in Asia* useful: it includes annotated streaming videos, an interactive catalogue of adaptations with faceted browsing, and dynamic maps to allow users to track the trajectory of an internationally released film or a touring production. While this continuously updated and open-access website was not created exclusively as a companion website for this book, Alexander Huang has been its core collaborator. The site is an interactive, web-based workspace designed to encourage not only further research on Shakespeare in Hollywood and Asia, but also critical reflection on motifs and questions such as cross-dressing, uses of mask, race-blind casting, and the nature of digital commentary and technologies of memory in the act of archiving and in films such as Michael Almereyda's *Hamlet*. The extended resource center on Asian-themed performances of Shakespeare (theater, film, TV) is based on Huang's research archive of videos and texts, including films, TV series, radio shows, videotaped stage productions, and cartoons from the Indian Subcontinent, Turkey, Southeast Asia, East Asia, Pacific Islands, New Zealand, Europe, and the US. Readers interested in details of the films, productions, or rewritings discussed in this collection can find on this website further transcriptions, translations, and critical notes (accompanied by videos and photographs), as well as interviews, reviews, stage bills, and primary research materials. The archive can provide rich opportunities for reflection on the ontology of performance.

It is hoped the articles in this collection and the critical apparatus will inspire more comparative studies of such topics as the appropriation of eastern spirituality in Almereyda's *Hamlet* and Kurosawa's *Throne of Blood*, and the intertextuality among the big-time and small-time screen Shakespeares: Baz Luhrmann's *William Shakespeare's Romeo+Juliet* and Anthony Chan's *One Husband Too Many*. As the essays demonstrate, variously articulated Shakespeares in Hollywood, Asia, and cyberspace have each evolved from something that is unfamiliar to something that is familiarly known on stages and screens big and small—something that now needs to be defamiliarized again. Just as Asian directors are no strangers to Shakespeare, the Anglo-European audience is growing familiar with Asian elements in Shakespearean performance, with Ariane Mnouchkine's and Yukio Ninagawa's productions being prominent examples. Whether watching these performances at their places of origin, on tour, or in cyberspace, with or without subtitles, readers, and audiences around the world, will continue to be inspired and provoked by the fascinating, although sometimes uncomfortable, gap between different cultures. The articles of the volume at hand provide an informative introduction on this important cultural exchange.

Acknowledgements

The editors would like to express their appreciation to editors at Purdue University Press and to Steven Tötösy de Zepetnek, editor of the Press's monograph series of Books in Comparative Cultural Studies, for their support of the publication of the present volume.

Works Cited

Arden: The World of Shakespeare. MMOG. <http://swi.indiana.edu/ardenworld.htm>.

Bristol, Michael. *Big-Time Shakespeare.* New York: Routledge, 1996.

Brown, John Russell. *New Sites for Shakespeare: Theatre, the Audience and Asia.* London: Routledge, 1999.

Bulman, James, ed. *Shakespeare, Theory, and Performance.* New York, Routledge, 1996.

Burt, Richard, ed. *Shakespeares after Shakespeare*. Westport: Greenwood P, 2006.

Cartmell, Deborah, and Imelda Whelehan, eds. *Adaptations: From Text to Screen, Screen to Text.* New York: Routledge, 1999.

Castronova, Edward, and Linda Charnes. *Arden: The World of William Shakespeare* (2006-): <http://swi.indiana.edu/ardenworld.htm>.

Derrida, Jacques. *Limited Inc.* Evanston: Northwestern UP, 1988.

Desmet, Christy, and Robert Sawyer, eds. *Shakespeare and Appropriation.* New York: Routledge, 1999.

Desmet, Christy and Sujata Iyengar, eds. *Borrowers and Lenders*: <http://www.borrowers.uga.edu>.

Dessen, Alan C. *Rescripting Shakespeare: The Text, the Director, and Modern Productions*. Cambridge: Cambridge UP, 2002.

Erickson, Peter. *Rewriting Shakespeare, Rewriting Ourselves.* Berkeley: U of California P, 1991.

Erne, Lucas, and Margaret Jane Kidnie, eds. *Textual Performances: The Modern Reproduction of Shakespeare's Drama*. Cambridge: Cambridge UP, 2004.

Esche, Edward J., ed. *Shakespeare and His Contemporaries in Performance.* Burlington: Ashgate, 2000.

Fischlin Daniel and Mark Fortier, eds. *Adaptations of Shakespeare: A Critical Anthology of Plays from the Seventeenth Century to the Present.* London: Routledge, 2000.

Gallimore, Daniel. "Measuring Distance: Tsubouchi Shōyō and the Myth of Shakespeare Translation." *Translating Others.* Ed. Theo Hermans. Manchester: St Jerome, 2006. Vol. 2, 483-92.

Griffith, James. *Adaptations as Imitations: Films from Novels.* Newark: U of Delaware P, 1997.

Hawkes, Terence. *Meaning by Shakespeare*. London: Routledge, 1992.

Hodgdon, Barbara. *The Shakespeare Trade: Performance and Appropriation.* Philadelphia: U of Pennsylvania P, 1998.

Hodgdon, Barbara, and W.B. Worthen, eds. *A Companion to Shakespeare and Performance.* Oxford: Wiley-Blackwell, 2005.

Hoenselaars, Ton, ed. *Shakespeare and the Language of Translation.* London: Arden Shakespeare, 2004.

Hoenselaars, Ton, ed. *Shakespeare's History Plays: Performance, Translation and Adaptation in Britain and Abroad.* Cambridge: Cambridge UP, 2004.

Holderness, Graham. *The Shakespeare Myth*. Manchester: Manchester UP, 1988.

Huang, Alexander C.Y. "Lin Shu, Invisible Translation, and Politics." *Perspectives: Studies in Translatology* 14.1 (2006): 55-65.

Hutcheon, Linda. *A Theory of Adaptation*. New York: Routledge, 2006.

Joughin, John J., ed. *Shakespeare and National Culture.* Manchester: Manchester UP, 1997.

Kennedy, Dennis. *Looking at Shakespeare: A Visual History of Twentieth-Century Performance*. Cambridge: Cambridge UP, 1993. Rpt. 2002.

Kennedy, Dennis. *Foreign Shakespeare: Contemporary Performance.* Cambridge: Cambridge UP, 1993.

Kishi, Tetsuo, Roger Pringle, and Stanley Wells, eds. *Shakespeare and Cultural Traditions: The Selected Proceedings of the International Shakespeare Association World Congress, Tokyo 1991.* Newark: U of Delaware P, 1994.

Landow, George P. *Hypertext: The Convergence of Contemporary Critical Theory and Technology*. Baltimore: Johns Hopkins UP, 1992.

Lavagnino, John. "Two Varieties of Digital Commentary." *Textual Performances: The Modern Reproduction of Shakespeare's Drama*. Ed. Lukas Erne and Margaret Jane Kidnie. Cambridge: Cambridge UP, 2004. 194-209.

Lehmann, Courtney. *Shakespeare Remains: Theater to Film, Early Modern to Postmodern*. Ithaca: Cornell UP, 2002.

Makaryk, Irena R. *Shakespeare in the Undiscovered Bourn: Les Kurbas, Ukrainian Modernism, and Early Soviet Cultural Politics*. Toronto: U of Toronto P, 2004.

Makaryk, Irena R., and Joseph G. Price, eds. *Shakespeare in the Worlds of Communism and Socialism*. Toronto: U of Toronto P, 2006.

Marcus, Leah. *Puzzling Shakespeare: Local Reading and Its Discontents*. Berkeley: U of California P, 1988.

Marsden, Jean I., ed. *The Appropriation of Shakespeare: Post-Renaissance Reconstruction of the Works and the Myth.* New York: Harvester Wheatsheaf, 1991.

Naremore, James, ed. *Film Adaptation.* New Brunswick: Rutgers UP, 2000.

Orkin, Martin. *Local Shakespeares.* New York: Routledge, 2005.

Ross, Charles, ed. *Shakespeare in Asia and Hollywood.* Thematic issue of *CLCWeb: Comparative Literature and Culture* 6.1 (2004) <http://docs.lib.purdue.edu/clcweb/vol6/iss1/>.

Royal Shakespeare Company's *Exploring Shakespeare* Project. <http://www/rsc/org.uk/learning/Learning.aspx>.

Shakespeare Performance in Asia. (2008): <http://web.mit.edu/shakespeare/asia/>.

Shaughnessy, Robert. *The Shakespeare Effect: A History of Twentieth-Century Performance.* New York: Palgrave, 2002.

Sukanta, Chaudhuri, and Chee Seng Lim, eds. *Shakespeare without English: The Reception of Shakespeare in Non-Anglophone Countries.* Delhi: Pearson Longman, 2006.

Taylor, Gary. *Reinventing Shakespeare: A Cultural History from the Restoration to the Present.* Oxford: Oxford UP, 1989.

Terdiman, Daniel. "Shakespeare Comes to a Virtual World." *cnet.news* (19 October 2006): <http://news.cnet.com/Shakespeare-coming-to-a-virtual-world/2100-1043_3-6127294.html?tag=mncol;txt>.

Worthen, W.B. *Shakespeare and the Authority of Performance.* Cambridge: Cambridge UP, 1997.

Worthen, W.B. *Shakespeare and the Force of Modern Performance.* Cambridge: Cambridge UP, 2003.

Part One

Shakespeare in Hollywood

Shakespeare's *Taming of the Shrew* and Screwball Comedy

Mei Zhu

Shakespeare's *Taming of the Shrew* is controversial owing to the subtlety and complexity of the text, especially its ending. The history of the play's reception is particularly contentious. Critics have long engaged in heated debates about how to interpret this play. As Deborah Cartmell points out, "The play's sexual politics are far too complex and problematic for a cinema audience at the end of the twentieth century" (214; for an overview of the Shrew theme in European literature and film, see Vasvári). Although the theme of the play is how to rule a wild wife and Zeffirelli's 1967 film version seems to follow closely the narrative structure of the original play, its effect is not contentious, mainly because Zeffirelli adopts the mode of Hollywood screwball comedy. Screwball comedy is a term one finds in filming contexts of all sorts, and it is not unfamiliar to mass audiences. However, no unanimously agreed upon definition can be found for it, neither among critics nor within the work of a single critic. As Wes D. Gehring observes, "Despite screwball comedy's significance in film and comedy history, its nature remains something of a mystery" (*Screwball Comedy* 10). Nevertheless, some general characteristics as well as a few screwball comedy classics are not difficult to identify. In Gehring's terms, screwball comedy is essentially "an eccentrically comic battle of the sexes, with the male generally losing." It is rooted in a chaotic world, in mid-1930s US-America: "In a world that seems more irrational every day, the antihero (the male) is fated to be forever frustrated. His frustration is the result of his attempt to create order in a world where order is impossible. The commonsense platitudes of any updated cracker-barrel philosopher are inadequate in today's crises. The vanishing of rigidity ... is the goal of all good screwball comedies" (11-14).

Zeffirelli's *Taming* is an early and substantial example of a marriage between Hollywood screwball comedy and Shakespearean comedy that influenced later filmmakers like Kenneth Branagh. Samuel Crowl argues that Branagh, in films like *Much Ado about Nothing*, reaches beyond even Zeffirelli in his willingness "to marry Shakespeare and Hollywood" and that "Branagh's greatest achievement is to link ideas in Shakespeare's play with the witty Hollywood comedies of the 1930s that have come to be labeled as 'screwball'" (111-12). I became interested in the topic because screwball comedy actually existed in Chinese culture, although it has never been widely recognized as a distinct film genre. In the 1940s, Shanghai was a universal metropolis and "New Woman" movements spread widely throughout China. A legendary Shanghai writer, Eileen Chang, was enchanted by Hollywood movies and wrote screenplays as well as popular fictions. Leo Ou-Fan Lee explored both the literary aspects of her screenplays and the cinematic aspects of her fiction, with particular attention to the screwball comedies, including her most famous story, "Love in the Fallen City" in *Shanghai Modern,* published in 1999. Generally speaking, Zeffirelli's version is more compatible with Chang's film conventions than Shakespeare's original play because it is always the ungrateful or picky husband (the male protagonist) who is eventually tamed in Chang's films. Most importantly, the wives are more intelligent and independent than the husbands.

To frame Branagh's achievement adequately, it will help analyze exactly how Zeffirelli created the precedent of using screwball comedy to present Shakespeare's most popular comedy. As his film opens, Zeffirelli invokes a festive atmosphere that prepares the way for the battle of the sexes, an integral part of screwball comedy. He shows Lucentio and his servant Tranio riding through a summer rain into idyllic Padua bathed in the golden and rose-colored light of a rainbow. They enter the beautiful city and then watch a solemn cathedral service in which everyone dresses decently and the music and prayers are handled properly. Suddenly, a book is burned and there is an explosion of color, music, masks, and costumes: a celebration of some kind. People carry the corpse-like body of a sick man who refuses to remain still. Masks represent a king and a queen. The camera moves from the legs to the top part of a prostitute's giant body to reveal a mountain of flesh. There is much chivalry. At the end of the procession, as the camera is positioned behind Lucentio and fixed on the veiled Bianca, a figure in a beaked mask lowers a hook to lift her veil while many young men surround her singing a licentious song. Everything at Padua seems fresh, funny, and crazy. Jorgens says that "Zeffirelli's major emphasis is upon farce" (71), but it is not slapstick so much as the particular romantic farce that we associate with Hollywood's screwball comedy. According to Leo McCarey, a key director of the genre, the point of these films is not to attack social problems but to entertain: "The way I look at it, it's larceny to remind people how lousy things are and call it entertainment" (qtd. in Gehring, *Screwball Comedy* 48). This fantastic opening of Zeffirelli's film turns out to be much more than a mere opening. It sets an entertaining mood for a movie in which Petruchio and Kate turn reason inside out and stand the everyday on its head.

Petruchio's role as an antihero perhaps prompted Zeffirelli to construct his film as a screwball comedy. Gehring summarizes five key elements of the comic antihero—his abundant leisure time, his childlike naïveté, his life in the city, his apolitical nature and his frustration (*Screwball Comedy* 10)—but one element missing is the class difference between the heroine and the hero that makes the male protagonist an antihero. Many screwball comedy classics, such as *It Happened One Night* (1934) and *My Man Godfrey* (1936), feature a male character whose social rank is beneath that of the heroine. The screwball comedy classics are usually romances between a selfish, spoiled, rich girl and a brash, out-of-work or lower-class man. Such films not only mock the pretensions and vanity of high society but also demonstrate that rich girls are often much better off with plebeians. In Shakespeare's original play, Petruchio is a gentleman with estates and servants. He is witty and kind. Although he is not the problem-solving cracker-barrel figure of traditional American humor, he is dominant and assertive, a gentleman (even a philosopher) who implements his strategic plan—"killing Kate with kindness." Radically different than other gentleman in the play, Petruchio in Zeffirelli's film is vulgar and not just greedy, as in Shakespeare's play, but almost impoverished. His friend Hortensio first sees him hitting his servant Grumio and is only willing to greet him when Petruchio recognizes him. After Petruchio is admitted into Hortensio's house, he behaves exactly like the tinker Christopher Sly in the Induction of the original play. He gets drunk and falls into bed still dressed. Next morning he recoils from a basin of rose-water brought by a servant, as unused to washing as Sly is unfamiliar with the "warm distilled waters" and "rose-water bestrew'd with flowers" (Induction 1.143) that greet him when he wakes. Zeffirelli's substitution of Sly's identity for Petruchio's changes Petruchio's social status. In his conversation with Hortensio, Petruchio does not ask about Katherina's father, as if he is unaware of the upper class's codes of marriage. Moreover, in his later negotiation with Baptista, he directly asks, "If I got her love, what the dowry would be?" He lacks the politeness and sophistication of Petruchio in the play. After he declares that "Petruchio is my name, Antonio's son, a man well known throughout all Italy," Baptista says nothing but distractedly shakes his head, implying that Petruchio is mad or a fortune hunter.

So far, we see a major difference between the play and the film. In the play, there is no class difference between Petruchio and Katherina. But the film boldly infuses class difference with gender difference. For Petruchio, the wooing is nothing but a game played for money. He even attempts to abandon Katherina on their journey to his house because he has never seriously thought about a married life up to that point. In many senses, this Petruchio is much more naïve than the character in the play, since he does not have a complete plan to deal with or tame Katherina. He plays the wooing game very well only because he is desperate and determined to get Baptista's money. He behaves horribly in the wedding ceremony and the wedding feast because he is an outsider, too brash and coarse to conform to genteel manners, or he simply does not care. His only plan is to leave Padua as soon as he gets his money. He is daffier than Shakespeare's character, and fits the model of a Hollywood antihero. Further, in a surprising twist that in part accounts for the brilliance of his film, Zeffirelli follows clues in Shakespeare's play and reverses the hero and heroine in the tradition of screwball comedy by making Petruchio more shrewish than Katherina. According to Fran Dolan, an important characteristic of a shrew in Shakespeare's day was "talking too much, or too loudly and publicly, or too crossly for a woman. Lacking other means to express anger to redress grievances, a shrew depended on her tongue" (9). Katherina in Shakespeare's play has a scolding, shrewish tongue that she uses as a weapon. Baptista warns Petruchio that he must be "armed for some unhappy words" (2.1.153) before he goes to see her. However, Katherina does not really talk more than many of the other characters; in the first scene she has only thirteen lines, all of them in response to provocation. In fact, at several crucial moments she remains silent. We don't have access to her psychological depth, and so we are uncertain what she actually thinks at those points. After her first fight with Petruchio Katherina declares that she wishes Petruchio be hanged rather than marry her (2.1.155). Immediately after that announcement, Petruchio boasts about their love and a marriage date is scheduled. Surprisingly, Katherina says nothing. When Petruchio disturbs the wedding ceremony, Katherina only trembles (3.2.158). After Katherina enters Petruchio's house, she speaks even less. In fact, Katherina is more marked by her physical violence than a sharp tongue: she ties up Bianca and whips her in act 1, scene 1. She breaks Hortensio's head with a musical instrument, and she strikes Petruchio not long after she meets him. Even in Petruchio's house, she beats Grumio because he refuses to feed her. She is also more frequently addressed as "mad" than "shrew" by almost everybody around her, including her father. Hortensio calls her a devil (1.1 147) and a "fiend of hell"; Gremio sees her as "the devil's dam" (1.1.147); her father accuses her "hiding of a devilish spirit" and confesses that she is an ill match for Petruchio—"She is not for your turn." (2.1.152). The men of Padua generally agree that Kate is unmarriageable "unless [she] were of gentler, milder mold" (1.1.147). Gremio concludes that "she's too rough" for him (1.1 147). In Shakespeare's play, her physical actions add to the farce.

In contrast, Katherina in Zeffirelli's film is very intelligent, sophisticated, and active, a much more fully developed character than in the play. In the film, it is clear that Katherina begins to change after she is tricked into believing that Petruchio really wants her. To reveal Kate's psyche, Zeffirelli first shoots Kate in profile over a stained window so that we see things through her perspective. She and we see Petruchio announce that he will buy beautiful clothes and make serious preparations for the wedding ceremony. Then we see a troubled and thinking Kate. Eventually we see a gentle and sweet smile on her face, a smile that humanizes her. This long take can be viewed as the epiphany moment because Kate starts intentionally and affectionately to tame herself according to genteel codes of manner. Much of the subtlety of this film comes from moments like this. In the original play, Kate is never seen alone. Every time she appears, she is with her father, sister, Petruchio, or servants. She is depicted, viewed, or commented on by others, who regard he as nothing but a crazy woman or a child. In Zeffirelli's film, audiences constantly see occasions when Katherina is alone. She is more sober (or less crazy) and intelligent than in the play. Katherina's first major scene, Petruchio's wooing game, continues the inexhaustible Dionysian energies and comically accelerated actions of the opening entertainment. Katherina's dress is extravagantly colorful and exaggerated. Her bosom is huge, symbolic of her shrewish energy. Petruchio's costume is like tarnished armor, partially revealing his strong muscles and hairy chest. His appearance resembles that of neither the effeminate Hortensio nor other lesser men. As soon as we set eyes on the heroine and hero, we know that they are perfect matches for each other. As a matter of fact, typical Hollywood techniques such as shot-reverse-shot, soft focus (on Katherina's face), and a freeze frame all demonstrate that Katherina loves Petruchio when she first sees him. However, I doubt that Zeffirelli's Petruchio falls in love at exactly the same moment, because Zeffirelli makes him behave cruelly toward Katherina in both the wooing scene and the journey to his house. In the wooing scene, Petruchio twists Katherina's by the wrist and hand. It would seem she is in severe pain were it not that the film is a farce. The wooing can be regarded as a game of chase, during which Petruchio pretends to be a great lover and Katherina plays hard to get. Petruchio participates in the action while engaging in witty dialogue, quarreling, cursing, and nagging Katherina. From the beginning to the end, this game lasts almost thirty minutes. Notably little of Shakespeare's witty dialogue is cut during this sequence, although Zeffirelli cut about seventy percent of the rest of the play. Thus Zeffirelli's film reaches one of its finest moments where the verbal flood in Shakespeare finds visual equivalents in shots full of motion, sound, and color. Screwball comedies use a similar combination of physical action and witty dialogue because they developed at the same time as the talkie: "Appropriately, only the picture-plus-sound could adequately showcase the marriage of slapstick to witty dialogue, which was screwball comedy's method of portraying of the antihero" (Gehring, *Screwball Comedy* 10).

The wooing game is but the first of several games that Petruchio and Katherina play. Hapgood notes eight distinct phrases of Katherina and Petruchio's witty battle and their progressions (91). What I see are two kinds of games in Zeffirelli's narrative. One of them is the game of pretension. The other kind can be roughly defined as a competition of courtesy between the married couple. The game of pretension starts with Petruchio's wooing and continues as Katherina sees Petruchio packing her father's money after the wedding ceremony. Once again, this shot-reverse-shot of Katherina gives her the prominence of an intense subject. Now that she knows that Petruchio's real interest is not her, she has to make a big decision. After being carried into a heavy rain and put on a horse, Katherina looks back again and again, struggling about whether to follow her husband or return to her father. Twice she chooses Petruchio. So far, she has been continuing the game of pretension invented by Petruchio—she has tried her best to keep her composure in public. After Katherina enters Petruchio's moth-beaten, all-male household, there is a subtle tension in the air. Petruchio is startled by Katherina's courageous action at first. Then, as if threatened by an intruding, shrewish, and higher-class wife, Petruchio defends his masculinity spontaneously by manipulating a disastrous dinner, as in the play. After the dinner, however, when he sees Katherina's ruined wedding dress, he is so moved by her courage that he cannot help kissing her and wanting her. He does not have a premeditated plan to tear up their bed. At this moment, as the film shies away from the possibility of marital rape, Katherina takes action by hitting Petruchio on the head with a warming pan. Enraged and embarrassed, Petruchio then improvises a plan to treat her as she treats him and tears up their bed. Unlike the play, Petruchio ends up spending his wedding night on a bench while Katherina lies on the bed, not unlike a scene from *It Happened One Night.* No different from antiheroes in the screwball comedies, Petruchio is the one who loses the battle of the sexes (on aspects of the shrew and society, see also Heffernan). And in a further domestic turn, a weeping then smiling Katherina not only greatly undermines the cruelty in the original play but also sheds some light on her indefatigable spirit—she loves the silly Petruchio and is determined to win his love and do something for their marriage. The next morning, she confidently orders the servants around, cheerfully cleaning up the house, completely in charge. At first, Petruchio is happy and satisfied. He greets Kate, "Good morning, Kate." Receiving not a single word from Katherina, he continues to greet her enthusiastically, "How is my fair queen?" This time one word, "ill," is squeezed out of Katherina's teeth with a grin. Then another shot-reverse-shot shows us that Katherina is busily befriending all the servants and Petruchio angrily watches her take control of his household. Later on, to revenge this humiliation, Petruchio invents a fashion show and destroys all the beautiful dresses in front of Katherina to establish his authority, as in the play. But the contest is reciprocal, not a plot by Petruchio. Zeffirelli elevates the film to the level of screwball comedy, a more sophisticated form than physical slapstick and farce.

Portrayed in an extremely subtle manner, Petruchio's anxiety and uneasiness evolve through two stages. Petruchio prefers a bachelor's life, and when he returns home to what is more or less a gangster's house, he is so happy that he throws his dowry money to his servants. In the film he then sings "Where is my life that once I lived? It's gone, it's gone," for he realizes marriage has changed his life. When Petruchio carries Katherina into his bedchamber, Grumio sings the same song in a sad and sorrowful tone because Petruchio's marriage threatens their male bonding. Interestingly, with Petruchio's gradually growing interest and love of Katherina, his uneasiness about marriage is gradually transformed into concerns about married life. He is rigid, anxious, and uneasy because he is not sure about Katherina's love. Then he starts to test, observe, and compete with Katherina. The film's series of competitions, the dominating female character, the anxiety of the hero, and his attempt to create order can all be linked to screwball comedies.

Zeffirelli's Petruchio is no less compromising than Cary Grant: the night before Petruchio and Katherina return to her father's house, Petruchio goes to Katherina's chamber and tells her they will wear fashionable and expensive clothes on this trip. As in *Bringing Up Baby*, where Cary Grant's brontosaurus collapses, a symbolic metaphor for the softening of Grant's rigidity and new appreciation for Katherine Hepburn, Petruchio's promise is a confession of his love for this earlier Katherina. After his promise of a return home, she stops competing because she has won. Later on, in the "Sun" and "Moon" scene and then the wager scene, she repeatedly reassures the worrying Petruchio by "obeying" him or surprising him with rather unexpected performances. Rather than codes of submission, these behaviors are actually codes of love. Zeffirelli's Katherina, by assuming control of Petruchio's domestic sphere, alleviates Petruchio's anxiety about marriage and leads him out of his bachelor's world.

Shakespeare's play and Zeffirelli's film are two different stories coming from different roots or traditions. Shakespeare's play is mainly a play of manners and the leader of the game is undoubtedly Petruchio. Although the irony in Katherina's final speech implies an unbroken spirit, it only presents a potential for Katherina to be the real leader in the future. Zeffirelli's film, by contrast, is a love romance in which Katherina plays a dominating role, not least because films like to look at women, as Carol Rutter has argued: "Cinema is a 'looking' medium that writes its texts in visual language, and cinema has always been interested in looking at women" (241). The physical aspects of Zeffirelli's Katherina constantly exceed the specifications of Shakespeare's theater texts. In the play, no detailed descriptions about either Katherina's appearance or her age can be found. Both the 1980 BBC version and Sam Taylor's 1929 version portray Katherina as a blonde. Zeffirelli's Katherina differs because she is played by Elizabeth Taylor, whose dark hair and legendary violet (dark) eyes immediately bring an extra text that is there to be read, a deeper contrast between her and other lesser women, symbolized by blondes such as Bianca and the widow. Moreover, Elizabeth Taylor makes Katherina a very strong subject. Her subjectivity not only comes from the shot-reverse-shots and her thinking moments but also from Taylor 's aggressive acting. Elizabeth Taylor has occasionally played intelligent, dominating women in films such as *Cleopatra* (1963) and *Who's Afraid of Virginia Woolf?* (1966). Her public image also enriches and alters Katherina's character. Almost everyone is aware of the off-and-on romance of Taylor and Richard Burton.

A final point on how Zeffirelli turned his Shakespearean source into a Hollywood film requires a look at the characters in what is technically the main plot of the play, the wooing of Bianca, although Zeffirelli makes it the subplot. Film writer Douglas Brode comments on the difficulty of filming *Taming*: "Also tricky is the balance of the Lucentio-Bianca plot, penned in the sophisticated style of Italian Renaissance comedy of intrigue, with the broad, burlesque-like Kate-Petruchio main plot" (18). Indeed, Zeffirelli's handling of the other plot is somewhat problematic and self-contradictory, as it steers between realism and fantasy. At the beginning of the movie, Lucentio and Tranio walk down the winding streets of Padua and see a series of outcasts or marginalized people: a drunkard locked in a cage, poor peasants, wandering men, an abandoned giant lady, and a grinning old woman. All these people imply that Padua is a rigid world with strict social norms. Anyone who does not follow the codes of the mainstream has been and will be abandoned as outcasts or treated with cruelty. It is a world of strict class distinctions. By juxtaposing the marginalized couple, poor Petruchio and crazy Katherina or the so-called "Lord and Lady of Misrule" with Lucentio and Bianca, the perfect genteel lovers, Zeffirelli puts the whole story in a big frame. At first he seems to be mocking the pretensions of high society. However, after Katherina determines to tame herself, she starts to imitate the manners of Bianca. She not only successfully tames herself but also tames

Petruchio, who is usually unconcerned for society's rules. When the couple returns to Padua, they are dressed up. Katherina behaves in a very careful way to avoid the disrespect.

Jack Jorgens interprets Katherina's departure from Bianca's banquet as a rebellion toward the old social order. He concludes that "For once the rebels in a comedy are not absorbed by society, but maintain their independence to the last" (155). I would argue that the irony in the ending does not lie in Katherina's speech. Instead, the film is ironic because both Katherina and Petruchio have unconsciously conformed to the values they are attacking or mocking. In this sense, Zeffirelli's film can be linked to screwball comedy again. Although screwball comedy tends to ridicule the stupidity, eccentricity, and sophistication of the upper class, and argues that a rich girl is much better off with a poor man, films like *My Man Godfrey* still end with compromise. In that movie, Godfrey eventually becomes a rich man and conforms to their manners. Petruchio and Katherina are compromised similarly.

Zeffirelli's film demonstrates an interesting marriage of Shakespeare and Hollywood. To me, this film is undeniably a screwball comedy. At first glance, it might be disappointing for Shakespearean scholars to see a Renaissance masterpiece distorted by popular culture. However, in turn, it is arguable that the entire tradition of screwball comedy has roots in Shakespearean comedies such as *Much Ado About Nothing, Love's Labor's Lost,* and *The Comedy of Errors*. Shakespeare gave these films the basic elements and stories. Most interestingly, Shakespeare's influence reached as far as China, although indirectly, by way of Hollywood. *Hamlet*, *Macbeth*, and *Lear* may be the most popular plays in Asia, but comedies are not absent, and *The Taming of the Shrew* has an interesting stage history in the Orient. Overall, the fact that different cultures or eras interpret the stories differently only proves that Shakespeare's themes have indeterminate spaces. His plays are neither limited to one period nor one place, not for an age, but for all time.

Works Cited

Brode, Douglas. *Shakespeare in the Movies: From the Silent Era to Shakespeare in Love*. Oxford: Oxford UP, 2000.

Cartmell, Deborah. "Franco Zeffirelli and Shakespeare." *The Cambridge Companion to Shakespeare on Film*. Ed. Russell Jackson. Cambridge: Cambridge UP, 2000. 212-21.

Crowl, Samuel. "The Marriage of Shakespeare and Hollywood: Kenneth Branagh's Much Ado About Nothing." *Spectacular Shakespeare: Critical Theory and Popular Cinema.* Ed. Courtney Lehmann and Lisa S. Starks. Madison: Fairleigh Dickinson UP, 2002. 111-24.

Dolan, Frances E. "Introduction." *The Taming of the Shrew: Texts and Contexts*. Ed. Frances E. Dolan. London: Bedford Books, 1996. 1-38.

Gehring, Wes D. *Screwball Comedy: A Genre of Madcap Romance*. New York: Greenwood P, 1986.

Gehring, Wes D. *Screwball Comedy: Defining a Film Genre*. Muncie: Ball State UP, 1983.

Hapgood, Robert. "Popularizing Shakespeare: The Artistry of Franco Zeffirelli." *Shakespeare, The Movie*. Ed. Lynda E. Boose and Richard Burt. London: Routledge, 1997. 80-94.

Heffernan, Carol F. "The Taming of the Shrew: The Bourgeoisie in Love." *William Shakespeare's* The Taming of the Shrew. Ed. Harold Bloom. New York: Chelsea House Publishers, 1988. 65-78.

Jorgens, Jack J. *Shakespeare on Film*. Bloomington: Indiana UP, 1977.

Rutter, Carol Chilington. "Looking at Shakespeare's Women on Film." *The Cambridge Companion to Shakespeare on Film*. Ed. Russell Jackson. Cambridge: Cambridge UP, 2000. 241-60.

Shakespeare, William. *The Riverside Shakespeare*. Ed. G. Blakemore Evans. Boston: Houghton Mifflin, 1997.

Vasvári, Louise O. "Examples of the Motif of the Shrew in European Literature and Film." *CLCWeb: Comparative Literature and Culture* 4.1 (2002): <http://docs.lib.purdue.edu/clcweb/vol4/iss1/3/>.

Method Acting and Pacino's *Looking for Richard*

Peirui Su

In 1996 Al Pacino released his docudrama *Looking for Richard*, forty-one years after Laurence Olivier's 1955 film version of *Richard III* and a year after Richard Loncraine filmed a modernized version of the play, set in a world of twentieth-century fascism, starring Ian McKellen. Critics hailed Pacino's *Looking for Richard* as "a solid entry among other Shakespeare films being produced in 1995-6" (Coursen 109-10). Even in his bitter review of the movie, Mark Leeper admitted it is "the first film about the making of a Shakespeare film," and that it "could not have been more timely." Not surprising, critics and audiences have wondered why Pacino chose this Shakespeare play and this method of production. He seems to have cared less about commercial profit than producing a labor of love. As director, coproducer, and cowriter, Pacino financed his film out of his own pocket, suggesting that at least in this instance, art is more important than money.

As a young actor, Pacino felt alien to Shakespeare, but as he grew older he found himself growing more familiar with Shakespeare's plays. It is his belief that only by playing Shakespeare can an actor understand the charm of his words and characters. Pacino himself appeared on stage in *Richard III* in Boston from December 1972 to January 1973 and again in New York City from 10 June to 15 July 1973. Both productions were directed by David Wheeler. Some reviews of those of his performances were quite encouraging: "One of the most credible—and creditable Richard IIIs ever to limp his way across the stage" (Yule 69). He also did *Hamlet* (1979, workshop only), *Othello* (1979, rehearsals only), and *Julius Caesar* (1986-87 in New York). However, according to Pacino, no one has asked him to play Hamlet or other roles of Shakespeare in film. Nearly twenty years later, Pacino was invited to play in a film version of *Richard III*. During four years of waiting, he made four other movies and did two plays, but at the same time, he was always haunted by the possibility of making his own version of *Richard III*. In September 1995, the American Film Institute announced a discovery of a nearly perfect copy of a 1912 film version of *The Life and Death of Richard III* which was believed to be the oldest surviving US-American feature film. This event probably spurred Pacino's passion further for shooting his own Richard III.

Once Pacino decided to direct the movie, the choice of form became dominant. He faced two trends in Shakespeare film adaptation: Olivier's theatrical and faithful version in the traditional Elizabethan drama or some kind of modernization. He rejected both approaches. Olivier's version is somewhat inaccessible for modern US-American audiences, whose knowledge of Shakespeare and Elizabethan theater is scarce. An updated modernization, on the other hand, is always anachronistic and sacrifices language and social context in favor of cinematic popularity. For actors in Pacino's mold, authenticity is always a primary concern. If British actors are nourished by the rich legacy of Shakespeare and verse play, their US-American counterparts emphasize the inner truth of the individual, the kind of thing international audiences who regard US-American literature associate with Holden Caulfield in J.D. Salinger's *The Catcher in the Rye*. Moreover, Pacino's education as a method actor prevented him from following the two approaches of period piece or modernization. Method is a system of acting techniques in the United States influenced by Russian theater director, teacher, and actor Constantin Stanislavsky, who developed his technique for the original production of the plays of Anton Checkov. Later it was extended by the leading figures of method acting, such as Lee Strasberg, Stella Adler, and Sanford Meisner. In method acting, stress is on "truthful behavior in imaginary circumstances" (Krasner 5). One necessary step for a method actor is to explore a character from inside out. The actor is supposed to experience and live through the role in order to create a convincing character. Stanislavsky suggests the magic "if" as a clue for how an actor should melt himself into a role. The actor should ask the question, if I am the character, how should I behave? In method acting honesty in performance is essential.

Contrary to the principle of "from inside out" in playing a role, Olivier insisted on working from the "outside in" (Olivier 118). He would paint a portrait of his character in his mind's eye first. Olivier believed that what mattered was the person. While British actors such as Olivier are famous for voice and movement, Pacino pays more attention to naturalism in his version. Therefore, in order to avoid "fake medievalism," which is how Peter Holland describes the stylized set of Olivier's *Richard III* (99), Pacino set most of his production of *Looking for Richard* in the Cloisters, a museum in Manhattan well known for its collections of ancient architecture and artifacts. It offered both a sense of history and also authenticity, since it is a real place in New York. By drawing on such a rich and real cultural context, Pacino was able to have his cake and eat it too. Pacino also rejected Olivier's highly theatrical style of acting, makeup, and voice, which in the case of *Richard III* Olivier termed "the thin reed of a sanctimonious scholar" (Olivier 119). Compared to Olivier's external entry to his character, a "venom coated with sugar" (119), Pacino approached Richard from the inside out, and his docudrama records his efforts to understand Shakespeare's story and characters at first. In the movie we see Pacino interrogating people on the street, conducting interviews with Shakespeare experts and actors, and discussing the history of the War of the Roses and life of Richard III. He tries to understand the soul of iambic pentameter, and he visits the birthplace of

Shakespeare and the Globe Theater in London. All these actions are closely connected with the principles of method acting of "motivation" and "justification." Method actors ask why does your role do this instead of that? How can you justify his behavior? The prerequisite for an actor is to understand, to find an epiphany, which means a special expression of someone's character. Having emotionally experienced a role, the method actor can then play the part. A method actor is always on the road, always searching. Once a method actor finds a cause, everything becomes believable and effective. In Pacino's case, this is the reason why the first part of *Looking for Richard* is entitled "Question," and consists of the questions Pacino poses during interviews with pedestrians as he asks people their opinions of Shakespeare and *Richard III*. "Question" then dissolves into "Quest." The point here is that Pacino is giving his production an inner frame. It is a spiritual odyssey in which Pacino looks for the meaning of the play *Richard III* as well as his own cinematic version. Pacino justified this meta-cinematic approach by playing someone who is a "quintessentially urban, American actor" (Dowd 357). It was his intention to correct the common belief that a method actor has difficulty in doing Shakespeare because of the utter dependence of the Stanislavsky-Strasberg training system on realistic texts: one "can play Chekhov, Odets, and Miller, but not Shakespeare" (Strasberg 175).

That Pacino adopted a documentary form for *Looking for Richard* was also based on his theory of communication. For Pacino, an actor must communicate with his audience. The significance of audience lies not in the fact that it determines the commercial profits of a film, but that Pacino—as a director and as an actor—has firm faith in the intelligence of the spectator. Contrary to Olivier's assertion that it is necessary to lead an audience by the nose and guide its thinking, in method acting the emphasis is on an audience's independent agency. If Stanislavsky says that actor is the soul of theater, Vsevolod Meyerhold believed it is the actor plus the audience. In method acting it is thought that the audience produces fifty percent of the performance. The empty space—the stage—is not void; rather, it is full of energy. An audience charges a stage with power, and only with its assistance can an actor release his creativity and consummate a role. Pacino's interviews with his audience not only show his concern for spectators, but also his intention to justify his making a movie as a means of popularizing Shakespeare in the United States. He tries to involve local people in his production. He wants to share with them his enthusiasm and obsession with the Bard. Furthermore, his communication with his audience can educate young actors. Pacino finds, from his personal experience, the importance of classics to the growth of young actors in the US, who can never grow if they are constantly doing the same thing.

Pacino learned the importance of growth from the work of Vittorio Gassman, who played in the original Italian version of *Scent of a Woman* (*Profumo di Donna*, directed by Dino Risi). In fact, he developed the education theme in *Looking for Richard* while studying Gassman's film for his own rendition. Pacino feels strongly that life and theater are always meeting in a kind of playful puzzle and that it is important to show what is behind the screen or the stage. He aims at communication with critics as well as the general audience by inserting clips of his rehearsals, one of the more charming aspects of his docudrama. In this he is actually similar to Olivier, who admitted that "critics are a grim necessity" (Olivier 362) and suggested that more critics ought to sit in on rehearsals "so that they could see the amount of work, concentration, belief and love that goes into the construction of a piece, before they take their inky swords to it" (363). Pacino uses his docudrama to present scenes of actors discussing their roles during rehearsals. He also recorded the multiple voices of Shakespearean experts. By making a movie about making a movie, Pacino is able to juxtapose Shakespeare's great story of violence, ambition, and lust for power with producers and actors. Some critics have objected to the frequent interruptions in the documentary but others believe that the double theme of making a movie about making a movie gives "life to the costumed segments" (Coursen 110). The fragments cohere as parts of a quest rather than a consequence. Pacino told a *Playboy* interviewer that when watching "regular movies you want the story to take us away and get us involved, but the nature of this film is showing process, and eventually you get into *Richard* and you forget about process. You're into the story and you don't know how you got there. That's the trick" (Grobel 136). This trick also appeals to the magic function of an audience's mental montage, which enables viewers to endow a movie with consistency and meaning even thought it is composed of fragmented cuts.

Pacino's reliance on his audience to superimpose unity also helps us to understand how he thinks about the character of Richard III. In fact, his Shakespearean villain is made up of pieces from his own former roles. For example, I believe the complex figure of Michael Corleone occupies Pacino in his Shakespearean role: Pacino first acted Richard III after his role in *The Godfather* had turned him from a stage actor to a movie star. Indeed, in my opinion we can detect the archetype of Michael Corleone in many of Pacino's films such Tony in *Scarface,* Frank Slade in the *Scent of a Woman*, Carlito Brigante in *Carlito's Way*, John Milton in *The Devil's Advocate*, or Walter Burke in *The Recruit*, not to mention his portrayal of King Herod in the play *Salome*. All these characters live at the edge of society physically and psychologically: the drug dealer, the Mafia don, the blind soldier, the veteran CIA agent, and finally, the Devil himself. Each character exhibits various and complex aspects of human nature: they are evil and violent but at the same time, charismatic, earthy, and vulnerable. They are mysterious and antiheroic, but also emotionally intense and explosive. For Pacino, such characters serve as stepping stones to develop his skill because to create them, he must experience what the characters feel, and their emotions must be genuinely acted, not pretended. The issue of what is genuine raises the question, among critics, as to the role that catharsis plays in method acting. Actors let off their inner tension, anxiety, or guilt through imitating their character. The result is similar to the effect of psychotherapy. For example, one of the most important techniques Stanislavsky developed was emotional recall, in which an actors turn to their own experiences or pasts to find feelings similar to those of their characters. In this context, Russian actor and theater director Yevgeni Vakhtangov pushed Stanislavsky's theory to an extreme, saying that "it is the actor's life, and not necessarily the role, that inspires" (qtd. in Krasner 29). Some teachers of method acting are accused of acting like psychoanalysts and invading an actor's psyche. Nevertheless Deb Margolin maintains that acting "is an emergency, and in an emergency you do whatever works" (128). In other words, method acting is legitimate as long as it helps an actors grasp a role.

For Pacino as a method actor, the motif of Michael Corleone thus resonates in Richard III: it is part of his own personal past, and it gave him an understanding of the lust for power and thirst for violence that marks Shakespeare's character. Both Michael and Richard are ambitious and cruel and their inner turbulence contrasts with their outer coolness. This contrast is especially evident in Pacino's acting in *The Godfather II*. We always see him as a blank face, calm and emotionless, without flashes in his eyes or anger in his voice, but he still gives the impression that he is a dormant volcano and nobody can predict when he will erupt, as when he learns that his wife has had an abortion. Like Michael Corleone, Richard III is transformed from a brave fighter to a villain. In Shakespeare's *Henry VI* (which precedes *Richard III*), Richard is able to face chaos and danger on the battlefield, but in *Richard III*, the same character alters, without losing his earlier intensity, into someone who does not hesitate to do anything in order to usurp the crown of England. He murders his brother and his two nephews, marries his niece, and exterminates ruthlessly his enemies and opponents, including Buckingham, his right-hand man, just as Michael pushes Tom Hagen aside in *The Godfather*. He trusts no one and suspects everyone. No creature loves him and he does not love himself. It is this balance between intensity and composure, between fire and ice, that makes the magic in Pacino's acting. It is also a symbol of his fatalistic split as an actor: he is inevitably torn between his role and himself, between an observer and a player. However, this schizophrenic state does not damage but reinforces Pacino's performances. The duality of this split identity allow the actor to immerse himself in his role by giving him a sense of success. It also allows him to observe everything as an outsider. In this sense, Richard III is an actor. When everybody believes that his heart is figured in his tongue, he is an actor. Richard is an actor when he determines to rip the crown of Hastings off his shoulder. He is melodramatic as he tells his cabinet that Queen Elizabeth and Shore, Hastings's mistress, have used their witchcraft to make his arm deformed, for no one believes him. As Hastings tries to defend his lover ("If they have done this deed, my noble lord," *Richard III* 3.4.73), Richard explodes and keeps stressing on the word "if" to stoke his rage: "If? Thou protector of this damned strumpet? / Talk'st thou to me of 'ifs'?" (3.4.74-75). Then, in a cool and calm tone, so familiar from the older Michael Corleone, he issues his orders: "Off with his head!" (3.4.76). At this moment, one can hardly distinguish Pacino from the Duke of Gloucester, since both are great actors, and both are able to move instantly from temper to self-control.

Another personality trait of Pacino's antiheroes is the innate loneliness they suffer, which always draws sympathy from the audience. In the last scene of *The Godfather II*, when Michael Corleone is left alone in his study, he recalls the sweet days of the past when his father was not dead. A camera shot of his study is superimposed on a flashback to a family party. Sonny, still alive, is talking and introducing Carlo to his sister. He quarrels with Michael for enlisting in the Marines. Michael sits alone, hearing the singing, and cheers for his father's surprise birthday party in the next room, on the right side of the frame, with some narrow paths and fallen leaves visible in the background. Next, the camera pulls toward him in a close-up to suggest that he is deep in memory and meditation. At the same time, however, his position is to the extreme right side of the frame, which creates, according to the visual habit of the audience, a sense of danger and instability, as if Michael is going to drop off from the edge of the screen to the unknown darkness. It follows a fade-out. This shot indicates that Michael Corleone, after committing so many crimes, has lost himself and his humanity. He must pay the price of loneliness for what he has done. Like Michael Corleone, Richard also lives in the abyss of solitude. His only friend, if there is one, is his horse, a symbol of loyalty, and at the same time, it stands for a lifestyle where Richard feels at home and in which his value of existence and bliss of passion can find proof and source. For Pacino's Richard, life is symbolized by and simplified into a riding crop that he always holds in his hands as he plays Richard. Like much of Pacino's method acting, the detail of using such a stage prop to represent the personality of a character comes from Lee Strasberg. Strasberg enumerated one principle among others: to use objects for their symbolic meaning (Krasner 6). It was Strasberg's custom to explain how actors bring roles to life by making their performances physical, "incorporating actions and behavior as means of embodying the role" (Krasner 6). When Kim Stanley played in Checkov's *Three Sisters* on Broadway, Strasberg provided her with a small tree branch to vent her feelings. During the whole play Stanley clutched this branch behind her back and won raves. The riding crop for Richard functions similarly. It stands for a desire for action and danger, a wish to engage in battle, and all in all, the passion of Richard's youth. It acts as a stimulus for his best memories, his wish for an ideal existence, a recurrence of creativity. At the same time, it serves as a reminder of sanity, self-knowledge, and strong will. It also symbolizes that Richard always takes fate, not only of his own, but others', in his control.

As in the case of Michael Corleone, Richard's loneliness is further strengthened by the frailty and stupidity of his enemies. Like "a Renaissance wolf among medieval sheep" (Coursen 99), Richard wins the crown without much labor, but then the rest is emptiness. The process is too short. His superior intelligence breeds irony, as it does in Pacino's portrait of Michael Corleone, especially in *Godfather III*, admittedly the least successful film in the series, where he utters a line suitable to the Reagan years of the US: "Never feel embarrassed with your wealth. It's only the trick of the rich to keep the poor without it." Successful or not in the earlier film, this irony helped Pacino play the most famous scene in Shakespeare's *Richard III*, the seduction of Anne. It helps him pretend to be religious when he seeks the coronation; it helps him surprise Buckingham. When Richard requests Buckingham to kill the princes as a means of reinforcing his position, Buckingham hesitates. But when he makes up his mind to follow Richard's edict, everything changes. As Pacino films the scene, Richard rearranges his dress, seems absent-minded, and smiles while Buckingham speaks off-screen. He touches his moustache to indicate thought and then shifts. He pushes Buckingham with his riding crop, mocks him, ignores him, suddenly stands up, and again using his riding crop, threatens Buckingham's doom, but he does so subtly and craftily, not violently. The climax of Richard's exhibiting the art of performance and inescapable split in his personality arrives in the scene of wooing Lady Anne, which determines the success of the play to great extent. Accordingly, Pacino's experiment on cinematic techniques reaches a culmination in the scene. In his search for motivation of the characters, of Richard and Anne, Pacino defines Anne as a very young girl who is unfortunately on the losing side. She has lost her husband in the war and has basically no future. Richard wants to defeat his rivals from the House of Lancaster; he intends to justify the legitimacy of his position through this marriage. It appears to me that this analysis of Shakespeare by Pacino is more convincing than Olivier's interpretation of Anne as a woman of loose morals who has got rid of her ring when she meets Richard the second time and already surrendered to Richard III before the seduction scene. If Olivier's understanding is logical, then Richard must have been an attractive man so that Anne cannot resist his charm. McKellen's portrait of Richard in the scene is no better. Terrence Rafferty complained that the sequence lacks an "appalling magnetism potent enough to win the grieving widow over. As the charmless McKellen play[s] it, Anne's capitulation is wholly incomprehensible" (Coursen 109).

The credibility of Pacino's version of the wooing episode depends on cinematic techniques. He uses a hand-held camera in keeping with the documentary style of the film. The scene also resembles a costumed rehearsal, again in keeping with the fragmented style Pacino conceived for his docudrama. This style also creates instability and uncertainty concerning the psychology of Richard's wooing and of Anne's hesitation. An interesting coincidence is that none of the three versions of the scene is faithful to the original script in which the parade of bearing Henry VI's corpse is going from Paul's toward Chertsey to be interred (1.2.29-30). According to the text, the event should take place on the street of London, but two of the film versions are set in the church and one in the mortuary. Pacino's scene takes place in the dark and vast interior of the Cloisters. This interior resembles a stage. It has minimal decor; only the crude stone columns and floor are visible. Contrary to the artificial lighting of daytime in Olivier's play and barren whiteness of McKellen's setting, Pacino's scene depends on low-key lighting, so that the whole stage, a spot in the Cloister, is covered in the heavy shadows. Low-key lighting usually contributes to hard-boiled suspense genres such as film noir, mystery, and sinister romance. According to classical narrative cinema, the standard illumination scheme is three-point lighting. In order to model an actor's face (or another object) with a sense of depth, light from three directions is used. The key light highlights an image or an area of greatest dramatic interest. Fill lights, which are less intense than the key light, soften the harshness of the main light source and reveal the subsidiary details hidden by shadows. The back light picks out the subject from its background, heightening the three-dimensional depth of an image (Giannetti 19). The low-key lighting in *Looking for Richard* employs very little fill light, creating strong contrasts between the brightest and darkest parts of the images and often producing strong shadows that obscure parts of the principal subjects. It suggests that Richard is one of the greatest villains in all Shakespeare's plays and implies a plot being processed. The low-key lighting, in this scene, is highly impractical in a true theater performance, because we are phototropic and our eyes tend to focus on the brightest object in a field of vision. Low-key lighting in the theater can cause visual fatigue in an audience, distracting their concentration. It is only feasible in a film.

It seems safe to say that Pacino borrows this low-key lighting and contrast from *The Godfather.* Gordon Willis, the cinematography of *The Godfather*, is famous for his low-key lighting magic: within the dark rooms, the Mafia dons plan their crimes. The contrasts between outside and inside, between brightness and darkness, are achieved through lighting. The same occurs in *Looking for Richard.* Even at the beginning of the film, as Richard speaks his opening soliloquy ("Now is the winter of our discontent") in the Cloisters Museum in New York, the shot brings us a glimpse of greenery outside through a window, a contrast between the coldness and barrenness of medieval architecture and the luxuriant and boisterous warmth of a summer day in the 1990s, between the winter of discontent of an ancient suffering soul and the noise of the postmodern metropolis. In the scene of wooing Lady Anne, the low-key lighting with its shadows and darkness produces a dour and obscure atmosphere, full of desire and unnamable malice.

Pacino also experiments with the speed and rhythm of his film. Compared to Olivier's six shots and McKellen's forty-five cuts within seven odd minutes, Pacino does ninety-eight in a similar duration, which means 4.8 seconds per take. That Pacino implements such an MTV-esque film technique of quick cuts creates a marvelous mosaic of spontaneity that adds to the quality of his docudrama and gives it the thrill of theatrical performance. The lack of the classic Hollywood establishing shot during these fast-moving sequences is characteristic of edgy and avant-garde filmmaking. These cuts, which follow the rhythm of the original play, adjust to the phases of a quarrel and fluctuate with Lady Anne's mental swirl. The marvelous melodrama of Richard's wooing begins with a shout: "Stay, you that bear the corpse, and set it down." Richard then emerges from darkness. A series of shots and reverse shots follows, then several long takes (mainly for the encounter of Richard with the guards), but mostly medium shots. This not only indicates the changing points of view of the Richard and Anne as they converse, but also signifies the physical and psychological distance between the two characters.

Adding to Pacino's documentation of *Richard III* as an actor's vehicle, his version also includes a number of dissolves in close-up, which give the effect of hallucination and suggest that Lady Anne is gradually mesmerized by the honey-coated words from Richard. Then comes the turning point of this dialogue: "Thy beauty was the cause of that effect, / Thy beauty, that did haunt me in my sleep / To undertake the death of all the world" (1.2.121-123), and for the first time the two appear in the same frame. The camera mimics the shrinking of their emotional and physical distance and hints that an intimacy is gradually building between them. What seem to defeat Anne are Al Pacino's eyes, which express the longing, care, weariness, and despair of his character. He looks at Anne with intensity and tenderness. This gaze hardly insinuates a lechery that flashes in eyes of Olivier and McKellen when they play this scene. If this is lust, it is well-disguised. Anne is moved, and a shift in the lighting registers her change of mood. Gradually Richard's face begins to shine, as if Anne is now seeing an angel rather than a devil. She herself is drawn more and more into the shadows, symbolizing that she has fallen into the grasp of the dark Richard. At the end of the scene, Anne retreats and is totally swallowed by the darkness.

Another dramatic aspect of Pacino's representation of Richard's wooing is the way he whispers. With the help of clever sound recording and close-up camera work, he can speak Shakespeare's verse as quietly as he wishes. The color in this scene also matches his wooing vein. The basic hues of costumes are black, red, silver and grey, signifying two rival houses of York and Lancaster and their symbols, the red and white roses. Richard's costume shows a silver flower embroidered on a black background—to me an echo of Baudelairean motives from his *Fleurs du mal*—and Satan in disguise of a sinister silver snake. The dark red (purple) of Anne's cloak symbolizes her desirability and fragility. Meanwhile, the score of Howard Shore provides a religious solemnity of medieval choir music that accompanies the bearing of Henry VI's body, while at the same time the music is ironic, since Richard's lewd play of wooing takes place as the coffin is carried. The scene ends as Pacino picks up Richard's riding crop, as if giving a sign that he has recovered his sobriety. To prove that his passion has not overcome his reason, Richard speaks his well-known lines: "Was ever woman in this humor wooed? / Was ever woman in this humor won? / I'll have her, but I will not keep her long" (1.2.227-229). Thus, Richard/Pacino completes his metacommentary on the actor's craft.

As one of the most prominent actors in the history of US-American film, Pacino is renowned for deep involvement and even obsession with his roles in consequence with his commitment to method acting. In *Looking for Richard* he identifies with the way Shakespeare's character combines fiction and reality. The result is a portrait of ambition and obstinate self-confidence. Life is, for both Pacino and Richard, "always on the wire, and the rest is just waiting" (Yule preface). The irony for Richard is that when he wins the crown, he needs to pretend no more and his wit and irony fade. Here, the great actor stops acting and ennui conquers him. Not until the battle of Bosworth does he recover his spirit. At that point Pacino and Richard again overlap in the final cry of "A horse, a horse, my kingdom for a horse!" (5.4.13). When Richard meets the fatal sword of Richmond, Richard/Pacino falls into the arms of Kimball, his cowriter, in a final superimposition of character and actor.

Works Cited

Coursen, H.R. "Filming Shakespeare's History: Three Films of *Richard III*." *The Cambridge Companion to Shakespeare on Film.* Ed. Russell Jackson. Cambridge: Cambridge UP, 2000. 99-116.

Dowd, Maureen. "Al Alone." *Gentleman's Quarterly* 62.9 (1992): 278-359.

Giannetti, Louis D. *Understanding Movies*. Englewood Cliffs: Prentice-Hall, 2001.

Grobel, Lawrence. "Looking for Al." *Playboy* 43.12 (1996): 124-96.

Holland, Peter. "Filming Shakespeare's History: Three Films of *Richard III*." *The Cambridge Companion to Shakespeare on Film.* Ed. Russell Jackson. Cambridge: Cambridge UP, 2000. 99-116.

Krasner, David, ed. *Method Acting Reconsidered.* New York: St. Martin's Press, 2000.

Leeper, Mark. "A Movie Review of *Looking for Richard.*" *Eclectica Magazine* (2004): <http://www.eclectica.org/v1n2/leeper.html>.

Margolin, Deb. "Mining My Own Business: Paths between Text and Self." *Method Acting Reconsidered.* Ed. David Krasner. New York: St. Martin's, 2000. 127-34.

Olivier, Laurence. *On Acting.* New York: Simon and Schuster, 1986.

The Riverside Shakespeare. Ed. G. Blakemore Evans. Boston: Houghton Mifflin, 1997.

Strasberg, Lee. *A Dream of Passion: The Development of the Method.* Ed. Evangeline Morphos. New York: Plume/Penguin, 1987.

Yule, Andrew. *Life on the Wire: The Life and Art of Al Pacino*. New York: SPI Books, 1992.

Underwater Women in Shakespeare on Film

Charles S. Ross

Underwater women are prominent in Hollywood films based on Shakespeare's plays, mainly from the 1990s, where a figure, usually a woman, floats underwater, silently and in slow motion, and then emerges, often as a changed person or in different circumstances. Sometimes clumsily handled, this symbolic immersion and miraculous release represents what Hélène Cixous calls the woman's "inevitable struggle against conventional man" (309). The symbolism of social oppression is not specific but general, what Diane Price Herndl calls the "systemic nature of women's oppression" (3). In other words, the immersion and surfacing of a woman does not express a complaint about a specific man, but a more general grievance about the way women are forced to exist in the world. Noticeably absent from Akira Kurosawa's versions of Shakespeare, although present in recent Asian fiction by women, the association of water and the social oppression of women has long been a symbol and theme in Western literature and more recently in film.

The addition to Shakespeare's text of water images in the form of rain or baths or near drownings is one of the ways that filmmakers substitute visual imagery, silence, or movement in space for the shifting effect of an actor's oratory. The Soviet director Grigori Kozintsev (*King Lear*, 1970) sums up the problem of filming Shakespeare as shifting the stress from the aural to the visual (Willems 72). Directors often hesitate to add words to Shakespeare, but few feel constrained not to employ normal cinemagraphic techniques. Filmmakers assume that cinema is a visual medium and that wherever possible images should reinforce if not replace dialogue. Long tracking scenes, for example, establish one of the main differences between theater and cinema. Despite movement up, down, and across stage, revolving sets, scrims, lighting changes, and other tricks, a stage is essentially a static place during a scene. A camera, by contrast, can move from place to place, and much of the art of cinema seems to be in making the most of that advantage (Kracauer 295). Yet movement is not a value in itself; it must be associated with something to have meaning: the countryside, city streets, the rooms of a house, or faces. Water scenes operate in a similar way. Often silent and in slow motion, they provide a visual mode of denotation (Metz 72). Thus minute after minute is spent tracking characters across a landscape in Lucentio's descent through rain—representing perhaps the sad world before he meets Bianca—to the sunshine of Padua in Franco Zeffirelli's *Taming of the Shrew* (1968), or, more spectacularly, the endless streaming of warriors across a notably dry Japanese landscape in Akira Kurosawa's *Ran*, where the aridity of the landscape seems to reflect the futility of the fighting.

The use of water or drowning as a metaphor for whatever oppresses women can be found as early as Homer's *Iliad*. At the beginning of the sixth book, Helen uses an image of waves sweeping her under to indicate her own innocence of the war that she brings to Troy. Conjuring a watery scene to express her alleged wish that she had never been born, or that she had been left exposed to die as an infant, she says that she would prefer that she had been cast "into the surf where the roaring breakers crash and drag / and the waves had swept me off before all this happened" (6.274). Helen's image culminates an amazing speech in which Helen anticipates Hector's argument that she causes Troy's suffering. To meet his objection before he can raise it, she calls herself a bitch and slut, thereby establishing her ethical appeal as a victim. This self-portrait allows her to persuade Troy's greatest warrior to continue defending her, an action that illustrates what Judith Butler in *Gender Trouble* (1992) calls the performance of gender. Helen then asks Hector to sit by her, a physical gesture that is both submissive and manipulative: "But come in, rest on this seat with me, dear brother." Although Hector understands the power of her performance and refuses to join her mini-drama, Helen's speech and acting establish a connection for women between drowning in the sea and survival.

Oppressed by their social position, women were often located underwater during the middle ages. In the thirteen-century *L'Atre perilleux*, Brun sans pitié (Brun the Pitiless) forces his damsel to immerse herself naked in a fountain, and then cuts off the heads of all knights who try to rescue her. He is jealous of the knights of the Round Table, whose merit, according to the damsel, is greater than his. Sir Gawain eventually defeats her terrible companion and liberates her. The scene was common, and we see it again in *Le Haut livre du Graal*. In one of the episodes of this version of the Grail story, Marin the Jealous, believing his wife has deceived him with Gawain, forces her to jump into the cold water of a lake before he savagely whips her. She is released only by death, as Marin kills her while fighting Gawain. Another version featuring another jealous man occurs in the *Continuation de Perceval* by Gerbert de Montreuil, where Brandin Dur Cuer (Brandin the Hard Hearted) makes his lover Dyonise, the most beautiful woman in the world, dwell nude in a fountain, submerged up to her neck. He castigates her because she says that Perceval is wiser, more valiant, more courteous, and more generous, than he is. Perceval frees her from her icy penitence, but in a surprise move that may register what her oppression has done to her, she turns around and tries to cut off Perceval's head (James-Raoul 388). In each case the women are dominated not just by men but feudal codes of behavior.

Water continued to be a sign of sensuality and oppression throughout the Renaissance. One has only to think of Cleopatra's association with sexuality, overflow, excess, and the Nile (Hall, *Things* 157), the imprisonment of Florimel undersea in Spenser's *Faerie Queene* (1596), or the ducking stool of the New England Puritans in the later seventeenth century. Of course, water imagery is not confined to women in a Western tradition where baptism represents the washing away of sins. Both Viola and her brother are nearly drowned before the comic action of *Twelfth Night* can begin, and Ferdinand's father lies full fathom five before he changes his evil ways in *The Tempest*. Prospero not only washes his enemies clean, but the play suggests a new, more tolerant worldview, if not a new way of thinking: "Nothing of him that doth fade / But doth suffer a sea-change / Into something rich and strange" (1.2.397), according to Ariel's song. Mind, for Andrew Marvell, was "that ocean where each kind / Does straight its own resemblance find" ("The Garden"), a place of expression and containment. For early authors men were as socially oppressed as women are treated today.

German literature makes full use of symbolic associations between women and water (see, e.g., Schmitz-Emans) and one has only to think of Heinrich Heine's *Die Lorelei.* In English there are few books where water in one of its forms of precipitation is more oppressive than Charles Dickens's *Bleak House*. The great fog in London represents the impenetrable ways of the Court of Chancery, which oppress male and female alike. At the center of the book is a woman, Esther Summerson. Rain dripping on the eaves of the country house of Esther's mother represents both boredom and the social constraints that separate her from her daughter. The use of water as a sign of the social oppression of women will became more powerful due to its association with mortal illness, as occurs when Esther takes sick and nearly dies during a period of transition from ward to recognized heiress. She herself connects her illness to the social limitations and difficulties that weigh her down, while Dickens's wet image of confinement prefigures—to take just one more example out of many—the boredom of the English countryside in Evelyn Waugh's *A Handful of Dust.* In this novel a dark and dank countryside forebodes the death, in a riding accident, of the heroine's young son John Andrew. This loss of a son adds to marital strains that Waugh represents by an underwater image. When her husband enters her separate bedroom and Evelyn kisses him, she is compared to a "Nereid emerging from fathomless depths of clear water" (16).

In the time between Dickens and Waugh, one of the most influential examples of water as a symbol of social oppression appeared in Kate Chopin's novel *The Awakening*. First published in 1898 and reprinted in paperback during the 1970s, the novel had become one of the major additions of women's literature by the 1980s, partly due to Annette Kolodny's 1980 essay "Dancing through the Minefield," which told how in 1979 an Oxford-trained colleague voted against letting her give English-department credit for teaching a seminar on the book. Today *The Awakening* has become a staple in American high school English classes. Throughout the United States, younger generations now read a novel in which learning to swim is Chopin's metaphor for a woman's gaining confidence to overcome her marital unhappiness. The title of Chopin's novel refers to its heroine Edna's awakening to her own sense of self, which is also compared to giving birth, "an awakening to find a little new life to which she had given being" (182). Much of *The Awakening* is set on the Gulf of Mexico, where the heroine's inability to swim is connected to her sense of oppression. Edna Pontellier's outer conformity belies her inner disturbances. Eventually she awakens to how her husband and children suffocate her. She expresses her new self-mastery by taking a few strokes during a midnight excursion to the Gulf: "A certain ungovernable dread hung about her when in the water, unless there was a hand near by that might reach out and reassure her. . . . But that night she was like the little tottering, stumbling, clutching child, who of a sudden realizes his powers, and walks for the first time alone, boldly and with over-confidence. She could have shouted for joy. She did shout for joy, as with a sweeping stroke or two she lifted her body to the surface of the water. . . . As she swam she seemed to be reaching out for the unlimited in which to lose herself" (46-47). Having learned to swim—a metaphor for her new-found independence—Edna gives up keeping house and trying to please her husband. At the end of the novel, perhaps because she no longer fears water, Edna drowns herself. It somehow seems natural, just as Chopin defines oppression as the inevitable suffering of women in childbirth or in marriage. The influence of Ophelia's death by drowning is palpable in Chopin's novel and helps explain the readiness with which recent directors of *Hamlet* have embraced the trope of the underwater woman. Both Shakespeare and Chopin resonate in recent Chinese fiction too. The image of a woman in a well is common in Chinese literature, with the obvious sense that it symbolizes her powerlessness. More horrifying is the torture of a child bride in Xiao Hong's *Tales of the Hulan River*, where a child bride's in-laws subject her to a series of hot and cold baths until she dies. Jia Zhang, in a story titled "Emerald," symbolizes the social constrictions of the protagonist by the drowning not of herself but of her husband. Her imagination of the ominous sea before his death is the key to the story's imagery and a comment on her place in society.

The cumulative impact of new additions to the canon by women writers and feminist scholarship during the 1980s coincides with the cinematic deployment of the underwater woman trope, despite its artistic limitations. Films like *Sleeping with the Enemy* (1991), starring Julia Roberts, and Jane Campion's *The Piano* (1993) repeat motifs found in feminist works such as Adrienne Rich's *Diving into the Wreck* (1973) or Margaret Atwood's *Sanctuary* (1972), where submersion in a lake stands for the psychological state of a woman who has had an abortion. These were far from the first films to illustrate the oppression of or danger to women through water imagery. One thinks of the threatening showers in *Psycho* or *They Shoot Horses, Don't They?* The problem with the trope of the underwater woman is it creates unrealistic situations to suit its symbolism. *Sleeping with the Enemy* and *The Piano* illustrate how the convention of the underwater woman became a cliché, as later directors told stories that overtly sympathize with women who suffer from controlling husbands, fathers, society, or nature, or themselves. *Sleeping with the Enemy*, based on a novel by Nancy Price but written and directed by men, illustrates the potential for melodramatic unreality of the topos when a woman named Laura (Julia Roberts), cruelly mistreated by her husband, escapes her entrapment in marriage by jumping off a sailboat, a move for which she has prepared by taking swimming lessons, despite her fear of water. In a scene so unrealistic that it must be symbolic, the film shows Laura clinging to a buoy in Long Island Sound after she jumps off her husband's sailboat. Her escape illustrates two essential features of the Hollywood trope, the near drowning of a woman and her subsequent release to represent her entrance to a new and better world. The actual underwater shot is a flashback to her lessons at the YWCA, which serves the dual purpose of symbolizing a woman's entrapment and showing off Julia Robert's legs.

Equally fantastic is the underwater scene near the end of Jane Campion's *The Piano*. This Academy Award winning film tells the story of a mute woman named Ada (Holly Hunter) who joins a man in New Zealand because he has agreed to marry her even though she has a daughter born out of wedlock. Ada is mute, and her inability or unwillingness to speak symbolizes her inner rebellion at the way society punishes her. To establish her identity, she hauls a huge piano through sea, beach, and jungle to her new home. This Victorian relic expresses her private sensuality and problems. She plays it beautifully, but its stolid and heavy mass symbolizes the way society appropriates and represses her sexuality. Cold toward her condescending and rather impotent husband, she soon has an affair with a Maori half-breed named Baines (Harvey Keitel). We wait for something horrible to happen to her, and it does when her husband chops off one of her fingers, symbolically castrating her (Campion uses psychoanalytic terms in her interviews).

The symbolism works despite the fantasy. Ada's redemption comes in three parts, and each relies on water imagery in ways that will be duplicated by Shakespeare films during the 1990s. Having lost her finger, Ada gazes upward into the rain even as her Victorian skirts drag her into the mud. The imagery suggests that she has been forced into the mud of illicit love before she can find true happiness, represented by her upward gaze. In the next scene, we see someone washing a pair of angel wings that are part of a costume her daughter wears, symbolizing Ada's moral innocence. After failing once again to experience arousal except when he is violent with her, Stewart tells Baines, the Maori lover, that he wants Baines to take away his wife. Ada's release is then represented by a third drenching, when she nearly drowns in the ocean. In Campion's lyrical ending for *The Piano*, Ada finds herself under the ocean before her release: Campion was looking for what she calls a "poetic or lyrical conclusion" rather than the "original ending with a classical settlement." As she is ferried away to a new life with Baines, Ada allows the crew of the Maori war canoe to slide her piano into the sea. At the last second, she reasserts her attachment to this clumsy reminder of her passion by allowing a trailing coil of rope to catch her foot. The piano drags her under the sea, where she stays for far longer than is humanly possible. The scene is silent and filmed in slow motion. Ada then does not so much struggle to escape from the rope knotted around her ankle as find herself miraculously freed and floating to the surface. She rises to the light of day and a happy life with her lover Barnes. The visual cliché of Holly Hunter submerging serenely in silence and then surfacing with equal serenity illustrates the topos of the underwater woman as a sign of social oppression and release (even if to death) from Helen of Troy to Sylvia Plath.

With its long literary history, it is natural that rain developed as a cinematic signifier and that directors of Shakespeare films often add rain where there is none in the text. Rain is a natural equivalent to tears, although it can be made to serve other purposes. Baz Luhrmann is said never to have met a scene he did not think would be improved by rain (*Romeo+Juliet* DVD). Cinematically, at least, there is nothing unusual about the thunder and rain that Welles (1952) added when Iago volunteers to kill Cassio or the puddles that Grigori Kozintsev's Russian *King Lear* (1971) adds to the king's funeral procession. In Shakespeare's play, a doctor orders music to soothe Lear's mind, but the film lingers over Lear's head as he is carried beside a stream, which flows turbulently and in the same direction as Lear is carried. The river suggests—and here as so often one can only make an educated guess as to the director's intentions—the flow and turbulence of his life, the swelling chaos of Lear's mind, and his movement through time toward death. The films Roman Polanski made in Poland before he directed *Macbeth* (1971) make full use of the element to find cinematic ways to express the position of women. *Knife in the Water* (1963), Polanski's first international success, associates a subservient woman with the placid lake on which she and two men sail and contrast her to the violence of the two men, whose struggle for power, often physical, is represented in the film by a knife. In *Repulsion* (1965), Polanski featured a woman who, having gone mad after she is raped, keeps her tormentor's body in a bathtub.

Not infrequently water images are inserted as visual equivalents for missing text. Nontextual rain soaks Callista Flockhart (Helena) as she pushes her bicycle after Demetrius, who scorns her in the 1999 *Midsummer Night's Dream*. Yet the scene seems to have been based on a metaphor in the text, which mentions Demetrius's "showers of oaths." Equally symbolic but less hoary are underwater scenes set in swimming pools. Most of the half a dozen or so scenes that show women moving slowly underwater in Shakespeare films take place in pools. These include Juliet's falling into her father's pool in Baz Luhrman's *Romeo+Juliet* (1996), the 1930s water ballet in Branagh's *Love's Labors Lost* (1999), where the female visitors to Navarre find themselves synchronously swimming underwater as soon as they are denied entrance to Ferdinand's court, and Ophelia's swimming in Claudius's high-rise in Michael Almereyda's *Hamlet* (2000).

The conventionality of the underwater scene reminds us of Vladimir Nabokov's disapproval of the ordinariness of sex scenes in cinema during the 1950s: "The scene with the water-ski girl, gulping and giggling, is exceptionally successful," wrote Nabokov. "But I was appalled by the commonplace quality of the sexual passages. I would like to say something about that. Clichés and conventions breed remarkably fast" (137). As if to illustrate Nabokov's point, Kenneth Branagh (1996) and Michael Almereyda seize every opportunity to make Ophelia as wet as possible in their films, in part to foreshadow Ophelia's death by drowning but also to symbolize the forces that constrain her. The brook where Gertrude says Ophelia drowns is already symbolic in the text, since apparently no one witnessed the event, or they would have assisted her, and Gertrude's lovely description of the drowning may be just a way the queen calms Ophelia's choleric brother. This symbolism lends itself to cinematic expansion, however, since Ophelia is already an underwater woman in the text. Earlier directors kept Ophelia dry, but by the 1990s Hollywood had created associations they both directors enlist. Branagh's water images are both clever and absurd. Laertes himself makes his sister an underwater woman by comparing Ophelia's youth and maidenhood to a dewed flower liable to rot before it blooms: "Too often before their buttons be disclos'd, / And in the morn and liquid dew of youth, / Contagious blastments are most imminent" (1.3.40-42). Consciously or not, the film draws on the trope when it sets Laertes' conversation with Ophelia against the fountains of a geometric garden. If we credit the camera with providing a visual image that expresses the core of this difficult line, it is nonetheless odd to see fountains full of water in winter, to judge by the snow on the ground. Real fountains would be drained to prevent their cracking. Such absurdities often indicate symbolism, and here it seems that Branagh not only represents Laertes's words and foreshadows Ophelia's watery demise, but also suggests a relationship between the water that will kill her and the oppressive social conventions that prevent her from loving Hamlet. Having overlooked the absurdity of an unfrozen fountain in winter, Branagh at first seems alert to the practical problem that Ophelia cannot possibly drown outdoors during the dead of a Danish winter. She accepts, or provokes, a hosing at the same time as she mouths a key that presumably allows her to escape from her cell. But the symbolism of the underwater woman carries Branagh away when he has guard aim a fire hose at Ophelia and soak her in her padded cell. The soaking of an oppressed woman whose madness may be socially induced carries with it images of the New England ducking stool for witches and scolds. Branagh could have let us imagine Ophelia freezing to death, but he inserts a quick clip of Ophelia underwater during Gertrude's speech. This addition to the play, where Shakespeare never shows Ophelia actually drowning, owes its existence to the trope of the underwater woman.

Michael Almereyda is equally intent to use water to express Ophelia's tragedy. He associates her watery conditional with Hamlet's "To be or not to be" speech by intercutting frames of Ophelia beside a fountain in New York City with Hamlet (Ethan Hawke) as he replays lines from the speech on various digital devices. This montage suggests that Hamlet is meditating not on death or suicide, the usual interpretations, but on his relationship with Ophelia. Later, as Hamlet views retrospective DVDs of his father, Ophelia shows up, not Gertrude (the wife who betrayed Hamlet, Sr.), and when the speech is over, the film cuts back to Ophelia at the fountain. She balances on the fountain's edge of the fountain, an action meant to connote her mental instability, before the film cuts again to Hamlet at home. Hamlet's meditation on a "sea of troubles" is focused almost exclusively on Ophelia in this film, which constantly associates water with the constraints that people and society place on Ophelia: Scorned by Hamlet and oppressed by her father, Ophelia imagines herself underwater in Almereyda's *Hamlet,* and a later scene also associates the men in Ophelia's life with the waters that will kill her. It takes place in a high-rise building where Polonius and Ophelia find Claudius swimming laps. Claudius's pool reflects Ophelia's red jacket as she listens to her father and Claudius discuss her impact on Hamlet. She stares in the pool while they talk, then, in what turns out to be a mental fantasy, she jumps in just as her father is saying that her relationship with Hamlet "must not be." Between her moment of reflection and fantasy of immersion, Ophelia walks as if she is having trouble keeping her balance, again fitting Hollywood's association between mental imbalances and being underwater. Ophelia seems to jump in and cover her face, to experience a wave of madness, but she recovers, this time, and only *feels* like she has been underwater. Hollywood takes full advantage of Ophelia's drowning as an image of her lack of power.

The lights of an urban waterfall illuminate Ophelia as the film once again creates a montage out of Hamlet muttering "to be" while Ophelia delivers Hamlet his remembrances of her. The water seems to fall in slow motion, an image of Ophelia's reluctance, sadness, and powerless condition. Her movements are suggestive, and ominous, like Garbo's in *Anna Karenina* (Panofsky 288). There is textual warrant and perhaps cinematic necessity for having fountains foreshadow Ophelia's madness and death. We are never clear, in this film of *Hamlet*, exactly how Ophelia dies. We see her lying in the pool of a fountain. She may have jumped, not drowned. No one understands her, but the images make the terrible pressures that drove her to her death plain enough. Less absurd, to my mind, is Baz Luhrmann's *Romeo+Juliet* (1997), which establishes baths as a sign of male power that endangers women. According to the director's conversation on the DVD, it was an afterthought, but the film crew set the second half of a meeting between Juliet's shady father and Paris in a steam bath because the heli-pad on top of Capulet's building that the script called for was not available. Nonetheless, the steam bath reinforces the themes of the first half of the conversation between Capulet and Paris. The two men smirk as they discuss Juliet's sexuality, her readiness for marriage, and her future motherhood. They wink and nod about the fresh young buds who will attend Capulet's party. The steam extrapolates their heated state. This association between water and male sexuality is reinforced by the first shots of the Capulet mansion, set behind a vertically gushing fountain whose bubbling spills onto our first view of Lady Capulet, who wears provocative underwear. She looks hideous without her wig or make-up, the image of a woman who defines herself by her attractiveness to men. By filming Capulet and Paris in a steam bath as they discuss Juliet's future, the film figures the way the male world of the Capulets skews Juliet's personality.

After establishing this connection between male power and water, Luhrman gives us our first glimpse of Juliet at home, happily innocent in her bathtub, but underwater. There is no bathtub in Shakespeare's text, and it is almost imperceptible in the film. Her nurse runs through the house at the bidding of Lady Capulet yelling for "Hooliet" as Juliet holds her breath. Her hair floats about her. The symbolism is multivalent. As a sign of male power, the water is ominous, like the fateful stars in the original text, giving a premonition of disaster to the audience that the fictional characters ignore. Yet Juliet's enigmatic expression also suggests that her free-floating experience also follows the symbolic pattern of a woman's oppression and spiritual release. According to meanings attached to the underwater woman by the 1990s, this scene suggests that Juliet, however confined, is an independent thinker. She will escape her parents' plans. She will not marry Paris, even if she has to die to escape the constrictions of the world.

The theory of semiotics is that anything can represent anything (Elam 14). Water works in the film like the stars in the text, both brilliant and ominous. This fluidity allows water imagery to establish a symmetry between Romeo and Juliet, since both are trapped by social forces and both seek a clearer, better world. Romeo therefore takes on the role of the underwater woman, just as in the text he worries that his association with Juliet makes him effeminate. We see him underwater when he must wash his face before meeting Juliet to cleanse himself of the drug that Mercutio has given him on the way to the ball, where the lovers first see each other through a fishtank that separates the washrooms for men and women in Capulet's mansion, and later when he leaves Juliet the morning after and falls into her swimming pool. After Romeo leaves the mask he had been wearing in the basin of water where he has washed away Mercutio's drug, he looks in a mirror; then he turns to stare at the fish. In three steps he leaves behind his false self, the one who loved Rosalind and lived in a world of misguided and immoral sexuality. He stops to see his true self in a mirror (figured in the film by the way DiCaprio moves his hair back into place), then he looks with awe into the medium that will first reveal Juliet. The way water is photographed provides a visual icon of social oppression, for the lovers lived in a world of hopeless taste, immoral behavior, and parental bickering and control that they cannot escape. Commenting on the fish tank through which Romeo and Juliet meet underwater, Luhrmann mentions that the water provides a transition to tragedy, which is similar to his comment on the beach scene after Romeo and Juliet are married, where the filmmakers added clouds to suggest the approaching storm. Luhrmann also says that the fish tank provided an excuse for silence as well as a way to create surprise.

What distinguishes Hollywood's scenes of underwater women is the way women immerse slowly and then ascend as if somehow transformed or released of some social weight. After Danes and DiCaprio fall into the Capulet pool that replaces Juliet's balcony as the place of their colloquy, they are first shown on security monitors in the room of a guard, then underwater, where Romeo turns in slow motion and faces a staring Juliet. Her arms make an angel-wing movement over her head, not to embrace Romeo but to move her to the surface. In Shakespeare's text, Juliet is always cleverer than Romeo, although he is not dull. In Luhrmann's film, she seeks the surface more openly than Romeo but then emerges more slowly, lingering, as it were, underwater, to stress her symbolic release. The ability of Juliet and a Romeo to wash themselves from their social conditions lies at the heart of the balcony scene that Lurhrann transfers into Capulet's swimming pool. The slow motion sensuality of the water meanwhile expresses the adolescent sexuality that overwhelms the couple.

Yet another water image symbolically expresses the constraints on Juliet after her father insists that she marry Paris. Her nurse draws a bath for her as soon as Juliet seems to relent and agree to marry Paris (we know from the text that she is lying). Again there is no bath in the text, and in the film we only catch a glimpse of it, but that glimpse suffices to establish how this modern Hollywood trope influences the cinematic representation of Juliet's quandary. For the nurse Angelica, water is a cleansing agent that symbolically allows Juliet to deny her marriage, but for the audience, it is a sign of Juliet's oppression. The film cuts most of the dialogue and instead finds an equivalent for Juliet's duplicity in this scene of her nurses turning on the taps. This image replaces a complicated set of double entendres, which start when Juliet weeps for Romeo but pretends, to her mother, to be weeping for Tybalt. Luhrman's use of the underwater woman images works throughout the film. At the very end, a series of flashbacks of Juliet underwater establishes a connection between her surfacing in a swimming pool and her death. The trope, which follows the pattern of Chopin's *Awakening*, moves from near drowning to some kind of release from the world that lead her to suicide.

More complicated than Juliet's sensual immersions, less obvious than Ophelia's drowning, perhaps the most complex example of the link between pools and social evils in recent Shakespeare films occurs in Julie Taymor's *Titus* (1999). Taymor stages an orgy set in a Roman pool that she adds to the text, and she pays special attention to the oppression of Tamora. In an interview with Dan Kleinman, Taymor admits to using images and influences from her own time: "I'm a person of this day and age, so my approach to the material is quite naturally influenced by all the movies, plays and paintings I've absorbed. You can't run away from all of them. It's how you twist and turn those influences that makes the work interesting" (Taymor disc 2). She admits the orgy does not come from the play, but argues that it opens the play, replacing the "elegant beauty of stylization" of theater with a "visceral reality" characteristic of TV or cinema. *Titus Andronicus*, for Taymor, is a dissertation on violence, and the swimming-pool orgy is meant to show Roman decadence. The result is a schematic but brilliant twist on the Hollywood trope of the underwater woman. Taymor, who studied puppetry in south Asia, has a complex and studied understanding of rituals. A bath that resembles the pouring of boiling oil from a rampart ironically cleanses Titus and his sons when they return from war. Swamps and rain surround the raped Lavinia, suggesting both tears and life-giving moisture. Bell jars encase the heads of Titus's sons, as if to ungender Sylvia Plath's image of despair; Titus retreats to his bath, like the dying Marat, but arises to take his awful revenge on Saturninus. Taymor drowns Virgo (Justice) in the emperor's pool and then releases Tamora, her double, to her wickedness and, ultimately, her death. Taymor uses the orgy not simply to signal Tamora's mistreatment as a Roman captive and mother, but to salute Shakespeare's freedom to envisage Tamora as a monster of revenge. As Taymor says in her interview with Dan Kleinman, Tamora is beautiful and smart, but she changes into a monster because "vengeance destroys her, it eats her up inside" (Taymor disc 2) and Taymor creates a watery equivalent for Tamora, the Goth victim of Roman power.

The film uses a Roman pool to combine into one scene the arrows of justice that Titus shoots toward heaven and Tamora's deception of the emperor. A large-breasted figure floats in a pool among couples engaged in a silent caricature of sex. And in an adjoining area, Saturninus lies exhausted, clutching Tamora's naked breasts. Marcus tells Titus's followers, who are supposed to be petitioning heaven for the return of Justice, to shoot into the atrium where the orgy takes place. Their arrows disperse the participants, and one hits the floating balloon, dousing whoever has received oral sex on its back (see Blumenthal 225). Outside, Titus says he has shot an arrow into Virgo's lap (Virgo is another name for Astraea, the goddess of justice who left the earth). The statue that receives the arrow is therefore an image of Justice. She deflates, as if returning to earth, but in this case into the water. The collapse of this figure of a woman signals the end of Saturninus's misrule and the start of Tamora's revenge on Rome, for which she has been coddling the emperor all this time and deceiving him while having Aaron's baby (for Tamora is horribly oppressed by Titus, who has murdered her son; by the emperor, who marries her to spite Titus and to indulge his perverse need to be mothered; and by society whose racial codes condemn her liaison with Aaron the Moor). The film does not fall into the trap of chick flicks like *Sleeping with the Enemy* or *The Piano*. There is no unrealistic submersion and resurfacing trope. But there is a *roman à clef* element. Properly tragic in Aristotle's terms, neither better nor worse than we are, Taymor's Tamora is the equivalent of Julie Taymor herself. The bosomy balloon that floats on the pool is the same golden color and as the same large breasts as Tamora, especially when her sons join her, while the name Tamora is uncannily close to Taymor. The balloon statue, designed by Dante Ferretti, is based on a work of art owned by Taymor herself: "Her cheeks and breasts distressed as if from years of sea winds, a giant figurehead labeled 'The Havoc' greets visitors to Julie Taymor's New York apartment" (Blumenthal 7). First published in 1995, before Taymor made *Titus*, Blumenthal's book includes a photograph of this figurehead. Material added in 1999 includes a still photo of the floating figure from the film. The balloon is Taymor's personal signature, a testimony to the vitality of Tamora as a character capable of both good and evil, for Taymor goes beyond the Hollywood cliché by insisting that Tamora's actions are not justice, but revenge.

Taymor's work, particularly her time studying rituals in Bali and refined by her association of women and water—an association she shares with Campion—makes it possible to compare the complexity of her imagery to that of Kurosawa. Kurosawa's explicit avoidance of water in *Ran* (1985) indicates a difference between the work of a Japanese artist and the standard semiotics of Hollywood. Although Hidetora (Lear) has sons instead of daughters to suit the earlier Japanese culture in which Kurosawa sets the scene, nonetheless the film includes women so oppressed by Hidetora and his world of violence that if the film had been made in the 1990s by a lesser artist they might have been shown swimming underwater. Taro's wife and Jiro's wife lose their families to Hidetora's violence before they marry his sons. Taro's wife Lady Kaede craves revenge; Jiro's wife Lady Sué, her opposite, finds solace in Buddhism. One feels the presence of the trope when Lady Kaede receives Lady Sué's head and announces her true goal, just before a stunned general cuts off her head and her blood splatters in a symbolic design on the wall behind her. Otherwise Kurosawa avoids water because the world of Samurai warriors is resolutely male. Several times the director shows fluffy white clouds, and later in the film these become ominously dark, but it never rains. The film is nearly waterless, like Hiroshi Teshigahara's *Woman in the Dunes* (1964), where social oppression is represented by life in a giant sand pit. In Shakespeare's play, the storm on the heath explicitly represents the mental chaos Lear experiences. But in the equivalent scene, when Hidetora (Lear) leaves the castle of his second son, Jiro, he goes out not into a storm but into parching heat and famine. Toward the end Kurosawa adds water to *Ran*, but it comes in the form not of rain but a river that Saburo, the third son, crosses to rescue his father. To Jiro, Saburo's crossing is a declaration of war (one thinks of Caesar crossing the Rubicon), and so Jiro (the Goneril figure) prepares to defend his castle. Saburo asks only for his father and is dismayed when Fujimaki, with whom he had spent his exile, arrives with his forces in white. Fujimaki is the France character, who maintains the offer of his daughter despite Saburo's rift with his father Hidetora. It is interesting that Saburo crosses a river, but Fujimaki, who must come from the same territory, does not, or at least we do not see him do so. This ambiguity indicates that like so many water scenes, the river has been added to the text and it plays a symbolic role. That is, the river serves Saburo the way water scenes reposition women: it signals a moment of recognition or release or a shedding of the past. Saburo, Hidetora's third son, crosses the river because he is now ready to fight his older brother and restore his father.

In recent Hollywood films the trope of the underwater woman offers a generalized symbol of oppression that goes beyond a specific problem—often a domineering husband—to suggest a wider need for women to move outside the confines of the world in which they find themselves. The trope itself is a variation of the ritual of bathing to rid one of one's earlier self or the stigma of the world, traces of which can even be found in Kurosawa's films. This symbolism seems to be universal, in contrast to shots of women moving slowly underwater, caressed by the camera, their hair moving in slow Medusa motions, which strike one as distractions. Part of the problem is that the scenes are often clumsily inserted, nowhere more so than in Branagh's *Hamlet,* when guards turn their fire hoses on Ophelia. Still, the trope has a powerful grip on Anglophile filmmakers looking for visual equivalents to Shakespeare's text. It accounts for the variety of ways that films have found to moisten Ophelia, Juliet, Viola, Miranda (who is first seen by a swimming pool in *Forbidden Planet*, 1956), Tamora, and Titania's fairies. By contrast, it does not seem to be a strong part of Chinese tradition. None of the women in the most influential of

Chinese novels, the eighteenth-century *The Dream of the Red Chamber,* undergoes immersion, although Baiyu's descent to the world and final apotheosis offers a paradigm for ritual renewal. Women are isolated on islands in the fantasy worlds of Chinese opera, and if not actually soaked can be surrounded on stage by waving banners to indicate immersion. I am not sure how it might work if a filmmaker like Ang Lee turned his attention to Shakespeare. But if the trend continues and is not co-opted as a sign of queerness (as it is in *Prospero's Books* [1991] or when Kevin Kline, playing a nineteenth century Bottom, is otherwise inexplicably soaked by a flagon of Chianti in *A Midsummer Night's Dream* [1999]), we may expect to see submerged Cordelias and Desdemonas in future films that with any luck will combine the aesthetics of Asia and the pleasures of Hollywood.

Works Cited

Blumenthal, Eileen. *Julie Taymor: Playing with Fire: Theater, Opera, Film.* New York: Harry N. Adams, 1999.

Chopin, Kate. *The Awakening.* New York: Bedford, 1972.

Cixous, Hélène. "The Laugh of the Medusa." Trans. Keith Cohen and Paula Cohen. *Critical Theory Since 1965.* Ed. Hazard Adams and Leroy Searle. Tallahassee: Florida State UP, 1986. 309-20.

Hall, Peter. "A Film Directors' Symposium." *Cineaste* 23.4 (1998): 48-55.

Hapgood, Robert. "The Artistry of Franco Zeffirelli." *Shakespeare the Movie.* Ed. Lynda E. Boose and Richard Burt. New York: Routledge, 1997. 80-94.

Hedrick, Donald K. "War is Mud: Branagh's *Harry V* and the Types of Political Ambiguity." *Shakespeare the Movie.* Ed. Lynda E. Boose and Richard Burt. New York: Routledge, 1997. 45-66.

Herndl, Diane Price. *Feminisms: An Anthology of Literary Theory and Practice.* Ed. Robyn R. Warhol and Diane Price Herndl. New Brunswick: Rutgers UP, 1997.

James-Raoul, Danièle, and Claude Thomasset. *Dans l'eau, sous l'eau. Le Monde aquatique au Moyen Age.* Paris: PU de Paris-Sorbonne, 2002.

Elam, Keir. *The Semiotics of Theatre and Drama.* London: Methuen, 1980.

Kolodny, Annette, "Dancing Through the Minefields: Some Observations on the Theory, Practice, and Politics of a Feminist Literary Criticism." *Critical Theory Since 1965.* Ed. Hazard Adams and Leroy Searle. Tallahassee: Florida State UP, 1986. 499-512.

Kracauer, Siegfried. "From *Theory of Film.*" *Film Theory and Criticism.* Ed. Leo Braudy and Marshall Cohen. New York: Oxford UP, 1999. 171-82.

Hamlet. Dir. Franco Zeffirelli. Hollywood: Warner Brothers, 1990.

Hamlet. Dir. Kenneth Branagh. Hollywood: Warner Brothers, 1996.

Hamlet. Dir. Michael Almereyda. Hollywood: Miramax, 2000.

Love's Labour's Lost. Dir. Kenneth Branagh. Hollywood: Miramax, 2000.

Marvell, Andrew. *The Poems of Andrew Marvell.* Ed. Nigel Smith. New York: Pearson Longman, 2007.

Metz, Christian. "Some Points in the Semiotics of Cinema." *Film Theory and Criticism*. Ed. Leo Braudy and Marshall Cohen. New York: Oxford UP, 1999. 68-89.

A Midsummer Night's Dream. Dir. Michael Hoffman. Hollywood: Fox Searchlight Pictures, 1999.

Nabokov, Vladimir. *Strong Opinions*. New York: McGraw-Hill, 1973.

Panofsky, Erwin. "Style and Medium in the Motion Pictures." Ed. Leo Braudy and Marshall Cohen. *Film Theory and Criticism*. New York: Oxford UP, 1999. 279-92.

Parker, Oliver. "Shakespeare in the Cinema: A Film Directors' Symposium." *Cineaste* 23.4 (1998): 48-55.

The Piano. Dir. Jane Campion. Hollywood: Miramax Films, 1993.

Prospero's Books. Dir. Peter Greenaway. Hollywood: Palace Films, 1991.

Ran. Dir. Akira Kurosawa. Tokyo: Fox Lorber, 1985.

Romeo+Juliet. Dir. Baz Luhrmann. Hollywood: Twentieth Century Fox, 1996.

Schmitz-Emans, Monika. *Seetiefen and Seelentiefen. Literarische Spiegelungen innerer und äusserer Fremde*. Würzburg: Königshausen & Neumann, 2003.

Taymor, Julie. "Interview at Columbia with Dan Kleinman." *Titus Andronicus*. DVD. Hollywood: Twentieth Century Fox Home Entertainment, 2000.

Waugh, Evelyn. *A Handful of Dust*. Harmondsworth: Penguin, 1999.

Willems, Michèle. "Verbal-Visual, Verbal-Pictorial or Textual-Televisual? Reflections on the BBC Shakespearean Series." *Shakespeare and the Moving Image*. Ed. Anthony Davies and Stanley Wells. Cambridge: Cambridge UP, 1994. 69-85.

Woman in the Dunes. Dir. Hiroshi Teshigahara. Tokyo: Toho, 1964.

Illustrations

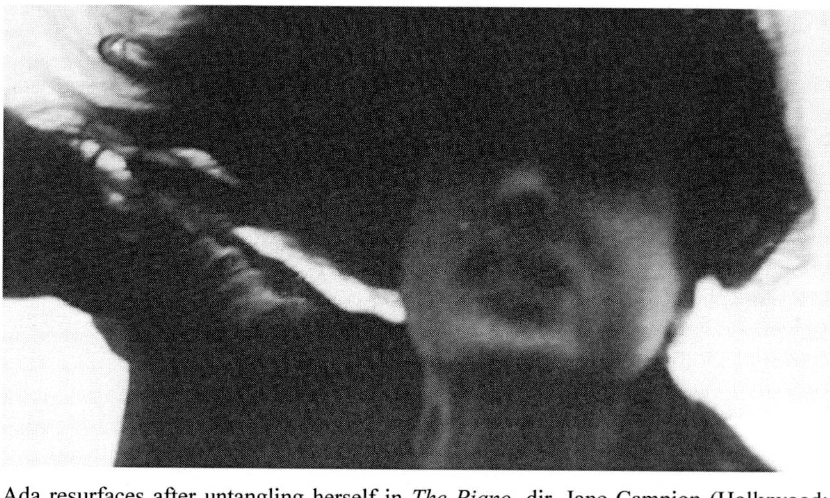

Ada resurfaces after untangling herself in *The Piano*, dir. Jane Campion (Hollywood: Miramax Films, 1993).

A synchronous swim in *Love's Labor's Lost,* dir. Kenneth Branagh (Hollywood: Miramax Films, 2000).

Branagh finds a way to dowse Ophelia in *Hamlet,* dir. Kenneth Branagh (Hollywood: Castle Rock Entertainment, 1996).

Ophelia, drowned, filmed underwater in Branagh's *Hamlet* (Hollywood: Castle Rock Entertainment, 1996).

Ophelia going mad goes underwater as her father speculates on the causes of Hamlet's madness, in *Hamlet*, dir. Michael Almereyda (Hollywood: Miramax Films, 2000).

Our first view of Juliet, in her bath, in *Romeo+Juliet*, dir. Baz Luhrmann (Hollywood: Twentieth Century Fox, 1996).

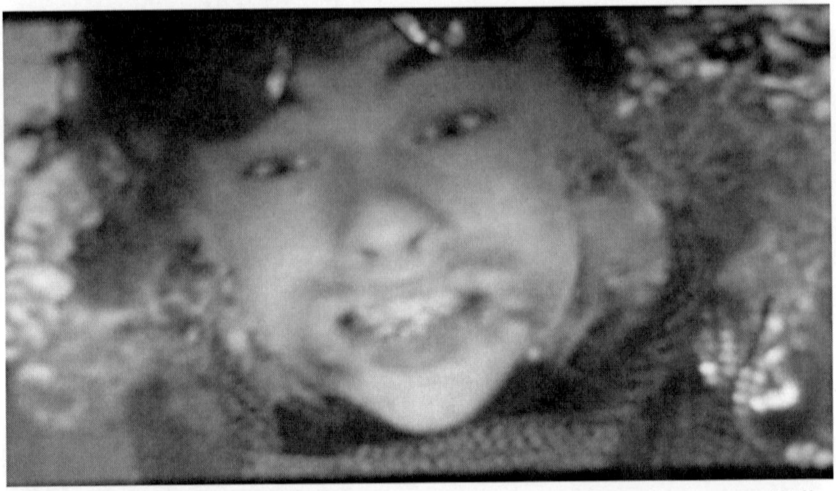

Romeo washes away the effects of drugs in *Romeo+Juliet,* dir. Baz Luhrmann (Hollywood: Twentieth Century Fox, 1996).

Romeo first sees Juliet underwater through a fish tank in *Romeo+Juliet*, dir. Baz Luhrmann (Hollywood: Twentieth Century Fox, 1996).

Juliet first sees Romeo underwater through the same fish tank in *Romeo+Juliet*, dir. Baz Luhrmann (Hollywood: Twentieth Century Fox, 1996).

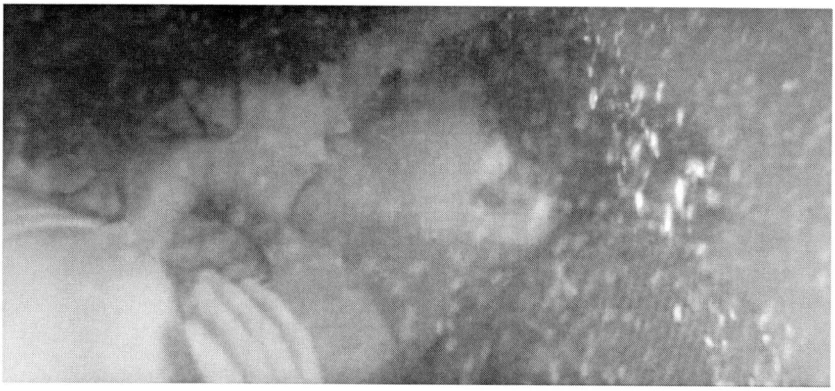

Baz Luhrmann's Hollywood version of the balcony scene in *Romeo+Juliet* (Hollywood: Twentieth Century Fox, 1996).

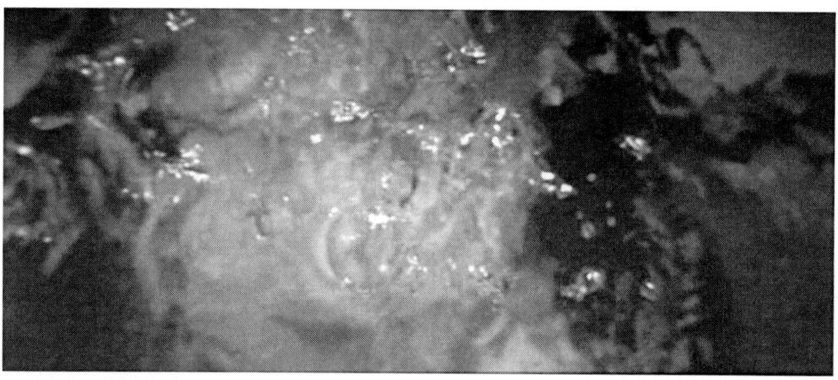

Romeo underwater, Hollywood's cinematic equivalent of Juliet's vision of the fate of Romeo, when he leaves her bedroom, in *Romeo+Juliet*, dir. Baz Luhrmann (Hollywood: Twentieth Century Fox, 1996).

Cultural Anxiety and the Female Body in Zeffirelli's *Hamlet*

Xianfeng Mou

When Franco Zeffirelli launched his shooting of *Hamlet* (released in 1990), he stated that he wanted to "present the play as Shakespeare 'meant' it to be performed" (Dawson 212). His invocation of Shakespeare's authority, together with his *auteur* interpretations and the huge commercial success of his two other Shakespeare plays, *Romeo and Juliet* and *The Taming of the Shrew*, seemed to invest his filmic interpretation of *Hamlet* with tremendous authority. Many critics have thought that Zeffirelli "focus[ed] on *Hamlet* as a family romance [and] plac[ed] Gertrude firmly at its center" (Crowl 67), thereby greatly "enhanc[ing] Gertrude's importance" (Weller 122). However, some feminist critics, such as Carol Chillington Rutter, refute the claim of political correctness and argue that rather than enhance women, the film further degrades Gertrude by portraying her as "behaving like an adolescent only just discovering the 'heyday in the blood'" (Rutter 304). William van Waston seconds Rutter's view and reads the film as manifesting not so much an advancing of the cause of women as "[Zeffirelli's] obsessive nostalgia for patriarchy which has led him into an increasingly reactionary position" (qtd. in Cartmell 217). These interpretations seem less aesthetic than ideologically at odds.

To explain how Zeffirelli can both seem to promote and degrade the female characters in *Hamlet*, partcularly Gertrude and Ophelia, I will analyze the director's handling of the Nunnery and Mousetrap scenes in terms of the female body. Compared to Shakespeare's original text, Zeffirelli's representations, although seemingly liberal, actually strip women of power. The result is that Zeffirelli grants more power to Hamlet, a cultural code for late twentieth-century North America, than the play warrants. Zeffirelli endows Hamlet with absolute power in the film to signal the increasing anxiety of contemporary culture over the progress of the women's movement and the increasing power of women in cultural production.

By analyzing the lines that the actors and actresses speak as well as Zeffirelli's visual narratives in the two scenes, I will show how the film's hidden desire regarding women is revealed by the way Zeffirelli constructs the meanings of the female body. To explain this process, I draw on Julia Kristeva's view that language reflects the desire of the subject: "*Desire* [is] where the subject is implicated (body and history), and *symbolic order*, reason, intelligibility. Critical knowledge ties and unties their imbrications" (116). Since literature and art give rise to applications of ideological doctrines (Kristeva 95), it follows that Zeffirelli's film reflects the cultural beliefs of contemporary North America (US and Canada). At the same time, Kristeva argues that interpretations of literature and art such as mine are necessarily varied and open: "an always infinite discourse, an always open enunciation of a search. . . . The *objective* of this search is to make *manifest* the very *procedure* through which this 'science,' its 'object' and their relationship are brought about" (95). My purpose, then, is to reveal the procedures by which the film represents and constructs meanings about the female body.

The theories on discourse and power of Judith Butler and Michel Foucault are useful guides as we go beyond the mere recognition that Zeffirelli's film degrades Gertrude and seek to find the workings of power that produce the feminist illusion. Foucault's theory of the regime of power-knowledge-pleasure further exposes the specific workings of power between Hamlet and Gertrude as well as those between Hamlet and Ophelia. In *The History of Sexuality*, Foucault proposes that the discourse on human sexuality is sustained by the regime of power-knowledge-pleasure (11). The four principal features of the regime are particularly relevant to our discussion: the negative relation, the insistence of the rule, the logic of censorship, and the uniformity of the apparatus. According to Foucault, any connection between power and sex is established in negative relationships. That is, where sex and pleasure are concerned, power always says no. Second, the legitimacy of sex is to be deciphered on the basis of its relation to the law laid down by power through language. Third, power censors sex in a logical sequence: sex is not permitted; it cannot be said; its existence is denied. Fourth, the apparatus of power is characterized by uniformity. In other words, power is exercised over sex at all levels (Foucault 83-84). Butler refines Foucault's thought by arguing that power is discursively constructed through the creation of sexual norms and the repeated citation of those norms (10). The subject who creates and cites the norms to discipline the object simultaneously establishes "an originary complicity with power in the formation of the 'I'" (Butler 15). In other words, the subject does not enjoy an anterior power. It is rather through a process of creation and reiteration of norms that he simultaneously invokes and constructs power for himself. Therefore, the negative meanings the two key women bear in the film—that Gertrude's sexuality is rampant and aberrant and that Ophelia is disloyal, insincere, and insignificant—are constructed discursively by Hamlet through the lines that he speaks. In creating the norms that demean the two women, Hamlet simultaneously constructs himself as virtuous and invests himself with power over Gertrude and Ophelia. In addition to these theories of discourse, we need to remember that films are not so much linguistic exercises as visual narratives. Besides analyzing Zeffirelli's discursive construction of power through each character's scripts, we must also draw attention to power communicated through the visual narratives created by camera placement, such as camera angles, the screen positions of characters, and above all Zeffirelli's masculine cinematic gaze. Zeffirelli employs a variety of visual techniques to invest Hamlet with predominant power as the active doer and gazer. At the same time, the film's superficial visual enhancement of Gertrude paradoxically, along with the textually sanctioned degradation of Ophelia, meets the cultural need of subjecting women to further control. Degradation camouflaged as enhancement, however, is where the film does its greatest harm.

The film's displays of verbal and physical violence first attracted me to the topic, but Zeffirelli's subtle choice of where to place Hamlet's "get thee to a nunnery" speech strikes me as one of his most telling editorial comments. Under Zeffirelli's direction, Hamlet delivers the lines to Ophelia not in the traditional Nunnery scene, but in the Mousetrap scene ("Get thee [to] a nunn'ry, why wouldst thou be a breeder of sinners? . . . Believe none of us" (3.1.120-28). Zeffirelli's move has invited a wealth of interpretations. Crowl thinks that the shift makes "'The Mousetrap' . . . less about Hamlet's power struggle with Claudius than about the conclusion of his relationship with Ophelia and the preparation for his confrontation with Gertrude" (59-61). Rutter disagrees with him. She believes that since most audiences know the Nunnery speech, its verbal violence already exists in their minds. The speech's absence in the film's Nunnery scene and unexpected appearance in the Mousetrap scene actually abuse Ophelia twice (306). They are both right and wrong. Crowl is right because the director is concerned with concluding Hamlet's relationship with Ophelia. Rutter is right because Zeffirelli's displacement carries the verbal violence over to the Mousetrap scene. But they both fail to see through Zeffirelli's strategic move to his primary motive of defining Ophelia as insignificant.

Does Ophelia's body matter? The answer becomes evident when we connect the verbal violence of the Nunnery speech to the physical violence with which Hamlet treats Ophelia in this particular scene. Compared to the play, these instances of physical violence betray Zeffirelli's added efforts to subjugate Ophelia. Such excessive physical violence lacks ground because of the film's macro-context as a family romance between Gertrude and Hamlet and the scene's micro-context of Hamlet's awareness of the spies at the beginning of the scene where he has spotted Polonius and Claudius hiding up (see Crowl 59). These two contexts lead to two conclusions: First, in the film, Hamlet does not love Ophelia, which differs from the situation of the play; second, in the film, he knows the spies are there, whereas he cannot be certain in the play. In fact, Zeffirelli has often been quoted as declaring that Hamlet does not love Ophelia (Hapgood 90). It follows that Zeffirelli should not make Hamlet act deeply hurt when Hamlet gets Ophelia's evasive answer "At home, my lord" to his question "Where is your father?" (3.1.129-30). From then on, Hamlet berates Ophelia, pinches her chin, thrusts her against the stone wall, and hurls the "remembrance" to the ground in front of her feet (3.1.142-49). The violence of his vituperation connects with the violence of the Nunnery speech Zeffirelli moves to the Mousetrap scene. Hamlet's ungrounded violence indicates Zeffirelli's hidden message that Ophelia does not matter.

Hamlet's cruelty further intensifies Ophelia's pain and marks her as unimportant when we consider that Zeffirelli insists that Ophelia loves Hamlet while never establishing any reciprocation on Hamlet's part. When Hamlet denies he has given her any remembrance, Ophelia objects: "My honor'd lord, you know right well you did / And with them words of so sweet breath compos'd / As made these things more rich" (3.1.96-98). Through her passionate tone, the sympathetic audience can almost feel her heart quivering. When Hamlet goes on to say, "I did love you once," the deep hurt in her tremulous reply—"Indeed, my lord, you made me believe so"—makes her pain almost tangible (3.1.114-15). In the Mousetrap scene, Hamlet continues to poke at her wounds by insulting her with his bantering about "country matters." This scene features a public environment for entertainment. That Zeffirelli instructs Hamlet to deliver the Nunnery speech under such a context suggests that his Hamlet trivializes Ophelia and her love. After confirming Claudius as the guilty murderer, Hamlet gives Ophelia a final, violent, and aggressive kiss. Then he finishes her off with a flippant "farewell," marking the end of his display of power and completing the violent circle. Rather than change and invent new lines, as he will do to demean Gertrude, Zeffirelli only changes the tones in which Hamlet and Ophelia deliver their lines to convey his subtle condemnation of her.

Besides rearranging the order of speeches to demean Ophelia, Zeffirelli draws on the language of the play to establish negative meanings for Ophelia and endow Hamlet with exclusive power of discourse. Hamlet defines Ophelia as unchaste, disloyal, and insincere. He finds faults with her physical beauty—"That if you be honest and fair, [your honesty] should admit no discourse to your beauty"—and accuses her of being unchaste; his main purpose, however, is to paint her as disloyal and insincere—"I'll give thee this plague for thy dowry: be thou as chaste as ice. . . . God hath given you one face, and you make yourself another" (3.1.102, 104, 106-07, 134-39, 142-49). Zeffirelli retains most of the key lines for Hamlet in the Nunnery scene but heavily cuts Ophelia's. At the crucial moment when Hamlet berates her, Zeffirelli makes Ophelia totally speechless to give Hamlet absolute discursive power. Regarding her answer "At home, my lord," Zeffirelli aligns his camera angle with Hamlet's male point of view. By making Hamlet aware of the presence of the spies, Zeffirelli leaves Ophelia no way out. She must choose either complete silence and loyalty to her father and the king, which she does, or loyalty to Hamlet, although he hardly earns her trust at this point. No matter what she chooses, she will be condemned. Ophelia receives a nominal nod for her resistance in the Mousetrap scene. Although despondent in love, she is still defiant at the beginning of the scene. When Hamlet stings her, "Do you think I meant country matters?" she emphatically retorts: "I think of nothing, my lord" (3.2.116-17). Her stress of "I" instead of "nothing" shows her subtle assertiveness. When Hamlet accuses Gertrude of a hasty remarriage, Ophelia cannot but correct him, "Nay, 'tis twice two months, my lord" (3.2.128). That insistence shows her courage and sympathy for Gertrude. Ophelia does not possess much discursive power to construct her selfhood, and the tremendous power of Hamlet's construction quickly washes away her subtle assertiveness and courage. Nonetheless, she still has her physical body. She resists with her face. Zeffirelli's sympathy for allowing that to happen may be misleading because he has repeatedly designated her as unimportant. He permits Ophelia only a very limited degree of agency. He turns her looks of rebellion gradually to those of confusion until finally she snaps. Besides a show of resistance, her looks simultaneously attest to her status of being written. In a way, Zeffirelli appropriates Ophelia's agency of resistance until he finally negates it in her madness.

In addition to his strategy of physical violence, discursive construction, and appropriation of Ophelia's resistance, Zeffirelli also employs such visual methods as costume and camera placement to prevent her from gaining symbolic and physical position. According to Rutter, the way Zeffirelli dresses Ophelia—the white embroidered cap, the dull, shapeless dresses, and her long, dark plaits—make her resemble a child, although Rutter believes that Ophelia's childlike face often registers the thoughts, emotions, and rebellion of a mature woman (304). But a child is not a fully developed human being. Compared to Gertrude's attractive dresses, Ophelia's shapeless dresses hide her and make her invisible. Zeffirelli's infantilizing strategies hinder Ophelia from reaching the autonomy of adulthood. His treatment reflects society's secret desire to reduce the intelligent Ophelia to a helpless figure who needs to be controlled. Ophelia is most disadvantaged by Zeffirelli's camera placement, which narrates the film from Hamlet's perspective. Besides spectator looks, he initiates almost all the shots from Hamlet's angle, looking at Ophelia. When the Nunnery scene begins, Zeffirelli lets Hamlet spot, from a high position, Polonius and Claudius using Ophelia to trap him. So Ophelia suffers from both objectification and moral degradation. She seldom possesses empowering point-of-view shots. Zeffirelli usually positions her at the lower part of the screen in long, high-angle shots in the Nunnery scene, or objectifies her in uncomfortable close-ups featuring her tortured face. Zeffirelli also diminishes her by the way he places her before Hamlet or against oppressive backgrounds like the massive watchtower in the Nunnery scene. The watchtower, together with Zeffirelli's high angle shots from Hamlet's point of view, reduces her to a tiny figure when Hamlet hurls his "remembrance" to the ground in front of her feet. These techniques disempower her and transform her into a powerless object passively receiving the gaze. She is constantly looked at; she does not see.

By contrast, Gertrude seems to occupy the visual center of Zeffirelli's film, something that many male critics have relished and praised. But what is problematic about Gertrude, both in the play and the film, is her sexuality. Indeed, Gertrude's maternal sexuality seems to occupy the center of Hamlet's consciousness. Janet Adelman holds that Gertrude's centrality in the play hinges on her maternal sexuality. Hamlet's obsessive fantasy regarding Gertrude's sexuality reflects his infantile fear and desire as well as the play's pervasive boundary panic (Adelman 12-19). Her centrality is not due only to Hamlet's infantile fear or desire but also to the patriarchal culture's disciplinary power over all female sexuality, which is implied in Hamlet's strategy of dealing with his mother—desexualizing Gertrude's maternal body through recreating a bodiless father (Adelman 18). This last point is problematic, since the film's recreation of a bodiless father plants the father's body, not Gertrude's body, firmly at its ideological center. Adelman's ideas, though valid, are not sufficient to analyze the film. In fact, the film demonstrates that men exercise tremendous power over Gertrude's sexuality on three levels: Hamlet's construction and citation of sexual norms for her, his strategy of desexualizing her, and the cinematic male maze reducing her to a passive, desired object. Butler's theory of discursive construction and "the law of sex" help us understand how Gertrude's sexuality constructs Hamlet's moral power and authority over her. Butler takes sex as a symbol for social commandment and believes that the subject creates compulsory sexual norms to govern the object and elevates the subjectively constructed norms as objective laws and ideals through repeated citation of the norms: "If 'sex' [a symbolic function understood as a kind of commandment or injunction] is assumed in the same way that a law is cited . . . then 'the law of sex' is repeatedly fortified and idealized only to the extent that it is reiterated as the law, produced as the law, the anterior and inapproximable ideal, by the very citations it is said to command" (14). During the process of construction and citation, the subject simultaneously constructs his self and power (see Butler 9, 15). In other words, the subject does not enjoy an anterior existence or disciplinary power prior to his construction and citation. Our detailed analyses of the process in the following paragraphs show that Zeffirelli makes Hamlet, the spokesman, establish his moral power over Gertrude in the Mousetrap scene through repeated discursive construction and reiteration of the sexual norms for Gertrude.

Hamlet's process of signifying Gertrude is complex. In the Mousetrap scene, after he stops insulting Ophelia, he shifts his focus to his mother, publicly accusing her: "Look how cheerfully my mother looks, and my father died within's two hours" (3.2.126-27). The norm he implies is that Gertrude should not have forgotten the sorrow of her husband's death and remarried so soon. After Ophelia comments, Hamlet confirms the norm yet again: "O heavens, died two months ago, and not forgotten yet? Then there's hope a great man's memory may outlive his life half a year" (3.2.130-32), lines that Zeffirelli takes directly from the play. The third time Hamlet berates Gertrude occurs at the end of the play-within-a-play's prologue. The line—"'Tis brief, my lord"—is directed at Ophelia in the play (3.2.153), but Zeffirelli purposefully changes it to "'Tis brief, my son" and forces it onto Gertrude to give Hamlet another chance to sting her. Her alleged crime is her transient love for Hamlet Senior. The fourth time Hamlet insists on a norm for Gertrude occurs in the lines he has added to the dialogue of the Player King and the Player Queen: "If once a widow, ever I be wife," which suggests that Gertrude should have remained a widow forever (3.2.223). Besides shortening and transposing lines, Zeffirelli invented a new line for the Player King, who says, in the film: "Should I die before a new sun shine / You might another husband soon entwine." The ugly image of entwining, which strongly hints at adultery, reinforces Hamlet's disgust at Gertrude's sexuality and the way he accuses her of misbehaving. The fifth time Hamlet reiterates his position, he addresses Gertrude directly to ensure she gets the message—"Madame, how like you this play?" (3.2.229)—giving Gertrude her only chance in Zeffirelli's scene to defend herself. Her answer, "The lady doth protest too much, methinks," stresses "protest" (3.2.230), not "too much," as if to say, in Zeffirelli's construction, that she believes the lady in the play-within-a-play should not have spoken prematurely, that she should in fact be allowed to seek new happiness. This answer no doubt does not satisfy Hamlet, so he stings her, for the sixth time, by comparing the Player Queen to the shameful Gertrude—"O but *she'll* keep her word" (3.2.231; emphasis added). Hamlet's irony is meant to remind Gertrude that she has breached a social norm.

Through his repeated discursive performances (six times in this scene alone), Hamlet constructs and reiterates constricting norms of widowhood for Gertrude. But neither the play nor the film has ever indicated these norms exist (see Ross 104-116). What the audience has is purely Hamlet's words, his own construction. In light of Butler's "law of sex," Hamlet carries out the construction and citation simultaneously. He derives his power from the very act of citing the norms which he himself produces. The norms of widowhood do not have a fixed form prior to his act of citation. That he cites them gives the audience the illusion that these norms possess factual existence prior to his citation. In other words, his citation endows his subjectively constructed norms with the objective status and power of obligatory laws—"the anterior and inapproximable ideal"—for Gertrude. Furthermore, during the process of construction and citation, Hamlet not only constructs Gertrude as negative, but also constructs himself as positive. In other words, during the process he establishes "an originary complicity with power in the formation of the 'I'" (Butler 15). The audience gets to know him, and in this film at least, approves of him because of the way he condemns his mother, presents himself as virtuous, and invests himself with the power to discipline. He is complicit with power from the very beginning, yet, it must be noted that "literature does not give rise to specific knowledge, but to *applications* of doctrines that are nothing but ideological exercises" (Kristeva 95). As a result, whether the norms exist or not does not concern Hamlet or Zeffirelli. What they desire is the power associated with their illusionary factual existence. And the desire for that power reflects the ideological exercises of late twentieth-century North America. Compared to the play, Zeffirelli's added effort of transposing one line from Ophelia to Gertrude and inventing a new line for the Player King underlies his as well as society's heightened anxiety and wish for control over female sexuality.

Zeffirelli does not allow Gertrude to possess the linguistic power to build her own norms to counter Hamlet's definition. Compared to Hamlet's six attacks, Gertrude only has two brief chances to speak. Furthermore, one line, the one Zeffirelli transposes from Ophelia to Gertrude—from "'Tis brief, my lord" in the play to "'Tis brief, my son" in the film—does not grant Gertrude, but Hamlet, the power to mark. Zeffirelli's invented couplet for the Player King serves the same function: it intensifies Hamlet's control over female sexuality and Zeffirelli's cinematic gaze also subjugates Gertrude by rendering her as a passive, desired object. In any film, high angle shots diminish characters while low angle shots enhance them. Therefore characters occupying high screen positions enjoy more power. In terms of the cinematic gaze, the initiator of the gaze possesses power while the gazed at does not. Close-up shots increase the intensity of the gaze, thereby reducing the power of the object. A film employs three looks, therefore, that differentiate characters in terms of power: "The look of the camera (at the profilmic), the look of the spectator (at the film projected on the screen), and the intradiegetic look of each character within the film (at other characters, objects, etc.) intersect, join, and relay one another in a complex system which structures vision and meaning and defines . . . the 'visible things of cinema'" (Lauretis 86-87).

Gertrude does not possess much power in either the Nunnery or the Mousetrap scene. At the beginning of the Nunnery scene, she only appears briefly, although she has a few point-of-view shots as she watches Ophelia and Polonius. In the Mousetrap scene, Zeffirelli makes the camera, aligned with Hamlet's point of view, constantly look at Gertrude to signify his control of her. Regarding screen position, Zeffirelli usually places her in upper or middle sections of the screen, thereby allowing her some degree of power. In the Mousetrap scene, Zeffirelli also features her in comfortable medium shots. Zeffirelli's techniques would convince the audience that he is enhancing Gertrude's importance. Indeed, that is the interpretation many male critics have picked up. But his real intention is to highlight Gertrude's attractiveness. For example, at the beginning of the Nunnery scene, he highlights her "girlishness," when Claudius touches her face—as an adult would touch a child. In the Mousetrap scene, Zeffirelli again emphasizes Gertrude's childlike appeal when the camera catches her happily clapping her hands when the play-within-a-play starts. These shots show that Gertrude's status is further reduced because Zeffirelli films her from the point of view of a male spectator, stressing her desirability. Compared to the way he films Ophelia, Zeffirelli's engagement with Gertrude is much simpler. Compared to his disguised degradation of Gertrude, his signification of Ophelia as disloyal, unimportant, underdeveloped, and completely powerless is much overt. His strategies mainly include displays of verbal and physical violence, discursive construction, appropriation of Ophelia's resistance, visual methods of infantilizing Ophelia, and camera placement. But they reflect the same cultural anxiety and desire for more control over the female body as the scenes that feature Gertrude.

My analysis of Zeffirelli's treatment of the Nunnery and Mousetrap scenes from the female body—its sexuality and physical body—locate power in the dynamics of discursive performances and the visual narratives of the film. In each case, Zeffirelli invests Hamlet—his spokesman and representative of the patriarchal society—with predominant power from multiple levels. Under his direction, Hamlet always negates Gertrude and Ophelia. Zeffirelli's creation of Hamlet as the consummate prince commanding absolute power and authority over the women reflects society's anxiety over women's ascending power in representation. Zeffirelli's approach kills three birds with one stone—"supplying a necessary aura of novelty and contemporaneity, adapting to new pressure, while at the same time bringing them under control" (Gledhill 172). With his profeminist colors, Zeffirelli not only provides the film industry with a sense of novelty, but also adjusts the industry to pressures from the women's movement. In absorbing and diffusing the pressure this way, he further consolidates the patriarchal society. That is exactly the danger of Gertrude's increased centrality and Ophelia's overtly intelligent performances that characterize Zeffirelli's film. I believe that to expose and counterattack such a strategy, women everywhere need to wield the power of representation to resist and question any discourse of dominance.

Works Cited

Adelman, Janet. *Suffocating Mothers: Fantasies of Maternal Origin in Shakespeare's Plays,* Hamlet *to* The Tempest. New York: Routledge, 1992.

Butler, Judith. *Bodies That Matter: On the Discursive Limits of Sex*. New York: Routledge, 1993.

Cartmell, Deborah. "Franco Zeffirelli and Shakespeare." *The Cambridge Companion to Shakespeare on Film*. Ed. Russel Jackson. Cambridge: Cambridge UP, 2000. 212-21.

Crowl, Samuel. "Zeffirelli's *Hamlet*: The Golden Girl and a Fistful of Dust." *Cinéaste* 24.1 (1998): 56-61.

Dawson, Anthony B. *Hamlet: Shakespeare in Performance*. Manchester: Manchester UP, 1995.

Foucault, Michel. *The History of Sexuality.* 3 Vols. Trans. Robert Hurley. New York: Vintage, 1990.

Gledhill, Christine. "Pleasurable Negotiations." *Feminist Film Theory: A Reader.* Ed. Sue Thornham. New York: New York UP, 1999. 166-79.

Hamlet. The Riverside Shakespeare. Ed. G. Blakemore Evans. Boston: Houghton Mifflin Company, 1997. 1183-245.

Hamlet. Dir. Franco Zeffirelli. Videocassette. Hollywood: Warner Home Video, 2001.

Hapgood, Robert. "Popularizing Shakespeare: The Artistry of Franco Zeffirelli." *Shakespeare, the Movie: Popularizing the Plays on Film, TV, and Video*. Ed. Lynda E. Boose and Richard Burt. New York: Routledge, 1997. 80-94.

Kristeva, Julia. *Desire in Language: A Semiotic Approach to Literature and Art*. Trans. Thomas Gora, Alice Jardine, and Leon S. Roudiez. New York: Columbia UP, 1980.

Lauretis, Teresa de. "Oedipus Interruptus." *Feminist Film Theory: A Reader.* Ed. Sue Thornham. New York: New York UP, 1999. 83-96.

Ross, Charles S. *The Custom of the Castle from Malory to Macbeth*. Berkeley: U of California P, 1997.

Rutter, Carol Chillington. "Snatched Bodies: Ophelia in the Grave." *Shakespeare Quarterly* 49.3 (1998): 299-319.

Traub, Valerie. "Jewels, Statues, and Corpses: Containment of Female Erotic Power in Shakespeare's Plays." *Shakespeare Studies* 20 (1988): 215-37.

Weller, Philip. "Freud's Footprints in Films of *Hamlet*." *Literature/Film Quarterly* 25.2 (1997): 119-24.

Illustration

Hamlet pinches Ophelia's face and treats her like a child in *Hamlet*, dir. Franco Zeffirelli (Hollywood: Warner Bros. 1990).

Part Two

Shakespeare in Asia

Imagining the East and Shakespeare's Asia

David Bevington

Early biographers of Shakespeare, confronting the problem of the so-called lost or dark years from 1585, in which year his twins Hamnet and Judith were born in Stratford, and 1592, when he first appears in London and was critically noticed by Robert Greene as an "upstart crow beautified with our feathers" (*Groatsworth of Wit*), speculated, in various ways, that Shakespeare taught school, that he served an apprenticeship in Stratford, or that he engaged in military service that took him abroad. Recent biographies discount these old speculations in favor of his having headed straight for London and its world of theatrical entrepreneurism (Honan 191). The only basis for the notion of military service, in fact, is a desire on the part of many readers to hope and even expect that Shakespeare did travel beyond the boundaries of his own country. He appears to know so much about Western Europe, and to be so curious about places like Venice, Aleppo, and India.

Yet Shakespeare was curious about many things. In much the way that he did not have to be a courtier to know the ways of courtiers, despite the claims of many anti-Stratfordians that he must have been well connected himself to be so intimately informed about the goings-on of the wealthy and powerful (see Whalen), Shakespeare did not need to travel to learn about the world beyond his immediate horizon. Most people then, as in many parts of the world today, did not travel beyond their own villages. Shakespeare got to London and lived there; we have no evidence that he got any further geographically. He sometimes makes revealing errors, as when he supposes in *The Two Gentlemen of Verona* that Valentine and then Proteus both must take shipping to journey from Verona to Milan (1.1.71-3, 2.2.14-15; in Bevington, *Shakespeare*; all line numbers and citations are to this edition); both cities are of course inland in northern Italy. Shakespeare is not even consistent in pursuing this misconception; Julia finds that she is able to make the same trip conveniently by land. Shakespeare imagines his outlaws to occupy a mountainous frontier of Mantua (see 5.2.49-50), evidently unaware that Mantua is located in the Po valley. One could compound this evidence of uncertain geographical knowledge with other examples, as one can also, for example, with Marlowe's knowledge of the Middle East: in

Tamburlaine, Part I, he places Damascus and Memphis within earshot of each other (4.1.1-3), evidently supposing that Syrian Damascus is in Egypt (see also 4.2.48, and 4.4.69 ff.); and he conflates similarly the River Gihon, one of the four rivers flowing out of Paradise through Eden, with the Nile (5.1.123), thereby further collapsing the geographical distinction between Egypt and the land of Mesopotamia (citations to works by Shakespeare's contemporary playwrights are from Bevington, *Drama*). The study of geography was then only in its infancy.

Like others of his day, Shakespeare traveled by book. The invention of printing brought with it the importation into England of a treasure trove of stories located in foreign lands, which were avidly rendered into English during one of the great ages of translation. Shakespeare need hardly have been able to read in foreign languages to capitalize on this influx of material, although he clearly did know some French (along with some Latin), and may have read at least a few stories from the Italian in the original language: his main source for *The Merchant of Venice*, *Il Pecorone* (*The Dunce*) by Ser Giovanni Fiorentino, does not appear to have been translated into English by the time Shakespeare encountered it, and so too with his main source for *Othello*, the *Hecatommithi* of G.B. Giraldi Cinthio, although here Shakespeare could have used a French translation by Gabriel Chappuys. More often, as in the case of *Much Ado About Nothing, The Merry Wives of Windsor, Twelfth Night*, and *Romeo and Juliet*, he availed himself of an English redaction. *Measure for Measure* was based on Cinthio's *Hecatommithi*, as was *Othello*, but in writing *Measure for Measure* he had easy access to George Whetstone's two-part play in English, *Promos and Cassandra*.

What did Shakespeare know of Asia, including China, and how does he portray the inhabitants of that part of the world? A central purpose of this article is to explore that question. We must do so, however, in the context of what he says about other foreigners and foreign locations, since from his insular perspective the great divide is between those who are English and those who are not. Even the Welsh, Scots, and Irish are significantly foreign in his dramatic world, though a play like *Henry V* does make a valiant attempt to harmonize the diversity of British cultural life into a kind of union capable of military and even imperial strength. The Welsh may speak strangely and indulge in a comic passion for cheese, but a stouthearted Welshman like Fluellen reminds us that the heir to the English throne was, after all, the Prince of Wales. Captain Jamie, in *Henry V*, atones for much that we learn about the Scots' habitual treachery in raiding England from the rear when she is involved in conflict with France. Even Captain Macmorris, for all his torturing of the English language and his hotheaded oversensitivity to the question, "What is your nation?," fights loyally for King Henry. The French, too, for important historical reasons, are also viewed in the history plays as assimilable into a world of enlightened British hegemony; the marriage of Henry V and Katharine of France is meant to atone for many misunderstandings between those two countries, although of course an awareness of fifteenth-century history prompts the audience to acknowledge that the peace symbolized by that marriage will break down in the reign of Henry V's underage son, Henry VI.

In general, the further we get from England, the more Shakespeare's language emphasizes strangeness, remoteness, otherness. The inhabitants of the Netherlands, relatively close at hand, are satirized repeatedly for their drunkenness (as are the Germans) and their Protestant hymn singing, but are at least Protestant in their faith. Thomas Dekker's *The Shoemaker's Holiday* reflects a similar ambivalence toward the foreigners who were flooding London with cheap labor and yet are seen in that play as potential fellow workers. The Italians are apt to be treacherous and hot-headed, like Iachimo in *Cymbeline* or Antonio and Sebastian in *The Tempest*, but Venice, Florence, Verona, and other Italian city-states are still centers of civilization. The Spanish are strangely absent from Shakespeare for the most part, other than in an occasional reference to a Spanish sword, presumably from Toledo (*All's Well* 4.1.47, *Romeo and Juliet* 1.4.84), and to a presumed penchant for bragging (*1 Henry IV* 5.3.119) and florid costuming (*Much Ado* 3.2.36). Don Armado in *Love's Labor's Lost* is a Spaniard (4.1.98), from a kingdom closely neighboring the Navarre where this play is set, although the reference to his nationality is a glancing one that occurs late in the play and seems only loosely connected to his chief humor, that of an affected sufferer of love melancholy. Ben Jonson, especially in *The Alchemist*, is considerably more inclined to exploit satirical attitudes toward the Spanish than is Shakespeare.

Similarly, Shakespeare is less given to defamatory allusions to the Greeks than are his contemporaries; except for the numerous references that are necessarily a part of *Troilus and Cressida*, with its Greek army and leaders onstage much of the time, Shakespeare is apt to use "Greek" in the neutral sense of referring to Greek and Latin books or to the warriors at Troy. To be sure, Sebastian does administer a put-down to Feste by calling him a "foolish Greek" (4.1.17), evidently meaning that as a fool he speaks gibberish (compare the famous line in *Julius* Caesar, 1.2.284, "It was Greek to me") and that Feste is a merry Greek or buffoon; and Cressida's wry remark about Helen that "she's a merry Greek indeed" (1.2.110) clearly plays on the Greek reputation for frivolity and moral laxity. More typical of Renaissance drama generally is the kind of epithet we find for example in *The Alchemist*: "heathen Greek" (2.5.16-45), or *The Shoemaker's Holiday*: "mad Greeks" (4.121). Elsewhere, "Lacedaemonians" is a common term of abuse signifying the kind of shiftiness attributed to Odysseus or Ulysses and to the devisers of the Trojan horse. In *The Shoemaker's Holiday*, moreover, the Greeks are paired with similar terms of sometimes friendly abuse drawn from Asia: Mesopotamians (7.80), Philistines (7.111), "Babylonian knaves" (11.160), and Trojans (11.163). Similarly we are told, by a madman, in *The Duchess of Malfi*, that "Greek has turned Turk" (4.2.91).

Once we stray beyond the bounds of West Europe, we encounter habits of speech that are inclined to be hostile or at least guarded, though also capable of wonderment and fascination. Shakespeare uses the word "China" only once, and not in a geographical sense: Pompey, in describing some fruit dishes in a Viennese house of prostitution, says that "they are not China dishes, but very good dishes" (*Measure for Measure* 2.1.92-5). The implication is that China dishes were of highly superior quality, as indeed they were. The Portuguese had first imported semi-transparent earthenware from China into Europe in the sixteenth century and had given it the name "porcelain," evidently from its resemblance to the polished surface of conch shells with their delicate iridescent colors; *pourcelaine* in the Romance languages signified a Venus shell, cowrie, or similar bivalve ("Porcelain," *Oxford English Dictionary*). Hakluyt's *Voyages* in 1579 refer to "Fine China-dishes of white earth." John Florio in 1598 speaks of "*Porcellana* . . . whereof they make China dishes, called Porcellan dishes" (see Florio, *World of Words*). Shakespeare's reference in *Measure for Measure* in 1603 is only the third listing given by the *OED*; its rareness bespeaks a sense of exotic and unbelievably expensive foreign imports. Ben Jonson speaks in *Epicene* of ladies "who are gone to the China houses" along the Strand and especially in the New Exchange (first opened in 1609) in search of luxury imports including porcelain (1.3.36-7).

Silk has a similar connotation in Shakespeare; it was a luxury item from the East that quickly became associated with wealth and rank. Queen Elizabeth I famously set a fashion for silk stockings at her court, and legislation from 1551 on decreed that "No man under the degree of a gentleman" is "to wear any silk points" ("Silk," *Oxford English Dictionary* 6). The protagonist of Marlowe's *Doctor Faustus* hopes to subvert such sartorial regulations when he dreams headily of filling "the public schools with silk, / Wherewith the students shall be bravely clad" (1.1.92-3). The silk trade was well established before the Renaissance. A similar aura of exotic luxury hovers over Shakespeare's references to imported spices, as in *A Midsummer Night's Dream*'s reference to the "spicèd Indian air" (2.1.124). Salerio, in *The Merchant of Venice*, imagines what it would be like to suffer the sad fate of a merchant, fearful lest a shipwreck on a return voyage from the East "Would scatter all her spices on the stream" and "Enrobe the roaring waters with my silks" (1.1.33-4).

If luxury goods from the Far East are thus invested with an aura of much-desired wealth and also danger, the few references we have in Shakespeare to Cathayans, or the people of China, are defamatory or merely incidental. Master Page in *The Merry Wives of Windsor* expresses his skepticism toward the allegations of Nym and Pistol that Falstaff is attempting the virtue of Mistresses Page and Ford by saying privately of Nym, "I will not believe such a Cathayan, though the priest o'the town commended him for a true man" (2.1.137-8). Anyone from Cathay, or China, is immediately assumed to be a sharper or scoundrel. The Folio spelling, *Cataian*, is characterized by the *Oxford English Dictionary* as a variant of *Cathaian*, a man of Cathay or China; "used also to signify a sharper, from the dexterous thieving of those people" (Nares); hence a thief, scoundrel, blackguard. The *Oxford English Dictionary*'s earliest citation, from 1577, uses the word in a neutral sense: "The Cataian king is woont to graunt free accesse vnto . . . forreiners" (Eden and Willes 237). Shakespeare's is the first citation in a negative sense, though it is supported by other Renaissance citations from Dekker's *The Honest Whore* Part II and other texts. The Nares *Glossary* is from 1822 and thus reflects an accretive tradition. We thus find Shakespeare perhaps first among those in print using "Cataian" in a pejorative sense.

His other use of the word, similarly spelled, is more ambiguous in connotation: a thoroughly drunk Sir Toby in *Twelfth Night*, challenged by Maria with a warning that the merrymakers are too noisy in a late hour of the night, chants, "My lady's a Cataian, we are politicians, Malvolio's a Peg-o'-Ramsey," and so on. The term "Cataian" could be derogatory here, but it may also be simple nonsense.

Although Cataians are thus only rarely and incidentally mentioned in Shakespeare, Turks, Tartars, Scythians, Saracens, and Indians are much more often in evidence, and in ways that often obscure geographical differences among these peoples and where they lived (Mongols are never mentioned [see Matar]). At times the confusion of races extends to Moors and those who inhabited Barbary in northwestern Africa. The uncertainty as to whether the term 'Moor' signifies Muslim peoples or Negroes is much debated, though the descriptions of both Othello and Aaron the Moor in *Titus Andronicus* present them physically as negroid. Indians sometimes appear to be from "the farthest step of India" (*A Midsummer Night's Dream* 2.1.69), presumably in south Asia, but may also appear to be blacks exploited in the slave trade and brought back from Africa or the Americas as curiosities to be put on display in a freak show, as Trinculo, Stephano, Antonio, and Sebastian would all like to do with Caliban in *The Tempest*. The confusion as to whether India is Asian India or the West Indies of the Caribbean, so common in the early modern period and responsible for the confusion of the names even today, appears in Shakespeare. One of Orlando's love poems in *As You Like It* begins, "From the east to western Ind, / No jewel is like Rosalind" (3.2.86-7). Falstaff, in *The Merry Wives of Windsor*, boasts that the two wives he is courting at least partly for their wealth "shall be exchequers to me. They shall be my East and West Indies, and I will trade to them both" (1.3.68-70). The confusion of course arose from the search westward from Europe to the fabled riches of "India," a search that reached land and native populations (and considerable amounts of gold) in the Americas. Often in Shakespeare one simply cannot tell whether he means east or west, as when Lord Mortimer, in *1 Henry IV*, praises his father-in-law Glendower by saying that he is "as bountiful / As mines of India" (3.1.164-5). All in all, this geographical and ethnic imprecision stands in direct proportion to the distance of such places from England, the infrequency of visits there by Westerners, and the unreliability and often fabulous exaggeration of stories arising from these lands, such as Othello's account of "the Cannibals that each other eat, / The Anthropophagi, and men whose heads / Do grow beneath their shoulders" (1.3.145-6).

Amazons in Shakespeare are no less hard to locate geographically, as is also true in the plays of his contemporaries. Amazons were reputedly a tribe of warrior women who cut off the right breast so as not to interfere with the use of the bow (hence a common supposed etymology of the word, from the Greek privative 'a' + mazos, breast), and were alleged by Herodotus to have inhabited wild regions of Syria and eastward to the Caspian Sea but who were later imagined also to have been found in parts of the New World where a great river bears the same name. Queen Titania, in *A Midsummer Night's Dream*, characterizes Hippolyta as "the bouncing

Amazon," formerly Oberon's "buskined mistress" and "warrior love," whom Oberon has come "from the farthest step of India" to see married to Theseus (2.1.69-71). Indeed, Theseus has won Hippolyta as his bride by defeating her in battle, wooing her with his sword (1.1.16-17). Hippolyta is described as a "Most dreaded Amazonian" in *The Two Noble Kinsmen* (1.1.78). Other Amazons (metaphorically) in Shakespeare are Joan of Arc in *1 Henry VI* (1.2.104) and Queen Margaret in *3 Henry VI* (1.4.114, 4.1.106). Coriolanus is Amazon-like when, as a still beardless youth but intrepid in battle, he drives older, bearded warriors before him (2.2.91). Amazons are thus, like Indians, a tribe with features typical of Asia and other far-off lands: they are strange, nearly inhuman, distant, fabulous, hard to place geographically but certainly associated with the steppes of Asia.

Let us consider some of the characteristics that Shakespeare's plays seem to associate with the peoples of Asia. A first impression is that they dwell in lands incredibly vast and distant from England and Western Europe. Pandarus, in *Troilus and Cressida*, can think of no more apt way to describe the unlikelihood of the lovesick Troilus being able to be his own best self than to cite a vivid impossibility: "Condition, I had gone barefoot to India" (1.2.75). No place on earth can be imagined as more distant and inaccessible. Bassanio reckons up the limitless extent of his friend Antonio's merchant venturings with a catalogue of places from which his ships might be expected: "What, not one hit? / From Tripolis, from Mexico, and England, / From Lisbon, Barbary, and India, / And not one vessel scape the dreadful touch / Of merchant-marring rocks?" (3.2.267-71). Titania refers, as we have seen, in *A Midsummer Night's Dream*, to "the farthest step of India" (2.1.69). This far-away land is also a place of ominous associations. King Henry V refers to "vasty Tartar" as the region of hell in which the devil himself assembles his legions. Dromio of Syracuse, in *The Comedy of Errors*, describes the incarceration of his master Antipholus as being "in Tartar limbo, worse than hell" (4.2.32). Sir Toby in *Twelfth Night* vows to follow Maria "to the gates of Tartar" (2.5.201). The name refers of course to Tartarus, the lowest of the infernal regions in classical mythology, but reminds us that Tartary is also the country of the Tartars, a region variously extending from the Black and Caspian Seas eastward into Mongolia. The names Tartarus and Tartary were often conflated, even though the peoples of that region are also known as the Tatars, both in eastern Asia and eastern Russia and in the area north of the Black Sea. The *Oxford English Dictionary* informs us that the term Tartar was "first known in the West as applied to the mingled host of Mongols, Tartars, Turks, etc., which under the leadership of Jenghiz Kahn (1202-1227) overran and devastated much of Asia and Eastern Europe."

A major reason for concern about east Asians from a west European point of view was, of course, the challenge that the Turks had posed with the siege and fall of Constantinople in 1453, followed by the subsequent arrival of the Turkish threat on the frontiers of Germany and in the Mediterranean. Shakespeare's one mention of Constantinople is bellicose in tone: Henry V proposes to Katharine that they breed an heir, "half French, half English, that shall go to Constantinople and take the Turk by the beard" (5.2.208-9). In *Othello*, the Turkish threat in the Mediterranean is a major motivating force of the play's action, as also in Marlowe's *The Jew of Malta*; in *Othello*, the Venetian leaders invite admiration for their canniness in outmaneuvering the Turks, whereas in Marlowe's play the Turks are ultimately bested by the Machiavellian Governor of Malta, Ferneze (see Bartels 82-108; Shepherd). Even if that remarkably skeptical play does not invest a moral superiority in the Christian West over the Turkish East, it characterizes the Turks as a dangerous superpower pitted against the Catholic Spaniards.

"Turk" is a common term of abuse in Shakespeare. Pistol can think of no more despicable term to throw at Falstaff than to call him "base Phrygian Turk" (*Merry Wives* 1.3.87). Perhaps no form of speech is more revealing of attitudes than such defamatory oaths, uttered for the most part without conscious awareness of what the speaker is implying about alien peoples. Shakespeare's characters occasionally refer to the Jews in a similar fashion, as when Benedick in *Much Ado* says of Beatrice, "If I do not love her, I am a Jew" (3.1.135). Benedick is not thinking about the Jews; he is wholly smitten with Beatrice's charms, and speaks of the Jews only by way of hyperbole. When Lysander heaps abuse on Hermia by calling her "Ethiope'" and "tawny Tartar" (*A Midsummer Night's Dream* 3.2.257-63), he means only that he finds Hermia's complexion unattractively dark. Dumaine in *Love's Labor's Lost* contrasts the fair beauty of his ladylove to the blackness of "an Ethiop" (4.3.114). The inconstant Proteus, in *The Two Gentlemen of Verona*, similarly declares that the fair Sylvia "Shows Julia but a swarthy Ethiop" (2.6.25-6). Rosalind in *As You Like It* speaks of "Ethiop words, blacker in their effect / Than in their countenance" (4.3.36-7). Shakespeare does not avail himself of the common proverb comparing an impossible task to the attempt to wash an Ethiop white, but it turns up often enough in other Renaissance dramatists (including *The Malcontent, The Roaring Girl, The Woman's Prize*, and *The White Devil*) and again illustrates the way in which proverbial utterances can reveal biases of which the speaker is only dimly aware (see Dent; Tokson 106-19; Barthelmey). In the mouth of a villain, on other occasions, the defamatory smear may be more deliberate. "Nay, it is true, or else I am a Turk," swears Iago (*Othello* 2.1.114), perhaps ironically aware that he uses this oath on an island (Cyprus) that has been under attack by Turkish naval forces.

Turks are open to such defamatory utterances in part because they are considered grotesque, even obscene. Among the revolting ingredients in the witches' brew of the Weird Sisters in *Macbeth* we find "Nose of Turk and Tartar's lips" (4.1.29). The nose reminds us of Barabas in Marlowe's *The Jew of Malta*, sardonically admired by the slave Ithamore (who may well be Turkish). More fundamentally, Turks are anathema because they are the militant enemies of Christian Europe and of the Holy Land in the Middle East. Rosalind, in *As You Like It*, speaks of Phoebe's defiant gaze as like that of "Turk to Christian" (4.3.34). Apostasy, whether in love or in religion, is often a matter of being "turned Turk"; see, for example, *Much Ado About Nothing* 3.4.52 and *Hamlet* 3.2.274. Turks and infidels are repeatedly equated as essentially synonymous. "Peace may go sleep with Turks and infidels," laments the

Bishop of Carlisle in *Richard II*, as he confronts the imminent threat of usurpation of the royal throne (4.1.140). "What, think you we are Turks or infidels?" Richard of Gloucester rhetorically asks the Mayor of London, by way of asserting that he, Richard, aims to govern through the forms of law (*Richard III*, 3.5.41). The Turks are pagans, a word that Shakespeare's characters repeatedly uses to characterize the enemies of Christ against whom a holy crusade must be waged; see, for example, Salisbury in *King John* 5.2.35-8, King Henry in *1 Henry IV* 1,1,24-7 and the Bishop of Carlisle in *Richard II* 4.1.95: "Against black pagans, Turks, and Saracens" (this is the only mention of "Saracens" in Shakespeare, by the way). The term can also connote Jews, as in *The Merchant of Venice* 2.3.11, and is more generally a term of abuse signifying "rascal," as in *1 Henry IV* 2.3.29, when Hotspur speaks of an unreliable potential ally: "What a pagan rascal is this, an infidel!" (see also *2 Henry IV* 2.2.154, where the term is applied to Doll Tearsheet).

Non-European peoples are accordingly sometimes viewed as savage in the sense of being untaught, credulous, naive, and idolatrous. This is more apt to be true of native peoples of the East and West Indies than of Scythians and Turks. Berowne, searching for a sufficiently grand hyperbole with which to praise Rosaline in *Love's Labor's Lost*, asks rhetorically whether even "a rude and savage man of Ind" beholding at dawn "the first opening of the gorgeous east," would not "Bow down his vassal head and, strucken blind," kiss "the base ground with obedient breast" (4.3.218-21). Stephano in *The Tempest*, trying to figure out what strange four-legged beast he has encountered on the beach, wonders if devils have "put tricks upon 's with savages and men of Ind" (2.2.58). Helena, in *All's Well*, confesses an element of idolatry in her worship of Bertram: '"Thus, Indian-like, / Religious in mine error, I adore / The sun" (1.3.201-2). The Dauphin Charles, in *1 Henry VI*, compares Joan of Arc's inspired visions to those that Mohammed reputedly received by means of a dove whispering in his ear (1.2.140)—the only reference to Mohammed in all Shakespeare. Othello sees himself at last as tragically too like "the base Indian" (thus in the quarto; "Iudean" in the folio) "who threw a pearl away / Richer than all his tribe" (5.2.357-8). The textual confusion of "Indian" and '"Iudean" may suggest a commonality of fatal ingenuousness in peoples of the New World and of the East. Such idolatry is in any case obviously related to what is perceived to be the anti-Christian error of most non-European peoples.

Turks, Tartars, Scythians, and other peoples from the East are regarded in Shakespeare and other Elizabethan dramatists as fearsome warriors. We learn this at times from glancing references, as when Puck in *A Midsummer Night's Dream* vows to go in search of Helena of Athens "Swifter than arrow from the Tartar's bow" (3.2.101). They have a reputation for valor. "Turk Gregory never did such deeds in arms as I have done this day," boasts Falstaff at the Battle of Shrewsbury (*1 Henry IV* 5.3.45-6). At sea, the Turks are regarded as pirates (Matar 55-63). By the same token, such peoples are reputed to be inhumanly cruel. Marlowe's Tamburlaine is but one example, though doubtless an influential one. Helena, in *All's Well That Ends Well*, speaks of the services she has done the French King as deserving gratitude which even "Through flinty Tartar's bosom would peep forth / And answer thanks" (4.4.6-8). In the famous courtroom scene of *The Merchant of Venice*, the Duke appeals to Shylock to find compassion in his heart for Antonio, a compassion that would be elicited even "From stubborn Turks and Tartars never trained / To offices of tender courtesy" (4.1.32-3).

Scythians are proverbially cruel. "Was never Scythia half so barbarous," exclaims Chiron in *Titus Andronicus*, as his hyperbolic way of deploring the "cruel, irreligious piety" of Titus in ordering the execution of Chiron's brother Alarbus (1.1.131). The Countess of Auvergne, in *1 Henry VI*, winds herself up to wreak vengeance on Lord Talbot by calling to mind the exploit of "Sythian Tomyris" in bringing about the death of Cyrus (2.3.5-6). King Lear, furious at Cordelia's refusal to flatter him as he wishes, protests that "The barbarous Scythian, / Or he that makes his generation messes / To gorge his appetite, shall to my bosom / Be as well neighbored, pitied, and relieved / As thou my sometime daughter" (1.1.116-20). In Lear's overraught imagination, Scythians are no better than cannibals. The impression of savagery is unrelieved in Shakespeare by any more kindly references. Further, Turkish and other Eastern rulers are despots: "This is the English, not the Turkish court," insists the young King Henry V as he assumes the throne in *2 Henry IV*. "Not Amurath an Amurath succeeds, / But Harry Harry" (5.2.47-9). Amurath was infamous as a Turkish sultan who, upon succeeding his father on the throne, ordered the strangulation of his brothers. As we have seen, Richard of Gloucester contrasts his presumed commitment to a rule of law to that of "Turks and infidels" (*Richard III*, 3.5.41). Tyrants of this magnitude are also imagined to hold vast areas under their cruel governance. Pucelle, in *1 Henry VI*, refers to "The Turk, that two-and-fifty kingdoms hath" (4.7.73), perhaps in recollection of the Turkish despot Bajazeth in Marlowe's *Tamburlaine* and indeed of Tamburlaine himself (although Tamburlaine is also an attractive figure in many ways). King Cambyses of Persia, in Thomas Preston's play of 1569-70, is held up as a negative model for his "many wicked deeds and tyrannous murders committed by and through him," leading to "his odious death by God's justice appointed" (title page).

Sexually, the peoples of the East (especially their rulers) are seen as exotically lecherous and quite immune to conventional Christian mores. Edgar, in his disguise as Poor Tom in *King Lear*, professes that "in women" he has "out-paramoured the Turk" (3.4.90-1). Turks are notorious for keeping eunuchs about them: as Lafew notes in *All's Well*, supposing that the courtiers are turning down a chance to be Helena's husband, "An they were sons of mine, I'd have them whipped, or I would send them to the Turk to make eunuchs of" (2.3.86-8). Cleopatra amuses herself, in *Antony and Cleopatra*, by taunting the eunuch Mardian with demeaning jokes about his lack of sexual potency. Indians are accused of being sexually voracious and possessed of outsized sexual organs: the Porter in *Henry VIII*, asks in a mocking rhetorical voice when commoners crowd at his door, "Have some strange Indian with the great tool come to court, the women so besiege us?" (5.4.32-4). Caliban in *The Tempest* is portrayed as quite unrepentant of his attempt to beget a race of little Calibans on Miranda; in his eyes, procreation and pleasure are what sex is all about. The presumption of sodomy among native Americans (not alluded to by Shakespeare) became a justification among European powers for conquest and possession (on sodomy, see Matar 109-27).

The East, most of all India, is a place of unimaginable wealth. The mines of India, whether East or West, are synonymous with bounty (*1 Henry IV* 3.1.164-5). When Troilus fantasizes about possessing Cressida, he thinks of her bed as India in which she lies, "a pearl" (*Troilus and Cressida* 1.1.103). To Sir Toby, Maria is "my metal of India" (*Twelfth Night* 13-14). The Field of Cloth of Gold in *Henry VIII* is so glitteringly extravagant that, in Norfolk's eyes, the participants have "Made Britain India" (1.1.21); later, when King Henry VIII forms an attachment for Anne Boleyn, a courtier notes approvingly that the "Our King has all the Indies in his arms" (4.1.45). The saintly King Henry in *3 Henry VI* eschews crowns that are "decked with diamonds and Indian stones" (3.1.63). Ethiopia shares too in this imagined wealth: in Romeo's eyes, Juliet "hangs upon the cheek of night / As a rich jewel in an Ethiop's ear" (1.5.46-7).

These images of extraordinary wealth bespeak a fascination with the world far beyond Europe to east and west that is not unattractive. And indeed there are glimmerings throughout the locutions of Shakespeare's characters that do homage to a romantic view. To be sure, "an Indian beauty" may be swarthy and even treacherous, as in *The Merchant of Venice* 3.2.99, but it is beauty nonetheless, and it is surprising and captivating in its strangeness. Trinculo in *The Tempest* assures us that Europeans will lay out a fair amount of money to see even "a dead Indian" (2.2.33), and it is for that reason that the clowns are so eager to get Caliban back to Italy where they can put him on show. The changeling boy in *A Midsummer Night's Dream*, "stolen from an Indian king," is the subject of one of that play's most exquisitely lyrical passages, of an experience among women "on Neptune's yellow sands" "in the spicèd Indian air by night"—a moment of womanly intimacy and great beauty (2.1.22, 123-34). The word "orient" has a generally positive connotation in Shakespeare, of the sun rising in majesty (Sonnet 7), and especially of orient (i.e., lustrous) pearls. Queen Elizabeth reflected her own interest, and that of her court, in things Oriental by financing revels costumes of Turks and Moors and by entertaining a "Masque of Moors" in 1560 (Bartels 55; see also Said). The world beyond Europe becomes preeminently a place of imagination, of the "marvelous" (see Greenblatt; Demaray). It is thus, at its best, like Shakespeare's own theater: a visionary world enabling English audiences to see themselves from others' point of view. For all the chauvinism we find in Shakespeare's characters, the experience of a new world is, for them and for us, an emancipating one.

Note

The above article is a revised version of David Bevington, "Imagining the East: Shakespeare's Asia," *NTU Studies in Language and Literature* 14 (2005): 107-22.

Works Cited

Bartels, Emily C. *Spectacles of Strangeness: Imperialism, Alienation, and Marlowe*. Philadelphia: U of Pennsylvania P, 1993.

Barthelmey, Anthony Gerard. *Black Face, Maligned Race: The Representation of Blacks in English Drama from Shakespeare to Southerne.* Baton Rouge: Louisiana State UP, 1987.

Bevington, David, ed. *The Complete Works of Shakespeare*. New York: Longman, 2009.

Bevington, David, Eric Rasmussen, Katharine Eisaman Maus, and Lars Engle, eds. *The Norton Anthology of Renaissance Drama*. New York: Norton, 2002.

Demaray, John G. *Shakespeare and the Spectacles of Strangeness: "The Tempest" and the Transformation of Renaissance Theatrical Forms*. Pittsburgh: Duquesne UP, 1998.

Dent, R.W. *Proverbial Language in English Drama Exclusive of Shakespeare, 1495-1616.* Berkeley: U of California P, 1984.

Florio, John. *A Worlde of Wordes*. London: Arnold Hatfield for Edward Blount, 1598. Rpt. Hildesheim: Georg Olms, 1972.

Greenblatt, Stephen. *Marvelous Possessions: The Wonder of the New World.* Chicago: U of Chicago P, 1988.

Greene, Robert. *Greene's Groatsworth of Wit Bought with a Million of Repentance*. London: J. Wolfe and J. Danter for William Wright, 1592.

Honan, Park. *Shakespeare: A Life*. Oxford: Oxford UP, 1998.

Matar, Nabil. *Turks, Moors, and Englishmen in the Age of Discovery*. New York: Columbia UP, 1999.

Nares, Robert. *A Glossary; or, Collection of Words, Phrases, Names, and Allusions to Customs, Proverbs, etc., Which Have Been Thought to Require Illustration, in the Words of English Authors, Particularly Shakespeare, and his Contemporaries.* London: J.R. Smith, 1822.

Said, Edward. *Orientalism*. New York: Vintage, 1979.

Shepherd, Simon. *Marlowe and the Politics of Elizabethan Theatre.* Sussex: Harvester, 1986.

Tokson, Elliot H. *The Popular Image of the Black Man in English Drama, 1550-1688*. Boston: G.K. Hall, 1982.

Whalen, Richard F. *Shakespeare: Who Was He? The Oxford Challenge to the Bard of Avon*. Westport: Praeger, 1994.

Kurosawa's *Throne of Blood* and East Asia's *Macbeth*

Yuwen Hsiung

Akira Kurosawa's *Throne of Blood* made its debut in 1957 and it remains a profound influence upon later adaptations of *Macbeth*. This legacy is apparent in East Asian countries that have a cultural closeness to Japan and therefore interpret the English play in similar ways. An adaptation of *Macbeth* entitled *Kingdom of Desire* (*Yuwang chengguo*) is a stage performance by the Taiwan theater Dangdai chuanqi juchang (The Contemporary Legend Theater) that blends traditional *jingju* (Beijing opera) style with the modern theater just as Kurosawa's *Throne of Blood* brings traditional Japanese theater, the *noh* conventions, into modern film. Although one is film and the other is stage performance, they are worth comparing because each envisions *Macbeth* from a particular cultural orientation. I focus on the role of the witch in order to argue that the heroic status of Macbeth in both works has been decreased considerably but in opposite ways. *Throne of Blood* asserts an experience of collectivity, whereas *Kingdom* shifts our attention back to individuality, like the original Shakespeare play. What they have in common is the Buddhist idea of relinquishing secular ambition and desire; otherwise, we lead ourselves into self-destruction and fall into a ceaseless, vicious circle of nothing.

My discussion of *Kingdom* is based on the script published in 2000, which includes script, stage directions, critical reviews, and photos of the original performance (see Wu). The Contemporary Legend Theater, which flourished during the latter part of the 1980s, is one of the leading theatrical troupes in Taiwan. It has distinguished itself from all the other troupes for its special artistic approaches in its attempts to incorporate some particular elements from Beijing opera, such as certain ways of speaking, singing, and performing, and especially acrobatics. The troupe not only makes the traditional more accessible, but also brings a new atmosphere to the multiplicity of contemporary Taiwan theater. Wu Hsing-kuo, the founder as well as the director of the troupe, exerts a shaping influence on the theater company. Many of their performances are adaptations of Western dramas, especially Shakespearean plays, such as *Revenge of the Prince*, based on *Hamlet*. In *Lear Is Here*, Wu played multiple roles including himself (Huang 31-47). So we can see that the significance of Wu to this troupe also lies in his being the leading character in most of the plays. Needless to say, in *Kingdom* he plays the role of General Ao (Macbeth).

Because Kurosawa's film had become such a landmark in Taiwan's theatrical circles, *Kingdom*, first performed in 1986, resembles *Throne of Blood* extensively in terms of plot. The time setting in *Throne of Blood* is sixteenth-century Japan, a period called gekoku-jo ("overthrown-by-underlings"), when the moral order started to get dissolved. Daisetz T. Suzuki reminds us of the traditional Japanese idea of a warrior: "Zen is indeed the religion of the samurai warrior" (84). Samurais believed in the Zen ideas of loyalty and sacrificing one's life for a worthy cause. Hence a treacherous warrior like Macbeth would be inconceivable in this early period of Japan. The sixteenth century, when the plot is set, was, however, the beginning of a period leading to turmoil and eventual downfall and *Throne of Blood* illustrates this period. The lord before Washizu and Washizu both commit illicit killings in order to get the throne and they themselves die in struggles for power. Although some scholars see new trouble brewing at the end of Shakespeare's *Macbeth*, in general it seems that Seward's forces are going to establish a new and unified sovereignty. *Throne of Blood* picks up Shakespeare's hint of irresolution because the film ends with a marching troop, which indicates that more fighting and killing would come and even will follow the death of Washizu.

Like *Throne of Blood*, *Kingdom* moves Shakespeare's play to pre-modern Asia. The time is the period of the Three Kingdoms (AD 220-277), an era of Chinese political degeneration after the stability and unity of the Han Dynasty. The country is separated into three main kingdoms and will be divided into more for another long period of time. After quelling a rebellion in the country, General Ao (Macbeth) and General Meng (Banquo) meet the mountain ghost on route back for court. The emperor then promotes their official positions, just as the mountain ghost prophesies. Aw's title changes from general to prime minister. Meng's decedents are promised power. In addition to cutting off the second half of the play drastically, as *Throne of Blood* does, *Kingdom* adopts some significant and similar changes in plot. For instance, where Kurosawa's Asaji cautions Washizu against the credibility of Miki and schemes for the killing of the lord, in *Kingdom*, Lady Ao (Lady Macbeth) arouses similarly Aw's disbelief in Meng. The relationship between Ao and Meng is further linked by their sworn brotherhood. Another resemblance is that between Asaji and Lady Aw: in both cases their pregnancy fuels the necessity of killing Miki or Meng and induces hallucinations. Ao, like Washizu, is shot to death by multiple arrows fired by his own troops, instead of fighting with Macduff in the field as Macbeth does. After the moving forest covers the whole stage, the play ends with the wild laughter of the mountain ghost while the curtain falls.

Neither the Japanese nor Chinese perspectives allow multiple witches. Rather than a collective group dedicated to malevolent acts against humans, Kurosawa's film and the Taiwan theater present figures closer to the shamans in East Asian culture who function between the human world and nature. These shamans practice witchcraft like witches, but their status is that of intermediary between the human community and the laws of nature; they are not, of themselves, makers of discord and disharmony. The adaptations therefore reduce the number of witches down to one, and also change the role of witch into that of a forest spirit in *Throne of Blood* and a mountain ghost in *Kingdom* while retaining the suggestion that they control human affairs. The archetype of Kurosawa's forest spirit is probably the *noh* play called Kurozuka (Black Tomb), which depicts the encounter of a traveling monk with a demon in the guise of an old woman, spinning on her wheel. Kurosawa's forest spirit, according to Jack Jorgens, is the "embodiment of an ironic, amoral Nature" (170). Nature, like the forest spirit, "is neither benign nor harmonious, but amorphous, changing shape, sex, and tone" (Jorgens 170). The answer to why a neutral spirit should appear to the two warriors can be seen by looking at the sequence of shots in the film. This sequence suggests that it is the unbalanced relationship between nature and men that gives rise to this encounter. Before we see the forest spirit, we hear a lord propose to use the Cobweb Forest as a weapon and we see Washizu and Miki shoot arrows at the forest to fight their way out. Their mistreatment of the Forest and their empty arrogance in their own power provokes the guardian forest spirit. It may be that the moving of the Forest to the castle symbolizes the power of nature over man in the end, but I agree with Peter Donaldson that Washizu's enemy uses the Forest as "a cultural artifact planted as a weapon of defense" (72). The trees are, in fact, cut down to cover human ambition, expelling the ravens and even the forest spirit from where they belong. Although humanity and nature should return to harmony, we see in the film's first and final scenes not only the disappearance of humans but also the barrenness of the land.

Like *Macbeth*, *Kingdom* begins with the supernatural, but like *Throne of Blood*, it transforms the agent, in this case to a figure called the mountain ghost. According to the stage directions, first, a high-pitched sound of *huqin* (two-stringed Chinese musical instrument) blasts out of the open, then a series of rapid drum beats indicates a war going on before the curtain rises. The stage curtain, which did not exist in the traditional theater and a clear import from Western drama, is adopted in *Kingdom*. Normally, the actor would get to his position or leave the stage in his particular movement according to the beats of the percussion. The first scene is particularly important in the traditional theater, because the first character on the stage is responsible for *bao jia men*, a special term used by Chinese theater. It literally means to report your family. After reciting a short poem, the character is supposed to not only identify himself or herself, but also give a brief introduction in the opening scene of the play. This is the function of the mountain ghost. She begins by telling about herself and what she intends to do afterwards: "I am the spirit of the mountain. Because the fire of Ji's (country name) civil war is going to be ceased, tomorrow, General Ao will return to the palace. This forest will he pass by. I shall wait for his arrival to make fun of him. Behold! The wind blows; the rain shouts; the light flashes; the thunder cracks. Let me take the cloud, ride the thunder-blast, pass the dark, and cross the light. This is what's on my mind. This is what's on my mind" (22; unless indicated otherwise, all translations are mine).

The introduction highlights her performance and turns the attention of the audience to the transition that the main character is going to experience. Although we do not find ghosts in traditional Chinese theater, it is common, especially in the beginning of short novels, for a ghost to play tricks, whether light or serious, upon humans. In the particular historical background of the Three Kingdoms, the lack of order in the human world easily conjures up the force of the supernatural, the negative force in nature. Moreover, the mountain spirit was also associated with the kind of abnormal weather that begins Shakespeare's play. As Garry Wills explains, the opening storm scene in *Macbeth* is "not just a matter of stage atmospherics or dramatic imagery. It is the necessary condition of the witches' abnormal activity by day" (54). We find the same association in *Kingdom*. In addition to her special function in the opening scene, the mountain spirit's symbolic meaning is embodied in her image and body movement. First of all, the degree of white on the face indicates the degree of evilness. The mountain spirit's face is painted white, as is Aw's face before his death. Moreover, each hand gesture has its designated meaning and varies according to the identity of the character. The basic hand gesture of a female role is called "open hand," with the third finger and thumb lightly touching each other. The much opener "open hand" symbolizes that something is "lacking." Here the suggestion is that the political ruler has lost control and also that there is a lack of controlling power over one's own behavior. These ritual gestures suggest a crisis in the individual's relation to the collective, a crisis that is also present in Washizu's reaction to the supernatural.

The reaction of Washizu and Ao to the supernatural illustrates how Asian directors find cultural equivalents, in theater and cinema, for the language and sentiments of Shakespeare's play. *Macbeth* is theatrical script, of course, and its concepts must be given equivalents. According to Gilles Deleuze, language gives rise to concepts and "Concepts are the images of thought" (xi). These concepts, not simply actions or language, determine the narrative structure of a film, by which Deleuze means its sequence of shots, or montage. Deleuze characterizes two different modes of image movement. In one case the camera focuses on one individual and then moves on to a broader frame that contains the individual. The second reverses this process: "One does not move from an unknown woman to the givens capable of determining her; one starts off from all the givens, and one moves down from them to mark the limits within which the unknown is contained" (188). *Throne of Blood* illustrates this second procedure. The film begins with a long prelude, a barren wasteland. No forest is in sight. There is chanting, and the camera lingers to show the scattered ruins of walls, perhaps the ruins of a castle. The camera then moves a little further down the slope. Through the mist, a deserted memorial statue is found. A fairly close shot is used to show the characters on the wood statue one by one: Zhi-zhu-chao-cheng-zhi ("the historical site of the Spiderweb Castle"). After this long exposition—a distinct characteristic Deleuze detects in Kurosawa's films—Spiderweb Castle finally reveals itself. Nevertheless, the sight of the inside of the castle is not available for the viewers directly. It is by way of the desperate messenger's repeated knocks on the gate door that we find a group of people sitting inside the limits of the castle. Through all these givens in the beginning, the shot zooms in on the specific. The givens, Gilles Deleuze states, "must be a complete exposition, are not simply those of the situation" (189). Thus we have to pay attention to both Washizu and the whole community, who are enwrapped within the same condition, which is exposed at the beginning, before any individual appears. Consequently it is important to observe how everyone involves and revolves around the challenge thrown down by the forest spirit.

In *Throne of Blood,* castles become the image of human ambition itself. In Kurosawa's work, castles are inseparable are from social concerns. In the beginning of the film, the lord and his councils prefer sticking to the castle until death rather than coming out of the castle to fight the enemy. The troops become more and more ambitious when they move to a higher positioned castle. The first castle Washizu moves to is the North Castle, his reward for success in the battle. The second one is the Spiderweb Castle, where he replaces the lord. Washizu's castle does not remain in the end, except as a ruin, yet that ruin is intimately connection to the fate of those who inhabit it. The various castles in *Macbeth*, according to Charles S. Ross in *The Custom of the Castle,* can eventually be purged of the sins and behaviors of the humans who inhabit them: "Macbeth's castles, once haunted by foul crimes, stand open to new masters, new customs" (119). By contrast, a castle is just one property in *Kingdom*, a static sign that is only important for its position. It does not function as a symbol of social behavior but of the individual, although these functions are really two sides of the same coin. The generals in *Kingdom* are rewarded with higher positions, and the emperor is willing to desert the castle at any minute. He would have fled to the other castle for protection if he were not afraid of being looked down as a coward, whereas in *Throne of Blood*, they are rewarded with a different castle as a sign of the change in their official position.

The castles in *Throne of Blood* operate diachronically as signs of the continuity of killing and the insatiable desire of human beings. It is this danger of collective mentality that Kurosawa warns us against when, almost without explanation, he shows Asaji dancing abruptly, as in *noh*, in the forbidden room while Washizu kills the lord. Following Ana Laura Zambrano's referrence to the forbidden room as the sign of "death and treachery" (269), Asaji's dance could be regarded as the actualization of that influence. During that scene, we see Asaji in a medium shot that focuses closely on her facial expression. She sits with her back to the wall but turns her head back twice to peek at the stain on the wall. Something seizes her attention there. Suddenly, the percussive *noh* music starts as she draws herself to the wall and dances. Finally the shot rests on her close and attentive look at the bloodstain. She kneels down before the wall as if she succumbs herself to the power of past treachery. She is less an individual than a victim of social customs and the ways of warriors.

Rather than illustrating collective guilt, *Kingdom* emphasizes the idea of individuality, of one person's response to a set of social conditions. Like *Throne of Blood*, *Kingdom* is set in a situation of decay and warfare, but it stresses the theme of individuality by depicting Macbeth as a character, as in traditional in Chinese theater, and in the way it structures his transformation. In Chinese culture, theater is directly linked to people's everyday lives. Its impact upon audience feeling is considered to be of practical value and importance. Therefore, moral lessons are straightforward in every traditional play. The distinction between a hero and a villain is clear, not to mention any abnormal mental condition that should occur to a hero, because a good man is believed to be essentially different from an evil one. More often than not, only heroes can be the main characters. Afraid of arousing an ambiguous response, a figure like Macbeth is not inconceivable, but unacceptable traditionally. In Shakespeare's play, Macbeth's moral character is ambiguous and Shakespeare has him come on stage relatively late, for example, to stress his social situation. *Kingdom* manages to give its Macbeth figure, Ao, a sense of individuality by the way it focuses on his transformation. I will explore this change of Ao in three scenes: the meeting with the mountain ghost, the banquet scene, and Aw's death scene.

Both General Ao and General Meng appear in the *jingju* role type known as *wusheng* (combatant male role). They dress in thick costumes and heavy armor, with four flags on their back, signifying their high position in the military. Upon their meeting with the mountain ghost, their reaction is different from that of Washizu and Miki in *Throne of Blood*. The mountain ghost equally prophecies each one's future; however Meng is able to pull himself out of the mire by saying to Aw, "General, why shall we get angry at her? If we are frank, a laugh at this would be enough" (37). Their different responses to the same situation not only reveal the differences in their natures but also foreshadow what they do next. That is why the mountain ghost says to Ao and Meng: "The moment between one move and one pause determines your future" (37). Ao moves. Haste and impatience is always negative in Chinese thinking. After Ao succeeds to the position of emperor, his costume is changed into that of lao-sheng (an old man), for he possesses more power now. His hat, with beaded curtains in the front and back ring, symbolizes his position. During the banquet scene, a three-mask dance is performed. The three masks not only make visible the sharp comparison between each stage of Aw's transformation but also foretell the destiny of Ao, as the dancer reveals the last face, a face painted white, as Ao shall be in the future. This focus on Aw's individuality is not only shown by a change in imagery but also by the changes in his relationships with Meng and Lady Ao. Ao becomes more and more isolated and distant from other characters. Unlike Miki, Meng does not assume any complicity in Aw's crime. What makes Aw's killing Meng worse is their sworn brotherhood, which is considered sacred traditionally. So Ao not only discredits trust, upon which friendship builds, but also his own vows. As to the relationship between Ao and Lady Ao, Lady Ao precipitates Aw's action in the beginning. However, as Lady Ao more and more hallucinates, Ao distances himself away from her. Washizu relies on the support from Asaji, but Ao counts more and more upon himself. He becomes more arrogant than before. His addressing to himself changes from wo to gu (from I to an addressing of a king to himself), and towards the end he uses, from time to time, an, a reflexive of vulgarity and conceit. His increasing isolation and evilness is symbolized by the white paint on his face until at last he looks as white as the mountain ghost.

The historical transition from *Throne of Blood* to *Kingdom* may be due, in part, to a shift away from the social feelings of collective guilt felt in Japan in the early 1950s to the capitalist focus on individual responsibility that characterizes, to whatever extent, later Taiwanese society. The result of this shift from the collective to the individual is, arguably, a more positive feeling. To conclude my study, I take one last scene as an example to explore whether Kurosawa provides us any way out of the mire of collectivity. Few audiences will fail to remember the death scene of Washizu, especially when the fatal shot of the arrow transfixing his neck stops him shouting. The frame is frozen for a second, no movement seen, no sound heard. Although too late, Washizu finally comes to understand himself and the situation he faces. Clumsily he steps down the stairs and stands before his men. Many critics argue that Washizu attempts to fight those who killed him by drawing his sword. On the contrary, I think that because he has a sudden realization, he actually seeks to commit *hara kiri* (the suicide of a samurai). Like the brave samurai he once was, he hopes to achieve his own integrity in accordance with the samurai code of honor. Here, ultimately, Kurosawa blurs the lines between the collective code and the individual, and it is this blurring that Taiwan theater may have found attractive. Representing Shakespeare's ambiguity rather than a Western notion of tragedy, in which a man essentially no better or worse than we are is undone by his own best qualities, the Asian versions of Macbeth draw on and twist their cultures' codes of heroism. But the final effect is quite different. Shakespeare's Macbeth fights Macduff until he dies, whereas both Washizu and Ao are killed by their own men. This dramatically decreases the heroic status of both of them. Judging from the closed form of this film, Kurosawa does not provide any answer as to how to be a hero free from the vicious circles imposed by society. Richie concludes that "for Kurosawa, the pattern of repetition is destructive and it is this pattern which his free heroes attempt to destroy" (115). But the Chinese believe that good will be rewarded with good, and evil with evil. The stress on individuality in *Kingdom* allows a way out of the problems of performing a play like Macbeth. Although in *Throne of Blood* it seems there is no escape from the collectivity and repetition as implied by Kurosawa, *Kingdom* suggests that justice has to be done to the individual who cannot hold himself together.

Works Cited

Deleuze, Gilles. *Cinema 1: The Movement Image*. Trans. Hugh Tomlinson and Barbara Habberjam. Minneapolis: U of Minnesota P, 1986.

Donaldson, Peter S. "Surface and Depth: *Throne of Blood* as Cinematic Allegory." *Shakespearean Films/Shakespearean Directors*. Boston: Unwin Hyman, 1990. 69-91.

Huang, Alexander C.Y. "Shakespeare, Performance, and Autobiographical Interventions." *Shakespeare Bulletin: A Journal of Performance Criticism and Scholarship* 24. 2 (2006): 31-47.

Jorgens, Jack J. "Kurosawa's *Throne of Blood*: Washizu and Miki Meet the Forest Spirit." *Literature/Film Quarterly* 11 (1983): 167-73.

Kurosawa, Akira. *Something Like an Autobiography*. Trans. Audie Bock. New York: Vintage, 1983.

Kurosawa, Akira, dir. *Throne of Blood*. 1957. *Macbeth*. DVD. Hong Kong: Mei Ah, 1995.

Richie, Donald. "The *Throne of Blood*." *The Films of Akira Kurosawa*. By Donald Richie. Berkeley: U of California P, 1965. 115-24.

Ross, Charles S. *The Custom of the Castle: From Malory to Macbeth*. Berkeley: U of California P, 1996.

Shakespeare, William. *Macbeth*. Ed. Kenneth Muir. New York: Methuen, 1951.

Suzuki, Daisetz Teitaro. "Zen and Samurai." *Zen and Japanese Culture*. By Daisetz Teitaro Suzuki. New York: MJF Books, 1958. 57-86.

Wills, Garry. *Witches and Jesuits: Shakespeare's Macbeth*. Oxford: Oxford UP, 1995.

Wu, Hsing-kuo. *Yuwang chengguo* (*Kingdom of Desire*). Taipei: Frankford International Workshop, 2000.

Zambrano, Ana Laura. "*Throne of Blood*: Kurosawa's *Macbeth*." *Literature/Film Quarterly* 2.3 (1974): 262-74.

Illustrations

Kurosawa's forest spirit, in *Throne of Blood: The Castle of the Spider's Web*, dir. Akira Kurosawa (Japan: TOHO Films, 1957).

Asaji dances, as in *noh*, in the forbidden room while Washizu kills the lord. *Throne of Blood: The Castle of the Spider's Web*, dir. Akira Kurosawa (Japan: TOHO Films, 1957).

Macbeth in *Kingdom of Desire* (Contemporary Legend Theater, Taipei, 1987).

The dancer reveals the last face of Awshu, painted white, as Awshu shall be in the future, more and more isolated and distant from other characters. *Kingdom of Desire*, dir. Wu Hsing-kuo (Contemporary Legend Theater, Taipei, 1987).

Silence and Sound in Kurosawa's *Throne of Blood*

Lei Jin

Silence and sound produce a compelling power in Akira Kurosawa's *Throne of Blood* (1957): the mysterious and pregnant silence carried on the harsh wind, the impatient silence intensified by the galloping hoof beats, the violent silence broken by the cry of the crow, and the ambiguous and suspenseful silence prolonged by the beating drum. These patterns intensify the characters' emotional turmoil, articulate their psychological struggle, and reinforce the narrative effect carried out through visual images in order to produce an aesthetically satisfying work of art. In the most critical moments of the movie, such as the murder scene, it is through the manipulation of silence and the interaction between silence, natural sound, and *noh* music that Kurosawa recreates the dramatic power of Shakespeare's *Macbeth* conveyed by dialogue. A close examination of a few selected moments of *Throne of Blood* shows that Kurosawa uses dramatic silence, natural sounds, and *noh* music as symbolic vehicles to explore the major themes of the movie—fate, ambition, and destruction.

The fact that *Throne of Blood* dispenses with Shakespeare's poetic dialogue has remained a contentious issue. Viewing it as "a great masterpiece," Geoffrey Reeves and Peter Brook refuse to recognize the movie as a Shakespeare film "because it doesn't use the text" (Reeves 316). However, more recent scholarship shows a more positive attitude. In Anthony Davies's view, the film "has made Western scholarship more aware of the universal appeal of Shakespeare's dramatic material" (154). Moreover, Davies's exploration of spatial relationships, particularly the conflict between horizontal and vertical, shows Kurosawa's craft and originality. And as Stephen Prince argues, Kurosawa "recognizes that the process of adapting literature to the screen is one not of translation but transformation. . . . The verbal texture of the play is transformed into a dense, elaborate patterning of image and sound" (142). Following this line of reasoning, I discuss how natural sounds, such as the cry of the owl and the hoof beats of horses, embody symbolic meanings that enforce not only the film's visual images but also the major themes of the movie.

In the early period of his work, Kurosawa showed a great sensibility toward the effect and power of silent movies: "I like silent pictures and always have. They are often so much more beautiful than sound pictures. Perhaps they have to be. At any rate, I wanted to restore some of this beauty" (qtd. in Richie, "Kurosawa" 112). In *Throne of Blood* Kurosawa invites his audience repeatedly to ponder brief or minutes-long moments of silence. Through these moments, he restores the great concentration of the silent movie. He recognizes that "depending on how the sound is put in, the visual image may strike the viewer in many different ways" (qtd. in Richie, "Kurosawa" 108). The way Kurosawa breaks the silence adds new meanings to visual images, and eventually he develops a symbolic sound and visual pattern that forms an aesthetic unity. Silence that infuses and is broken by natural sound forms one of the most significant patterns in the film. At the beginning of *Throne of Blood*, the camera moves slowly from a vast bleak landscape to the site of a deserted castle, where only the stone foundation remains. The chorus chants the warrior's doomed fate: "Behold within this place / Now desolate, stood / Once a mighty fortress / Lived a proud warrior / Murdered by ambition / His spirit walking still." After the chant fades away, there is a moment of silence. The fog rises and flows more and more densely, eventually shrouding the landscape. For a transcendental moment, the audience beholds nothing but void and hears nothing but silence. The sound of harsh wind counterpoints the silence, and the silence deepens the mysterious and ambiguous feeling evoked by the heavy fog. Silence compels the audience to penetrate the inscrutable fog. The image of the creeping metamorphic fog emphasizes that all earthy things are illusory. Silence not only enforces but also transcends the particular historical moment to a timeless frame. Gradually the Forest Castle emerges on the screen, and the silence is broken by hoof beats. A wounded soldier knocks at the castle's heavy wooden gate and delivers a message: the North Fort has rebelled. Besides being a conventional characteristic of the war movie, the hoof beats here declare the major themes of the film—ambition, perfidy, treachery, and war. This pattern is further developed and illustrated in two other important scenes: the forest scene in which Washizu (Macbeth) and Miki (Banquo) gallop aimlessly in the foggy forest and the scene in which the murder is being planned in Washizu's castle.

After hearing the Forest Spirit's prophecy, Washizu and Miki try to find their way anxiously out of the forest. A dozen times the two samurai gallop through the dense fog, then rush back again. After hours of vain struggle, the two warriors discover that they have ridden in a circle. The ringing hoof beats break the forest's silence, and in return, a crack of thunder and hollow laughter threatens and mocks the two warriors' aimless struggle. This eloquent shot is held for more than four minutes. Eventually the impatient and vigorous hoof beats articulate the two samurais' suddenly kindled ambition. Their ambition, however, is doomed to fail, a failure represented by the metaphorical circle, which the two warriors exit and enter. The audience finds that the forest, whose silence is violated, not only threatens and mocks the two intruders, but also asks for revenge. The psychological implication of the metaphorical visual pattern—labyrinth forest and circled movement—and the particular sound pattern—silence and the intrusion of hoof beats—set up the symbolic texture of the film. At the end of the movie, the forest advances to the castle in a slow-motion shot, ending Washizu's ambition and his life.

In addition to the forest scene and the end of the film, the circling gallop is seen in another crucial scene--the plotting of the murder. The only bright yet ironically serene scene is depicted right after Washizu becomes the lord of the North Castle. In his courtyard, Washizu's samurais are relaxing in the sunshine—walking a horse in lazy steps, sitting on the porch, and enjoying the shade, and chatting as one of the samurai proclaims: "how peaceful!" This contented mood and atmosphere, however, are subverted by a sudden whinny. The camera shifts to the porch where Washizu appears: Silently and restlessly he stands there for a brief moment, then returns to his chamber. Inside the chamber, the warrior paces back and forth, trying to suppress his ambition and resist the attempts of Lady Asaji (Lady Macbeth) to persuade him to rebel. The warrior exclaims: "I want to live in peace!" His claim is immediately mocked by another loud whinny. In the rest of the scene, the conversation between Washizu and Asaji concerning the treacherous plot is coupled with and disrupted by the sound of the horse's whinny and hoof beats, and one can see through the open door of the room the horse circling in the courtyard. Washizu's moral struggle, suppressed ambition, and deepened suspicions are vividly illustrated through the image of the circling horse, and intensified by the sharp whinny and the restless hoof beats. Prince suggests that the repeated metaphorical circling movement of the film embodies "ideas of temporal circularity and the fatedness of violence and evil" (Prince 144). "Kurosawa seems closely allied to the Spirit," Jack Jorgens notes, as "he too enmeshes his characters in a format pattern so rigid that it becomes an aesthetic equivalent of Fate" (172). Suppressed silence, hoof beats, and the circled movement are interwoven, and the repetition of this sound and visual pattern emphasizes the world of *Throne of Blood*, a world in which humans are caught in the cycle of ambition, treachery, and war.

Although the symbolic sound and visual images convey the complicated psychological conflict of the characters and fathom the depth of human fate, their elements are surprisingly simple. "Visually," Donald Richie observes, "the film is a marvel because it is made of so little: fog, wind, trees, mist—the forest and castle" (*The Films of Akira Kurosawa* 120). The same simplicity is applied to the sound pattern and technique. Silence, natural sound, and *noh*-music—mainly the sound of flute and drum—are the main aural components in the movie. Moreover, both sound and visual images are shaped in a restricted pattern. The solitary flute and the contrast between its high pitch and a deep drum function as soliloquy and dialogue, conveying the characters' wide range of emotional stress, as well as the conflicts among different characters. The harmony of stylized performance and restricted music ironically amplifies the disharmonious relationships and the emotional and mental crises that follow.

A glance at the Japanese theatrical tradition, *noh*, helps us to better understand the significant relationship between silence and the music. Both the visual and sound patterns of *Throne of Blood* are heavily influenced by *noh* tradition, which flourished in the later fourteenth century. The ideal *noh* performance offers the audience a profound theatric experience of ritual dance, song, chant, and poetry. Comparisons of

Throne of Blood and *noh* have stressed the affinity between this theatrical tradition and the performance of the characters in the movie, particularly the "stylized performance" and the "masklike presentation of characters" (Prince 146). The stylization of the two female figures—Asaji and the Forest Spirit—and "the formal, closed, ritual, limited quality of the Noh" has also been noticed (Richie, *The Films of Akira Kurosawa* 118). The relationship between the convention of *noh* performance and the auditory perception of the film, however, has received little attention. Yet the connection is very strong, since the interval and silence between two physical actions has a fascinating and important effect. At the moment when the dance has stopped, or the chant has ceased, or indeed in any of those intervals that can occur during the performance of a role or during any pause or interval, the actor must never abandon his concentration but must keep his consciousness of inner tension. It is the sense of inner concentration that manifests itself to the audience and makes that moment enjoyable (Zeami 97).

The concentration and intensity of silence, a legacy of the pauses between chants and songs in the *noh* tradition, creates the compelling force of the pivotal scene in *Throne of Blood,* the equivalent of Duncan's murder in Shakespeare's play. Lasting six minutes and broken only briefly by nonverbal sound and music, silence dominates the action. It deepens the dark mood of the movie, enhances the narrative effect of the visual images, and conveys the broad range of the characters' emotional struggles from hesitation to determination, fear, and eventually terror. Having been persuaded and now determined to murder the Lord, Washizu sits still on the floor of his chamber, his face contorting as he breathes heavily. In contrast to her husband's still position, Asaji glides around the room. Against the deep silence, the swishing sound of her silk kimono is sharp, clear, and forceful. Soon the gentle and feminine sound of silk is transformed into the creeping and threatening glide of a vicious snake. Sliding into a side chamber, Asaji disappears into the deep darkness. Reappearing a few seconds later, she has a jar of tempered wine in her hands. One shot of the particular jar sufficiently tells the lady's success. The drugged guards sleep soundly, and a profound silence pervades the entire castle.

The apparent silence, however, is deceiving, for soon the sharp swish is heard again. In concert with Asaji's appearance on the porch, a thin-pitched flute melody rises. On one hand, the elegant music forms an aesthetic harmony with Asaji's body movement. On the other hand, it infuses a creeping, haunting sensation into the tense atmosphere. The camera quietly moves into the chamber in which the couple plans to stay for the night. It was once occupied by a traitor who killed himself after his treachery failed, and now hideous bloodstains cover the wall. The audience beholds Washizu, again sitting intensely on the floor. As Kurosawa explains, the low ceiling and the mattress that lies in front of the warrior create "the effect of oppression" and emphasize the hero's psychological struggle (Richie, *The Films of Akira Kurosawa* 123). The haunting sound of the flute persists, and the eerie sensation is made visual by the grotesque bloodstained walls, within which Washizu is physically and psychologically trapped. Asaji enters the room and places a spear in his hand, and all is silent. The silence and the swish associated with Washizu and Asaji indicate respectively their roles in the conspiracy. The forceful sounds of her garment symbolize the lady's aggression, which breaks the silence. Thus the ongoing psychological battle between the warrior and his wife is not only revealed by the spatial arrangement of the two characters—stillness versus movement, low position versus high—but is also illustrated by the auditory contrast between silence and her forceful swish. This implication is made clearer by a significant moment in which the two characters appear frozen, face to face, both with their hands on a spear. Unable to speak, Washizu glares at his wife violently, as if trying to gather all his strength to resist her evil force, his face twisting like the *noh* mask of an ancient warrior as his shoulders shake. In contrast, his wife remains emotionless, yet her eyes project a compelling force. Although Lady Macbeth's introspective speech and most of the dialogue between the couple are eliminated, silence bespeaks Asaji's unfathomable evil. Asaji's silence proclaims her determination, ambition, and thirst for blood and power, as well as a pure evil force.

Although the virtues of Shakespeare's King Duncan have been subverted by the treachery of Kurosawa's Lord, still the social code of the samurai emphasizes loyalty, duty, and trust. Facing the dreadful idea of violating the samurai code, Washizu wages a psychological battle both within and without himself. On one level, he desperately struggles between ambition, moral consciousness, and the social code of the samurai. On another level, he wrestles with Asaji's arguments. Her words from an earlier scene, "there cannot be any peace if Miki tells what happened in the forest," root suspicions in his mind, and the Lord's disguised military movements further muddies the unclear water. Washizu is confused. The warrior's inner struggle is so furious that ultimately he reaches its limitation. As if his nerve has been extended to the utmost limit and snapped, a sudden screech of an owl breaks the unbearable silence. The screech simultaneously conveys an ominous cry of murder, the mocking of the Forest Spirit, and a lamentation on the fate of a doomed human. It is also a cry of Washizu's defeated moral consciousness and destroyed samurai's confidence. Finally, the warrior takes the fatal spear and makes his way to the treacherous murder.

The power of silence is further manifested through the dynamic interfusion with *noh* music. Although marked as "a good deal more evil than Lady Macbeth" (Richie, *The Films of Akira Kurosawa* 119), and "lacking of the human dimension of Shakespeare's character" (Prince 143), Asaji also reveals her inner fear and realizes her doomed fate. Sitting on the floor, she waits noiselessly. The silence that symbolizes Washizu's fear and resistance in the earlier scene accompanies her, until the haunting solitary flute recurs. As if listening to the flute, Asaji slowly turns her face to the bloodstained wall and rests her eyes on the grotesque scene. Although only partially visible, Asaji's masklike face alters and betrays her fear. As the haunting flute begins to play, fear apparently creeps out from beneath her mask-like face. The music persists, and the lady's fear increases. A sudden shrill note and a driving drumbeat intensify Asaji's emotion. She abruptly rises and quickly walks toward the bloodstained wall. Staring at the hideous image, terrified, she circles frenziedly in front of the graphic wall. Her circular movement emphasizes the metaphoric cycles of the movie—ambition, treachery, and hideous death. Ironically, she is one who draws the circle and sets the trap. The sharp contrast between silence and the driving *noh* music, which frame the transition from Asaji's stillness to her sudden frenzied movement, prove that "the whole energy system of the film derives from the pattern of extreme containment followed by explosive release that characterizes the rhythm of Noh" (Hapgood 239).

The silence of the murder scene finally reaches its full power as Kurosawa reveals the destruction of the great warrior. Washizu returns with the bloody spear and drops himself on the floor without realizing that the deadly weapon is still in his hands. The spear remains locked in his lethal posture even after Asaji takes it away by force. The warrior appears to sink to a moment of "frozen immobility," to borrow Noel Burch's phrase (310). Where in the early scene silence conveys Washizu's wavering mental state, at the end of the scene it bespeaks his destruction. Commenting upon this breath taking scene, John Gerlach argues that "Kurosawa eliminates the contrast between act and reflection and gives only acts performed in mitigating circumstances" (357). From my point of view, however, the psychological complexity and conflict in the murder scene are extended and intensified to the extreme. This scene demonstrates the most distinctive characteristics of Kurosawa's general approach to Shakespeare's play: simple, dense, intense, and compelling.

The mysterious silence of the beginning of the movie and the violent silence of the murder scene are matched by the ambiguous and suspenseful silence of the funeral scene. Here Miki's failure to speak contains a paradox of perfidy and loyalty. First, it can be understood as a denunciation of his loyalty to the murdered Lord. Chased by Washizu and his soldiers, Master Kunimaru (Malcolm) and General Noriyasu (Macduff) narrowly make their way back to the Forest Castle, and in a life and death moment, they demand that Miki open the gate. Instead of fulfilling his duty and demonstrating loyalty, Miki sends down a shower of arrows, wounding and driving his young master away. Since his rejection of Kunimaru, the legitimate heir, is treacherous, it would not be surprising to see Miki take a chance and strike for power. But Miki's ambiguous silence remains when Washizu first arrives at the gate. In contrast to the presentation of Washizu's psychological struggle, which is conveyed by the warrior's contorted face and glaring eyes, Miki is absent from the screen and only appears at the end.

Rather than giving his audience the privilege of witnessing the character's mental stress from a distance as in the cases of Asaji and Washizu, Kurosawa involves the audience in the process of interpreting Miki's ambiguous silence. A long-shot first reveals the slow funeral procession as Washizu approaches the castle for a second time. In addition to suspenseful music, a suddenly rising mist heightens the uncertainly of the situation. A few close-shots show the alert and tense facial expressions of Washizu and his soldiers, while a pounding drum dramatically resonates the beating of the warriors' hearts. The funeral procession is viewed for a long time and shot from different angles and distances, compelling the audience to perceive Miki's silence through the mist. The sense of danger heightens as the procession gets closer and closer to the castle and the drum pounds even more heavily. Eventually, at an effective moment, the distance between the observer and the observed—the audience and Washizu—is erased. In a low-angle shot the viewer finds himself placed in Washizu's position: looked down upon by those hidden behind the castle walls, and exposed to potential attack. A ringing gong heightens the threatening sensation. A low-shot of numerous arrow-holes of the high castle gate implicates the potential danger and viciousness of Miki's silence and projects Washizu's fear. Finally, the long suspenseful silence contrasts with the movie's intense rhythm. Kurosawa's portrait of Miki's ambiguous silence manifests his masterful skill and demonstrates the power of silence in the movie from a different aspect. The gate finally opens, Washizu encounters Miki, but one finds no certain answer to Miki's ambiguous silence over the murder that Washizu committed. Although Miki casts a condemning glance at Washizu, Miki's voluntary suggestion that the murderer is the Lord of the Forest Castle betrays his complicity, while his comment that "the Forest Spirit sees the future very clearly" reveals his own ambition. Miki's ambiguity enforces the observation that "the world of *Throne of Blood* is morally ambiguous" (Clifton 56)—a theme that Kurosawa illustrates through the repeating symbolic circular motif.

As these three examples show, silence and the interactions between silence, natural sound—wind, hoof beats, the horse's whinny, the owl's cry, and *noh* music, mainly flute and drum—enhance the effect of Kurosawa's dramatic visual images, enforcing their symbolic messages, and proclaiming the major themes of the movie. The hoof beats symbolize suppressed ambition, war, violence, and the chaos. Parallel to the repeated circular movement of the galloping horse is the sound pattern of silence broken by hoof beats. Together they emphasize the cycle of doomed fate. The forest, whose silence is interrupted and broken by the violent hoof beats, sends the cracking thunder as a message of anger and revenge, foretelling the destructive result, that no voice will remain, only silence.

As in the original play, where Macbeth and Lady Macbeth startle at every little noise after the murder of Duncan, Kurosawa's soundtrack conveys the characters' inner stress and conflict. While silence conveys Washizu's hesitation and fear, the swishing sound of Asaji's silk kimono proclaims her determination and force. The couple's psychological battle of desire and resistance, of treachery and moral and social consciousness are expressed through stylized performance and constricted music, both of which derive from the *noh* tradition that offers a visual and auditory harmony. At the same time, an elegant flute creates a disharmony that reflects the characters' inner world, intensifying the characters' psychological conflicts. The owl's cry over Washizu's defeated moral consciousness and the lost confidence of the samurai mocks the couple's doomed fate and echoes the Forest Spirit's hollow laugher. While Asaji's fear is betrayed by the driving drumbeats and the sound of the shrill flute, silence and immobility accentuate Washizu's destruction. Finally, by employing different strategies to construct silence, Kurosawa not only reveals the psychological depth and conflict of this great story, but also forces his audience to participate in and interpret his film. Miki's inner tension is portrayed through an ambiguous silence, which reveals a moral ambiguity—the lasting truth of *Throne of Blood.* Shakespeare's introspective speeches have been transformed into a contrast between silence and sounds.

Works Cited

Clifton, Charles H. "Making an Old Thing New: Kurosawa's Film Adaptation of Shakespeare's *Macbeth.*" *Ideas of Order in Literature & Film.* Ed. Peter Ruppert. Tallahassee: UP of Florida, 1980. 51-58.

Davies, Anthony. *Filming Shakespeare's Plays: The Adaptations of Laurence Olivier, Orson Welles, Peter Brook and Akira Kurosawa.* Cambridge: Cambridge UP, 1988.

Gerlach, John. "Shakespeare, Kurosawa and Macbeth: A Response to J. Blumenthal." *Literature/Film Quarterly* 1.4 (1973): 352-59.

Hapgood, Rovert. "Kurosawa's Shakespeare Films: *Throne of Blood*, *The Bad Sleep Well*, and *Ran.*" *Shakespeare and the Moving Image: The Plays on Film and Television.* Ed. Anthony Davies and Stanley Wells. Cambridge: Cambridge UP, 1994. 234-49.

Jorgens, Jack J. "Kurosawa's *Throne of Blood*: Washizu and Miki Meet the Forest Spirit." *Literature/Film Quarterly* 66.3 (1983): 167-73.

Kurosawa, Akira, dir. *Throne of Blood.* New York: Public Home Video, 1957.

Kurosawa, Akira. *Something Like an Autobiography.* Trans. Audie E. Bock. New York: Knopf, 1982.

Prince, Stephen. *The Warrior's Camera: The Cinema of Akira Kurosawa.* Princeton: Princeton UP, 1991.

Reeves, Geoffrey. "Finding Shakespeare on Film: From an Interview with Peter Brook." *Film Theory and Criticism: Introductory Readings.* Ed. Gerald Mast and Marshall Cohen. Oxford: Oxford UP, 1974. 234-49.

Richie, Donald. *The Films of Akira Kurosawa.* Berkeley: U of California P, 1965.

Richie, Donald. "Kurosawa on Kurosawa." *Sight and Sound* 33 (1964): 108-13.

Shakespeare, William. *William Shakespeare: The Complete Works.* Ed. Stanley Wells and Gary Taylor. Oxford: Clarendon, 1988.

Zeami, Motokiyo. *On the Art of the Noh Drama: The Major Treatises of Zeami.* Trans. Thomas J. Rimer and Yamazaki Maskazu. Princeton: Princeton UP, 1984.

Illustrations

Silence broken by natural sounds in a bleak landscape in *Throne of Blood: The Castle of the Spider's Web*, dir. Akira Kurosawa (Japan: TOHO Films, 1957).

A sudden whinny and the camera shifts to Washizu, silent and restless. *Throne of Blood: The Castle of the Spider's Web*, dir. Akira Kurosawa (Japan: TOHO Films, 1957).

Elegant flute music forms an aesthetic harmony with Asaji's body movement. *Throne of Blood: The Castle of the Spider's Web*, dir. Akira Kurosawa (Japan: TOHO Films, 1957).

Asaji stares at the bloodstained wall, illusrating ambition, treachery, and hideous death. *Throne of Blood: The Castle of the Spider's Web*, dir. Akira Kurosawa (Japan: TOHO Films, 1957).

The Visualization of Metaphor in Two Chinese Versions of *Macbeth*

Alexander C.Y. Huang

The past ten years have witnessed drastic changes in the dynamic relationship between writing (drama and literary translation) and other forms of cultural production (mass media, theater, and film). Chinese opera adaptations exhibit unique strategies to negotiate different terrains of meanings through cultural translation, a form of rewriting that is distinct from printed literary translation. Cultural translations often involve verbal and nonverbal signs. Many Chinese operas rewrite Shakespeare in visual terms and use stylization to translate verbal metaphors. Wu Hsing-kuo's *jingju* (Beijing opera) *Kingdom of Desire* became part of the repertoire of his troupe, the Contemporary Legend Theatre Company, based in Taipei. Wu's *Mabeth* has toured internationally several times since its premiere in Taipei in 1986. As a comparison, the Kunqu opera *Macbeth* (*Story of Bloody Hands*), directed by Huang Zuolin and Li Jiayao and staged by the Shanghai Kunqu Opera Theatre Company, was specifically commissioned for the spectacles of the first Chinese Shakespeare Festival in Shanghai and Beijing. These two Chinese opera *Macbeth*'s were planned and staged across the Taiwan Straight, independent of each other, in 1986. Both productions localized the story but nonetheless captured both local and international audiences.

Running through the press reviews and audience responses is a strong current of nationalistic and pseudo-cosmopolitanist narrative, as it were, that by staging and enjoying plays by a world dramatist like Shakespeare, China is initiated and requalified to join the world. This was only ten years after the devastating experiences of the Cultural Revolution (1966-1976) and still a few years before the official opening of China's door to the world. On the other hand, the Beijing opera *Macbeth* in Taipei, initiated by the innovative Beijing opera actor, Wu Hsing-kuo, who, like Ma Yong'an, specializes in male martial roles, took on a commercial and practical concern from its inception. Its purpose was to astound and amaze, with spectacles and Shakespeare, so as to attract audiences back to the decaying Beijing opera theater. Unlike the Kunqu *Macbeth*, the Beijing opera *Macbeth* toured in Continental Europe and England successfully and has since entered the repertoire of the Contemporary Legend Theatre of Taiwan. In fact, it is the most profitable production for the company since its founding in the 1980s. The diverse fates of these two productions have bearings on their political and cultural environs. These two productions also invariably translate their cultures onto the stage. They have been met with severe criticism from avid lovers of traditional Chinese opera theaters, as both Taiwanese and Western critics have questioned their fidelity to Shakespeare. Not heard in that debate, however, were the ways in which the structure of emotions of a foreign play found their way onto the intercultural stage. Both modern stages (English or Chinese) and modern media (films or multimedia) deviate from Shakespeare so widely that stage translations should be understood in terms of the structure of emotions and metaphors rather than the language of the original text.

In these dramatic adaptations, the plot and the spirit of Shakespeare are preserved but also relocated into characteristically Chinese contexts. As in Kurosawa's *Throne of Blood*, Shakespeare's metaphors and plot lines in these two *Macbeth*s are given local contexts and restaged with characters and behavior patterns in Chinese terms. The significance of this transformation goes beyond the invention of Chinese names for characters and places. Ariane Mnouchkine (Théâtre du Soleil, France) understood how the Chinese version modified the original and jumped at the idea of making an intercultural performance a way to undermine both hierarchies and difference (see, e.g., Singleton). When conventional methods of expression can no longer communicate the foreignness of Shakespeare and of the theatrical selves, the directors turn to signs wholly foreign to their spectators. Li Jiaoyao, the director of a Kunqu opera adaptation of *Macbeth* in 1986, and Wu Hsing-kuo in Taipei use Shakespeare's foreign aesthetics and metaphors to refresh the Chinese formalistic style of presentation. In the trajectories of intercultural transplantation of Shakespeare into Chinese opera forms, such as those that distinguish the Taipei and Shanghai productions, directors find inspirations from one another's work and move toward various versions of *Macbeth* with East Asian characteristics.

Li Jiayao admitted he encountered many difficulties in staging Shakespeare as a Chinese opera, but he also claimed that it was the foreignness of Shakespeare that enriched and expanded the performing techniques of traditional Chinese theater (see Yu). The directors of these two productions and many other Chinese adaptations share a common agenda to reform and save the traditional theater from the aesthetic, political, and pragmatic perspectives. The experience of staging and attending intercultural performances of Shakespeare resembles that of writing and reading a palimpsest on which modern rewrites never quite conceal the writings of the past that are written over. East Asian Shakespeares sometimes refer to one another, as in the case of Wu's *The Kingdom of Desire* and Kurosawa's *Throne of Blood*, as well as to a mystified premodern Chinese identity, as in the case of Li's *Story of the Bloody Hands*. It is not always a pleasant experience, because these radical dislocations challenge the conventionalized meanings of Shakespeare and Chinese theater. One of the crucial components of such reworking of a foreign text is the transformation and metamorphosis of metaphor, not only from page to stage but also from Early Modern England to the Sinophone world of the modern and postmodern era.

These transformations and stage translations necessarily call into question the ways in which Shakespeare's plays are represented on Chinese-language stages. Metaphors are transformed in accordance with specific dramatic codes, Chinese conventional mixtures of the serious and the comic, as well as interpersonal relationships in the Chinese cultural landscape. However, cultures do not interact with each other in a mechanical way, and metaphors in dramas are not simply replaced by another set of words in a successful stage translation. All bilingual dictionaries and line-by-line translations of plays are based on a powerful but questionable assumption that language and signs are made of equivalent counterparts. Metaphor, more so than words, operates on a constantly transforming plane of consciousness. The earliest model is offered by Aristotle, who believes that metaphor serves to divert and give pleasure, and the meanings of a metaphor can therefore be expressed in alternative modes. Max Black sums up different conceptualizations of metaphor throughout the history of Western philosophy. I suggest that, at least in theater, metaphor is simply a better expression for specific emotions or situations, and there are no literal equivalences. Metaphors have to be staged, which is even more urgent in intercultural theater. The best and most effective way to translate cultural texts would be to translate semantically or, in the language of theater, to translate visually and acoustically, with colors, dance, steps, gestures, and songs in a stylized performance like Chinese opera.

In the cases of Chinese operatic adaptations of *Macbeth*, the Shakespearean metaphors are not transformed or translated mechanically into neatly assigned, compartmentalized Chinese counterparts. Not only do religious, cultural, political, and social codes get replaced, but a matrix of moral valences, connotations of gestures and actions, as well as visual metaphors, has to be recreated in the Chinese theater to effectively Sinicize its cultural Other. It can be more accurately described as rewriting, like a palimpsest, rather than a one-to-one, itemized cross-cultural transformation of signs. The result is a mode of representation heavily dependent on gestural and other modes of visualization that in turn depend on metaphors to convey verbal messages. The term visual here relates not only to the stage design and setting but to the physicality and physical embodiment of metaphors on the particular stages of Beijing and Kunqu opera. For example, the metaphors of destiny, the supernatural, and ambition are embodied in the three witches, who, when transformed onto the Chinese operatic stage, become mountain ghosts and deformed spirits known to divert, pervert, and confuse the minds of heroes. Word-to-word accuracy is not the central concern for this transformation of Shakespearean metaphor. The Chinese theater has neither the English Elizabethan concept of ghosts nor the Jacobean obsession with the witches. If, like novels, the play also contains what Raymond Williams terms "the structure of feelings" that holds the piece together, this structure must be the core of the transformation operation that crosses cultural boundaries (133-34). The first priority of the production is audience acceptance, as directors seek to preserve the play's feelings and emotions. *Macbeth*, a play with the most visually striking and humbly simple imagery and metaphor, suits such cultural crossings, since it can be boiled down to a set of emotions and mental pictorial images rather than culturally or historically specific allusions in history plays, as Elizabeth Wichmann-Walczak also argues in this volume.

Other aspects of *Macbeth* foregrounded in the two adaptations are the politics of signs and the visual nature of its metaphors. Verbal messages sustain the play. Colors take on meaning. Visual impressions we recall after reading the play include the red of dripping blood, crimson stains that would "incarnadine" the green "multitudinous seas" (2.2.60-2) the glow of an imagined dagger at night, the limbo light of dawn, the unnatural pitch of black night, the transparent devil that would "damn [one] black" (5.3.11-12), and the equivocal colors associated with the deformed images conjured up by the watches in act four. Several critics and directors, from A.C. Bradley to Wu, have noticed these vivid visual images. The two Chinese versions of *Macbeth* exploited the connection between the symbolic nature of the play's language and the symbolic Chinese operatic stage and used the connection to transform and sustain otherwise untranslatable Shakespearean metaphors. In the stage design of *Story of Bloody Hands*, the color red is featured prominently throughout the production in its costume, lighting, and stage design. In the *Kingdom of Desire* the contrast between red and black is deployed to construct a palpable, violet world. Both directors rendered in colors, dance, and music the metaphors for unnatural crime, disillusioned overreaching, and the anxiety of adulteration and the loss of masculinity in the face of different forms of femininity ranging from Lady Macbeth to the witches. Of course, Li and Wu are not the first ones to render *Macbeth* in stylized performance. The operatic adaptation of Sir William Davenant, their English predecessor, held the English stage from 1663 to 1744, with the witches dancing, singing, and flying through the air on machines (see Barnet 187-88). If the Anglophone theater, and stage productions in general, has already been translating Shakespeare into visual and audio metaphors, what would the difference be between the English and the Chinese operatic adaptations? The answer lies in the metaphorical transformation of plots and language that the Chinese operatic adaptations sustain. *Story of Bloody Hands* and the *Kingdom of Desire* are plays and displays of colors and gestures within the codes of the forms in which they are performed. Unlike Davenant's operatic adaptation, the physical and the visual in intercultural theater are not expressions of Shakespearean metaphors but the metaphors themselves.

Not only is the color red an important metaphor, but natural and painted colors in general become metaphorical during the course of the play (a different thing from predetermined color symbolism). Lady Macbeth says that her hands "are of [Macbeth's] color" in the murder scene (2.2.54-60). She also tries to comfort Macbeth by comparing the illusory nature of "the sleep and the dead" to pictures that cannot pose threats. Only "the eye of childhood" will fear a "painted devil." (2.2.50-51). The production creatively converges the three weird sisters, Furies, or biblical demons into three grotesque figures. Combining the role types of dwarf specter and a taller ghost, the spirits of *The Story of Bloody Hands* find a way to represent the grotesque in the Kunqu universe. This version effectively transforms the metaphors of a "painted devil" and the illusions of the "pictures" in Macbeth's mind's eye. *The Story of Bloody Hands* opens with a spectacle of painted devils. A gender-neutral witch stands at the center of the stage with a long cloak that wavers as the witch moves. This witch says that "I am good and evil." At the same time, with a sudden move he shakes the figure of a dwarf witch out of one side of his cloak. The dwarf says, "I am true and false," and then another dwarf appears in the same manner from the other side and chants that "I am the beautiful and the repulsive." The three witches sway and swirl as they turn their heads to reveal grotesque masks on the back of their heads. Metaphors for fluidity of words, double takes, evanescences, and inconstancies become a stunning spectacle of movements and masks. The witches are visually striking as they physically embody the doubleness that lies behind the plays theme of equivocation. Ma Pei, the Kunqu opera's version of *Macbeth*, sees only half of the witches' faces and destroys himself because he believes in their prophecy.

In the scene the production titles "Seeking Advice [from the witches]," Ma Pei is surrounded by the three deformed mountain spirits and dances with them as prophecies are poured out. His dance and movements eventually harmonize with those of the spirits, signifying his thought is being synchronized with deformity. Dance and music occupy a strikingly important place in this adaptation, as metaphors are danced out and sung. In the following scene the play's version of Lady Macbeth is surrounded by ghosts of people she and her husband have murdered, as the royal doctor watches from the dark her sleepwalking. She also ends up dancing in synchronization with the ghosts. The three mountain spirits return to the stage at the very end of the play to comment on Macbeth's actions and thereby offer some kind of a moral lesson. They turn their heads, altering between their smiling and grotesque faces. The program note for the production self-consciously exploits this sensuality and claims that the *Story of the Bloody Hands* replaces Shakespeare's metaphors with spectacles. Lois Potter's amazement at the spectacle of the *Story of Bloody Hands* confirms this point. She writes: "Whereas Shakespeare's play stages the supernatural but keeps most 'real' events offstage . . . [*Story of Bloody Hands*] is almost pure spectacle. It shows everything except the murder of Duncan and even that is so audible that the royal physician rushes off to tell the heir-apparent to escape" (1253). However candid this observation is, scholars such as Catherine Diamond and Antony Tatlow have pointed out the tendency, especially by Western audiences not familiar with codes of stylization, to concentrate on sheer spectacle and to ignore the language of the body. Still others point toward a consumerist attitude toward Shakespeare in rendering his plays as spectacles. However, such an emphasis on the effect of the spectacles will lead to a demise of performance. Stylized performance and the visual representation of verbal metaphors can easily be confused with pantomime and said to be child's play imitating a higher art form. The speech of the body incorporated and newly forged speeches on stage combine to bring forth a new mode of expressing emotions. As metaphors are unique and do not have literal equivalences either in the same language or in a different language, the stage serves as a venue of cultural translation through enactment of emotions conjured up by foreign metaphors.

Kingdom of Desire also uses dance and mask to create a sense of fluidity and uncertainty. The famous dance of Lin Hsiu-wei (Wu's wife and founder of the Taigu Tales Dance Theater) in the banquet scene is almost a parallel to the three witches in the *Story of Bloody Hands*. In a costume and style with Japanese elements, she plays a dancer entertaining Macbeth and the lords of the court. She holds two masks in her hands and alternately covers her face with them as she swirls, bends, and crosses the stage. She dances with three masks on her face and in her hands. When the dance is over, she reveals a third mask on her face, which has been covered by the two masks she holds in her hands. After Duncan is murdered and the ambition of Macbeth realized, this interlude ironically comments on Duncan's own words: "There's no art / To find the mind's construction in the face" (1.4.10-11). The dance itself is also an intervention to the narrative and to the harmony of forms, since it combines Japanese techniques and ballet steps and does not align itself to the norms of the Beijing opera.

In both versions of *Macbeth*, encounters with the supernatural and the anxiety of the unnatural take the form of whirling dance movements performed by masks or deformed bodies. While linguistic codes strike faster and gestural codes move more slowly, the visual metaphors are more memorable and impressive. Excess dance and singing concentrate such adaptations on selected episodes. The conventions of the Chinese operatic stage call for the condensation of the plot of an already short play, the shortest of Shakespeare's tragedies. This shortening also contributes to the intensified visual and gestural metaphors on stage, which serve to synthesize the emotions and not to analyze them. For example, in the episode, "Madness in the Chamber," in the *Story of Bloody Hands*, Lady Macbeth is dressed up in a red robe washing her hands in a crimson-red chamber. Haimin Wei as Lady Macbeth in *A Kingdom of Desire*, just like *The Story of Bloody Hands*, foregrounds the gestural codes and heightened emotions in the hand-washing scene through contrasting colors. While Lady Macbeth wears a red robe in *The Story of Bloody Hands*, the character is dressed in white in *A Kingdom of Desire*. The red of her robe corresponds to the color of the royal chamber and the color for joyful occasions in Chinese contexts, especially weddings, although it is also the color of crime and danger. Red also symbolizes various feminine codes, including the birth of a child. In this creative and imaginative lyrical transposition of actions into song, dance, and devouring, the color denotes terror, madness, and death, as Lady Macbeth encounters the ghost of Lady Macduff. It is a perplexing moment for anyone familiar with Chinese social codes, as the connotations of red on stage are joy and social connections, such as marriage. Later, the very same red robe transgresses the conventional connotation and comes to signify the schizophrenia of Lady Macbeth. Colors are charged with psychological and moral allusions, and the irony and tension successfully transform the Shakespearean metaphor of anxiety and guilt into a matrix of conflicting connotations on stage represented by dance and stage sets.

The transformations of *Macbeth* into *The Story of Bloody Hands* and *The Kingdom of Desire* have a significance that goes beyond the invention of Chinese names for characters and places, or the reconfiguration of Chinese counterparts of the story of Macbeth. The enactment of the foreign and of its Chinese counterpart necessarily threatens and modifies the original. Mnouchkine jumped at this idea and takes intercultural performance as a way to undermine both hierarchies and difference. The director of *Kingdom* was also primarily interested in tackling the established yet stifled notion of what Beijing opera is or should be, deploying the psychological depth of the characters in *Macbeth* to construct a new Beijing opera. The director of *Bloody Hands*, on the other hand, was less interested in undermining hierarchies. He used Shakespeare as a ticket to promote Kunqu at international venues.

Second, when conventional methods of expression can no longer communicate the foreignness of Shakespeare and theatrical personae, directors turn to signs wholly foreign to their spectators. Mnouchkine turns to signs used by the Japanese theater, including masks, steps, and styles of speaking. Li and Wu turn to Shakespeare and attempt to use his foreign aesthetics and metaphors to refresh the formalistic style of Chinese presentation. In the trajectories of intercultural transplantation of Shakespeare into Chinese opera forms, directors find inspirations from one another's work and move toward various versions of *Macbeth* with East Asian characteristics. A proliferation of East Asian types combine to define Macbeth, as these intercultural texts refer to one another and implicitly to Shakespeare. Performance is a palimpsest.

In both works, cultural signs intersect on stage not only through an amalgamation of Shakespeare's texts and Chinese opera verse, but through actors who embody different cultural signs as well. *Kingdom of Desire* and *Story of the Bloody Handss* concentrate on color symbolism and the visual aspects of the verbal metaphors found in key scenes in *Macbeth*. They epitomize a paradigm shift from seeking authenticity to foregrounding artistic subjectivity in modes of cultural production that re-produce global texts. Changing modes in the representational practice of stylized theaters have induced changing attitudes to Shakespeare and to Western classics. This shift has received increased scholarly attention. Michael Billington, for example, is struck by Shakespeare's "infinite adaptability" in productions in "a variety of cultures and languages." He suspects "something more significant is going on" and notices "changing attitudes to Shakespeare, particularly in performance" (15). On the other hand, Asian stylized appropriations of Shakespeare's plays share some features of what Stephen Greenblatt terms "appropriative mimesis" in cross-cultural encounters and identifies a cross-cultural strategy to domesticate the foreign by linguistic means: this kind of imitation is carried out "in the interest of acquisition" and does not "entail any grasp of the cultural reality of the other, only a willingness to make contact and to effect some kind of exchange" (99). Early modern European colonizers did not invest interests in the cultural reality of the Other as such; the intercultural directors and actors of *Kingdom of Desire* and *Story of Bloody Handss* were also not interested in the Elizabethan field of reception, which was either vague or intentionally lost. However, the two cases I discuss ultimately depart from European "appropriative mimesis." While the European travelers in Greenblatt's case imitated only to possess the Other, inter-cultural travelers in these two Chinese production of

Macbeth did not share any anxiety of acquisition. Images of the Other presented on stage were connected to images of the self. Further, these two productions demonstrate a very different force of performance. Critics of culture such as Theodor W. Adorno and Max Horkheimer have expressed concerns about the machinations of the culture industry and, by extension, the ways in which global dissemination of Shakespeare's name and plays might eradicate "the personal, the local, [and] the different" (Desmet 5). *The Kingdom of Desire* and *Story of Bloody Handss* consciously mobilize cultural differences to create new performing styles. The local and the different are foregrounded in this cultural translation. These two plays reveal exactly the opposite potential of cultural appropriation. They fuse foreign verbal metaphors with local visual signs and non-verbal codes. Re-imagined metaphors on stage bear out histories of the evolving inventory of appropriative modes off stage.

Works Cited

Adorno, Theodor W., and Max Horkheimer. "The Culture Industry: Enlightenment as Mass Deception." 1944. *Dialectic of Enlightenment*. Trans. John Cumming. New York: Continuum, 1977. 120-67.

Barnet, Sylvan. "Macbeth on Stage and Screen." *Macbeth*. Ed. Sylvan Barnet. New York: Penguin, 1998. 186-200.

Billington, Michael. "Was Shakespeare English?" *Shakespeare: World Views*. Ed. Heather Kerr, Robin Eaden, and Madge Mitton. London: Associated UP, 1996. 15-28.

Black, Max. *Models and Metaphors: Studies in Language and Philosophy*. Ithaca: Cornell UP, 1962.

Desmet, Christy. "Introduction." *Shakespeare and Appropriation*. Ed. Christy Desmet and Robert Sawyer. London: Routledge, 1999. 1-14.

Diamond, Catherine. "Kingdom of Desire: The Three Faces of Macbeth." *Asian Theatre Journal* 11.1 (1994): 114-33.

Greenblatt, Stephen. *Marvellous Possessions: The Wonder of the New World*. Chicago: U of Chicago P, 1991.

Potter, Lois. "The Spectacle of Macbeth." *Times Literary Supplement* (13 November 1987): 1253.

Shakespeare, William. *The Riverside Shakespeare*. Ed. G. Blakemore Evans. Boston: Houghton Mifflin, 1974.

Singleton, Brian. "Mnouchkine and Shakespeare: Intercultural Theatre Practice." *Shakespeare and France*. Ed. Holger Klein and J.M. Maguin. Lewiston: Edwin Mellen P, 1995. 307-26.

Tatlow, Antony. "*Macbeth* and Kunju Opera." *Shakespeare in Comparison: A Politics of the Sign*. Hong Kong: Department of Comparative Literature, U of Hong Kong, 1995. 169-201.

Williams, Raymond. *Marxism and Literature*. Oxford: Oxford UP, 1977.

Yu, Qiuyu. "Shashibiya zai dangdai zhongguo" ("Shakespeare in Contemporary China"). *Wenhui Bao* (28 April 1986): n.p.

Illustrations

Ji Zhenhua as Macbeth (left) in *Story of Bloody Hands*, directed by Huang Zuolin and performed in Edinburgh, Shanghai Kunju Company, 1986.

Stage design for the banquet scene, *Story of Bloody Hands*, directed by Huang Zuolin, Shanghai Kunju Company, 1986.

Lin Xiouwei (Lin Hsiu-wei) as the triple masked dancer in the banquet scene in Wu Hsing-kuo's *Kingdom of Desire* (*Macbeth*).

Zhang Jingxian as Lady Macbeth in the sleepwalking scene in Huang's *Story of Bloody Hands*, dir. Huang Zuolin (Shanghai Kunju Company, 1986).

Shakespeare in Contemporary Japan

Daniel Gallimore

Shakespeare production in Japan is arguably as ephemeral as cyberspace in its detachment from any integrative tradition, and will often need to explain itself. Like Hollywood also, it has tended to be dominated by auteurs: translators such as Shōyō Tsubouchi and Tsuneari Fukuda through to the 1970s, and with the commercialization of the modern theater in the 1980s by directors such as Yukio Ninagawa. The ambiguity of this space grants exponents considerable freedom in reinterpreting Shakespeare according to their agendas, and can also be said to save them from any responsibility for artistic traditions other than their own. It is, in other words, problematic to detect any overarching purpose of Shakespeare production in Japan other than the parochial. In their moments of awakening, Japanese Shakespeareans compare themselves with both Shakespeare's old world and the old world of their cultural traditions. This comparison is intercultural in the sense that any comparison with another may promote self-awareness, but as a comparison of like with unlike it is also metaphorical, realizing a dual indebtedness to the old and respect for one's own creative potential.

If the ideal of intercultural understanding is an apolitical one, then at least the aesthetic can be ideologized. In this article I refer to some of the aesthetic problems encountered in Shakespeare's reception in Japan, suggesting that they each in their way have ideological implications for modern Japanese culture. Rather than adopting a historical approach, I illustrate these problems with a series of short case studies to show how the overarching problem of "newness" may be encountered in its time and place. In other words, I am concerned with identifying cultural rather than historical trends. The ideal of newness is a traditional characteristic of Japanese culture, typified for example by the reconstruction of wooden shrine buildings every thirty years, the admiration of cherry blossoms in spring, and the delectation of raw fish. The problems described in this article have both an open or universal and a closed or local aspect, acquiring newness through the mutuality of the two aspects. Novelty is acquired not through the application of universal principles or specific details but rather the interaction of the two aspects to address a changing situation. The

Japanese biologist Kinji Imanishi observed that "[e]volution is not brought about by the freedom of certainty, but originates in the constraints of chance" (75). The plays of Shakespeare have been received in Japan not as objects but as agents of evolution. As Imanishi writes, "It is not that something becomes food after being ingested, or becomes prey after being eaten, or becomes a mate after copulation. Only when living things react, does the environment make them live. If organisms do not react, the environment presumably kills them and transforms them into matter. The recognition of the environment is the organism's reaction to it; it is the choice of living things in the environment" (74).

To apply Imanishi's metaphor of determinacy and indeterminacy, the trajectory of Shakespeare in Japan may be seen to develop not in agreement with its local environment but as a positive reaction. I argue, then, that Shakespeare in Japan will always strive for the patina of newness because it is always in the process of becoming itself, a genuinely Japanese Shakespeare that is elusive because Shakespeare can never be authentically replicated outside his originating culture and because the reception of Shakespeare in Japan is too diffuse to amount to a composite cultural tradition like *noh* or *kabuki*. In the 1890s, Tsubouchi argued that Shakespeare was a writer whose ideals could never be fully realized. The newness of his representation may therefore depend—as an artistic ideal—on the respect with which the interiority of Shakespeare is treated.

Room for Shakespeare

From a Japanese point of view, the two most striking characteristics of Shakespearean drama are its scope and diversity. The plays draw on a range of sources and geographical and historical settings that are without parallel in traditional Japanese culture. They also display a lexical and rhetorical range that is unusual even in the context of the reforms of the Japanese language over the last hundred years. Shakespeare's tendency to transcend generic boundaries is unusual as well, and although he has always been perceived as a foreign writer in Japan, or one who can be expected to break the rules, the problem of finding suitable sites for his production continues to intrigue Japanese Shakespeareans. It is not that the plays demand a particular theatrical design like the *hashigakari* in *noh* or *hanamichi* in *kabuki* (the *hashigakari* is a covered bridge connecting the stage with the wings, and the *hanamichi* is a raised aisle projecting from stage right through the audience to the back of the theater). Shakespeare can be staged in any kind of venue, large or small. Rather, the problem is that of finding a niche for Shakespeare in a culture of niches.

Although the myth of Japan as a homogeneous society prevails, and is justified to some extent by the influence of the bureaucracy and education system, this myth conceals a considerable heterogeneity in the tendency for organizations to preserve and enhance their hierarchies and territories, no more so than in the theatrical world. There is, for example, no national system of drama schooling in Japan. Instead, actors receive most of the necessary training from whichever company they happen to join in their youth. The parochialism of the Japanese theater may be difficult to reconcile with the inclusiveness of Shakespeare's vision. The historical solution has been to stage Shakespeare as a modern or contemporary writer, although there have been numerous experiments in traditional genres, hinging on perceived similarities of dramaturgy. In 2005, Ninagawa directed a full-scale *kabuki* version of *Twelfth Night* at the Kabukiza theater in Tokyo, exploring similarities between the homoeroticism of Shakespeare's comedy with the tradition of female impersonators (*onnagata*) in *kabuki*.

Ryūtopia is a new company that has sought a novel approach to the problem of framing Shakespearean rhetoric within a heterogeneous culture. Founded in 2003 as part of a local arts organization in the north-western city of Niigata, Ryūtopia looks both to the traditional culture of *ura Nihon* (literally "nether Japan," the prefectures overlooking the Japan Sea) and the culture of the Tokyo metropolis. Their twice-yearly Shakespeare productions are staged in both Niigata and Tokyo, and while their director Yoshihiro Kurita was trained in the Tokyo theater, their actors are drawn partly from the Niigata area. Moreover, Ryūtopia combines traditional with contemporary techniques, using both *kabuki* and mainstream actors to perform Shakespeare in contemporary translations by the female translator Kazuko Matsuoka, and in a contemporary *mise-en-scène*, but on a *noh* stage, Ryūtopia's own theater in Niigata and the Tessenkai and Umewaka theaters in Tokyo. Given the company's background, its work can be said to address not only the problem of Shakespeare's rhetoric but also the topical issue of the impact of globalization on local communities.

Like globalization, a world poet such as Shakespeare can be seen either to disrupt local identities or else sacrifice his own identity for the sake of tradition. The point at which such loss occurs is subjective. Ninagawa's 1994 *Tempest* was criticized for its liberal use of *noh* motifs (see Kishi 110-11), and because this controversial production was set on Sadō, an island off the Niigata mainland known for its historical associations with *noh* drama, one of the contexts for Ryūtopia's own work. Yet rather than using Shakespeare to foster the *noh* tradition with which their locality is associated, the company can be said to pose a significant question as to why Shakespeare should continue to matter in a global age. In other words, neither Shakespeare nor the native tradition are taken for granted, and this dual perspective is suggested in the company's name: *ryū* meaning "stream," but also metonymically for a school of one of the traditional arts (e.g., *ikebana*), combined with "utopia." The rationale of organizations such as Ryūtopia is that there lies within the local a niche for the global as well, on the assumption that Shakespeare's plays are sufficient within themselves to locate and fill that space. Ryūtopia's productions represent this rhetorical interface as theater. In the current climate of global tensions erupting into localized violence, it is no doubt unsurprising that three out of the nine productions mounted since the company's début in May 2003 have been of *Macbeth*, but I start by focusing on the third of their productions, *The Winter's Tale* of 2005. This I saw at the Tessenkai theater, and my initial concern was to how a play on the geographical scale of Shakespeare's late romance, spanning twenty years, could be crammed into the confined space of a *noh* theater, which is a little more than 33 square meters in size. The sense of confinement was made even more conspicuous by the casting of Ayumi Tanida, who is unusually tall for a Japanese man, as Leontes against a classically tender Haruyo Yamaga as Hermione.

Leontes has been labeled a suppressed homosexual, but in this production the problem was not so much psychological, rather that he was just too big, too hot, for a confined space. Rather than negotiating a way through this space, Leontes seemed oblivious to the calming austerities of time, which ultimately reconcile him to the wife he rejects in the first half of the play. Time was represented through the physical features of the *noh* tradition—the *hashigakari*, main stage and painted pine tree—and through a chorus of four shrine maidens in white robes who lined one side of the stage throughout the performance in what seemed an imitation of *noh*. They held globe-shaped lanterns, which they moved slowly up and down during the first half and then clasped at arm's length during the second. This change in direction may have denoted the change in Leontes' mood from jealous and possessive in the first half to one transfixed and so stabilized by grief after the loss of his son and apparent loss of Hermione. This contrast was also represented by a contrast between the innocent horseplay of Hermione and Polixenes beneath a blanket and, in the second half, Hermione's concealment within a brocade tent used in *noh* performances before appearing for the recognition scene in the mask of a beautiful woman. These contrasts seemed to present two characteristically Shakespearean notions of time: time as an oppressive, unpredictable force that threatens to cuckold and usurp its victims' authority and time as a pacifying force, forever in the present. Shakespearean rhetoric embraces both dimensions: the force and drift of the line containing the measure of its own regularity as well as debt to the classical tradition. Recent productions by Ryūtopia of *Macbeth* and *Othello* have gone even further by employing *kabuki* actors in lead roles. Whereas mainstream actors like Tanida suggest the limitations as well as possibilities of psychological determinism in interpreting Shakespeare, *kabuki* actors such as Ukon Ichikawa in the role of Macbeth and the *onnagata* Emiya Ichikawa as Desdemona and Lady Macbeth suggest the limitations of stylization.

Kurosawa's film of *Macbeth*, *The Throne of Blood* (1957), portrayed the Macbeth character (Washizu) as a man whose only real fault "is his failure to realize himself completely" (Richie 115). Social role in *kabuki* is indicated by gesture, so that a *kabuki* Macbeth can be expected to demonstrate an increasingly frenetic detachment of gesture from reality; one of the effects of Kurosawa's film, although not *kabuki* but in the same feudal environment of traditional *kabuki*, is that Washizu maintains his samurai gestures to the bitter end. In the Ryūtopia *Macbeth*, Ichikawa's equivocation of style and role was profoundly challenged by six identical witches: dressed in black with shiny black wigs and deathly white makeup. The witches represented a typical postmodern assumption that all women can made to look the same, that "bad" women may be made to look good and vice versa, which can only undermine the *kabuki* actor's stylistic assumption that there is a right and wrong way of doing things. In an interview for the Ryūtopia magazine (*Ryūtopia Magazine* 30), Ukon also commented on Shakespeare's "remarkable verbal imagination" in contrast to the recitative of *kabuki*; for Ukon personally, this style of production freed him from the normal professional constraints.

The Ryūtopia *Winter's Tale* generated a sense of time as a comic force that heals the tensions between the local and global, while the *Macbeth* responded to the rhetoric of Shakespeare's tragedy by representing the conflict between nature and the supernatural as a conflict between traditional and postmodern. The overall effect may be too knowing for audiences used to either mainstream or traditional theater but then no more knowing or presumptuous than Shakespeare's own rhetoric. Moreover, the *noh* stage provides a simplicity of focus, a notion of a Japanese Shakespeare, which perhaps the success of *Throne of Blood* has left other practitioners reluctant to explore.

Transcending Shakespeare

In the spirituality of Japanese Buddhism, awareness is *satori* from the verb *satoru*, to see or perceive the reality of phenomena. In a comparison with Meister Eckhart, D.T. Suzuki described *satori* as "a little point" where we can look in two directions: "God-way and creature-way. Expressed in another form, the finite is infinite and the infinite is finite" (70). The goal of *satori*, as of all Buddhist practice, is release from the chain of suffering and desire and a mature apprehension of the animate world in which suffering is conditioned. Shakespeare offers opportunities for various levels of awareness, spatial, temporal, Buddhist, or otherwise. When Matsuoka writes of "countless discoveries" she has made as a Shakespeare translator, "derived from the interest of the plays as they are and from the depth and diversity of Shakespeare's language" (199), she is not referring explicitly to a *satori* of translation but reflecting on what Shakespeare means to Japanese readers in general terms: a writer who neither affirms nor rejects cultural assumptions but facilitates a richly cognitive process. This process may be conceived as "baroque" in the tradition circumscribed by Toshio Kawatake: "What I call 'baroque theater' includes Greek *mimos*, Roman *mimus*, pantomime and other theatrical traditions that originated in popular, improvizational theater; Commedia dell'Arte; the plays of Shakespeare and other Elizabethan dramatists; the baroque theaters of Spain and Italy; Italian, German and Austrian opera; *Musikdrama*; all the way down to expressionism and Brecht. . . . Dynamic instead of static, wild and extravagant, versatile and adaptable, spectacular and ever-changing . . . theatrical rather than text-oriented and essentially centrifugal and outwardly-directed instead of centripetal and inward-looking" (Kawatake 74-75).

Shakespeare in Japan is an heir to this tradition, not least because of the influence by Brecht on Shakespeare directors such as Koreya Senda. The danger of such spectacular theater is that the wood is lost for the trees, and it is no doubt for this reason that one of Matsuoka's most emphatic realizations as a translator is not to over-interpret. In the Japanese context the tendency to interpret or explain Shakespeare is a compelling one. Interpretation may indeed compensate for the lack of a native tradition of Shakespeare performance in Japan, for the foreignness of Shakespeare. Conversely, with a history of reception going back to the 1870s, the temptation to add one's own individual interpretation to the pile is also strong. Yet as Matsuoka suggests in the example discussed below, excessive interpretation can compromise further a work of art that has already been compromised by four hundred years of cultural history. This concern is echoed by a typical observation by Suzuki: "The idea of participation or empathy is an intellectual interpretation of the primary experience, while as far as the experience itself is concerned, there is no room for any sort of dichotomy. The intellect, however, obtrudes itself and breaks up the experience in order to make it amenable to intellectual treatment, which means a discrimination or bifurcation. The original feeling of identity is then lost and intellect is allowed to have its characteristic way of breaking up reality into pieces. Participation or empathy is the result of intellectualization" (Suzuki 92).

Such processes of awareness can be seen in the interaction of cultural myths with a translator's apprehension of an original text. In certain situations Japanese discourse prefers *haragei*, literally "the art of the stomach," a terse style of communication depending on subtle body language, but this discourse, an established technique in the Japanese theater, functions mainly among members of social networks who can be expected to know each other's feelings. Another myth common in both Japanese and Western discourse suggests that it is "unmanly" for men to express their feelings openly to each other, and this too is situational. As the following example suggests, these myths can be overdone as suggested by Kazuko Matsuoka:

> In an unpredictable play like *Hamlet*, where every word counts, translation is unforgettably a matter of trial and error. Just before the play within the play, Hamlet turns to Horatio, asking him to keep his eyes on Claudius during the performance, but before doing so he praises his friend unreservedly. What he says next is "Something too much of this" (3.2.72; i.e., "I've said too much"). "This is what he's been rabbiting on about up to then, and I first translated it as *Chotto yokeina koto wo shaberisugita*. My translation was first staged in the autumn of 1995 at the Ginza Saison Theater, and before rehearsals began I had a meeting with the director Yukio Ninagawa to discuss possible cuts, and suggested cutting the above line. "He is talking about his own speech. Wouldn't it be better to cut it?" On the way back home after the meeting, I started to wonder why I had cut this line. A voice whispered inside me: "Hang on a moment. Do you really need to cut it?" "It's you who's doing 'too much of this.'" There needn't be anything excessive about Hamlet's praise for Horatio. The image of a bashful Horatio, embarrassed by Hamlet's praise, came to mind. Seeing the perplexed Horatio, Hamlet is embarrassed by his intense effusion of feeling. The line reveals the gentleness of a Hamlet trying to save his friend from squirming, a model of charming and manly embarrassment and self-control. That's what I thought, so I changed it to "Now I've overdone it!" Early the next morning I rang Ninagawa, and told him what I wanted to do. Without asking for a

> reason, he simply said, "OK, let's do it. It'll make a great scene." What one has to consider is why these words need to be spoken in performance, their deeper meanings, the relationship between Hamlet and Horatio, and more generally the dynamics between speaker and recipient. Thus, translation and the process of translation do themselves belong to the overall process of staging a play. Yet, one shouldn't overinterpret—just as overdirecting is wrong—that's what I've learnt time and time again. (210-12)

This holistic view of stage translation may be thought to differ from that of Matsuoka's predecessor, Yūshi Odashima, who, although an avid Shakespeare watcher, never took an active part in rehearsals by the Shakespeare Theater company as the company staged his translations of the complete works in the 1970s and 1980s. Yet Odashima does maintain a belief in the idea that Shakespeare is "good for you" in numerous newspaper articles and books with titles like *Kōhīten* no *Sheikusupia* ("Coffee Shop Shakespeare," 1978), and it is arguably his detachment from the rehearsal process that allows him to take this point of view. Odashima's translations belong to the previous generation of Shakespeare's reception in Japan, the period of high economic growth that marked the second half of the Shōwa Era, influenced by Jan Kott's *Shakespeare Our Contemporary*. Preceded by the existentialism of figures like Tsuneari Fukuda, who in the 1950s sought to fill a void left by the relegation of the Shōwa Emperor from divine status to symbolic head of state, Odashima's Shakespeare is multifarious and Bakhtinian in tone, typified by his treatment of the Shakespearean Fool (Odashima), whose aphoristic wisdom often exceeds that of actual authority figures.

Shakespeare's status has always been marginal to the mainstream culture, but whereas prewar Shakespeareans such as Tsubouchi tended to emphasize the conservatism of Shakespeare as a humanistic reflection of the status quo, Odashima's position reflects the radical economic and social changes of the postwar era, in particular the mobility than may in turn reflect Shakespeare's own transition from country boy to city sophisticate. The dual perspective which mobility generates runs counter to Matsuoka's apologetic "matter of trial and error" (Matsuoka 210). Just as characters such as Touchstone seek to hide their social status through their rhetorical skill, Odashima's Shakespeare seems directed at a state of pure linguistic awareness. This trajectory is not without its dangers, as Odashima admits in an anecdote he tells of the day he finished translating *Macbeth*, a play in which "illusion holds a real strength greater than reality" (Odashima 26). He went drinking at a bar with a friend, feeling that after a month in "Macbethland," he was suffering not from the time difference (*jisa*) of the international traveller but from spatial difference (*basa*): "My friend teased me in a hearty voice. "So then, doesn't the *mamasan* look like a witch to you?" I replied in a voice suspiciously like Macbeth's, "Yes, and I think I want to turn you into a ghost" (Odashima 27).

To wit to woo

Wit in both Shakespeare's England and modern Japan denotes the remarkable or unusual, even when used to seek attention. The word is derived from Old English *witan* "to know," and indeed Shakespeare's witticisms often drive at some truth beyond the text. The Japanese word *share* does not have this etymology, although it does usually imply some hidden knowledge or propriety, and can nowadays mean chic or fashionable. Wit can be an uncomfortable device, as when Berowne charges Rosaline in *Love's Labours Lost*, "Your wit's too hot, it speeds too fast, 'twill tire" (2.1.119), and is not necessarily humorous. In Japanese poetics, a distinction is made between *senryū*, comic, often ribald verses of seventeen syllables (5-7-5), and haiku, which are profound rather than humorous, although using the same meter. Haiku are not even clever in the way of a metaphysical conceit, but depend for their effect on naturalistic syntheses of images and sensations; it demands *hai* or wit to make such correspondences. Although haiku is still a popular pastime in Japan, it is nevertheless surprising to find contemporary translators like Kazuko Matsuoka and Shōichirō Kawai sometimes adopting syllabic meter (*shichigochō*) in their translations. Their intention is not to render Shakespeare as *kabuki*, which are predominantly metrical, but for contextual rhetorical effect in a form sufficiently understood by contemporary Japanese. This effect could even be called postmodern in the sense that the translator's contemporary reading of the play is framed within a traditional form, and if that is the case, the purpose must be to locate a point of reference between his own and Shakespeare's culture: to add depth to a text that can otherwise seem obscure and banal. Kawai gives a striking example in a note provided for a recent production of his own translation of *Romeo and Juliet*: "Romeo and Juliet get to kiss just fourteen lines into their first dialogue! Before wondering how such a passionate love could transpire in so short a time, I wanted to know why the fourteenth line? Kawai gives a brief account of the Shakespearean sonnet: As you can see, *Romeo and Juliet* is a very symmetrical work. . . . In my translation, I have not only tried to convey these special qualities of the original but also to make sense of the difficult bits. It really is a labour of love!" Kawai gives a number of examples from his translation, including from the love sonnet: "When Romeo takes Juliet's hand for the first time, I again tried to bring out a poetic feeling through the use of seven-five meter. *Iyashii waga te* [7] *ga, moshimo kono* [7 including comma], *seinaru mido wo,* [7] *kegasu nara,* [5], *douka yasashii* [7], *otogame wo* [5]. " "If I profane with my unworthiest hand / This holy shrine, the gentler sin is this" (1.5.92-3). He adds that "Even when it is possible to rhyme in Japanese, the effect is weak, and so I gave up the idea of repeating the same sound at the end of lines, although there are still a few places where I try such rhymes."

Kawai's observations on prosody, a key concern for all Japanese translators of Shakespeare, are developed at length in his study of Shakespearean dramaturgy, *Romio to Jurietto—koi ni ochiru engekijutsu* ("*Romeo and Juliet*: Dramaturgy in Love"), and they contain a number of significant sub-texts. One is surprised that the love of Romeo and Juliet should be consummated with a kiss in so short a time. Another surprise is that their love is expressed in beautiful and poetic language in the original, which demands some level of response in Japanese, and a third, more subtle point that Shakespeare's pursuit of order and symmetry sometimes makes his language difficult. These sub-texts correspond to the Shakespearean meaning of wit. Its usage can yield rapid and positive results, especially when used collaboratively: the concentration of sense and meaning enables the couple to acquire sufficient knowledge of each other to risk the intimacy of a kiss after only fourteen lines. As Kawai acknowledges, the point is not whether the scene is realistic. Even in contemporary Japan, where couples rarely kiss in public, the kiss is seen as a more specifically erotic gesture than in Western society. Shakespeare is demonstrating a potential for love. Moreover, wit involves an elegant use of language as an aid or enticement to its multiple audiences: the heartbeat rhythm of blank verse. A final point is that wit after all implies a search for order or symmetry that may be tragically lacking in the outer world.

These functions make equal sense in the context of Japanese poetics. The traditional Japanese love lyric is the 31-syllable *waka* or *tanka*, rather than 17-syllable haiku. Its greater length suggests that love demands a slightly more elongated expression of feeling than is possible within the haiku but equally its formal symmetry fits the same archetype of lyrical expression as does the Shakespearean sonnet: that the ontological truth of love will engender an aesthetic beauty. Yet Kawai's third sub-text hints that one difference between Shakespearean and Japanese wit is that models of rhetorical symmetry are arguably less available in Japanese poetics than in Shakespeare's: not just the weakness of rhyme, but also the shift to the regularity of syllabic meter when the standard prosody of the translation is irregular prose. Of course, there are devices for making even prose rhythmical in Japanese, but the prosodic contrast is greater than in Shakespeare's original, where the iambic pentameter of the sonnet follows the same metrical pattern of the rest of the play. These two rather different prosodies may still serve a similar contextual purpose: to enable Romeo and Juliet to detach themselves from their families for the moment and devote themselves to each other. In other words, they articulate a need for attachment to another that is compromised or taken for granted within their established networks. One might even argue that just as the sonnet formalizes a Platonic idea of unity that is latent in the underlying symmetry of blank verse, so too does seven-five meter express an ideal of perfection, related to Chinese culture from which the poetic was originally derived. Both poetics also assume that it is by showing loyalty to tradition that the two lovers find the strength to express their individuality. This discovery of perfection can only depend on the possibility of imperfection, and so Juliet's admonition that Romeo kisses "by th' book" (1.5.109) is a tacit recognition of the finitude of their love.

Kawai's purpose in using this prosody is to do justice to what he calls the poetic beauty of Shakespeare's language and to make that beauty accessible to theater audiences as well as readers. Yet in a distinctly postmodern slant, he is also dramatizing the act of love—knowing another—as the relationship between the traditional and contemporary. It is as if no one can know exactly why blank verse or *shichigochō* are such perfect forms. Their elusiveness makes the attempt to know (or translate) them a veritable "labor of love." The pursuit of perfection may sometimes yield comic results: a sense of the ridiculous. The use of a familiar meter can only heighten the appreciation of Japanese audiences of Shakespeare's wittiest tragedy.

The Meaning of Shakespeare in Japan

The three examples discussed in this article are examples of how the recipient culture reacts to Shakespeare and Shakespeare to the recipient culture. Shakespeare production in Japan has declined (and stabilized) since the boom period of the late 1980s, and continues to be shared between large-scale commercial theater and small theaters, each with devoted followings. Although neither forum advocates a radical political message, my examples—if not exactly radical—suggest subtle ways in which translation and production may subvert endemic features of Japanese society: above all the parochialism, but also the loss of traditions. In this sense, the lesson that Shakespeare has for Japanese culture is that the culture has the answers to its own problems. One reason for Shakespeare's foreignness is that the plays are the product of a Christian heritage that is historically alien to Japan. Although Shakespeare's beliefs remain a controversial topic and should be seen in the context of his dramatic art, his plays must seem slightly detached from the reality of ordinary non-Christian Japanese, albeit infused with an enriching and entertaining imaginative power. One influential approach to Shakespeare's beliefs is the theory of "hidden ideals" (*botsu risō*). Tsubouchi in the 1890s espoused this notion that Shakespeare, supreme above other writers, lacks an overt message; rather, his plays expose the character and diversity of those individuals, cultures, and societies that receive him. This theory can be turned on its head and applied to Tsubouchi's individual response to Shakespeare as a representative figure in the history of modern Japanese culture. In fact, Tsubouchi's theory of hidden ideals runs through the whole of his career, and can be linked to Buddhist philosophy, which accepts a void at the core of existence. If suffering is caused by material desire, the acceptance of nothingness can relieve suffering and lead to spiritual wholeness. As numerous writers have observed, the obsession of tragic characters such as Lear and Hamlet with the illusion of being leads ultimately to their downfalls. By contrast, the comedies hinge on a mature awareness of the transience of life. Tsubouchi himself was not particularly interested in Buddhism as a religion, and seems quite modern in his substitution of culture for religious practice; nonetheless, his writings on Shakespeare are rich with references to Buddhist cosmology. The act of Shakespeare translation can be seen as a dramatic emptying of self, driven both by a need to overcome the numerous illusions Shakespeare presents his readers and to accept the illusoriness within the translator, although Tsubouchi is always modest about his achievements in this regard. Shakespeare is sufficiently distant in time and space from Tsubouchi's reality to present characters who have the semblance at least of detachment from the path of cause and effect. He writes that there are "no Buddhas in paradise, no puppets dancing along the path of cause and effect" (qtd. in Kawatake and Yanagida 722). What in terms of language and rhetoric seems a supremely difficult writer may turn out to be a highly effective mentor, and from the 1890s onwards Tsubouchi comes increasingly to regard Shakespeare in that role. In Tsubouchi's way of thinking, Shakespeare is not in paradise because he is himself an embodiment of paradise, inimitable yet leading others on.

The opening of Japan to the West in the Meiji era heralded an era of Christian influence, especially in education, but Tsubouchi himself never studied under missionaries and had no apparent interest in Christianity, although his study and translation of Shakespeare would have introduced him to the Bible and the basic doctrines. An essay he wrote in 1934 on the madness of Ophelia hints at what must have been a stumbling block towards acceptance of a Christian worldview. As a Buddhist, he would have believed that, short of complete insanity, individuals retain responsibility for their actions and point of view, however distorted. Tsubouchi insisted that Ophelia still had something to say in her madness and that it would be a universal shame if that point of view were ignored. Even in modern Japanese thought, the private world of the insane person is thought to belong less partially to the public domain of shared experience and to have spiritual value (for example in the *noh* tradition of "mad plays"), whereas in Christian (and even modern psychiatric) tradition the substance of madness has no such value. As the product of a strict Confucianist upbringing, Tsubouchi would also have had difficulties accepting the contempt sometimes shown for parental authority. Under Confucianism, respect for parents (especially the father) is paramount, in contrast to *The Merchant of Venice*, where a Christian context seems to justify Jessica's desertion of her father Shylock. In Shakespeare's plays generally, kingship is a more central theme than filial piety. The particular fascination of the early Japanese Shakespeareans for *Hamlet* is that the protagonist is driven by filial piety. The revenge plot is similar to *kabuki* tragedies such as *Kanadehon Chūshingura* (1748). Tsubouchi's sensitivity to the connections within the hierarchy, as comprising dramatic as well as ethical relationships, is comparable to the sophistication that Neo-Confucianism had achieved by the time of his birth in 1859. Confucianism had been revitalized in the eighteenth century beyond a set of principles to a coherent philosophy in the way that monarchy was reinvented under the reigns of Elizabeth and James. Tsubouchi's model was always the Confucian scholar, dispensing moral instruction as well as critical insight, and he would have agreed with the advice of one late nineteenth-century Confucianist that the "learning of human nature and principle does not esteem *extensive* reading; rather it esteems *energetic* reading" (Okada 233). The relationship between teacher and pupil in Oriental tradition survives only so long as the teacher conceals his own hidden ideals.

In conclusion, Shakespeare in Japan is a resourceful creature, adapting to the culture by using a variety of styles and rhetorical devices. Yet, as Tsubouchi argued, Shakespeare's meaning remains elusive, expressed in only the broadest terms, as Odashima suggests: "To know Shakespeare is to know love. That is to say, people who know about love already know what they need to know about Shakespeare" (24).

Works Cited

Gallimore, Daniel. "Measuring Distance: Tsubouchi Shōyō and the Myth of Shakespeare Translation." *Translating Others*. Vol. 2. Ed. Theo Hermans. Manchester: St Jerome's P, 2006. 438-92.

Imanishi, Kinji. *A Japanese View of Nature: The World of Living Things*. 1941. Trans. Pamela J. Asquith. London: Routledge Curzon, 2002.

Kawai, Shōichirō. "*Romio to Jurietto* shin'yaku no urabanashi" ("Notes on a New Translation of *Romeo and Juliet*"). Programme, *Romeo and Juliet, The Globe Tokyo* (15 January - 7 February 2004): n.p.

Kawai, Shoichiro. Romio to Jurietto—*koi ni ochiru engekijutsu* (Romeo and Juliet: *Dramaturgy in Love*). Tokyo: Misuzu Shobo, 2005.

Kawatake, Shigetoshi, and Izumi Yanagida. *Tsubouchi Shōyō*. 1939. Tokyo: Daiichi Shobo, 1988.

Kawatake, Toshio. *Kabuki: Baroque Fusion of the Arts* (2001). Trans. Frank Connell Hoff and Jean Connell Hoff. Tokyo: International House of Japan, 2003.

Kishi, Tetsuo. "Japanese Shakespeare and English Reviewers." *Shakespeare and the Japanese* Stage. Ed. Sasayama Takashi. Cambridge: Cambridge UP, 1998. 110-23.

Matsuoka, Kazuko. "Hon'yaku kara mita Sheikusupia" ("Shakespeare from a Translator's Perspective"). *Sheikusupia e no kakehashi* (Getting Across to Shakespeare). Ed. Yasunari Takada, Shōichirō Kawai, and Manabu Noda. Tokyo: Tokyo UP, 1998. 199-223.

Odashima, Yūshi. *Kōhīten no Sheikusupia* (Coffee Shop Shakespeare). Tokyo: Shōbunsha, 1978.

Odashima, Yūshi. *Dōke no me* (The Eyes of the Fool). Tokyo: Hakusuisha, 1990.

Odashima, Yūshi. "Sheikusupia ni miru ai 1: *Romio to Jurietto*" ("Love in Shakespeare, Pt. 1: *Romeo and Juliet*"). *Nihon Keizai Shimbun* (1 March 2007 [evening ed.]): 24.

Okada, Takehiko. "Neo-Confucian Thinkers in Nineteenth-Century Japan." *Confucianism and Tokugawa Culture*. Ed. Peter Nosco. Honolulu: U of Hawaii P, 1997. 215-50.

Richie, Donald. *The Films of Akira Kurosawa*. Berkeley: U of California P, 1996.

Ryūtopia Magazine 7 (2006): 29-30.

Tsubouchi, Shōyō. "Ofīriya no seikaku" ("The Character of Ophelia"). *Shōyō senshū bekkan daigo* (Selected Works of Shōyō Tsubouchi). Ed. Shōyō Kyōkai. Tokyo: Daiichi Shobō, 1934. 320-25.

The Tokyo Globe Years 1988-2002

Michiko Suematsu

In the last years of the twentieth century, a company that experimented with various blends of Shakespeare, local tradition, and creativity, the first Tokyo Globe opened in 1988 and closed in 2002. The goal was to find what worked in performance, as it was in Korea, Malaya, Okinawa, Cambodia, Indonesia, China, and Hong Kong, the geographical subjects of the next set of articles. Postwar Japanese theater thus saw the popularization, diversification, and decanonization of Shakespeare. The new movement replaced *Shingeki* Shakespeare, which dominated the Japanese stage until the late 1960s. The Globe no longer belongs exclusively to England. The United States has the Old Globe (San Diego) and the Globe of the Great Southwest (Odessa College) apart from the New Globe Theater in New York Harbor, while Germany and Japan each boasts its own replica: the Nuess Globe and the Tokyo Globe. Although the Globe Theater in Tokyo did not close to the design of the original, its dedication to Shakespeare's works was more than unusually thorough and consistent. Besides staging Shakespeare exclusively, it housed Shakespeare productions throughout the year unlike other Globes with limited opening seasons. Moreover, because the privileged space of the Tokyo Globe sanctioned theatrical experiments related to Shakespeare, it functioned as a radical site for fantasizing and imagining his works. Within a little more than a decade, the Tokyo Globe consequently changed the way of understanding and performing Shakespeare in Japan.

The first Tokyo Globe opened in 1988 and closed in 2002. The present Tokyo Globe re-opened in 2004 after refurbishment under the new ownership of an entertainment company, the Jonny's Office. Only the theater's name remains intact, since the artistic principles of the second Globe have been geared drastically toward populist commercialism, and Shakespeare occupies a minor part in its repertoire. Historically, the Tokyo Globe's opening in 1988 was the second biggest event in the postwar history of Japanese Shakespeare productions. The first was the visit of Peter Brook's production of *A Midsummer Night's Dream* in 1975. Admittedly, Brook's Kottian staging of Shakespeare as a representation of "here and now" changed the Japanese approach to Shakespeare. When the possibility of staging a Japanese Shakespeare speaking directly to people became a reality, copying past Western models looked outdated. A decade later, the Tokyo Globe dispelled successfully the last remains of Japan's century-long servitude to the authority and authenticity of the West and in this sense the theater's significance should not be underestimated. The first Globe was a liberated and exciting space where both actors and audience could fantasize Shakespeare uninhibitedly and give their ideas the force of performance.

Postwar Japanese theater saw the popularization, diversification, and decanonization of Shakespeare. The new movement replaced *Shingeki* Shakespeare, which dominated the Japanese stage until the late 1960s. From its start in the early twentieth century, *shingeki,* or the new theater (a term to differentiate it from the old theater, *kabuki*), aimed at introducing the Western classics to Japan. In their belief in the superiority of the West, *shingeki* theater companies tried to stage Shakespeare in what they considered an authentic style. It even became a norm for *shingeki* actors to play with red wigs and padded nose to impersonate Western characters in what was thought to be a realistic style. At the same time, Shakespeare was not exempt from the influence of the underground theater movement, or the Little Theater Movement, which reflected the students' anti-establishment movement of the 1960s. No longer a medium of enlightenment for the general public, theater then became part of a counter-culture that promoted a powerful political message. Shakespearean theater also had to prove its validity as a form of self-expression, and naturally this change in intention accompanied a change in style—a marked shift in Japanese Shakespeare from a cultural icon of the establishment to the privatized vehicle of propaganda, and then to the most sought-after commodity of mass culture. By incorporating elements of indigenous theatrical traditions, or by modernized staging in jeans, or by overall radical adaptation, producers of Shakespeare advanced their particular concepts and messages.

Japan's unprecedented economic growth in the following decade steered Japanese Shakespeare further into popularization and commercialization. Backed by the superfluous capital of the market, theater itself became a thriving commercial industry. New theaters were built one after another in the Tokyo area, and to satisfy the demand of these new theaters, an increasing number of salable shows, including Shakespeare's, were staged (see Suematsu 101). In this sense, the Tokyo Globe was a child of the age. The Tokyo Globe was a by-product of land development, driven by what was called the "bubble economy," which ransacked available urban space in the 1980s. The Tokyo Metropolitan Government demanded that large housing estates be equipped with at least one cultural facility for residents, and so a development corporation called Toyama Kaihatsu decided to build a theater in Shinjuku, one of the busiest commercial districts in central Tokyo (see Takao 145-47). The idea was to build a theater to outdo rival theaters newly built in the greater Tokyo Area, and a renowned designer Arata Isozaki chose the original Globe Theater as his model. Unlike its counterpart in London, Shakespeare's Globe Theatre, the Tokyo Globe was not a reconstruction of the original but replica intended exclusively for Shakespeare production. This Globe enjoyed its privileged economical condition from its start (see Takahagi). Sufficient funds contributed by the country's first-class businesses guaranteed artistic freedom to stage Shakespeare creatively. Buoyed by this freedom to experiment, the Tokyo Globe accelerated the transformation of Japanese Shakespeare productions in terms of quantity and quality.

A review of the Tokyo Globe years

Over fourteen years, from 1988-2002, the Tokyo Globe staged nearly two hundred Shakespeare productions, including adaptations. The theater's repertory falls into two categories according to nationality: productions by Japanese theater companies and those by overseas theater companies. At the start, the theater made a name by hosting productions of visiting companies from abroad. It opened with English Shakespeare Company's *The War of the Roses*, and major British companies such as the Royal Shakespeare Company (1988, 1991, 1993, 1994, 1995, 1998, 2000, 2001, 2002) and the National Theatre (1988, 1989, 1990, 1991) followed. These giant, subsidized theaters continually fascinated the audience at the Globe, as did touring or regional British companies like the Renaissance Theatre Company (1990), the Compass Theatre Company (1990, 1991, 1992, 1993, 1995), Cheek By Jowl (1992 and 1994), the Watermill Theatre Company (1992, 1995), the Nottingham Playhouse (1995), and the Shared Experience Theatre (1996). Visiting companies from outside Britain were no less illustrious, including Ingmar Bergman's *Hamlet* (Sweden, 1988), Andrzej Wajda's *Hamlet* (Poland, 1990), the Cliova Theater's *Titus Andronicus* (Romania, 1992), Robert Lepage's *Coriolanus* and *Macbeth* (Canada, 1993), and the Beijing People's Arts Theater's *Hamlet* (China, 1995). While these overseas productions at the Tokyo Globe were straight Shakespeare, Japanese productions varied in genre. The Globe staged extensively Shakespeare, adapted to such indigenous performance traditions as *kabuki, kyōgen* and *bunraku* as well as dance, ballet, and opera. It also offered straight production by *shingeki* theater companies and young small-scale companies (*sho-gekijo*). In short, the Globe became a cultural matrix where Shakespeare merged with almost all theater forms existing in Japan.

To explore new ways of staging Shakespeare, in 1989 the Globe formed its own troupe, the Tokyo Globe Company. From this attempt emerged two highly popular series, *Shakespeare for Children* and *BROKEN Shakespeare*. The children's series was and still is popular among young and old. It successfully engages the attention of children by introducing a simplified narrative, energetic physical movements, and a Shakespeare doll who comments sagely and humorously on key moments. The other series is one of the forerunners of Japanized Shakespeare, dislocating the setting to Japan, and not necessarily modern Japan. In addition to these two series, the Globe Company stages frequently intercultural productions and works in collaboration with directors from abroad such as Peter Stormare (Sweden), Gerald Murphy (UK), Robert Lepage (Canada), and John Retallack (UK).

An appraisal of the Tokyo Globe years

The Tokyo Globe contributed to a significant increase in the number of Shakespeare productions in the greater Tokyo area. In the pre-Globe period, the approximate

Table 1. The approximate number of Shakespeare productions (including adaptations) in the greater Tokyo area.

Year	1985	1986	1987	1988	1989	1990	1991	1992	1993
Number	21	23	27	33	68	119	120	70	105
Year	1994	1995	1996	1997	1998	1999	2000	2001	2002
Number	67	71	69	54	46	70	82	47	30

Table 2. The approximate number of Shakespeare productions (including adaptations) at the Tokyo Globe Theater.

Year	1988	1989	1990	1991	1992	1993	1994	1995	1996	1997	1998	1999	2000	2001	2002	Total
Total number	17	12	14	22	17	24	21	18	12	10	6	7	4	5	3	192
UK productions	13	1	7	4	7	5	6	3	2	2	3	1	2	2	1	59
Other overseas productions	1	0	0	1	0	4	1	3	0	0	0	0	0	0	0	10
Japanese productions	3	10	6	15	7	10	10	10	9	6	3	5	2	3	2	101
Intercultural productions	0	1	1	2	3	5	4	2	1	2	0	1	0	0	0	22

number of annual Shakespeare productions was a dozen in the 1960s, and 30 in the 1970s. However, as is shown in table 1, the number reached 120 in 1991, which means that one could see ten Shakespeare productions a month if one wanted to. On average, the Tokyo Globe staged fourteen productions a year (see table 2), and this influenced a boost in number both directly and indirectly.

In retrospect, the Globe years changed not only the quantity but, more important, the condition and style of staging Shakespeare in Japan. First of all, the Globe contributed to the removal of Japan's principle drawbacks in staging Shakespeare: geographical distance and time lag. Before the Globe's opening, Japan, as with the rest of non-Western countries, had always remained second-class and out-of-date in terms of staging Shakespeare. In those days, to see British productions used to be a privilege because they usually visited Japan once every two or three years as a part of official cultural exchange under government sponsorship. For example, the tour by the Royal Shakespeare Company in 1970 (*The Winter's Tale* and *The Merry Wives of Windsor*) caused a cultural sensation in Tokyo. Audiences flocked in from all over Japan to honor this rare occasion. Major TV stations and newspapers featured the wave of excitement. However, once overseas companies established regular yearly visits these productions became a usual part of the Japanese theater-going experience. Because it was included in a global circuit of touring productions, the Globe could put on the overseas productions immediately after their initial run and thereby secure the contemporaneity between the East and the West.

The increased staging of overseas production at the Globe also encouraged the objective repositioning of Japanese Shakespeare in a global perspective. For example, Ingmar Bergman's shockingly violent *Hamlet* (1988) or Lin Zhaohua's metaphysical Chinese *Hamlet* (1995) by the Beijing People's Art Theater, in which Hamlet was split among several characters, demonstrated that Britain no longer had the monopoly on Shakespeare and that all nationalities had an equal right to stage Shakespeare according to how they chose to engage with the issues of the text. Japanese Shakespeare had always been subjected to a binary relationship with British Shakespeare, giving it a constant second-class position. As Shakespeare productions increased around the world, however, Japanese Shakespeare strove to contribute to and rank itself among such first-rate specimens of world-wide Shakespeare. In fact, the Tokyo Globe eventually contributed to challenging the older British model of authenticity. Since its opening, the Globe had regularly staged British productions (see table 2). After a flurry of opening productions by prestigious companies such as the Royal Shakespeare Society, British Shakespeare broadened its stylistic range. Heterogeneous productions like Cheek by Jowl's all-male *As You Like It* (1992), Michael Bogdanov's radical modern-dress *Macbeth* (1992), and the Shared Experience's *The Tempest* (1996), physical and rich in visual imagery, showed that Britishness became merely an expedient term for classification by nationality.

Today, Japanese Shakespeare is neither bound by the authority of the West nor part of a simplistic West-East dichotomy. The experience of the Tokyo Globe allowed Japanese Shakespeare an unbridled license that resulted in almost limitless experimentation. It is no exaggeration to say that at the Tokyo Globe Shakespeare received treatment in almost all Japanese performance genres. The two most remarkable examples are the *kabuki Hamlet, Hamuretto Yamato Nishikie* (1991), and the *kyōgen* version of *The Merry Wives of Windsor*, *Hora-Samurai* (1994). Although heavily cut, the former wonderfully proved Shakespeare's adaptability to the very formal acting style of *kabuki*. Amazingly, the roles of Hamlet and Ophelia were created by a single male actor, who took advantage of the common theatrical device of *hayagawari* (a quick change of roles). The *kyōgen Merry Wives of Windsor* was also staged in an abridged form, and yet it successfully brought out the ethos of this comedy. It was indeed a fortuitous discovery that the formalistic style of these indigenous theater traditions worked so wonderfully with Shakespeare.

Stylization can bring out the bold and archetypal narrative of the plays powerfully, which the language-centered productions at times miss out in their emphasis on detailed realism. Not only these traditional theater forms but also other genres of performing arts including dance, ballet and opera joined in fantasizing Shakespeare. Certainly this cultural mix was not new but these attempts at the Globe were more than one-off experiments. The creative license there developed into a series of dedicated explorations of theatrical identity through Shakespeare, and they led on to successful post-Globe localized productions such as *Comedy of Kyōgen,* a *kyōgen* version of *Comedy of Errors* (2001, 2005), Yukio Ninagawa's *Kabuki Twelfth Night* (2005, 2007, 2009), and the Ryutopia Noh Shakespeare series, which stages modern productions on a bare *noh* stage. In addition, this cultural fusion at the Globe developed into a more literal and wider mixture of cultures. In some cases, directors from abroad worked with Japanese actors, or an entire company was formed of actors and staff from several countries. The actors of the Globe Company also regularly collaborated with non-Japanese directors such as Peter Stormare, Edward Hall, and Robert Lepage. They acquainted themselves with different modes of staging Shakespeare and managed to find a middle ground through cultural negotiation.

Perhaps the most astonishing intercultural achievement at the Globe was the ITI (International Theater Institute) production of *King Lear* in 1997. Directed by Korean director Kim Jeong Ok, this production featured casts from Korea, the U.S., Germany, Japan, Bulgaria, and Mexico. Kim aimed to stage an international Shakespeare production from an Asian perspective. Taking advantage of actors' multiple cultural backgrounds, he mixed languages, acting styles, and physical movements to present a primitive and chaotic Asian society onstage. Although the resulting production proved little more than a juxtaposition of different cultures, it was regarded as a worthwhile attempt to check Western domination of international theatrical projects and established the Globe as a site of cultural contest in Japan, a place where actors as well as staff can accumulate experiences and strategies to tackle intercultural projects. In this sense, the Globe paved the way for subsequent cultural cross-breeding in Shakespeare such as Jonathan Kent's production of *Hamlet* (2003) staged both in Japan and in the UK using a Japanese cast and British staff.

The Tokyo Globe's greatest contribution was that it pushed Japan's naturalization of Shakespeare to the extreme by accelerating the increase of radical modern adaptation in the 1990s. Incorporating indigenous traditional theatrical practices into Shakespeare was one type of adaptation, but the search for national identity through localization still depended on Shakespeare's authority. In the case of modern adaptations, however, they appropriated Shakespeare with such audacity that his texts degenerated into supplementary materials. Productions such as Takeshi Kawamura's *Makubesu to Iu Nano Otoko* (A Man Named Macbeth, 1990) and Takeshi Muramatsu's *Dopondo Benisu de Oborete* (Drowned in Venice, 1998) retained only a hint of the original plot. Young postmodernist directors felt no need to respect or even challenge the cultural authority of Shakespeare by which the older generation had been bound because Shakespeare had long become a part of their cultural and dramatic tradition even before they were born. They could imagine Shakespeare in the wildest sense and naively explore their own theatrical creativity through his works. If there was any localization, it was merely subsidiary. In other words, the naturalization of

Table 3. The approximate number of straight and adapted Shakespeare productions in the greater Tokyo area.

Year	Straight productions		Adapted productions
	Japanese	Overseas	
1985	18	0	3
1995	15	13	34
2005	14	3	31

Shakespeare in Japan has come to a point when Japanization becomes a mere matter of aesthetic choice. It no longer is a self-conscious statement of defiance or an attempt to match one's culture against another. These adaptations are uninhibited by any form of authority—authority of the West, authority of Shakespeare's canon, and authority of *shingeki* Shakespeare, the dominant prototype in Japan. Modernized adaptations of Shakespeare continued to increase after the closure of the Tokyo Globe Theater in 2002, and as table 3 shows, they continue to outnumber straight Shakespeare productions.

Despite the Tokyo Globe Theater's contribution to Japanese Shakespeare, the theater was not exempt from criticisms. As mentioned earlier, the Globe was originally run by a group of land-developing companies and they had to resort to the British Council and a group of academics for advice on the choice of overseas productions. This influence resulted in an erratic choice of seasonal repertoires besides giving a certain elitist and unfriendly atmosphere to the theater. Ironically, the theater was not even physically audience-friendly at the start; some of the seats had a severely restricted view. Several columns were eventually cut down to improve sightlines. Partly due to the impact of economic recession in the late 1990s and partly due to the increasing discord within the governing body of the theater, the first Globe closed after fourteen years. Within that period, however, the venue proved itself more than a bureaucratic cultural showcase. In staging an impressive array of overseas productions, and in affording Japanese theater companies of any genre an opportunity to experiment with Shakespeare, it functioned as a site of cultural contest, and a force for repositioning Japanese Shakespeare in worldwide perspective. Authenticity of the "original" theater made the Globe a unique space to imagine Shakespeare.

The Globe's freedom to fantasize Shakespeare is the greatest legacy of the years 1988-2002. Even after its closure, this license and repositioning has pushed Japanese Shakespeare productions further toward radical modern adaptation. At the turn of the century, Japanese Shakespeare has gone beyond a self-effacing imitation of Western models or localized productions incorporating indigenous theater forms or intercultural productions that negotiate values of different cultures. No longer subject to the authority of Shakespeare and the West, the prevalent mode of creative vandalism flourishes by producing radically privatized dramatizations of his plays.

Works Cited

Minami, Ryuta, Ian Carruthers, and John Gillies, eds. *Performing Shakespeare in Japan.* Cambridge: Cambridge UP, 2001.

Suematsu, Michiko. "Shakespeare on the Recent Japanese Stage." *Shakespeare Yearbook IX: Shakespeare in Japan.* Ed. Tetsuo Anzai, Soji Iwasaki, and Peter Milward. New York: Edwin Mellen, 1999. 92-104.

Takahagi, Hiroshi. Personal interview (2 October 2005).

Takao, Koji. "The Tokyo Globe in the Context of Shakespeare in Japan." *Shakespeare Global/Local.* Ed. Kwok-kan Tam, Andrew Parkin, and Terry Siu-han Yip. Frankfurt: Peter Lang, 2002. 143-52.

Hamlet in Korea

Meewon Lee

Shakespeare's work was first introduced to Korea at the beginning of the twentieth century as a Western cultural artifact rather than as the work of a dramatist. The first full version of a Shakespeare play in Korea was a 1917 film of *Macbeth.* A film of *Romeo and Juliet* appeared in 1922. These two films made Shakespeare somewhat familiar to Korean audiences, but it was *Tales from Shakespeare* by Charles Lamb and Mary Lamb that made Shakespeare widely known. Five plays, *Cymbeline, Othello, Tempest, The Merchant Venice,* and *Romeo and Juliet*, were translated in the 1920s. The translation of *Cymbeline* was faithful to the original text, while *Othello* in 1924 was freely translated but kept the essence of Shakespeare. *The Merchant of Venice* was translated three times under different titles: *A Lady Pleader*, *A Trial of Human Flesh*, and *The Merchant of Venice*. *Romeo and Juliet,* translated as *A Regrettable Love*, seems to have been especially popular, since a second edition was printed after three months. The Lambs' texts of Shakespeare were easier than the original plays to understand and remained popular through the 1940s. At the same time, during the 1920s full versions of *Hamlet* and *The Merchant of Venice,* and a partial version of *Julius Caesar* were translated into Korean, probably from Japanese intermediaries. *Hamlet* appeared in a milestone translation during the1920s. Hyun Chol, the translator, said he tried to describe in detail the inner psychology of the hero and to pay special attention to the way characters interacted in dialogues. There was also an adaptation of *King Lear*, which had a happy ending where the French king, husband of Cordelia, conquers the armies of the two sisters, and King Lear and Cordelia are happily reunited.

Translations of Shakespearean plays in the 1930s were less frequent, but they were mostly full versions and based directly on the English texts. In addition, productions of Shakespeare plays were not rare. The first Shakespearean production was *Julius Caesar* by Kyungsong Commercial High School in 1925 and student productions were widespread among university students in the 1930s. For example, *The Taming of the Shrew* was produced in 1931 by Ehwa Women's University and *Romeo and Juliet* in 1932 by Yeonsae University, a leading university of the time. It is noticeable that students were the first to show interest in performing Shakespeare.

In other words, it was the educated elites that realized the value of Shakespeare. But before long, theater specialist groups such as Kugyeosul Yonguhoe produced the court scene of *The Merchant of Venice* and commercial theater groups such as Nangmanchwa produced an adaptation titled *The Scene of Grave in Hamlet* in the 1930s.

Despite the attention paid to Shakespeare in the 1930s, few Shakespearean plays were produced in the first half of the 1940s due to World War II, as not only Shakespearean productions but also most cultural events were suppressed by the Japanese military government and only propaganda was allowed in theaters. In fact, Korea was under Japanese colonial occupation between 1910 and 1945, and Shakespeare was introduced to Korea as a part of Western civilization. Playwrights such as Chijin Yoo, however, showed influences of Shakespeare for the first time in this period. For example, the play *The Jujube Tree* took a motif of love and hate from *Romeo and Juliet* and the play acquired the reputation of propaganda by the Japanese occupying forces. In scholarship, few articles on Shakespeare were published and they were mainly on the introductory level.

Ideological conflict divided the democrats and the communists between the emancipation from the Japanese in 1945 and the end of the Korean War in 1953. During this time a full-length *Hamlet* was produced by Jungang University in 1949. Although a student production, it was directed by Haerang Lee, a professional director who would lead Korean theater during the next four decades. The production was successful and showed the magnitude of Shakespearean tragedy. The National Theater finally came into being in 1950 right before the Korean War broke out. It employed two theater companies, and one, called Sinhyup, continued to produce plays during the war. *Hamlet* was perhaps the most famous production of the Shinhyup Theater Company, and is still remembered today. This *Hamlet* expedited the translation of Shakespeare and two translations of his complete works were published in 1964, the 400th anniversary of Shakespeare's birth. One version was done by an English literature scholar named Jaenam Kim and the other was the collective work of nineteen English literature scholars of the time (see Shin, *Shakespeare* 93). There were also many university student productions in the 1950s. *A Midsummer's Night* in 1958 by Ewha Women's University and *The Merchant of Venice* in 1959 by Jungang University to celebrate the foundation of the first Department of Theater in Korea are still well remembered and it was said that *A Midsummer Night* made great use of the stage space while *The Merchant of Venice* had a very good acting.

A theater called "The Drama Center" opened in 1962 with a production of *Hamlet*. This theater was the brainchild of Chijin Yoo, a pioneer of modern Korean theater who received seed money from the Rockefeller Foundation and managed to build a modern mid-sized theater. This production of *Hamlet* drew the attention of the theater intelligentsia. Its director was Haerang Lee, who already directed *Hamlet* several times including successful productions for Jungang University and the Sinhyup Theater Company. The production reviews complimented the acting of the hero, played by Dongwon Kim, but criticized the lighting and mechanical operation of the stage. It seems that technical staff did not know how to operate the new systems of the theater. The production was double cast with young actors, and five new acting stars in the future came into being from this production. *Hamlet* remained the most popular play. A 1962 production was repeated in 1964 for the 400th Anniversary Shakespeare Festival. During the 1970s *Hamlet* was again performed, this time by the London Shakespeare Company led by director Peter Potter. The company's highlight performance of *Hamlet* was accompanied by performances of *The Winter's Tale, Othello,* and *Twelfth Night* in authentic Elizabethan costumes. In contrast to these traditional productions, Korean directors incorporated Korean culture into Shakespeare's dramas. Representative of these efforts to create a Korean context was *The Prince of Hamyul*, a 1974 adaptation of *Hamlet* by Minsoo Ahn, who gave characters Korean names and costumes and also employed Korean traditional movement and dance. This adaptation toured in the West and advanced Korea's reputation. Korea experienced severe political oppression under the military regime of the 1980s. Although few theatrical events were allowed, the *Hamlet* series of Kukseo Ki succeeded in making a roundabout but keen satire of the political situation by deconstructing the plot and rearranging episodes, providing, too, a harbinger for the introduction of the concept of postmodernism to Korea in the 1990s. The end of the military regime and the hosting of the 1988 Summer Olympics opened Korea to the rest of the world. Shakespeare productions were more diverse than ever, bringing popularity and modernity to tradition. *Hamlet* by Yeontaek Lee in 1996 was representative of the use of Korean traditions and freedom from the effort to reproduce any kind of historical authenticity.

The fusions of intercultural productions have become common in the new millennium. Popular modernity now combines with traditional Korean culture. *A Midsummer Night's Dream* by Junguong Yang, who received a directing prize at the Cairo Experimental Theater Festival, is one such production. In addition, adaptations of Shakespeare plays from a particular perspective are very popular: it became widespread to interpret Shakespeare from a minor character's perspective rather than that of the hero's. For example, *Lady Macbeth*, by Taesook Han, is a rewriting of *Macbeth* from a feminist point of view. Indeed, productions of *Hamlet* illustrate the development of Shakespeare productions in Korea that occurred against the broader theatrical backdrop that I have sketched. Next, I focus on six productions of *Hamlet*, one from each decade since the Republic of Korea was established in order to illustrate how cultural theories influenced the mainstream depiction of Shakespeare in Korea.

Hamlet in 1950 by the Sinhyop Theater Company

Sinhyop was probably the first theater company mature enough to produce Shakespeare; it had educated directors and well-trained actors with a stable financial situation. In spite of the Korean War, in 1951 Sinhyop produced *Hamlet* directed by Haerang Lee, who had already directed Jungang University's *Hamlet* in 1949. It was played on a proscenium stage similar to other productions of the time. According to the recollection of Dongwon Kim, who played the title role, the lines were not projected as everyday speech, but poetically (see Kim 192-93). Kim has said that he tried to portray a Hamlet in action rather than a Hamlet in thought, which had been the style since the performance of a "thinking" Hamlet by a leading Japanese theater group in the 1930s. When Kim later saw Laurence Olivier's performance of *Hamlet* on film, he realized his interpretation was similar to Olivier's. In fact, after that film, he became known as the Olivier of Korea. There are several reasons for this production's success: Kim was an elite actor, educated in Japan; the Queen was played by Jungsoon Hwang, one of the best actresses of the 1960s and 1970s; and the King was played by Haerang Lee, the director himself. The translator Nodan Han had studied theater and was more than a good literary scholar. Moreover, Haerang Lee understood that while realistic plays describe everyday life through small events, Shakespearean plays have strong plots. He interpreted Hamlet as a man of revenge rather than as a man of hesitation. Thus, the production accentuated the tension and suspense of the play, since the conflicts in the mind of Hamlet resolved themselves in action. Another reason for the play's success was that Jungwhan Kim, the best stage designer of the time, joined the production staff. In spite of wartime economy, he made a wonderful set including stairs. Bokja Kim, who played Ophelia, once fell down the stairs during a performance, but she carried on her mad scene in spite of the pain. She illustrates the most important reason for the success of this performance, namely that those in the cast rehearsed very hard and did their best. For example, Kim used to rehearse about 16-17 hours a day, although the rehearsal period was relatively short. In addition, he was concerned with his appearance: he stood in profile to the audience in order to look taller and he made his costume personally from military blankets. Although he played the role of Hamlet again later, he thought his first Hamlet in Sinhyop Theater Company was the best of all (Kim 199). Even after the opening, the director kept suggesting new improvements to the actors and the actresses. The opening night event is talked about even today: the performers were so focused on listening to the director's new pointers that they forgot the opening time and the evening night performance started late. All these worked together to make a famous production of *Hamlet*. In fact, this *Hamlet* was influenced by a *Hamlet* in one act by Kugyeosul Yonguhoe in the 1930s and continued to be influential until the production of *Hamlet* in 1964. It was the first full version of professional performance of *Hamlet*.

Hamlet in the 1960s and the opening of the Drama Center

The opening of the Drama Center in 1962 was a dream came true for Korean theater people. Koreans had not had a theatrical venue since the Dongyang Theater in the 1930s, which had lasted only briefly. The Drama Center chose *Hamlet* as its opening production. Although it was double cast for its long run, the main members were those of the Sinhyop Theater Company. Haerang Lee, who had directed the Sinhyop's *Hamlet*, directed this production, and Dongwon Kim again played the title role. The acting and the directing style were not very much different from the former production, although the circumstances for the production were much better than they had been in the 1950s, during the Korean War. The Drama Center used a semi-circular stage, similar to the Globe Theater, rather than a *proscenium*. The actors felt awkward on this new stage; in his memoir, Dongwon Kim remembers that the audience was so close to the forestage that he had trouble concentrating on his acting (see Kim 199). Nonetheless, this theater became the center of the avant-garde experimental theater movement. Music and sound effects were excellent, owing to the new sound system, although reviewers were less pleased by the lighting, costumes, and scenery. One reviewer said that "the sound effects heightened the atmosphere of the play well . . . but the production did not fully make use of its new lighting system due to the lack of operating skills" (Kyunghyang Daily Newspaper, Theatre Review section). Another said that Dongwon Kim's *Hamlet* had appealed to the audience, but the lighting, costumes, and scenery did not meet expectations (Chosun Daily Newspaper, Theatre Review section). Still, this Hamlet was well received: "*Hamlet* indicates the hopeful future of our theaters. . . . Owing to the good translation of the translator and the skillful directing of the director, it was a really fruitful production. Especially, the director coordinated the movements well, making best use of the semi-arena stage of the Drama Center" (Hanguk Daily Newspaper, Theatre Review section).

Many new faces became distinguished from this *Hamlet,* owing to the double cast. A newspaper review foretold the rise of new five stars, generally from university theater clubs; most of them became leading actors and actresses in Korean theater afterward. Another factor for the success of this *Hamlet* was the presence of new scholars and directors such as Keunsam Lee, Sukgi Yeo, and Jongok Kim, who had studied abroad. They provided this production with new and profound knowledge of Shakespeare in general. The interest of the press was also an important factor. Because the opening of the Drama Center theater itself was big news, the mass media paid special attention to the production of *Hamlet*. The Drama Center's *Hamlet* at the Shakespeare Festival for the 400th Anniversary in 1964 was an extension of *Hamlet* in 1962. In addition, the main theater companies at the time each played one Shakespearean play, including *The Merchant of Venice, Othello, King Lear, Antony and Cleopatra, The Taming of the Shrew, As You Like It,* and *Hamlet. Hamlet,* by the Drama Center Academy, was newly translated by a young English-trained scholar Sukgi Yeo, and directed by a new director, Sarang Oh. Although they were young, they were both under the influence of the Drama Center. In other words, *Hamlet* in 1964 was not much different from *Hamlet* in 1962, although the members were changed. Thus it seemed not to get as much attention from the media as *Hamlet* in 1962 had. But overall, the Shakespeare Festival drew the attention of the public and increased the size of theater audiences.

Hamlet in the 1970s and *The Prince of Hamyul* (an adaptation)

In the 1970s Koreans began paying attention to the avant-garde theater of the West and to their national identity. They revived the traditional Korean theatrical heritage and experimented with its application to the modern theater. Representative theater companies were the Minye Theater Company, the Jayu Theater Company, and the Drama Center. While the Minye worked hard to revive the authentic theatrical tradition of Korea, the Jayu concentrated on the traditional images and sounds, and the Drama Center mainly used them for avant-garde experiments.

The Prince of Hamyul, directed by Minsoo Ahn for the Center, applied traditional Korean heritage to Shakespeare's *Hamlet* and also drew on other Asian cultures. It changed the setting from Denmark to an Oriental country and drew characters' names from the ancient Kingdom of Silla in Korea. *The Prince of Hamyul* was also based on an understanding of Oriental philosophy. The stage space was empty, indicating the philosophy of nothingness in the Orient, especially Taoism. The floor space consisted of a few wooden boards to reflect the oriental constitution of the world (Shin, "The Prince of Hamlet" 219-20). Props heightened the atmosphere of tradition. For example, a mourner's walking stick in Korea was the symbol of un-dutifulness and grief. This symbol extended to the world of death and sin. Thus Hamyul, whose destiny included both sin and death, held this stick in the play. Costumes were also old Korean style. Hamyul wore traditional mourning and the King and the Queen wore royal family robes. Ophelia was robed in white, the mourning color of traditional Korean society. When she was dying in the river, she beautifully performed the traditional slow Buddhist dance of Seongmu. All these props, costumes, and dances made *The Prince of Hamyul* traditional and Korean. Some elements from Japanese tradition, such as the white facial make-up of *noh*, were criticized by people who had strongly anti-Japanese sentiments (Ko, 237). Yet Ahn's directing was an avant-garde intercultural experiment in oriental traditions, not English authenticity, in order to discover what would be effective in *Hamlet.* Further, new interpretations and theatrical productions of *Hamlet* occurred in the 1970s, along with the avant-garde theater movement. Realistic theaters gave way to the theatrical theaters, and national identity became an important issue of Korean theaters. Charles Marowitz's *Hamlet* was translated and produced by Dongguk University theater students in 1974. Also the production of professional theater company Kagyo in 1975 emphasized "the theme of death. The gravedigger scene was emphasized, while the tragic atmosphere changed to comic with the deconstruction of authentic Shakespeare" ("The 10th Anniversary of 'Kagyo' Company"). It is said that Kagyo's *Hamlet* was the forerunner of the variations and the rearrangement of *Hamlet* to come thereafter.

Hamlet as political theater in the 1980s

The massacre of Kwangju citizens by government military forces in 1980 cast a political shadow over most of the decade. The military government led by President Jun suppressed not only the freedom of the press but also student demonstrations. The atmosphere of the whole society was depressed, and some were even tortured to death, such as Jongchul Park, a student of Seoul National University. Thus, society in general was silenced, and so were the most of the arts. Under these circumstances, a political *Hamlet* came into being. Director Kukseo Ki adapted *Hamlet* and made it into a series of political confrontations. Owing to the fame of Shakespeare, the changes went relatively unnoticed by the government. Ki made a series of five *Hamlets* between 1981 and 1990.

Hamlet 1 in 1981 was set in modern times and played by seventy young people in jeans referencing the numb outsiders of history rather than the intrigue of the murder of Hamlet's father in Denmark. In other words, Ki tried to criticize the indifferent people of the day by showing the incompetent outsiders in *Hamlet* and his adaptation showed subtle similarities between the murder of King Hamlet and the massacre of the people in Kwangju. There were so many "plays within a play" that the production looked like a rehearsal and Ki used more than twenty human-sized dummies and fifty ghosts in vinyl costumes, mixing scenes with illusions. In addition, he employed slang and profanity to mock and caricature reality.

Hamlet 2 in 1982 was adapted even more freely, as Ki changed Hamlet's personal troubles to social ones. Thus the question of the play became not to be or not, but to be true or not. *Hamlet* was interpreted as a tragedy of the madness and terror of society, not as a tragedy of inner instinct and human desires. The seventy characters in *Hamlet 1* were compressed into thirteen and conveyed clearer messages about social and historical events. The director tried to express how the collapse of politics had spread over society like opium, creating collective madness and terror. It seemed that the political messages were clearer than ever in *Hamlet 3* of 1985, about which no records or comments can be found owing to censorship (it is said that the theater was surrounded by 500 police during performances). After the military government ended, *Hamlet 4* in February of 1990 changed its mockery from the foibles of politicians to the incompetence of the intelligentsia. Hamlet was not a prince of Denmark looking for revenge against his uncle but a helpless young man living in modern Korean society. His appearance was not princely but that of commoner in blue jeans. The hero had to experience the tyranny of power, corrupt political situations, sexual corruption, the labor movement, and so on. He instantly suffered from social injustices, and questioned himself helplessly whether to wake or not to wake. This *Hamlet* also employed many ghosts besides King Hamlet and portrayed the deaths of many innocents. In fact, the ghosts symbolized the victims of the military suppression in the city of Kwangju in 1980. *Hamlet 5* in September of 1990 was the extension of *Hamlet* 4. It criticized the military government's political brutality, tortures, and murders as well as the suppression in Kwangju. Its subjects of satire and the formal structure were similar to *Hamlet* 4, but this production employed more bawdy talk and words of abuse than *Hamlet* 4. Thus, it had the atmosphere of corrupt capitalist society overall. It likened King Hamlet to the innocents who died, the Queen to the incarnation of capitalist extravagance, the gravedigger to modern commoners of Korea.

This *Hamlet* series gained attention owing to its rearrangements of the story as well as its satire. For example, *Hamlet 4* consisted of three acts and six scenes without any direct connection between the scenes. The first act was the rehearsal of *Ham-*

let in modern times, which provided the frame of the play. The second act consisted of six scenes; the first scene was a dream where Hamlet is troubled by many ghosts of those who died unfairly; the second scene showed how Hamlet falls in love with a pure girl who does social work for the poor; the third scene focused on terrorism, as murderers like Rosen and Gilberstin confess their crimes during inner monologues; the fourth scene was a play within a play through which the dictator reveals his hidden thoughts; the fifth scene was "the rendezvous of the mother," where various social problems such as sexual corruption, drug abuse, and human trafficking are discussed; the sixth scene was "the tomb of philosophy," where the matter of life and death is agonized over. The third act concluded the play with a series of deaths. The King is shot to death, Hamlet is killed by torture, and so on. This scene structure shows how director Kukseo Ki broke down the motifs of *Hamlet* and arranged them to dramatize the issues of society. Although some critics pointed that Ki's *Hamlet* series were oversimplified and destructive of the original artistic dignity because of its crudeness, slang, and bawdy talk, the series criticized the political and social situation of modern Korea. Owing to the fame of the original *Hamlet*, these satires could be performed under the military government; in addition, the rearrangements of the plot were forerunners of the new deconstruction experiments in near future in Korea. Indeed, *Hamle*t in the 1980s is the forerunner of the new era of postmodernism, which stressed multicentered interpretations.

Yeontaek Lee's *Hamlet* (1996)

The *Hamlet* directed by Yeontaek Lee was heavily rooted in Shamanism. Lee said that his interpretation of *Hamlet* traced the carnival between life and death ("The Director's Words"). He stressed the body rather than Shakespeare's poetic words as a medium of the production. The body movements were based on Korean traditional theater and martial arts, a fusion of tradition and the modern. The meeting of the ghost and Hamlet and the madness of Ophelia were expressed as shamanic possessions. Hamlet's feigned madness was compared to a shaman illness. In fact, the structure of the appearance of the grudge-bearing ghost King Hamlet, his venting of his spite, and Hamlet's final revenge were similar to the basic structure of a shaman ritual, where a grudged spirit appears, appeases, and returns peacefully to the dead. Kwangdae, the traditional actors of Korea, played various roles in this *Hamlet*, including the actors in the play within a play, the grave-diggers, and commentators and entertainers between scenes. They heightened the merry atmosphere of the production in spite of the play's serious theme. For example, the gravedigger scene extended to the carnival of life, thus employing the traditional Namsadag plays with wandering players. All these were based on Korean traditional theatrical arts, modified for modern understanding.

In addition to making the best use of the traditional theatrical arts, the scene of the play within a play was further estranged from reality. The actors and actresses acted like puppets, and spoke in English to create a defamiliarizing effect. It was also one of the first attempts to use more than one language in a production in Korea. Although it was not well received by audiences, it was an interesting attempt. Sexual connotations were also maximized in this interpretation. An Oedipus complex was obvious in the scene between Hamlet and the Queen. Hamlet made aggressive sexual attacks on the Queen, far beyond the normal relationship of son and mother. Ophelia and her brother Laertes showed signs of incest; they actively touched and hugged. The behavior of the King and Ophelia also indicated possible sexual relations. The stage was designed like the inside of a tomb, indicating that life itself is a part of death. In addition, a grave of yellow ocher was located in the middle of stage. Thus, the stage appeared to symbolize the border between life and death. Many masks and props were from Korean traditional theater, but they were neither solely Korean nor authentic. Overall, the movement, dances, music and songs were Korean, but also from many cultures, including the West and Japan. In other words, the production was multicultural in spite of its strong Korean influences. The actors' bodies spoke more than their languages did. The conflicts of sexual connotation heightened the tensions. The grave on the stage indicated the world of death nearby. The use of masks gave the atmosphere an exotic and oriental feel. It was intercultural performance of the traditional and the modern, as well as the Korean and the Western.

In conclusion, starting from imitations of English productions in the 1950s and the 1960s, Shakespeare in Korea has reflected a variety of domestic and international influences. His works have inspired many directors to produce Shakespeare as expressions of their own situations and cultures and thus the more variations of his work emerged, the more audiences have seen the richness of his plays.

Works Cited

"Chongbajirul Ipeun 70 chulmunieu Silhumguk" ("Shakespeare's *Hamlet*, an Experimental Production with 70 Young People"). *Chosun Ilbo* (Chosun Daily News) (15 April 1981): n.p.

"*Hamlet* ui Samchawonjuk Mudae" ("The Three Dimensional Stage of *Hamlet*"). *Chosun Ilbo* (Chosun Daily News) (15 April 1962): n.p.

"*Hamlet* yeso Ttoeorunen Pyul Taseotmyungui" ("The Profiles of Five Rising Stars in *Hamlet*). *Kyunghayng Ilbo* (Kyunghyang Daily News) (3 May 1962): n.p.

"Kakyo sipjuneon Kineom" ("The 10th Anniversary of 'Kagyo' Company"). *Hanguk Ilbo Hanguk* (Hanguk Daily News) (4 May 1975): n.p.

Kim, Dongwon. *Misueu* (Curtain Call). Seoul: Taehaksa, 2003.

Ko, Seunggil. "Hanguk Yeonguk kwa Shakespeare" ("Korean Theatre and Shakespeare"). *Daewha* (Dialogue) 78 (1977): 201-43.

Lee, Yeontaek. "The Director's Words." *Hamlet* Pamphlet (1996): n.p.

"*The Prince of Hamyul* Stands for Japanese Traditions" ("Hamyul Taeja, Weisaekgi Chitta"). *Hanguk Ilbo* (Hanguk Daily News) (24 June 1977): n.p.

Shin, Hyunsook. "Hamyul Taeja" ("The Prince of Hamlet"). *Hanguk Yeongukhak* (Journal of the Korean Theater Research Association) 6 (1994): n.p.

Shin, Jungok. *Shakespeare Hangukei Oda* (Shakespeare Came to Korea). Seoul: Baeksin, 1998.

Theatre Critics Association. *80 yeondae Yeonguk Pyongron Jaryojip* (Collection of 1980s Theatre Criticism). Seoul: Theatre Critics Association, 1993.

Theatre Critics Association. *80 yeondae Yeonguk Pyongron Jaryojip* (Collection of 1990s Theatre Criticism). Seoul: Theatre Critics Association, 1996.

"Yeonguk Pipyong" ("Theater Review"). *Hanguk Ilbo* (Hanguk Daily News) (14 April 1962): n.p.

"Ydeonguk Pipyong" ("Theatre Review"). *Kyunghyang Ilbo* (Kyunghyang Daily News) (16 April 1962): n.p.

Yoo, Minyoung. *Lee Haerang Pyung Chon* (Biography of Haerang Lee). Seoul: Taehaksa, 1999.

Bangsawan Shakespeare in Colonial Malaya

Nurul Farhana Low bt Abdullah

The earliest record of Shakespeare performance in Malaya occurred during the latter half of the nineteenth century. This was a fluid period for the Malay states, during which they were in the midst of a long and complex conversion from being a collection of autonomous sultanates to a British colony. The states, while contiguous in geography and culture, had no history as a unified political whole. The exact levels of independence varied between three main groups, namely 1) the Straits Settlements (Penang, Malacca, and Singapore), which were crown colonies and directly under British rule; 2) the Federated states, which had a British Resident advising on all matters save religion and culture; and 3) the Unfederated states, which were nominally independent, although subject to increasing trade pressures. Neither recordings nor scripts nor indigenous reactions to performances of Shakespeare plays have yet surfaced; the only records are reviews written for the British press. Moreover, these loose adaptations of Shakespeare took such liberties with the plays that they were more often showcases of Malay adaptations than dramatizations of Shakespeare's characters. As artifacts of the earliest modern (Western-influenced) commercial Malay theater, however, they make an interesting sociohistorical vignette of the convergence between English culture and Malayan society in a colonial context.

Bangsawan theater appeared during a period of transition when the British colonial presence meant increased urbanization and Western influence in the country (see Zuhra). It is described as a commercial theater that evolved initially from local imitations of Wayang Parsi (Parsi theater), which first came to Penang in the 1870s from India (see Bujang). Cantius Leo Camoens describes Parsi theater as a semi-operatic style of Indian theater, performed in the Hindustani language. Large numbers of northern Indian traders established trading bases in Malaya, especially Penang, and by keeping in touch with cultural developments in India brought the first Parsi theater troupe to Malaya. This entertainment was considered modern and innovative at the time because it emphasized elaborate sets and costumes designed to create sensational effects (Camoens 66-67). Parsi theater troupes such as the New Elphinstone Theatrical Company of Bombay performed local Indian stories, adaptations of Shakespeare, and Arabic fairy tales (see Tan 16). When the troupes returned to India, all their sets, costumes, stage, and sound props were bought by Mamak Pushi, a wealthy Indian Muslim trader who lived in Penang. He then formed his own troupe in 1885, which he named Pushi Indera Bangsawan of Penang. This was the first Bangsawan troupe in Malaya or, as Sooi Beng Tan notes, the first theater troupe to call itself "bangsawan" (16). Derived from the Malay word *bangsawan*, which means "of aristocratic class," R.J. Wilkinson describes the bangsawan as a form of Malay opera. In these operas, Malay songs are sung to European tunes and the plot is built around some story borrowed from a European play or the *Arabian Nights*, and whatever the plot, there is always a comic element which is considered the best part of the show.

The Peranakan (or Indian Muslim) community in Penang established troupes like The Prince of Wales Theatrical Company and Sri Indramawan (Camoens 69). Although bangsawan performers frequently comprised Malays, Eurasians, and Chinese, performances were predominantly in Malay, including the Shakespeare adaptations. In the late 1880s Penang was the center of wayang activity and Penang troupes visited the mining towns of the Larut district in Perak (Camoens 74). As commercial theater, bangsawan was entertainment. Performances were publicized through advertisements and leaflets or handbills and to ensure high audience turn-out for each performance, troupes staged a different play each night of their run in a particular town. An advertisement for the Opera Indra Permata in the newspaper *Straits Echo* for example proclaimed: "Tonight! Tonight!! Dedicated to the loving memory of our beloved Wm. Shakespeare, The Opera Indra Permata Company of Selangor will stage the sensational tragedy Prince Hamlet by the best actors and actresses procurable in Java. Our clowns are without rivals! New dresses! New scenery!! Excellent music!!! The Orchestra plays from 8 to 9 before the performance" (16 February 1907). The one-off nature of bangsawan performances unfortunately meant that published reviews were infrequent, available only if a member of the audience or a journalist bothered to write them. The boast of the above *Hamlet* advertisement indicates that the troupe's "unrivalled" clowns were the main attraction rather than the tragic styling of the hero. Thus, the unscripted, impromptu nature of bangsawan performances would probably have caused local (British) journalists at the time to deem such performances unworthy of serious artistic or literary review. The unscripted nature of performance appears to be a characteristic peculiar to Asian forms of theater at that time. As an unnamed writer for *The Straits Times* of 12 May 1924 observed in his article on a translation of Tibetan drama: "The actors, who specialize in particular parts, are by no means bound by the written word, but on the contrary, use it with a great deal of freedom, putting in much of their own. . . . It may be remarked in parenthesis that this freedom of treatment seems to be peculiar to the Asiatic genius, for we find it also in the highly developed Indian art of music. Europe regards the text as sacred; it is a crime to take liberties with the text of *Hamlet* or with a Beethoven symphony. Asia prefers to introduce the personality of the performers, regarding the performance of the literal text as tending to lifelessness" (n.p).

The same sensational tragedy of *Hamlet* mentioned above, fortunately, warranted brief comment from the *Straits Echo* the following week. The performance had indeed attracted a full house. The anonymous reviewer also noted: "The plot of the English play was departed from in several cases; for instance, in the Malay version both 'Hamlet' and 'Ophelia' remained thoroughly sane throughout, and two humorous characters—a P.C. 142 and his sergeant—were introduced to provide the comic element, which Mohamed Noor and Abubakar did right loyally, the audience almost splitting their sides with laughter over the antics of the twain. Salley, as 'Hamlet,' worked hard and gave a very creditable interpretation of the part, although, of course, as has been said, not quite Shakespeare's" (18 February 1907). This departure from the original plot was a common feature of bangsawan Shakespeare. *Hamlet* was a popular choice, probably because the supernatural element in its plot held much promise for creative innovation. Reviewers, however, were not always impressed by the liberal improvisations. R.O. Winstedt, in a detailed description of a bangsawan *Hamlet* by the "King Edward's heart-soothing play company" written for the *Malay Mail*, then reproduced in the *Straits Echo* on 14 November 1908, and later included in his book *Malayan Memories* wrote as follows:

> The next scene is a garden . . . with a large coffin or box on trestles in the centre. The clown enters and goes to sleep at the foot of the trestles. . . . The ghost of Hamlet's father, a fearful figure in white, with ghastly chalked face, comes from behind the coffin and executes a slow dance between a minuet and a cake-walk. The clown wakes and rolls himself head over heels across the stage in terror. . . . [s]uddenly the ghost vanishes behind the coffin, the clown jumps up, opens the side of the box and peeps. Hamlet's father lies inside, a decorous corpse. The clown shuts the box, opens it again. The corpse has gone. . . . It is an odd performance, bizarre scenery, strangely translated plot: but interesting, perhaps, as a perverted example of Shakespeare's world-wide popularity. I have seen women weep at the pity of the tragedy, though that, to be sure, was not at the pathetic cadence of the line or any turn of the plot, but when the ghost of Hamlet's father was stalking across the boards, and again, when the "dumb-show" poison was poured into the old King's ear! (78-81)

The actors in Winstedt's review were possibly from The Emperor Edward Theatrical Company of Perak that had won wide acclaim in the state. Camoens writes that the company made a performing tour of Penang and played at a theater in King Street in January 1904 (121). Although this piece is written some four years later, it is entirely possible that a successful company, such as this appears to have been, would have enjoyed such longevity similar to the Indra Zanzibar Royal Theatrical Company of Singapore (Wayang Kassim) which was formed in 1902 and performed in Penang in 1909, yet was still in existence well past 1915 (see Bujang).

Another version of *Hamlet*, *Hamlet Rajah of Denmark*, was performed by the Straits Opera Company at the Tek Soon Theater in January 1912 and received a full-length review in the *Straits Echo*, reproduced in the *Times of Malaya* on 11 January 1912. The reviewer comments satirically: "At the outset we may summarize our criticism by saying that the actors were worthier of a better piece. Mr Shakespeare's idea of a play is crude, and his construction amateurish. Apparently his studies in dramatic authorship have not led him beyond third rate melodramatic standards. The plot was a mass of improbabilities, and the incidents unnecessarily 'bluggy'" (n.p.). A note of exasperation permeates the review as details of the myriad improbabilities unfold and the anonymous reviewer discusses issues such as the fact that the play opens with the murder of the Sultan of Denmark by Sultana Gertrude who is in love with her brother-in-law, Claudius. Claudius supplies her with a packet of poison that she pokes into the sleeping Sultan's ear. Since the play is an opera, much singing accompanies the action. Hamlet or H.H. Pramas Hamlet, son of the murdered Sultan, makes a brief appearance, clad entirely in black, and sings a soliloquy beginning "*Idop-ka? Mati ka?*," a very truncated and colloquial rendering of the most famous Shakespearean line. The reviewer then describes the scene in the graveyard, which turns out to be a crowd pleaser. A comic character, P.C. 22, and his superior officer are introduced and so is the ghost of the murdered Sultan: "Number Dua-puloh-dua [twenty two] was set to jaga [watch over] the kubor [graveyard] which contained five tombstones inscribed in English. P.C. 22 was very much scared by a ghost which walked among the tombs, and the unfeeling audience laughed at his tremors. So did his superior officer, summoned to the place by telephone. But the ghost appeared again, and the officer was even more scared. He fell over his sword and was too fat to get up again" (n.p.). The reviewer continues to describe how in the play a report about the ghost is made to Hamlet, who together with Horatio decides to wait for it to reappear that night. Hamlet's ability to recognize the ghost as his father's draws admiration from the reviewer, for it is described as looking "more like a hollow turnip than the handsome sultan who was earwigged." Hamlet's re-enactment of his father's murder is also detailed. For this scene the troupe has apparently taken the opportunity to include a somewhat lengthy albeit comic portrayal of a local theater audience attending a performance. The reviewer observes: "[Hamlet] got [the players at a neighbouring theater] to stage a representation of his Papa's murder, and invited his Mama and Claudius to go to see it. They were admitted free, as if they had been members of the Press, or Police. A towkay [a rich Straits-born Chinese businessman] and his nonia [wife] had to pay. The ticket seller at the door said that satu class was satu ringgit, dua class dua ringgit, and so on. A Malay fisherman and an Indian lady got in for twenty-cents each, but so far as we could understand, that was due to favouritism. The ticket-seller, a handsome youth, had a penchant for the Indian lady. . . . Even a blind Sikh tapped his way in, and the inhuman ticket-seller mocked his blindness, to the inhuman amusement of the audience" (n.p.).

Such scenes were included to elicit as much laughter and enjoyment as possible from the audience, even though they compromised the plot. The rest of the play remains reasonably faithful to Shakespeare's story, albeit condensed. The scenes with Ophelia or Opeelyer are somewhat crudely fashioned, for after she is introduced, singing and sobbing, Hamlet mistakenly kills her father Tungku Polonius and then knocks her about the stage before snatching back the diamond solitaire engagement ring he had given her. Subsequently she jumps into the sea and kills herself. Hamlet is sent off after Laertes (who was briefly shown leaving for France before Ophelia's death) with a letter but literally jumps ship mid-voyage: "When in mid-ocean, on a one funnel steamer called 'The Star Line,' he met a cruiser going back to Denmark, and just as they were passing, he jumped from one to the other" (n.p.). Back home in Denmark, Hamlet lies to his mother the Sultana about all he had seen in England, describing it as a "negeri banyak bagus" [very good country]. The wicked Claudius nevertheless has other plans for Hamlet and introduces a tumbler of poisoned raspberryade. When that fails, he supplies a cutlass with poisoned tip for Laertes to use in a duel with Hamlet, who is armed only with a light rapier. Despite being jabbed on the wrist by the poisoned tip, Hamlet manages to slay Laertes. Upon seeing this Gertrude drinks the poisoned raspberryade while Claudius is given the choice whether to die by the sword or drink the poison: The reviewer ends his piece satirically, criticizing the play and its author while praising the actors: "As we said, we do not think much of the play itself. It may be classed as more promising than achieving. The author will improve with practice. The players were the thing. Miss Gaffor as the Sultana, Gertrude was very tragically wicked, and Miss Nita as Opee-lyer imported a pathos into her part for which Mr. Shakespeare must not get all the credit" (n.p.). And herein lay the central characteristic of the bangsawan: Hamlet's "Mousetrap" notwithstanding, the play was not the thing. It served merely as a vehicle to showcase the singing, acting, or comedic talents of the actors, and in some cases, the artistic innovations of the prop masters.

Perennial favourite *Hamlet* (or 'Omlet), is once again reviewed, this time by R.P Hunter in the August 1926 edition of *British Malaya*, who gives details of the encounter between the ghost of Hamlet's father and a sentry: "Enter a sentry, dressed as a cross between a Malay *mata-mata* (constable) and a sea-booted fisherman. A clown this fellow. He sets the audience rocking with an anecdote, and gestures to our standard of the crudest. He is obviously trying to think of another when—enter the Ghost. . . . 'What have you come back to this place for?' he [the sentry] asks. The Ghost replies that there is a little affair about which he wishes to speak with his son Prins 'Omlet. With an air of the most indescribable boredom the Sentry strolls to the battlements, grinds the handle of an imaginary telephone, and says 'O, Serjin, there is the ghost of 'Omlet's father here and he wishes to speak to him. You will tell him? *baik*'" (115). The scene continues with 'Omlet's reaction to his father's ghost: "Omlet was evidently waiting for such a call for he appears at once. One cannot help feeling that they must have always been an undemonstrative couple, for quite calmly 'Omlet says, 'What news, my father?' and the reply, 'Good news!' comes rather curiously from the sometime murdered. The spirit of the injured sovereign then goes on to relate in the flattest of flat voices the manner in which he was assisted to shuffle off his mortal coil. At last the kingly Ghost concludes. . . . And now comes indisputable evidence of the supernatural character of the visitor, for a ballet of fairies troop in to lead him away. . . . Their costumes have received the addition which marks the fairy of the Malayan stage—heavy anklets of brass bells, from which the maximum of sound is obtained by the simple expedient of stumping along on the heels" (Hunter 115-16). The telephone, whether real or imaginary, was evidently a popular prop in the bangsawan *Hamlet*s of the 1920s. A review of "Pantomime Hamlet" written for the *Straits Echo* of 4 June 1923, describes how "the ghost turned out to be a comic character, introducing a scene of excellent burlesque in which the sleeping soldiers awake and in the extremity of terror ring up the guardroom." Richard Sidney writes in 1923 about "A Malay Production of Hamlet," probably the same production as *Pantomime Hamlet* also staged by the Indra Zanzibar Royal Theatrical Company of Singapore: "We do not have to wait for humor until the gravedigger's scene, for it begins as soon as the first clown (the sentry) meets the ghost! This is really funny! A telephone has been introduced into the castle grounds in Elsinore . . . by means of which the comic sentry tries his best to call up the rest of the guard. The ghost, however, will stand none of this nonsense, and continually frightens the sentry, so much that he falls down on the stage, kicking up his legs in the air" (247).

The comic elements in these adaptations commanded the most attention from commentators. The Wayang Kassim troupe from Singapore, which appears to have made a point of including a Shakespeare adaptation or two in its repertoire, often had comedic extra turns or interludes between acts while the stage was being rearranged and these extra turns in themselves were enough to attract the crowds (see Tan 35). The *Straits Echo* of 11 December 1909, reported on Wayang Kassim's successful performance of *The Merchant of Venice*, including the extra turns which bore no relation to the play. In fact, the play itself seemed to be secondary to the comic sketches performed during the intervals: "The house was crowded, owing to the fact that some extra 'turns' which promised to be interesting and attractive were billed" (n.p.). These were described in some detail. For example, "Instantaneous Photographer Clown Klimanoff will make a photo in five minutes time and present it to the public for inspection. If not satisfactory Clown Klimanoff will pay $100 to the person who condemns it so" (*Straits of Echo* n.p.). The instantaneous photo was a joke: Clown Klimanoff adjusted the camera as if he were taking a snap-shot of the whole house. In five minutes' time, he came down the stage, with a number of packets done up in paper, and distributed them among the audience. The eager recipient opened the packet to have a look at his photo—he saw a reflection of his face in a small looking glass. This was Wayang Kassim's second run in Penang for the year, having already performed earlier that same year. Commenting on their earlier performance of *The Merchant of Venice*, the anonymous reviewer for the *Straits Echo* on 18 January 1909, generously conceded: "It is impossible to compare the performance with a reproduction of the piece at Home; still, the play, as acted by the Wayang Kassim, was not uninteresting, the lighter parts especially being creditably done" (n.p.).

Indeed, the adaptation of Shakespeare appears to have provoked unusual attention to the Bard in the press. In the very same issue of the *Straits Echo* two lengthy articles appeared that same day, the first on page two titled "Among the

Gods," containing comments by Cockney audiences made during Shakespeare performances in England, while another article on page ten described stage costumes in England during Shakespeare's time. It seemed as if the editors, who were almost certainly British, were responding ambivalently to the idea of Malayans adapting Shakespeare for their stage while ignoring the original text while not necessarily aspiring to evoke undue reverence for the English Shakespeare. As mentioned, the first article was devoted to amusing anecdotes of Shakespearean actor Sir Henry Irving and some Cockney audiences he had encountered, whereas the second article on stage costumes acknowledged that even in Shakespeare's day stage costumes for his various plays were seldom historically accurate. Although the appearance of the former could possibly be interpreted as the aligning of local Malayan audiences with the lowest class of English theater-goers thereby commenting obliquely on the social status of local audiences and, by extension, on the troupes performing for their entertainment, the second article implies that although bangsawan costumes were less than satisfactory, even Shakespeare himself had to contend with this common technicality. Thus, the newspaper appears more concerned to reconcile its readers (of whom the majority must have been English or at the very least English educated) to Malayan appropriations of Shakespeare than to condemn these productions, thereby encouraging its readers to view such performances with an open mind.

Laughter in these early Shakespeare adaptations was frequently procured at the expense of members of the English administrative machine and, indirectly, the Malay royalty or *bangsawan* as portrayed in the characters of Hamlet, Claudius, and the ghost. The police were a popular target for ridicule, prompting Hunter to make the following comments on the comic skills of the Malay actor: "The Malay is a natural mimic, with quite a pronounced sense of humor. Far more sensitive to sarcasm than the average inhabitant of the East, he is very prone to use it, in a crude form, and so long as only buffoonery, with a gentle dig at somebody, is called for, he quite equals the average actor of the West" (114). Hunter describes at length the character of Hamlet's friend, the police inspector, an extra character who is introduced for comic effect: "The police inspector idea is introduced for the sole purpose of giving the funny man a bit of congenial business. It is an excellent opportunity for the mimic to play havoc with the peculiarities of the white man, and if the joke be but directed against a representative of law and order, the most respectable old *Haji* will roll in his seat from sheer enjoyment. . . . ['Omlet] sends for his friend, and for a short period there are noises off [stage]. Then [there] staggers on to the stage an individual who is disputing hotly with some person behind the wings. He clinches the discussion with the hidden one by saying '*Nanti sahya minum s'tengah, sahya pukol sama lu*' (Wait until I've had a whisky and soda and I'll beat you)" (116). From here, the Inspector steals the show, upstaging Hamlet/'Omlet as he proceeds to apprehend the usurper Claudius: "From behind the backs of his constables [the Inspector] introduces himself to the villain and cautions him to '*jaga baik baik*' (be careful) and remember that he is dealing with a Government Servant, but to his evident consternation the usurper advances. Ever and always behind somebody's back, the Inspector encourages his constables with shrill cries, and eventually the wanted man is down and bound hand and foot. Then he cautiously approaches, inspects the bonds, satisfies himself that there is no danger, and planting one foot upon the prostrate form, raises high his sword and cries, '*Sahya sudah tangkap sendiri*' (I arrested him myself), and the curtain falls upon this tableau" (Hunter 116).

Despite the "indiscriminate slaughter" (Winstedt, "Hamlet in Malay") of plot and character, bangsawan productions of Shakespeare were well received by local audiences. For the expatriates however, they were ludicrous and grotesque. An article on the bangsawan written for *The Straits Echo* in 1928 elaborates: "The pieces chosen for presentation are most frequently taken either from the 'Thousand and One Nights' or from Shakespeare. In either case the result is grotesque, since the production—invariably musical—is interlarded with countless topical allusions, and with songs that have once been popular in England or America. A Shakespearean entertainment is particularly ludicrous to European spectators by reason of their familiarity with the original but players and Oriental play-goers perpetrate and accept the wildest incongruities with intense gravity" (n.p.). Such reviews indicate that extraneous comic scenes appear to have been a staple of Shakespeare bangsawan and that these were no doubt included because they proved to be very popular with the audience. Tan describes this phenomenon: "As commercial theater, bangsawan was extremely responsive to audience preferences. Dependent as they were on their performances' popular appeal for survival, opera companies were known 'carefully' to study 'the likes and dislikes of the *bangsawan* enthusiasts'" (44).

It is reasonable to assume that the audience consisted primarily of town folk who lived in and around the areas where bangsawan troupes set up their stage. These urban dwellers could be anyone from the white Tuans to their Malay punkah pullers and anyone else in-between. Winstedt in his memoir *Start from Alif, Count from One* recalls that he once gave his punkah puller Ngah fifty cents to go to the Malay Opera, "where Horatio in the uniform of a police sergeant was telephoning to a palace of Reckitt's blue canvas that the ghost of Hamlet's father had arrived on that tropical stage!" (22). The audience could also be illiterate farmers from nearby villages or schoolboys from English schools who stayed out late to attend these performances. During the period between the World Wars, Europeans in Malaya—at least officials or government servants living in the towns—enjoyed a luxurious lifestyle. Margaret Shennan (115) notes that they usually had automobiles and enjoyed membership at exclusive expatriate clubs besides possessing "a retinue of domestic servants [who] sustained the kind of privileged lifestyle which had disappeared from middle-class Britain" (137). These normally consisted of "a cook, a 'boy' or two to clean and run the household, a *syce* or chauffeur to drive and look after the car, an *amah* or *ayah* as nursemaid for the children, and, lower in the pecking order, a gardener or *kebun*, a *dhobi* or laundryman and a *tukang ayer* to take care of water and sanitary needs" (137). They were also fond of throwing parties and get-togethers during the weekends for tennis, picnics, swimming, or golf. Lifestyles and friendships, however, "were governed by occupation and a man's position in the hierarchy" (Shennan 137).

Of the local population, the Malay princes in particular enjoyed a social relationship with the British. The Malay sultans "entered into European social life and shared the British passion for sport" (Shennan 142). Some European women also socialized with their Asian neighbors; for example, Shennan quotes Nancy Wynne, who wrote: "Yesterday . . . I went out to tiffin with two Chinese ladies, Mrs. Eng and Mrs. Lim, at a Malay lady's house" (145). The degree of social contact between Europeans and non-Europeans varied from state to state and Shennan also writes that Roger Barrett, who grew up near Sungei Petani in the Unfederated Malay State of Kedah, recalled that as a child he had friends of all races, while Agnes Davison had the same experience in Alor Star (145).

Although there are accounts of European clubs admitting members from the Asian communities, the European population on the whole tended to seek the company of fellow nationals. In the hierarchical society of Malaya during this period, bangsawan gained popularity as the non-European version of Western theater, modified and adapted to suit local tastes. While it was an imitation of Western culture and thus considered modern, bangsawan was nevertheless open to all and sundry—rich, poor, Malay, Chinese, Indian, Arab, even European (see Tan 31). It was during this period too that Malays began to appreciate the importance of education, especially English education: "One of the effects of the low standard in Malay education, combined with its lack of utility in obtaining government employment except as a low-paid schoolteacher, was that there was increasing pressure from Malays, especially in the developed areas, to be given greater opportunities to receive English education" (Roff 136). The British, however, were still reluctant to expand educational opportunities for the rural Malay population, fearing the disruptive effect it might have on peasant life. They endeavoured instead to strengthen and develop the vernacular school system "to make it a fit instrument with which to breed a vigorous and self-respecting agricultural peasantry such as must form the backbone of every nation" (Roff 138-39 quoting the 1920 "Federal Council Proceedings"). In order to train teachers who would staff the ever-increasing number of vernacular schools, the Sultan Idris Training College (SITC) was set up in Tanjong Malim, Perak, in 1922. The importance of this college towards the growth of Malay nationalism is well documented and where Shakespeare is concerned, it is important for the contribution of its Translation Bureau, which translated several Shakespeare plays into Malay, part of college principal O.T Dussek's efforts to educate his teacher trainees so that the standard of vernacular education could gradually be raised. The 1920s thus have been described by William R. Roff as "years of political change and political discussion, directed for the most part toward a redefinition of the relationship between the British and the Malays" (148). Roff suggests that SITC students who read the local vernacular press, knew Indonesian literature, and learned from each other about the various Malay states were acutely aware of social change and its attendant problems for the Malays. They may also have influenced the Malay population among the town dwellers and those from nearby villages. As the British increasingly promoted vernacular Malay education, more and more Malay boys were able to read the Malay newspapers and journals that circulated at the time, both for themselves and aloud to their mostly illiterate fathers. Roff lists the titles of ten Malay newspapers and journals published before 1900, and notes that by 1900 there were at least sixteen Malay language journals established in Singapore, Penang and Perak (49).

At the higher levels of officialdom there was much discussion throughout the decade about the decentralization of the federation and the restoration of power to the sultans. Comparisons were drawn between the federated and unfederated states and to the greater degree of Malay participation in the government and administration of the latter. To appease the Malays, attempts had been made to allocate to them a proportion of subordinate administrative, clerical and technical jobs in government. There was an avowedly pro-Malay preferential policy in recruitment to the lower ranks of the Federated Malay States' public services introduced in the early 1920s, designed as much to cut down expenditure on overseas staff as to restore to the Malays a more active role in the affairs of their own state (see Roff 118). Meanwhile, the local-born Chinese were becoming increasingly discontented at their virtual exclusion from the apparatus of government and this was expressed overtly by the late 1920s (see Roff 149). Their discontent could not compare, however, to the despair felt by the Malays at their lot, which was enunciated by Zainal Abidin bin Ahmad or Za'ba in 1923: "The Malays, as a whole, are a particularly poor people. Poverty is their most outstanding characteristic and their greatest handicap in the race of [sic] progress. Poor in money, poor in education, poor in intellectual equipment and moral qualities. . . . The poverty of the Malays is an all-round poverty" (qtd. in Roff 151). Such laments were a common subject in the vernacular press of the period and this awareness was not confined to the Malay states alone, for as early as 1906 members of the Malay community in the Straits Settlement of Singapore had begun publishing a Malay periodical, *Al-Imam*, through which they aspired "to remind those who are forgetful, arouse those who sleep, guide those who stray, and give a voice to those who speak with wisdom" (Roff 56). Although concerned mainly with religion, *Al-Imam*'s articles nevertheless would have raised the Malays' awareness of the necessity to better themselves in all aspects of life so as to become better Muslims. At the same time, however, editors of early Malay periodicals were careful not to point the finger of blame at others for the Malay predicament, placing the responsibility for improving their lot on the Malays' own shoulders. Newspapers such as *Utusan Melayu* and *Lembaga Melayu* were controlled by the English language press and helmed by loyalist Malays in the confidence of the government but represented for the urban middle-class Malays the voice of moderate, progressive Malay opinion. There were other independent Malay periodicals that emerged by the 1920s such as the *Majallah Guru*, published by the Malay Teachers Association of Selangor, Negri Sembilan, and Malacca, and the Penang reformist newspaper, *Idaran Zaman*. These newspapers discussed matters related to Malay life but seldom expressed radical views or touched directly upon political matters.

Another avenue for social interaction during the 1920s was enabled through the forming of clubs and associations. These groups were, however, purely social, cultural, or economic in nature. Roff states that none of the Malay and Malayo-Muslim organizations sought to exercise direct political influence or suggested that they spoke for a political as distinct from a socio-cultural group. Most societies and vernacular newspapers in fact took care at the outset to disclaim explicitly any desire to contravene or act outside the laws of the state. This reflects awareness, even fear on their part towards repressive British attitudes against secret societies in general and toward anything resembling political activity in particular (Roff 187). It would appear that although the British brought law and order to the Malay states, there were aspects of life that were less than satisfactory to the local population and that this dissatisfaction could not be voiced. Therefore it is not surprising to find that local audiences at bangsawan performances, particularly Shakespeare adaptations, revelled in the comic portrayals of police inspectors and other British officials that depicted them in the silliest light possible, exaggerating their officious mannerisms. As commercial entertainment, bangsawan troupes depended on paying audiences for their survival. The actors played to the audiences, often lengthening scenes that elicited the most interest. The various improvisations introduced to *Hamlet*, such as the comic sequences discussed above involving the ghost and the sentry or the police were well received by audiences and were therefore rehashed in later productions through the years. Bangsawan Shakespeare articulated the dissatisfaction, conscious or otherwise, of its audiences, yet disguised this in humor to make it palatable to everyone including the butts of the jokes. As a result, the plot in bangsawan, whether adapted from Shakespeare or any other source, was ultimately secondary to other elements: individual actors, special effects, or audience enjoyment. For the occasional European members of the audience familiar with the original plays, the improvisations were comical at best but at the end of the day, these plays were "not quite Shakespeare's," as one reviewer politely put it. So long as the performances remained purely entertainment and not expressions of political dissent or incitement, the British were happy to allow bangsawan actors to continue producing such versions of Shakespeare.

In conclusion, the adaptation of Shakespeare by Malayan bangsawan troupes was motivated by profit. The managers of the various troupes, often Straits-born Chinese who had been English educated, were aware of the prestige attached to the name hence capitalized on it. While Shakespeare's name was appropriated primarily for its commercial value, it is probable that the inclusion of a *Hamlet* or *Merchant of Venice* also aimed to cater to the taste of a specific segment of the audience or simply to add variety to to the troupe's repertoire. At the same time, the performance had to be entertaining to other members of the audience who may not have been aware of the literary and canonical status of Shakespeare, hence the inclusion of extraneous characters and scenes, and the extra turns. The text therefore was really of little consequence. As a student, identified only by his initials L.C.S., states in an article titled "Wayang" for *The Free School Magazine* of 1912, the plays "are always so much Malayanised that the brilliancy of Shakespeare's art has to give place to that of the Malay" (34). This sums up the effect of the bangsawan appropriation of Shakespeare.

Works Cited

Andaya, Barbara Watson, and Leonard Andaya. *A History of Malaysia*. Hampshire: Palgrave, 2001.

Bujang, Rahmah. *Sejarah Perkembangan Drama Bangsawan di Tanah Melayu dan Singapura* (*A History of the Development of Bangsawan Drama in Malaya and Singapore*). Kuala Lumpur: Dewan Bahasa dan Pustaka, 1975.

Camoens, Cantius Leo. *History and Development of Malay Theater*. M.A. thesis. Kuala Lumpur: U of Malaya, 1981.

Hunter, R.P. "*Hamlet* as She is Played." *British Malaya* (August 1926): 114-16.

L.C.S. "Wayang." *The Free School Magazine October* 2.5 (1912): 32-36.

Roff, William R. *The Origins of Malay Nationalism*. New Haven: Yale UP, 1967.

Shennan, Margaret. *Out in the Midday Sun: The British in Malaya 1880-1960*. London: John Murray, 2000.

Sidney, Richard. "A Malay Production of *Hamlet.*" *They Came to Malaya*. Ed. J.M Gullick. Oxford: Oxford UP, 1993. 245-48.

Tan, Sooi Beng. *Bangsawan: A Social and Stylistic History of Popular Malay Opera*. Penang: The Asian Centre, 1997.

Wilkinson, R.J. *A Malay English Dictionary (Romanized)*. London: Macmillan, 1957.

Winstedt, R.O, *Malayan Memories*. Singapore: Kelly and Walsh Ltd., 1916.

Winstedt, R.O. "Hamlet in Malay." *The Straits Echo* (14 November 1908): n.p.

Winstedt, R.O. *Start from Alif: Count from One*. Oxford: Oxford UP, 1969.

Zuhra, Nur Nina. *An Analysis of Modern Malay Drama*. Shah Alam: Biroteks, 1992.

Illustration

Bangsawan troupe at the Prince of Wales Theatrical Company (reprinted with permission from the National Archives, Kuala Lumpur, 2007).

Shakespeare, *Noh*, *Kyōgen*, and *Okinawa Shibai*

Masae Suzuki

In recent years, the study of the intercultural productions of Shakespeare in non-English speaking countries, including those in Asia, has attracted widespread scholarly interest, as we can see from the programs of the World Shakespeare Congress and other international theater conferences and colloquiums. There also seems to be an increasing number of East-West fusion productions of Shakespeare, using (or borrowing) the techniques of indigenous or traditional theater.

Josette Feral points out that two reactions to intercultural productions have been identified in the past: "euphoric" and what is termed "dysphoric." The first group describes the bases of an emerging global culture: this is the position of artists such as Eugenio Barba and Peter Brook, whose theater is based on the merging of traditions where audiences are confronted with the specific as well as the universal truth by virtue of performances that blend various cultures. The second type of reaction is that of critics like Carl Weber or Rustom Bharucha, who criticize the former as representing the danger of a ruling culture unduly appropriating other cultures and traditions without offering anything in return, having little regard for the historicity of the chosen material and using the alien component as a spicy sauce to make some old familiar food. Though basically supporting the euphoric point of view that borrowing has always been the way art has developed, Ferral also states that the concern of the dysphoric point of view should not be dismissed, for it "should encourage us to treat the intercultural phenomenon more carefully, to reflect on what it implies at the social, political and aesthetic levels. We must therefore be lucid, prudent, and re-assess our behaviour" (Feral 33).

This vision can also be suited to Japanese and other East Asian Shakespeare productions where works such as those of Yukio Ninagawa, Tadashi Suzuki, Ku Nau'ka or Ong Keng Sen have allowed crossings between dramatic arts, technical play, and systems of representation, including the use of images and techniques from *noh*.

On the other hand, Japan has national theaters for all of the genres it acknowledged as traditional drama : *kabuki*, *noh* (and its comic interlude, *kyōgen*), *Bunraku*, and Okinawan Drama to preserve and promote those arts. Most of the professional artists in those genres are raised in native traditions with strict conventions of connoisseurship and must build up their careers within the traditional repertoires. As a matter of fact, despite the movement to make use of traditional conventions as spices or for intercultural Shakespearean productions for the global market, most scholars and practitioners of authentic traditional theater, especially of *noh* drama, seem to have been relatively indifferent to such experiments. When we look back to the history of the Japanese reception of Shakespeare, however, it is also true that Shakespearean themes or titles of Shakespearean plays had been made use of in the local theater whenever it needed to expand its traditional repertoire and strengthen its popularity.

The aim of this paper is not to examine the pros and cons of the euphoric and dysphoric trends of the intercultural Shakespeare productions using Japanese traditional theater, which is often misrepresented in the world market, but to see how Shakespeare can strengthen and recreate the indigenous traditional theater for the local audience.

Though Shakespeare and *kabuki* is an important field to discuss to show how Shakespeare as a representative of Western culture has influenced or stimulated the theater of Japan, my focus will be more on *noh* (including its comic version *kyōgen*), as a representative of national traditional drama and Okinawan Drama as a representative of local traditional drama form would be the center of discussion.

Shakespeare and the traditional theater in the historical context of Japan

While Shakespeare's works in many parts of Asia and Africa often represented the importation of a foreign and potentially dominant culture, in most parts of the East Asia, including Japan, his plays were imported deliberately to modernize their indigenous theater and to show Western countries the level of their civilization.

Before the 1868 Meiji Restoration, Japan was controlled for more than 260 years by the Tokugawa Shogunate, which exercised central authority from Edo (present-day Tokyo) over some three hundred feudal domains ruled by individual feudal lords, as well as over the Ryukyu Islands (present Okinawa), a kingdom acknowledged by the emperor of China and the Japanese Emperor remained in his court in Kyoto as the figurehead of Japan.

Since the seventh century, tribes from Okinawa (Ryukyu) Islands, then referred as the "Southern Islands" in Japanese documents, had been sending tributes to the early Japanese Imperial Court (the Yamato Court) , but after the islands were unified as a kingdom during the fourteenth to fifteenth centuries, Okinawa (Ryukyu) established tributary relations with China during its Ming and Qing Dynasties. In the early seventeenth century, the Tokugawa Shogunate authorized the Shimazu family of the Satsuma domain (present-day Kagoshima prefecture) to send an expeditionary force to conquer the Ryukyus. As a result, though the kingdom technically came under the control of Satsuma, the kingdom also remained a tributary state of China and was given a considerable degree of autonomy to serve the interests of the Satsuma daimyo and those of the Shogunate in trade. The formal annexation of the islands as one of Japanese prefectures and the abolition of the kindom did not occur till 1879. To be precise, "Okinawa" or "Uchinah" is what the Okinawans had been calling themselves, while "Ryukyu" or "Ryuchus" was what those islands were called in China. There is a continuous debate over whether people of Okinawa are of the same ethnic strain as those of mainland Japan (often referred to as "Yamato" by the Okinawans), for northern island groups of this region (Amami-Oshima and main Okinawa Island) show evidence of migration from Kyushu, whereas in the two southern island groups (Miyako and Yaeyama), evidence points to Melanesian cultural strains. In this paper, I am including Okinawa as part of Japan, but considering the area as a possible link between mainland Japan and other east-Asian countries.

Now, among the indigenous theater in mainland Japan, *noh* was considered the most elaborate and sophisticated form of drama and was put under the direct control of government officials in charge of all performing arts for official ceremonies. *Noh* had been established during the fourteenth century in the capital Kyoto, patronized by the Ashikaga Shogunate of the Muromachi period. It was also patronized by the Tokugawa Shogunate during the Edo period (1603-1868) and most feudal lords followed the Shogun's taste and employed actors of the lineage of "the four troupes and one school" (Kanze, Hosho, Konparu, and the Kongo troupe and the newly established Kita school) in their domains. Being basically the art form of performance of the ruling samurai class, as well as the aristocrat, the general public had limited opportunity to see *noh* productions, but *Utai-bon*, or the chant-books of the words of the songs chanted within the plays were popularized and circulated around the country. As the people's interest in *noh* and *kyōgen* grew high, special performances for the public was also held for the citizens. In contrast, *kabuki*, the vulgar form of theater that emerged from the seventeenth century was considered the theater for commoners, but feudal lords sometimes invited the actors to their mansions so they can see the highlight scenes of famous *kabuki* performances.

In the case of Okinawa (Ryukyu), its classical traditional theater, now designated as important cultural asset by the Okinawa Prefecture and the Japanese government, was formed in the Ryukyu Court in order to entertaining foreign envoys during its period of dual subordination to Japan and China. As mentioned before, from 1404 to 1875, Okinawa (Ryukyu) had sent tribute missions to China (Ming and Quing), and in turn, the Chinese emperor had sent Sappu-shi, an envoy that acknowledged the region as the Ryukyuan Kingdom. Hundreds of Chinese government officials visited the Ryukyuan Court with the *sappu-shi*, and the king entertained them with dance performances which were later developed as a form of dance-drama called Kumiodori. The form of *kumiodori* was created by Tamagusuku Chōkun (1684-1734), a government official in charge of court performances, who was later called "the Shakespeare of Okinawa." This drama form, though with heavy Confucius themes in order to be presented to the Chinese officials, drew style and source from *noh* and *kabuki* plays in mainland Japan as well as from old ballads and local folk songs. This theater form, however, was strictly for ceremonial occasions and was not shown to the general public.

When Commodore Perry sailed to Japan with his black ships to force trade relations with the United States in the 1850s, he first stopped in Okinawa and then Edo and forced Ryukyu Kingdom and the Tokugawa Shogunate to sign unequal treaties to open up to American trade. Thus, Japan and Okinawa opened the doors to the hegemonic West, and suddenly, Europe and America became the new model of civilization.

In 1868, revolutionaries, including many from the ex-Satsuma domain, ousted the ancient regime of the Tokugawa government and set up a new government, restoring the Japanese Emperor as its symbolic head. According to Tsutsumi Harue, the Japanese newly appointed diplomats and politicians who were dispatched to Western countries first brought the idea that the Meiji government should target theater as one of the chief areas in which the western culture could be imitated. The Japanese mission members were exposed to Western theatrical genres such as opera, ballet, burlesque, and melodrama as well as Shakespeare and other classical plays, all at once. As Tsutsumi points out, the new Japanese leaders chose *kabuki* as a vehicle for a new form of drama, judging that "Kabuki's popularity among the commoners also appeared to be potentially a wonderful tool by which the leaders could enlighten and influence the people of Japan" (3-4). Those leaders also showed the *kabuki* play to the emperor for the first time in Japanese history, in order to elevate its status.

Since the early meeting between *kabuki* and Shakespeare in Japan has been already discussed thoroughly by Tsutsumi Harue and James Brandon, I will just summarize their opinion here that, in response to the new policy of theater reformation, there were mainly two movements to introduce Shakespeare on stage to the Japanese public the Meiji era. The first was the movement centering on Morita Kan'ya XII in his intercultural Kabuki (Brandon 33-53), and the second was that of Kawakami Otojiro (1864-1911) in his early Shakespeare productions in modern style (see also Suzuki, "Shakespeare Recreated " 117-38).

The first modern Japanese theatrical movement began in 1888 as a political form of drama. Although actors in such drama never had much formal training and the plays and productions were far from refined, the genre achieved a certain amount of fame, partly because the plays conveyed anti-Meiji government messages and gained favor from the audience. The achievements of Kawakami Otojirō were considered a part of this. Between 1899 and 1902, Kawakami Otojirō, his wife Sada-Yakko, and other members of his troupe made two tours to the United States and Europe. Using his first-hand knowledge of Western theater, Otojirō started to call his production *seigeki* (true theater) in order to produce adaptations of Shakespeare. Though Kawakami's attempts were later criticized by the *shingeki* (new drama) movement, which aimed to introduce Shakespeare and other Western plays in translations more faithful to the original texts, it is interesting that both the newly created plays and old *kabuki* plays from mainland Japan were accepted in Okinawa in those days as something new. Also, it is worth noting that the formation of modern spoken drama in both China and Korea had some influence from the theater reformation movement in Japan during this time._

Meanwhile, as one result of the fall of the Edo government and the samurai class, the world of *noh* and *kyōgen*, which had been basically supported by them, lost their financial foundation. Though *noh* was still considered a theater for educated people with some continuation of support by the aristocrats, many actors who lost the patronage of the samurai had to seek other jobs. To protect this art form, *nohgaku kai* was established in 1881, and owing to the effort of actors and scholars, its popularity spread among people again, with more people becoming amateur disciples of the *noh* masters. Some people thought that the rhythm of *noh* was the essence of the Japanese elocution, while others thought learning *noh* was associated with high culture.

It is well known in Japan that Natsume Soseki (1867-1916), who studied English literature in London for a year under W.J. Craig, the first general editor of the Arden Shakespeare, was not satisfied with the way Tsubouchi Shōyō (1859-1935) produced his version of *Hamlet* that was performed at Teikoku Gekijo theater in 1911. Shōyō, the first Japanese translator of the complete works of Shakespeare, admired Chikamatsu Monzaemon (1653-1724), the Edo period playwright of Joruri and Kabuki productions, and compared Shakespeare to *kabuki*. Soseki saw the production on 26 May and in a review he wrote for the *Tokyo Asahi Shimbun* on 5 and 6 June, he suggested that Shakespeare's lines should have been chanted in the rhythm of *noh* or Yokyoku. In spite of Soseki's opinion, it took more than another half-century for audiences to see Shakespeare on the *noh* stage and listen to the chanting of professional *noh* actors._

Okinawan drama and the early Japanese Shakespeare plays

A phenomenon similar to the fate of the *noh* actors happened to the court entertainers of the Ryukyu Kingdom, following the annexation of the islands to Japan as Okinawa Prefecture in 1879. The Kingdom was abolished, and King Shotai, the last king of the Ryukyus, was moved to Tokyo and was made a Marquis, just like the last Tokugawa Shogun and the other ex-feudal lords of mainland Japan. This also meant the majority of the samurai class officials who worked for the Ryukyu kingdom, including the government officials for court entertainment. Thus, the ex-samurais who were trained in court entertainment started to make their living by performing dance and drama in the playhouses newly built in town and this is how the art of the court performance was spread to the common people and absorbed more of their taste. At the same time, there was a strong movement in the urban areas of Okinawa to follow the modernization policy of central Japan. Okinawan playhouses started seeking out what was in vogue in Tokyo or Osaka in order to create new plays that would draw a large audience. Thus, the popular entertainment called *Okinawa shibai* was formed under the influence of both *kabuki* and modern plays from the mainland Japan. It was this boom to imitate plays from mainland Japan that introduced Shakespeare to Okinawa.

To be precise, in this paper, I include both *Okinawa shibai* and *kumiodori* as "Okinawan Drama," as well as the pre-forms of *Okinawa Shibai*, but in fact, *Okinawa shibai* is the genre that has been long neglected by theater scholars and government officials. For example, when the plan to build a National Theater in Okinawa emerged at the end of the twentieth century, it was temporarily named *Kokuritsu Kumiodori Gekijo* ("National Theater for Kumiodori"). After various debates, it is now renamed *Kokuritsu Gekijo Okinawa* ("National Theater Okinawa") to include all genres of Okinawan performances, including *Okinawa shibai* and *Ryukyu Buyo* ("Okinawan dances"), but the academic research on *Okinawa Shibai*, including its pre-form that included Shakespearean themes, is still staggering.

The transition of the definition of the Japanese word "Shibai" could be one hint to consider the reason why. Shibai, which literally means "sitting on the lawn," originally meant the spectators at the time when *Sarugaku-no-noh* and other forms of entertainment were usually performed outdoors. In modern terms, *shibai* means "plays," including opera and *kabuki*. Present *noh*, which is now considered a refined art, is often excluded from this category.

When *Okinawa shibai* was created under the influence of various genres of plays from mainland Japan, it became customary to refer to this new local drama genre as their "Shibai," hinting that it is their own popular theater that can draw large local audiences, while some Okinawan artists refer to the more classical *kumiodori* as their *noh*, indicating that it is more refined and meant for a more educated audience.

However, there seems to be no *shinsaku* ("newly created") *kumiodori* with Shakespearean themes, just as there had been no *shinsaku noh* with Shakespearean themes for a long time. As mentioned before, to find the trace of Shakespearean plays, we must examine *Okinawa shibai* and its pre-forms, produced in the commercial playhouses in Naha where some ex-samurai class entertainers with their knowledge of Kumiodori plunged themselves as actors and strived to attract the mass audience in order to make their living.

The first Shakespearean play introduced in Okinawa, an adapted version of *Othello,* was produced by the theatrical troupe *Kyuuyooza*, at a popular playhouse in Naha, in 1906. The play was modeled after the Kawakami Otojiro-Emi Suiin version of *Othello*, which was first produced in Tokyo in 1903. Following the first Shakespeare boom in mainland Japan, for two years, two theaters in Okinawa competed in producing adaptations of Shakespeare, including *Romeo and Juliet, Hamlet,* and *The Merchant of Venice,* all modeled after the productions in mainland Japan. Unfortunately, no script remains (for they usually took the *kuchidate*, or the "mouth-to mouth" training system), but it is obvious that the plays were adaptations in Okinawa dialect, and it is likely that the costumes were quite different from those worn by actors in Tokyo, let alone from Elizabethan costumes.

Meanwhile, intellectuals in mainland Japan who were dissatisfied with the way Shakespeare was presented to the Japanese public started the *shingeki* (new drama) movement, introducing Shakespeare and other Western plays in translations more faithful to the original texts. This movement, however, did not seem to affect the Okinawan theater world, and the title of Shakespeare plays in the Okinawan playhouses disappeared after 1908. One reason for the Okinawan rejection of *shingeki*-style Shakespeare is that by this time, *Okinawa shibai* had created a distinctive language style, a combination of dialects used in central Okinawa. It had a certain rhythm of *shingeki,* based on the then newly created standard Japanese failed to create.

After a period of imitation of the plays from central Japan, *Okinawa shibai* succeeded in producing two unique genres using *Kumiodori* as a base: *shigeki* (straight history plays) and *kageki* (Okinawan style opera), both of which deal with Okinawan legends and history. Accompanied by *sanshin* music and lyrics based on a rhythm with 8-8-8-6 syllables, the styles of these plays were very effective in expressing Okinawan passion and sentiment. The 8-8-8-6 syllables rhythm can also be seen in the old poetry in *Yamato* (mainland Japan) composed before the eighth century, but the basic rhythm of the poetry in *Yamato* was later changed to 5-7-5-7-7, as seen in the *noh* rhythm.

As theaters in Okinawa depended entirely on local audiences, it is natural that *Shingeki*-style Shakespeare, or *shingeki* plays in general, which were performed in standard Japanese and had educational purposes, could not draw large crowds in Okinawa. Titles of Shakespeare seem to have disappeared from the theater scenes in this region, while *Okinawa shibai* in Okinawan language with local themes apparently continued to flourish.

However, Shakespearean titles appeared in Okinawa again in the form of adaptations to the local theater form, as something like a touchstone to re-examine cultural identity. They arrived whenever the local theater faced a crisis of existence, such as the time of US-American occupation after World War II, disappeared again when they recovered their strength, and then appeared again in more varied styles (Suzuki, "Shakespeare in Okinawa"145-156).

One of the most significant intercultural Shakespeare productions in this region in recent years was the production of *English Noh Hamlet* by Ueda (Munakata) Kuniyoshi in October 2006. The production was held to commemorate the anniversary of the new Miyako City of the Miyakojima Island, where *noh* productions or Shakespeare productions are not easily accessed. Therefore, this intercultural production seems to have given a considerable impact on this small island of poets, and have proved that both *noh* and Shakespeare still have the power to vitalize the local culture.

Shakespeare and *noh*

Then how and when did the fusion of Shakespeare into *noh* ever start? One early example can be when Akira Kurosawa shot his film *Throne of Blood* (the Japanese title was *Kumonosu Jo* or the "Spider Castle"), based on *Macbeth*, in 1957, and used some techniques halfway between *noh* and adventure cinema. *Jiutai*-like chorus was used in the beginning and end in 7-5 rhythm.

In his 1971 interview with film critic Sato Tadao, Kurosawa said that he showed the main actors photographs of *noh* masks he believed that were the image of their roles. Toshiro Mifune (Washizu, equivalent to Macbeth) was shown the mask called *Heita*, the warrior mask, and Isuzu Yamada (Asaji, Washizu's wife) was shown *Shakumi*, the mask for a beautiful woman whose youth is waning. Chieko Naniwa (the witch) was shown the mask of *Yamamba*, the mountain witch. Their make-up was done according to those masks, and *noh* music and *noh*-like *suriashi* movements were used in crucial scenes instead of the poetic language written by Shakespeare. We can say that this Kurosawa film was the first post-World War attempt to borrow *noh* conventions to express Shakespeare's poetic language.

Since the 1970s, there have been attempts to mount *noh* Shakespeare productions by scholar-directors such as Ueda Munakata Kuniyoshi (see Ueda) and Jonah Salz, who created *Noho Gekidan* with the Kyogen actor Shigeyama Sengoro and produced *Ophelia* at Otsuki *noh* Theater, Kyoto, in 1971. Akira Matsui, the *noh* master of Kita School, who had appeared in Jonah Saltz's *Noho Gekidan* from an early stage, can be named as one example of the exceptional professional *noh* actor who has been involved in numerous intercultural performances. His key role in *Ur-Hamlet* (2006), directed by Eugenio Barba at the Kronborg Castle showed how the *noh* style can be fused with the avante-garde adaptation of Shakespeare. In addition, performances on *noh* stage by non-*noh* actors in fusion style are now in vogue, as in the case of Ryutopia Shakespeare series and "Mugen *noh* na Othello" by Ku Nauka in 2005.

Such attempts, however, with a few exceptions, are considered experimental and do not necessarily mean that Shakespeare plays are now included in the repertoire of authentic *noh* plays acknowledged by the association for *noh* actors. Although there have been some new *noh* plays written over the years, the repertoire of *noh* drama has shrunk since the Muromachi period, when there were over one thousand plays, and most of the professional *noh* actors are just busy performing the 200 or so classical pieces that are still frequently played in the style they believe to be the oldest and yet most avant-garde theater style in the world.

The *Noh Macbeth* project

One notable attempt to include Shakespeare in authentic *noh* repertoire is the "*Noh Macbeth* Project": in 2002, Noriko Izumi of Hagoromo University, together with Manjiro Tatsumi, the *noh* master of the Shite family of the Hosho School, launched a project to create a *noh* play based on Shakespeare's *Macbeth.* Izumi, a scholar of Japanese classics and also a semi-professional performer of *noh*, wrote the play in the form of *fukushiki- mugen noh* and Tatsumi created the rhythm and music for the play. The project had its first production at *Sakai Nohgaku Kaikan* Theater on 16 October 2005 and another production at *Osaka Nohgaku Kaikan* Theater on 31 March 2006. A third production was planned for the MOA Museum in the east of Japan, with the Kyogen part supervised by Mansai Nomura. This *shinsaku noh*, fit in well as a traditional style of warrior *noh* in *fukushiki-mugen noh* style and also fused the poetic language of Shakespeare naturally into the language of *noh*. Therefore, this was acknowledged as a new repertoire added to the Hosho school of *noh*.

In all three productions, Tatsumi himself was in the role of the *shite*, the ghost of Macbeth who retells his story to *waki*, a traveling priest. The synopsis is as follows:

> A traveling priest from London loses his way in a misty forest of Scotland. There he meets a man who offers him a night's lodging and is led to an old castle which suddenly appears under the moonlight.
>
> The priest asks his host, who introduces himself as the keeper of the castle, the history of this mysterious building. The keeper says, "This was a castle of the good king Duncan who was killed by Macbeth, his general. Macbeth took the throne and castle and also killed his friend and colleague Banquo. Scotland was in disorder and Macbeth was finally killed by Duncan's son. The castle was abandoned, and I have kept it since then."
>
> However, after he finishes his story, the keeper reveals that he is actually the ghost of Macbeth, and melts into the candle light.
>
> Then appears an odd-looking creature, neither male nor female, announcing "I am the one who ruined Macbeth by drawing out his evil spirit hidden behind his loyal heart."
>
> Next, appears the ghost of Lady Macbeth, who has fallen into the Hell of Solitude. While explaining how she encouraged her husband to murder the king, she rubs her hands, grieving that the blood does not come off. She then disappears, still longing for light, as well as her husband. The odd-looking creature watches all this and laughs at her, telling how easy it is to control the human heart. Then sighting another victim, the creature too disappears in the mist, repeating "fair is foul and foul is fair." The priest understands the real story behind the murder and pitying the souls of Macbeth and Lady Macbeth, starts chanting sutras.
>
> Led by the holy sutra, the ghost of Macbeth appears in full armor, chanting "*shogyo mujo*" ("everything is evanescent"). As the priest suggests to him to confess how he has fallen into the Warrior's Hell, he describes how he killed Duncan and Banquo. He also tells of his glorious days when he bravely fought as the king's loyal general, but then remembers his sin for which he is now punished in hell. He grieves, crying "is this a dream or reality?" when he notices his name being called to attend another battle amidst a desperate war.
>
> Macbeth watches himself losing the battle and being beheaded. He shudders with fear and shame and asks the priest to pray for the salvation of his soul.
>
> Thus, Macbeth disappears, and the priest finds himself amidst a ruin of a castle hid in a deep mist. Only the voice of the grasshoppers is heard in the tranquility, as the priest stands in amazement. (Izumi, translated by Izumi and myself)

One innovation of this new *noh* was to enroll Kyogen actors for "odd-looking creature" (equivalent to the witch) and Lady Macbeth, and therefore adding another dimension to its *Fukushiki-mugen-noh* style. *Kyōgen*, a colloquial interlude to *noh*, though included in *noh*gaku as one genre, seems to have accepted western themes with less trouble than the more formalized and ritualistic style in genuine *noh*. Flexible use of Kyogen actors in addition to the *noh shite* and *waki* actors can be one key to the success of adapting Shakespeare to the style of *noh*.

Kyōgen and Shakespeare

Another *noh*-master and scholar, Masaru Sekine, seems to have been enchanted with the use of the flexibility of Kyogen, when he started seeking the possibility of incorporation Shakespeare in *noh-kyōgen* style. In 2004, Sekine produced *Yopparai no Shikaeshi* (*The Drunkard's Revenge*) and *Sakaino Shonin* (*The Merchant of Sakai*) at the Japanese Culture Center in Rome, with six students from La Sapienza University as the cast. *Yopparai no Shikaeshi*, an adaptation of a subplot of Shakespeare's *Twelfth Night*, was produced in Japanese, while *Sakaino Shonin*, an adaptation of *The Merchant of Venice*, was produced in Italian. Also in 2004, Sekine and his *Roma kyōgen Ichiza* toured to Tokyo, Yokohama, and Kyoto, producing *Yopparai no Shikaeshi* for the Japanese audience; and in 2005 they produced their new play *Koi no Honeori* (*Love's Labor*) in Rome and they produced both *Yopparai no Shikaeshi* and *Koi no Honeori* in Fukuoka, Nagoya, Kyoto, Osaka, Yokohama, and Tokyo.

When asked why he chose *kyōgen*, not *noh*, for his intercultural work with Italian students, Sekine wrote "Why I chose *kyōgen*? Well, the *kyōgen* world may get angry at my honest answer, but it is simply because it is easier (than *noh*). The University of Rome initially asked for a *noh* workshop, but it takes ten years training to get (actors) to look right on stage. Of course, it also takes ten years to have them master a real classical *kyōgen*, but at least we do not need *hayashi* or *jiutai* and they don't have to master *yokyoku*. If I put a classical *kyōgen* on stage, it is up to the skills of the actors whether the audience laughs. But if I put on my own *kyōgen*, I can make people laugh just with the plot of the play. Thus I created *Sekine kyōgen* with *shingeki*-like ideas. That is the difference between a real classical *kyōgen* and my *Sekine kyōgen*, or *Roma kyōgen*" (e-mail letter 14 February 2006; my translation).

It is true that *kyōgen* seems to have accepted Shakespeare with less trouble than *noh*, which is considered a more distinguished form of art. *Kyōgen*, though still considered subordinate to *noh*, has also grown popular as an independent genre after World War II, and in need to challenge new themes, *kyōgen* actors have been challenging incorporating Shakespeare much earlier than *noh* actors.

In his article "On Shakespeare *Kyōgen*," Takashi Sasaki categorizes the Shakespeare *kyōgen* as 1) Shakespeare plays in completely *kyōgen*ized style and language; 2) *kyōgen*-like Shakespeare, or Shakespeare plays with ideas from *kyōgen*; and 3) *kyōgen* Shakespeare in original English (18).

The first category includes the *Shinsaku kyōgen* (newly created *kyōgen*) based on *A Midsummer Night's Dream* and *Twelfth Night* (entitled *Kiiroi Koi*, or *Yellow*

Love), both written and produced by Motohide Izumi in 1990. Those two new *kyōgen*s, together with Miyake Tokuro's adaptation of *The Taming of the Shrew*, were reproduced in August 2005 by his son Motoya and daughters Junko and Shoko .The Izumi family also performed Shakespeare *kyōgen* at the Japan Festival in London in 1991 (*The Taming of the Shrew*, *Twelfth Night* and *A Midsummer Night's Dream*).

The second category of adaptation is not as strictly bound to *kyōgen* style as the first. Typical productions are *Horazamurai* (1992) and *The Kyōgen of Errors* (2001) adapted from *Falstaff* and *The Comedy of Errors* by the English scholar Yasunari Takahashi. This type is written to be produced in a Western theater, not on a *noh kyōgen* stage, and usually has five or six acts, while a real *kyōgen* play only has one or two acts.

The third category is *kyōgen* written in English, using the original Shakespearean text. The target audience is English speaking people or people outside Japan. Together with various adaptations by British and American *kyōgen* specialists, these include works by Motohide Izumi and Yoshio Arai such as "A Love Letter" and "The Lovesick in Yellow," both adapted from *Twelfth Night.*

Where the adaptations of *Twelfth Night* by the Izumi family were just very short skits, in the length of traditional *kyōgens*, Sekine's adaptation was fully developed as drama, using his knowledge of both Japanese and Western classical theater. Sekine made his actors speak in *kyōgen* rhythm and dressed them in kimono, but did not insist on the use of traditional costumes of *kyōgen*. *Yopparai no Shikaeshi* was the adaptation based on a subplot of *Twelfth Night*, with the "drunkard" Sir Toby Belch, called "Yamashiro-no-Kami" in this play, as a hero. The comical revenge on the proud Malvolio was indeed suitable to the subversive nature of *kyōgen*, and though Malvolio's anger in Act V of *Twelfth Night*, which is expressed in the scene when all the characters in the main plot are happily married or re-united, sometimes cast a dark shadow on the otherwise perfect happy ending, the ending of "Drunkard's Revenge," with Malvolio-Taizen chasing Yamashiro-Belch saying *yaru maizo, yaru maizo* and disappearing from the Hashigakari, summed up everything in the familiar *kyōgen* pattern and made the audience laugh with a light heart. *Love's Labor* was based on the theme of Viola in *Twelfth Night*, but was a freer adaptation better classified as a newly created play by Sekine with hints from Shakespeare, *kyōgen*, and Commedia dell'Arte. Sekine's new experiments, relatively free from the constraints of academia or the traditional *noh-kyōgen* world, added another dimension to the intercultural theater.

In June 2008, Sekine started his "Theater Project Si" and produced *Hamlet*, fusing *kyōgen* and Opera. It was a *kyōgen* (comedy) version of Shakespeare's tragedy because it cut most of the subplots and many of the characters and was made into a thirty-minute play, an usual length for a *kyōgen*, and also because professional *kyōgen* players were cast in the role of Hamlet, Ghost of the King, Gertrude, Claudius, Polonius and Laertes. As part of the challenge of merging the East and West, a Japanese opera singer was cast in the role of Ophelia (alias Ayuhime in this production) while the European and American players from the Roma Kyogen

Ichiza, the group Sekine formed for his previous Shakespeare *kyōgen* series appeared as the mousetrap actors for the play-within-the play. Full of the spirit of festivity and enjoyable music, the production seems to have been successful as an entertainment and as an attempt of West-East fusion.

The attempt to blend in the comical essence of *kyōgen* to cast new light on Shakespeare's tragedy was also attempted by Mansai Nomura and Shoichiro Kawai's production of *Kuni Nusubito* (2006). It was an adaptation of *Richard III,* fusing Shingeki and *kyōgen* style with some pop music, showing that this second generation *kyōgen* Shakespeare (Mansai is the son to Mannojo Nomura, who directed and starred in *Horazamurai,* and Kawai is the son-in-law to late Takahashi Yasunari who wrote *Horazamurai* and *Kyogen of Errors*) is less conservative in style and was moving much closer to the attempts by non-*noh*- *kyōgen* actors like Ryutopian *noh* series.

Conclusion

The reception and adaptations of Shakespeare plays in Japan work as a touchstone to indigenous theater and even have worked as the catalyst of creating another local theater genre such as *Okinawa Shibai.* Shakespeare plays have also been a good material to fuse one theater genre to another. Though the traditional *noh* world has been reluctant in its attempt to include Shakespeare in their repertoire, there have been some recent attempts like *Shinsaku noh Macbeth* of the Hosho School. Kyogen actors have been more involved in Shakespeare plays, and the further involvements of professional *noh* actors and *Kumiodori* actors in Okinawa are awaited. The involvement of those authentic actors of traditional theater genres could be crucial to bridge between euphoric and dysphoric intercultural Shakespeare productions.

Works Cited

Brandon, James. "Shakespeare in Kabuki." *Performing Shakespeare in Japan.* Ed. Minami Ryuta, Ian Carruthers, and John Gillies. Cambridge: Cambridge UP, 2001. 33-53.

Feral, Josette. "Beyond the Cultural Perspective toward Transcultural Identities, or Is Interculturalism Possible?" *The IV International Colloquium of Theatre Studies in Tokyo March 26-April 1, 2006.* Ed. Mitsuya Mori. Seijo University, 2006. 33-52.

Izumi, Noriko. *Noh Macbeth* (*Utai bon*). Osaka: Hagoromo International U, 2002.

Sasaki, Takashi. "Kyogen to Sheikusupia kigek ino hikaku kenkyu" ("A Comparative Study of Kyogen and Shakespearen Comedy"). *Sheikusupia to Kyogen:Tozai higeki hikaku kenkyu* (*Shakespeare and Kyogen; Comparative Research in Eastern and Western Comedy*). Ed. Taki Seiju. Tokyo: Shinjusha. 18.

Sato, Tadao. "Interview with Kurosawa." *Shakespeare Kenkyu Shiryo Shusei* (30): 387-90.

Sekine, Masaru. Email to Masae Suzuki. February 14, 2006.

Soseki, Natsume. "Tsubouchi Hakase to Hamuretto." ("Dr. Tsubouchi and *Hamlet*.") *Tokyo Asahi Shinbun*. June 5-6, 1911.

Suzuki, Masae. "Shakespeare in Okinawa." *A Collection of Thesis: International Conference on Shakespeare in China—Performances and Perspectives*. Ed. Shanghai Theater Academy, Hong Kong Baptist University, La Trobe University. Shanghai: Shanghai Theater Academy, 1999. 145-56.

Suzuki, Masae. "Shakespeare Recreated by Tsutsumi Harue." *Journal of Osaka University of Commerce* 109 (1997): 117-38.

Tsutsumi, Harue. *Kabuki Encounters the East: Morita Kan'ya's Shintomi-za Productions, 1878-79*. Dissertation. Indiana University, 2004.

Ueda Munakata, Kuniyoshi. "Some *noh* adaptations of Shakespeare in England and Japanese," *Performing Shakespeare in Japan*. Ed. Minami Ryuta, Ian Carruthers, and John Gillies. Cambridge: Cambridge UP, 2001. 67-77.

Illustrations

The ghost of Macbeth enacts the scene when he kills Duncan (*Noh Macbeth*, Sakai Noh-gaku Kaikan Theater, Osaka, 2005).

The odd-looking creature (equivalent to the three witches) laughs at the ghost of Lady Macbeth who is condemned to the Hell of Solitude (*Noh Macbeth*, Sakai Nohgaku Kaikan Theater, Osaka, 2005).

Samritechak and Intercultural Shakespeare in Cambodia

Kevin J. Wetmore, Jr.

There is, comparatively speaking, not much Shakespeare in Cambodia, certainly not as much as in South and East Asia. There are many reasons for this: first, Cambodia was a French colony, not an English one. From 1863 to 1953, it was French protectorate as part of the colony of *Indochine*, except during a brief occupation by the Japanese during World War II. While the English certainly utilized Shakespeare within their colonies to assert the superiority of British culture and to justify the presence of the Empire, to the French, Shakespeare was *persona non grata*. Instead, French comedies would be presented, mostly Molière, Courteline, Labiche, and Racine, along with French religious plays in Roman Catholic schools, similar to Francophone Africa and Francophone America (see Conteh-Morgan 49-60). Second, European theater in Cambodia was a theater of the elite. Traditional theater remained a favorite of the indigenous masses, although certain traditional theaters, such as court dances, were also reserved for the elite. And both theaters suffered in the 1970s as a result of Cambodia's sociopolitical history. The French and Japanese colonizations were followed by independence on 9 November 1953, resulting in rule by constitutional monarchy under King Norodom Sihanouk. Sihanouk was ousted by military coup in 1970, resulting in the founding of the Républic Khmère, which was itself overthrown in 1975 by the Khmer Rouge. Under Pol Pot, ninety percent of all classical performing artists (including dancers, musicians, actors, and playwrights) were killed. Likewise, practitioners of modern, French-based drama were either driven from the country or killed. Thus, Cambodia has been particularly challenged to preserve traditional forms of theater that the Khmer Rouge attempted to obliterate, to engage in the development, production and consumption of a modern theater, to engage the plays of Shakespeare, and to develop an intercultural theater that combines indigenous traditional theater with texts and elements from external (often Western) cultures. This is not to say that Shakespeare was absent from Cambodia. Ironically, Khieu Thirith, who married Pol Pot's top lieutenant Ieng Sary and is sister of Khieu Ponnary, Pol Pot's first wife, majored in English literature with a focus on Shakespeare at the Sorbonne, where her sister studied Khmer linguistics (see Sambath). It was in Paris that all four met and married before returning to Cambodia. They later would earn collectively the pejorative nickname "the Cambodian Gang of Four," for their similarity to the Chinese group of the same name (see Ana and Doyle). Other elites sent their children to France to study, some of whom encountered Shakespeare in French and English as well. Thus, Shakespeare was presented in Cambodian culture as twice-foreign and elite.

Contemporary use of Shakespeare within Cambodia falls within one of four categories. The first is international tours of Cambodia by foreign companies presenting Shakespeare, often in English and sometimes in French, such as the Royal Shakespeare Company, which has performed several times in Cambodia. Such presentations fall again into the category of both foreign and elite. Second is the educational use of Shakespeare: universities that offer degrees in English such as Royal University of Phnom Pehn and Cambodian Mekong University allow for advanced students to read Shakespeare. Again, such encounters are in the contexts of foreign (Department of English) and elite (in the university). Third is the use of Shakespeare as an outside matrix of interpretation for Cambodian history, often by those from outside Cambodia, such as Hélène Cixous's *The Terrible but Unfinished Story of Norodom Sihanouk, King of Cambodia*. Fourth, and final, is the sole example of Cambodian intercultural Shakespeare thus far, *Samritechak*. In this article, I focus on the latter two as examples of intercultural Shakespeare in Cambodia.

Cixous's *The Terrible but Unfinished Story of Norodom Sihanouk, King of Cambodia* uses Shakespearean narrative as an outside matrix of interpretation for an indigenous story. This strategy imposes Western culture onto Asian history. The play was first performed in Paris in September 1985 at the Thèâtre du Soleil, produced by Ariane Mnouchkine (herself known for intercultural appropriations in producing Shakespeare and Greek tragedy). According to David Williams, *Norodom Sihanouk* "represents a conscious attempt to apprehend and represent contemporary history in the light of a recuperated Shakespearean dramaturgy" (198). In other words, this lengthy play about the rise of and coup against Sihanouk is patterned after the form and structure of Shakespeare's history plays. Sihanouk becomes the equivalent of Henry VI, Richard II, and King John. As Cixous herself writes in the preface to the published English edition of the play, "I just want to follow [Shakespeare's] path" (xvii). In doing so, however, she imposes a Western dramaturgy on an Eastern history. Within the play the characters praise Shakespeare. In part I, act 2, scene 2, Sihanouk names the stars after the ones he loves. His friend Penn Nouth asks him, "And which one is Shakespeare?" Sihanouk does not answer, but asks instead, "Do you like William Shakespeare, Penn Nouth?" The following exchange is very telling in its construction of the importance of Shakespeare in Asia in Cixous's Western mind: "Penn Nouth: As much as our own Royal Chronicles. Don't you admire William Shakespeare, your Grace? Sihanouk: Of course I admire William Shakespeare. But he is a little big. . . . William Shakespeare is immeasurable, like an empire. He is a gigantic giant" (44).

Penn Nouth equates the plays of Shakespeare with the royal history of Cambodia and Sihanouk also admires Shakespeare, but he recognizes the imperialism behind Shakespeare. Cixous thus posits two models of viewing Shakespeare from the point of view of the colonized: his work is seen as either the equivalent of the best in the indigenous tradition, or it is the product of "gigantic giant": something that threatens to overwhelm and conquer indigenous culture, not from its own inherent greatness, but from the force of Western culture behind it, insisting on its own superiority. In other words, it is almost impossible to "like" William Shakespeare because "SHAKESPEARE" is behind the plays. While the play contains what Williams refers to as "self-conscious Shakespeare intertexts," he also notes correctly that Cixous has not "chosen to address the profoundly ironic implications of her choice of model in the context of a play about colonialism and cultural imperialism" (198). Instead, Shakespeare is at the center, a matrix for understanding Cambodia and its king. Not so the adaptation of *Othello* by Sophiline Cheam Shapiro, which represents an attempt to engage this challenge, including preserving traditional forms and developing modern and intercultural theater in contemporary Cambodia. *Samritechak* places Shakespeare's narrative (and none of his language) in the traditional setting and style of Cambodian classical dance drama *robam kbach boraan*. Unlike Mnouchkine's adaptations of Shakespeare, which use the external forms and images of non-Western cultures in order to tell Western stories, Shapiro's play reverses the appropriation and places the foreign story in traditional form. *Robam kbach boraan* is a court dance form (still elite, even if indigenous) that consists of pure dance pieces, of which there are about sixty pieces in the current repertory, and traditionally performed by an all-female company.

Shapiro is part of the first generation of dancers to graduate from the Royal University of Fine Arts (RUFA) after the killing fields. She states in the *Samritechak* program that she considers her first job to be preservation (all references to the *Samritechak* program and uncited quotations about the characters are from the program of the performance at the Carpenter Performing Arts Center at the California State University at Long Beach on 30 January 2003; the Program is unpaginated and contains a note from Shapiro). Her second job, apparently, is "to use the tale as an artistic bridge between Cambodia and the West," so that "Westerners can gain access to traditional Cambodian aesthetics." This goal is also embodied in the person of Shapiro herself, who, classically trained at RUFA, has lived in the United States for over a decade, and has served as a bridge between cultures. Her work has toured throughout the United States, Europe and Asia, including performances in Japan and Hong Kong.

Othello was also a practical and serviceable choice due to its similarities to characters from indigenous narratives. Shapiro was inspired by the similarities between Desdemona and the female characters in Cambodian narratives, in particular the story of Sita, the heroine in the Khmer version of the *Ramayana* whose husband unjustly rejects her on grounds of infidelity. In Shapiro's play Desdemona becomes "Kanitha Devi," a beautiful princess. Iago, represented in Shapiro's play as the angry monkey Virul, is less malevolent than in Shakespeare's play, and often a figure of amusement for the audience, through his tumbling, acrobatics and comic scratching. While not inherently evil, the monkey is a trickster who utilizes one's own weaknesses against one, such as Hanuman, the more heroic trickster monkey in the *Ramayana*. Othello himself is Samritechak, which means "Dark Prince" in Khmer. In an inversion from Shakespeare, the Cambodian moor's face is coated in white makeup—this warrior ruler is marked by his whiteness as a visual reminder of difference. White is also associated with spirit mediumship in Khmer culture, connecting Samritechak's skills as a leader and a warrior with the supernatural world. Samritechak is a *Nguah*, the product of the union between a human and a demon, making him a whole other species than the humans with whom he interacts. He is a giant, although his size is indicated through dance rather than any naturalistic attempt to make the actress taller than the others. Although the adaptation is not faithful to Shakespeare, its story comes from *Othello*. Shapiro's play begins as Samritechak's lieutenant Virul, the "spiteful trickster monkey," witnesses the secret wedding of Samritechak and Khanitha Devi. Played by the company's only male, he is is also the only masked character. All others wear makeup. Following this wedding, Virul tricks Samritechak into believing that Kanitha Devi betrays him, causing him to murder her. Within this broad outline minor plot differences make the cultural differences visible.

Cambodian aesthetics, for example, prohibit showing death on stage and thus Samritechak cannot smother Khanitha. Instead, Samritechak kills her by magic as she dances, pleading for her life. Nor can Samritechak kill himself onstage, as Othello does. Instead, he asks her ghost to name her punishment. She asks him to join her in death, and he magically commits suicide. Shapiro's stated hope is that the Khmer Rouge will see the lesson in the play: as she observed in an interview, the play is about the need to acknowledge guilt and take responsibility for what one does (see Pasles 14). In this sense, as a traditional dance interpretation of a Western narrative, the piece reflects contemporary Cambodia, and Shakespeare becomes the vehicle by which local concerns are addressed, although we must acknowledge the international context of Shapiro's work in the Los Angeles area. There are approximately 55,000 Cambodian expatriates in Long Beach, the largest population of Cambodians outside of Cambodia itself, many of whom came to California fleeing the Khmer Rouge and the subsequent Vietnamese-backed government. When the play was performed in Los Angeles, therefore, the audience had members both familiar with the form and the cultural context as well as those less familiar with Cambodia, but perhaps more familiar with Shakespeare (although it is dangerous in this multicultural age of globalization to make any assumptions about the knowledge of any audience member, regardless of background). There is little spoken text in the performance, as *robam kbach boraan* employs gesture, music, and movement to convey meaning, rather than speech. There is sung narrative, but all lines are performed by the narrator. Thus the transculturation of Shakespeare to a Khmer context is not merely one of finding cultural equivalencies within the story and between the characters and translating from Renaissance English to classical Khmer, but of translation from textual language to physical language. The translation is less linguistic than formal, as Cambodian dance focuses on the beauty of the costumes and the movement of the dancers rather than dramatic tension to appeal to the audience.

Shapiro's adaptation raises the issue of other Asian productions, including films, that transpose the text of Shakespeare in order to fit it, in this case, into the postcolonial world of Southeast Asia. One must ask if Shakespeare without his language is still Shakespeare. For example, how is *Samritechak* not as much an adaptation of Cinthio's "The Unfaithfulness of Husbands and Wives" from *Hecatomithi* (1565), Shakespeare's source for *Othello*, as it is an adaptation of *Othello*? Many scholars, both of Shakespeare and of Asian culture, regard Akira Kurosawa's adaptations of *Macbeth* (*Kumonosu-jo*) and *Ran* (*King Lear*) as the best Shakespeare films in the world. But how much of Shakespeare is actually present in those films, especially if the stories are from Holinshed and the *mise-en-scène* is from pre-modern and early modern Japan? The answer, perhaps, is that *Samritechak* embodies the duality of Shakespeare as at once familiar and foreign. Indigenous performance transforms Shakespeare by using forms that create tension for all viewers, regardless of culture of origin. As Dennis Kennedy argues, even in the West Shakespeare is at once foreign and familiar (145). In the United States and Europe Shakespeare is encountered in a variety of forms in education, literature, popular culture and so on, and is therefore familiar, but the distance of four centuries also makes him unfamiliar. Despite our cultural familiarity with Shakespeare as part of the English literary and theatrical tradition, Shakespeare's texts are another matter. One can argue that despite his presence in the secondary school curricula of nearly every state, Shakespeare is as much a foreigner in the US as elsewhere in the world.

Performed using non-Western performance techniques, Shakespeare's plays are removed even further from the English language and Anglocentric culture. Thus, Kennedy would argue, productions such as *Samritechak* further familiarize Shakespeare to Western audiences by the distancing use of the foreign, which, inversely, is rendered more exotic by its proximity to Shakespeare (145). Yet even this idea is both simplistic and Eurocentric, as in Cambodia it is *robam kbach boraan* that is both familiar and, thanks to the efforts of the Khmer Rouge, foreign as well. As court dance it embodies Cambodian aesthetics, but it is not a form that would have been available to average Cambodians, even before the Khmer Rouge. "*Robam kbach boraan* Shakespeare" is thus a foreign story in a somewhat familiar form to a Cambodian audience and a somewhat familiar story in a foreign form to a Western audience.

There seems to be a need to commodify theater in nations with emerging economies in order to make it accessible to international audiences as a product for tours and invitations to international festivals. Catherine Diamond observes that having seen all the performances of the wide variety of Cambodian dance drama at the Royal University of Performing Arts at Phenom Pehn available for tours outside of Cambodia, the US-American producers preferred *Samritechak*, which was "already headed for the Hong Kong Arts Festival" (148). In other words, traditional Cambodian theater was of less interest internationally than dance drama with the name of Shakespeare attached. This popularity does not rob the individual piece (in this case, *Samritechak*) of artistic or cultural validity. But, as many recent examples demonstrate, too often "intercultural theater" means non-Western productions of Shakespeare using indigenous technique and placing the Shakespeare play in an indigenous context, whether Welcome Msomi's *uMabatha* (a Zulu *Macbeth*), Suzuki Tadashi's *The Tale of Lear*, or O T'ae-sok's Korean *Romeo and Juliet*. It is these pieces that often tour to other nations (as all three of these examples did) for the legitimate reason of greater accessibility, but with the result of obscuring more authentic indigenous narratives. Given all this, however, if Shapiro's objectives have been the preservation of a classical Cambodian dance form and the building of a bridge through which Westerners may experience Cambodian theater (with the added goal of calling on the Khmer Rouge to account for their sins), then *Samritechak* is a success. I would argue, however, that it is also a success at raising the key issues of the primacy of Shakespeare in international theater, intercultural theater as commodity and constructor of identity, and the complex nature of interculturalism in a global village full of immigrants.

Works Cited

Ana, Phann and Kevin Doyle. "Retired Ideals." *The Cambodia Daily* (5 October 2001): <http://www.camnet.com/kh/Cambodia.daily/selected_features/retired_ideal.htm>.

Cixous, Hélène. *The Terrible but Unfinished Story of Norodom Sihanouk, King of Cambodia*. Trans. Juliet Flower MacCamell, Judith Pike, and Lollie Groth. Lincoln: U of Nebraska P, 1994.

Conteh-Morgan, John. *Theater and Drama in Francophone Africa*. Cambridge: Cambridge UP, 1994.

Diamond, Catherine. "Emptying the Sea by the Bucketful: The Dilemma in Cambodian Theater." *Asian Theater Journal* 20.2 (2003): 147-78.

Kennedy, Dennis. "Shakespeare without His Language." *Shakespeare, Theory and Performance*. Ed. James C. Bulman. London: Routledge, 1996.

Pasles, Chris. "'Samritechak' transplants the Bard." *Los Angeles Times* (1 February 2003): Section E.

Sambath, Thet. "Sister No. 1." *The Cambodia Daily* (20 October 2001): <http://www.camnet.com/kh/Cambodia.daily/selected_features/khiev.htm>.

Shapiro, Sophiline Cheam. "Note." Program, *Samritechak*. Long Beach: Carpenter Performing Arts Center, California State U Long Beach, 30 January 2003. n.p.

Turnbull, Robert. "A Khmer Test for *Othello*" *International Herald Tribune* (22 October 2003): n.p.

Wetmore, Kevin J., Jr. "Performance Review: *Samritechak*." *Asian Theater Journal* 22.2 (2005): 348-52.

Williams, David. "Book Review: *The Terrible but Unfinished Story of Norodom Sihanouk, King of Cambodia*." *TDR: The Drama Review* 40.3 (1996): 198-200.

Spectres of *Hamlet* in Colonial and Postcolonial Indonesia

Evan Darwin Winet

On the first of April (Easter Monday) 1619, employees of the Dutch East Indies Company (VOC) performed what may have been the first production of *Hamlet* in Asia. The venue was a warehouse theater: the company's fortified complex of storehouses (*godowns*) just north of the Sundanese town of Jayakerta (see Winet; all English translations from Bahasa Indonesian are the author's own). The Dutch commander, Jan Pieterszoon Coen, had built fortifications around the "Nassau" and "Mauritz" storehouses the previous year. This military escalation of the *godowns* into a *kasteel* precipitated a four-way conflict between the Dutch, the Sultan of Banten, the English (who had also just established an outpost in Jayakerta), and Prince Wijayakrama of Jayakerta, who had allied with the English to strengthen his position vis-à-vis the Sultan. In December 1618, a British fleet surprised the few Dutch ships in the harbor, sending Coen in flight to seek reinforcements in Ambon. The Prince and his English allies proceeded to lay siege to the Dutch *kasteel*. Encircled and outnumbered, the Dutch would have surrendered in January 1619, but were "saved" by the Sultan. Wary of allowing the Prince to nurture a preferential alliance with one European power at the expense of another, the Sultan scattered the Prince's forces and drove the English back to their ships, only to settle down to their own siege of the *kasteel*. Less inclined to surrender to the Sultan than the British, the Dutch held their ground and waited. So things stood on 1 April 1619.

The Dutch players as well as the audience were drawn from approximately three hundred and fifty company employees living in the *kasteel*. Only half of them were actually Dutch. About a fifth of them were slaves. There were slave owners and native concubines; free and enslaved Asians; European merchants, settlers, soldiers, shipwrights, carpenters, sailmakers and other artisans. The non-Dutch included Germans, French, Scots, English, Danes, Flemish, and Walloons. It was, by all reports, a rowdy lot. A court established in 1617 had regularly heard cases of insubordination, blasphemy, brawling, and drunkenness. M.C. Ricklefs described them as "spending their time in a mixture of debauchery and prayer" (30). One anonymous journal from the time of the siege reported "nightly orgies within the Dutch compound, and marriages rowdily celebrated between Company servants and 'black women,' the Reverend Evert Hermans conveniently being one of the company" (Taylor, *The Social World of Batavia* 15). In an exceptional display of hubris, the assembly had determined twenty days previously to name their little *kasteel*, "Batavia," after the Roman name for the founding tribe of the Netherlands (in Dutch nationalist rhetoric, "Batavia" associates the origin of the Netherlands with Tacitus's notion of the noble Germanic primitive; it purports a cultural independence useful to patriotism although inaccurate insofar as there were numerous "founding" tribes in the ancient Rhine delta region. Likewise, the motley VOC contingent in Jayakerta was, through the image of "Batavia," reduced to a strategic Dutch homogeneity). When Coen returned with seventeen ships on 30 May, defeated the British fleet, broke the Sultan's siege, and burned Jayakerta to ashes, this fanciful name was taken for the new Dutch town built on the ruins.

The event of 1 April may not have been a production of *Hamlet*. A brief reference in de Jonge's *De Opkomst van het Nederlandsch gezag in Oost-Indie* (1610-1814) to a play recorded as "van den Conninck van Denemarcken en van den Conninck van Sweden" (153) leaves room for doubt. Dutch theater historian, J.A. Worp, suggests that it was more likely a familiar play by a Dutch playwright, L. van Wassenburgh, called *Historiaal spel van Koningh Reynier van Norwegen ende de schoone Langerte* (first printed in Rotterdam in 1612), but offers no argument other than this play's familiarity. Indeed, the named relation between kings of Denmark and Sweden would seem closer to the story of *Hamlet* than of this other play (amusingly, the second kingdom was recorded as "Sweden" in the original journal entry; whether the play performed was this work by Wassenburgh or Shakespeare's *Hamlet*, the players apparently mistook Norway for Sweden). N.P. van den Berg, who first suggested in 1881 that the play was indeed *Hamlet*, reasons that someone present may have witnessed a production in Europe by a traveling English troupe (*Hamlet* was being performed by such troupes in Germany as early as 1603). For that matter, one of that well-traveled bunch might have witnessed the original London production. There is, however, a possibility more elegant than all of these conjectures. William Keeling, well known to Shakespeare scholars as the eccentric British ship captain who conducted morale-boosting performances of *Hamlet* and *Richard III* off the coast of Sierra Leone in 1607, did so while en route to West Java. His ship docked at Banten in 1609. From there, numerous possibilities emerge as to how *Hamlet* might have traversed the seventy-odd kilometers between Banten and Jayakerta in the ensuing decade. Members of Keeling's crew might have performed again in Banten or in the English camp at Jayakerta and been seen by a later inhabitant of the Batavian *kasteel*. Perhaps a member of Keeling's crew switched employers or perhaps a later Batavian acquired a manuscript of *Hamlet* through one of Keeling's men. If, through any of these means, some version of the play text passed into the Dutch *kasteel*, perhaps it emerged with the new Batavians to the apocalypse of Jayakerta and the birth of a new colonial state.

Presuming that this was indeed the first "colonial" production of Shakespeare in what would become the Dutch East Indies, it does not fit easily into the "canonical discourse" to which postcolonial Shakespeares are imagined typically to run counter. Indeed, there are many aspects of this performance that are arguably already post-colonial. An already heterogeneous, diasporic, transnational population sits under existential threat, first by a coalition of a greater imperial power with a local prince, and then by a greater monarch suppressing the maneuvers of his vassal. A few weeks earlier, the defenders had reached back into their primordial past for a heroic image (Batavia) through which to imagine a more robust present nation than their current degradation would suggest. Now, they took a play by Shakespeare, which for them in this context was not a canonical work from their own national literature, but, rather, a text appropriated from the damnable English. This text they localized undoubtedly in various ways. As in Keeling's shipboard productions, the Batavian production would surely have been multilingual, including the use of Portuguese (then the most common European language in global trade) and, presumably, Dutch. Might a Sundanese woman, the recent wife of some company man, have played Gertrude or Ophelia? The themes of *Hamlet*—burdens of inheritance, duty to kin and nation, search for identity—would all have taken significance within the particular context of a heterotopia awaiting conquest. Perhaps the players saw their own *kasteel* as the embattled Elsinore or perhaps thought of the hapless Prince Wijayakrama, whose treachery to his relative and liege (as that of Claudius to the elder Hamlet), would ultimately bring his small state to ruin. However the topicality of the play may have been parsed, the situation of *Hamlet* fit the moment: a castle caught in a tide of war, spurred on by ghosts and racked by doubt, a fortress shaken by fundamental ontological questions.

According to Indonesian theater historian Jacob Sumardjo, the next recorded production of *Hamlet* in Batavia occurred nearly two centuries later, in 1816 as what would turn out to be the final performance of the Military Bachelor's Theater during the British interregnum. However, this amateur performance by British soldiers was interrupted by a Dutch mob that demolished the bamboo playhouse, apparently in a patriotic display at the news that the Indies would be returned to Dutch rule. The British *Java Government Gazette* referred to these vandals as "mercenaries of Jan Pieterszoon Coen," casting the attack as a reperformance of the founding of Batavia itself (see Sumardjo 90). From this perspective, the British military production of *Hamlet*, which might itself be understood as a more typical "colonial" Shakespeare (universalizing the high culture of the colonizing civilization), precipitates a postcolonial counter-discourse from the Dutch Batavians. Thus the Batavians "deconstruct" *Hamlet* patriotically in violent fashion (Sumardjo 90). Peculiarities of circumstance give these two productions a postcolonial character vis-à-vis Dutch Batavia. There were certainly more typically "colonial" literary and theatrical discourses implemented by the Dutch during their time in Batavia. However, for the reasons demonstrated by these productions, Shakespeare never operated comfortably as part of the culture of the colonizers in the Dutch East Indies. Indeed, when, in the late eighteenth century, Dutch partisans first attempted in earnest to establish a Dutch theater in Batavia, they ran into difficulties that would recur throughout the nineteenth century, and still plague the ongoing struggles to establish an Indonesian theater in Jakarta. Better funded and more professional foreign repertories keep the nationalist repertoire at a disadvantage. In colonial Batavia, this most commonly took the form of French theater and opera troupes against which Dutch thespians constantly struggled to attract audiences and sponsors. French troupes, besides attracting greater cultural prestige with audiences, commanded a reputation as professionals against which Dutch troupes were always seen as amateurs. As one striking indication, the sole theatrical newspaper ever published in the Dutch East Indies, *La Lorgnette* (1875-76), was printed in French. Against military and cultural dominance from the British and the French, Dutch Batavians were marginalized paradoxically even at the center of their own colonial empire. In these two instances, *Hamlet* served as a battleground for that sense of dislocation, marking the difference between Elsinore (and London and Paris) and Batavia.

W.S. Rendra's *Hamlet*

When, after Indonesian Independence in 1950, the Western dramatic canon began to be translated in earnest for newly emerging theater troupes, Asrul Sani and Trisno Sumardjo gained some recognition as translators of Shakespeare. Sumardjo, whose 1950s translations are still regarded as the literary standard used in most Indonesian productions, was almost single-handedly responsible for establishing a reverence for Shakespeare in Indonesian literary circles. His romanticist assessment of *Hamlet* is typical:

> This work of Shakespeare is considered the best drama in all of English literature up to now. Thoughts that are lofty and penetrating, the poet's resources of beautiful language, portraying a time of constant suffering, and above all the extraordinary romantic power of the imagery all combine to give the play a special place in the world of literature. This tragedy consists in the tragedy of an individual filled with ideas, but gloomy and sorrowful, feeble in coming to a decision, and unwilling to fulfill the heavy duty with which he has been charged. Then Hamlet only fulfills his destiny in the final pressing moment, when he himself is beyond all hope. (qtd. in Machdan 557)

However, despite Sumardjo's promotion, the performance records of the Soekarno regime (1950-1966) evince only occasional interest in actually producing these works. W.S. Rendra's more colloquial translations and locally colored productions in the 1970s did promote numerous imitators of "Indonesianized" Shakespeares (e.g., a Balinese *Macbeth*, a Batak *Romeo and Juliet*). Nevertheless, the overall record of Indonesian production, publication, and criticism shows a paucity of specific interest in Shakespeare that challenges the universality of his postcolonial relevance. Bakdi

Soemanto, in one of the more extensive recent Indonesian surveys of Western drama, considers absurdism, *Oedipus*, and realism (in that order), referring to Shakespeare merely for comparison. Saini K.M., another leading New Order theater historian, sandwiches a discussion of *Hamlet* between *Tristan and Isolde* and *Ibsen and Chekhov* in his 1981 monograph on Western drama, *Beberapa Gagasan Teater* (Several Ideas of Theater). There is, in these works, what might appear to Anglophone observers a shocking indifference to our well-rehearsed periodizations and notions of style. It might be seen as an inversion of Orientalist interculturalism, leveling the foreign culture to a banquet of available texts, shorn of complex historical contexts, none of any greater intrinsic value than the others. One young Jakarta-based director suggested to me that the beauty of Shakespeare's poetry is comparable to that of Khalil Gibrain, but that economic considerations preclude frequent production of his plays. With huge casts, and difficult language, they are simply too colossal for most Indonesian theater troupes.

In light of this situation, I focus in this article on three productions of *Hamlet* undertaken by Rendra and his *Bengkel Teater* in 1971, 1976, and 1994. These cannot be seen as representative of Indonesian Shakespeares. On the contrary, they demonstrate a convergence of exceptionalisms: that of a play frequently regarded as beyond the reach of Indonesian troupes, and an actor often lauded (paradoxically) as the singular epitome of modern Indonesian theater, the one actor whose personal mystique has been regarded as commensurate to the role. Rendra began to devote himself to theater in the early 1960s, when he first experimented with intercultural techniques for adapting Western plays. In 1962, for example, he adapted Eugene Ionesco's *Les Chaises* in a work he called *Kereta Kencana* (Golden Chariot). *Kereta Kencana* preserves the basic structure of Ionesco's parable, but fills the imaginative world of the play's elderly couple with imagery more congenial to Rendra's own romantic and mystical palatte and verbal etiquette more closely aligned to Javanese and Indonesian conversation patterns. The culminating suicidal defenestration of *Les Chaises* becomes for Rendra's couple a more mystically optimistic passage. They ascend via a golden chariot, invoking the wondrous chariot of Krishna that carries Prince Arjuna in the *Bhagavadgita*. Although Rendra's theatrical work of this period was not overtly didactic, he did criticize publicly President Soekarno and communism. He was harassed and imprisoned in 1962 and 1963, which apparently influenced him to flee the country. In 1964, he attended an international humanities seminar for anticommunist youth at Harvard University and afterwards attempted to remain in New York City. Fortuitously, Rendra stayed in the United States during the years of Indonesia's bloodiest reckoning, a failed communist coup in 1965, followed by witch hunts that destroyed the party in one of the most terrible genocides of the twentieth century and catapulted General Suharto to power. Rendra studied social sciences and humanities at New York University where he first began to think of art in relation to "structural analysis" and communal activism. At the same time, he received his first (and only) formal theater training at the American Academy of Dramatic Arts. Although American

Method acting had been known in Indonesia since the 1950s, it was here that Rendra first became acquainted with improvisational rehearsal techniques (see Cohen; Gillitt; Winet).

When Rendra returned to Indonesia in 1967, he began to produce a kind of modern theater Indonesia had not seen before: ensemble-based, improvisational, abstract, and theatrical; a theater that privileged action over text, visual over linguistic composition, and the company over the individual actor. Goenawan Mohamad called the style *mini-kata* (minimal word). The bulk of critics saw it as pointing to a significant shift from the literary, realistic Indonesian theater of the 1950s and early 1960s. There are certainly historical affinities between *Bengkel*'s early experiments and the contemporaneous work of Jerzy Grotowski, Peter Brook, and Eugenio Barba. Nevertheless, it would seem that Rendra came to his own methods from the mixture of his training in US-American social sciences and method acting with the Javanese *kampongan* (village, neighborhood) culture of Yogyakarta. This was not so much an imitation of currents in the Western avant garde as an original Indonesian inter-cultural and intra-cultural experiment. Indonesian artists and political activists met the first years of Suharto's presidency in the late 1960s with a great sense of optimism following the political turmoil of the preceding decade. By and large, they expected that Suharto would put the nation back on course towards development and democracy, and Suharto, for his part, seemed eager to inspire confidence in his new regime. The *mini-kata* aesthetic suited such times. It was political, but in an exploratory rather than an ideological mode. It represented what many Indonesians regarded as the enduring political and social question for the nation—that is, how to balance leadership and freedom—without the use of polarizing language. Rendra came to be regarded as an artistic prophet. In this extraordinary transitional moment, people in Yogyakarta claimed him as "our Rendra," scholars praised him as a cultural hero, and, in 1969, the Indonesian government presented him with a National Arts Award.

However, by the early 1970s, it became clear to progressive students that Suharto had assumed a familiarly paternalistic and authoritarian stance, and was settling into the role of a latter day Javanese king. They began to demonstrate against the same sorts of political and economic abuses and "prestige projects" they had seen under Soekarno. In particular, the construction of the *Taman Mini* amusement park on the Southern outskirts of Jakarta and the open manipulation of the first post-Soekarno election in 1971 convinced many student activists that the new regime was not committed to improving the plight of the poor. Rendra allied himself with the student movement and its critique of Suharto. Once again, so soon after being hailed at all levels of society as a cultural treasure of the nation, Rendra found himself at odds with official state nationalism. He was first detained briefly in 1970 for taking part in a "night of prayer for the nation," beginning a new period of police harassment. Such were the conditions as Rendra entered the most productive period of his career, from around 1971 to 1978; a period during which he produced his most acclaimed work and the government increasingly harassed him, banning him from performance in Yogya (1973) and ultimately throughout Indonesia (1978).

Rendra staged *Hamlet* twice during this period: once in 1971 and then again in 1976. The 1971 staging reflected the simple, contemporary aesthetics of *mini-kata*. A setting characterized primarily by green and orange acting areas and with an ordinary wooden chair standing for the throne. Claudius wore a simple star on his chest to signify his rank, the Queen wore a simple contemporary nightgown, and Ophelia dressed like a contemporary Indonesian student. Rendra, in the role of Hamlet, wore blue jeans and a sweater, looking like a student, or as if he had just come from one of his own poetry readings. What impressed the critics (and apparently audiences) most about this production, however, was a liberal use of colloquial dialect (especially Javanese words). Many critics, no doubt raised on Sumardjo's literary translations, were shocked and reacted like British conservative writers reviewing some avant garde outrage. Audiences found the production entertaining, prompting some critics to denounce Rendra's lack of gravity and others to praise him for bringing the modern theater closer to such populist genres as *lenong*, *ludruk*, and *kethopra*—a connection heightened by the fact that it had been staged in the open amphitheater of the Taman Ismail Marzuki (TIM) arts complex.

The 1976 staging was different in many respects. It played for two nights (rather than three, as previously) in TIM's Closed Theater (a medium-sized proscenium stage)—a much smaller audience in a more intimate and controlled environment supporting a more carefully composed *mise-en-scène*. Indonesia's eminent scenic designer, Roedjito, used bamboo scaffoldings, ten blocks, and multicolored lights to create numerous specific delineated acting areas. One reviewer described it as reminiscent of a traditional *wayang orang* stage mixed with contemporary elements. Likewise, the costuming was more suggestive of Javanese traditional garb and Rendra himself (again as Hamlet) wore the batik *kain* (wrapped cloth) of an aristocrat from the Javanese traditional stage. A *gamelan* and *gending* ensemble led by Rendra's spouse, Sunarti, provided music (whereas the previous production had featured an ensemble singing Simon and Garfunkel tunes). Various explanations might be given for this different approach. One significant factor, however, was that between 1971 and 1976, government pressure on Rendra had increased such that he had become more careful to frame his social criticism within traditional culture. Whereas in October 1971 he had held a meditation and improvisation workshop at Parangtritis beach explicitly as an alternative to the absent civil society of Suharto's regime, his 1975 play, *Struggles of the Naga Tribe*, had adopted the frame of *goro-goro* (clown scenes) from the *wayang* shadow theater to defend against anticipated censorship. In the play within a play scene (III:ii), for example, the king asks, "Isn't this play of yours dangerous?" to which Hamlet/Rendra replies, "This play clearly is not dangerous, Sire. It's nothing but shadows. Only make-believe. Just look, the one who plays the king just feigns kingliness, the one who plays an adviser just gives pretend advice. Also that throne is just a play-throne. So, it's no problem, man! (*enggak berbahaya dong*)."

After 1978, Rendra's credentials as an oppositional figure lost some of their luster. After the performance ban against him was lifted in 1985, a prominent investor, Djody Setiawin, sponsored *Bengkel*'s relocation to Depok, a relatively upscale community on the outskirts of Jakarta. Many critics and old admirers judged Rendra hypocritical for accepting the aid of an investor and moving into an exclusive development (Depok itself epitomizes Rendra's contradictions; the town has enjoyed a certain privileged position in relation to colonial and subsequent postcolonial governments; Cornelis Chastelein, whose estate encompassed Depok, freed his slaves and bequeathed them the grounds in the early seventeenth century and the slaves became landlords and in 1871 were even granted a degree of administrative autonomy from Batavia; today, as site of the main branch of the University of Indonesia and three other universities, Depok has a large student population and it is an elite, yet marginal community within metropolitan Jakarta yet at its periphery). However, in 1991 Rendra moved a little further out from Depok to the village of Cipayung where he re-established a *padepokan* (training compound) for *Teater Bengkel*. Since then, new *Bengkel* recruits have trained and worked on the extensive grounds while numerous old *Bengkel* actors have settled nearby, partially transforming *kampong* Cipayung into *kampong Bengkel*. Meanwhile, a period of self-censoring depoliticization of the arts accompanying the New Order's height in the early 1980s started to change by the end of the decade. A growing Indonesian middle class began clamoring for greater freedoms and real civil society. Suharto, responding to Gorbachev's *glasnost*, declared *keterbukaan* in 1990. Artists began immediately testing this "openness" and some censorship and performance bans followed. The hollowness of *keterbukaan* was disheartening, but many artists kept pushing. From the early 1990s to Suharto's resignation in May of 1998, such theater artists as Emha Ainun Nadjib, Ratna Sarumpaet, and Butet Kartaredjasa gave voice to a growing consensus of dissatisfaction with the regime and called for reform and real democracy. Despite the doubts against him, Rendra was very much a part of this movement when he staged *Hamlet* a third time in 1994.

The 1971 production had been striking for its colloquial language and the 1976 production for its more extensive Javanization, each of these an early example of approaches that would become commonplace to staging Western drama in Indonesia. The 1994 production, however, heralded a new trend in corporate sponsorship that had previously been seen only with Teater Koma, then as now Jakarta's most commercially successful company). Rendra's 1994 *Hamlet* was sponsored by *Djarum* clove cigarettes, marketed through a special-edition cigarette packet with an image of Rendra in the starring role. The economics of theater production had changed in the intervening years, with government subsidy for the arts minimal and rental costs for rehearsal and performance space in Jakarta on the rise. *Hamlet* played for five performances at TIM's Graha Bhakti Budaya (a large proscenium space) at a cost of 150 million rupiah, at that time one of the most expensive productions ever staged. This expense, did not, however, translate to elaborate design. Setting and costumes were as simple, if not more so, than before. The setting was simply a series of platforms providing acting areas at different levels. The costuming suggested a greater mixing of styles than in previous productions. Rendra (as Hamlet, of course) was once again in blue jeans, but was also the only character to carry a *kris panjang* (a long sword believed to channel mystical princely power), indicating (as Radha Panca Dahana suggests) his connection with traditional Javanese society. Claudius (like Gertrude and the rest of the court) wears a mix of Betawi, Javanese, and contemporary Western upper class garb, but instead of a scepter, wields a military crop—an indication that he is an army man, like Suharto, but also reminiscent of the crop Soekarno habitually brandished. The radical student still rooted in Javanese tradition opposes the military dictator who has no authentic connection to the people.

One thread running through reviews of all three productions is the force and unique authority of Rendra in the role of Hamlet. There is an awareness, implicit and sometime explicit, of the role of Hamlet as the ultimate test for Western actors, and hence of Rendra's attempt as the ultimate test of how Indonesia's best actor measures up. Asrul Sani had written, in the introduction to his 1960 translation of Richard Boleslavsky's *Acting: The First Six Lessons*, that the Indonesian postcolonial actor encounters the difference between these canonical Western roles and his own experience, and in this very difference finds the substance for a new modern identity as an Indonesian. Rendra, likewise, had filled the role of Hamlet with his own existential doubt and humor, and located the role in his own habitus as modern Western-educated youth (in 1971 and 1994) and traditional Javanese man (1976 and 1994). In the 1994 production, however, the additional element of his advanced age added a new dimension of complexity and difference between actor and role. Reviewer E.H. Kartanegara describes the image of Rendra in the role with some trepidation: "Rendra's chubby body, his sluggish movements, the furrowed skin of his face (remember, Brother, Rendra is already 58), reveal some difficulty at portraying the seething soul of Hamlet, who is surely just in his twenties. . . . The face of Hamlet-Rendra now has more the kneaded (*lenjeh*) look of a 'native.' Putting on his bell-bottom jeans and jacket, sometimes wearing an *overcoat* (like a New Yorker in December), juxtaposed with a *keris* (Javanese sword) and fan, the meaning of which is unclear" (631). For some reviewers, however, this complexity adds another dimension of political meaning to the portrayal. For Hari Prasetyo, this Hamlet is simultaneously Danish noble, Javanese revolutionary aristocrat, and contemporary middle class, all looking for a way out of their social cages (627). Muji Sutrisno goes further to see this last *Hamlet* as Rendra's depiction of widespread Indonesian social stagnation. In these latter days of Soeharto's Indonesia, the aging actor dons paradoxically the blue jeans of youth and takes up the traditional Javanese sword, warning Indonesian society to shake off its "Hamletization" and recover its progressive culture (qtd. in "Rendra, Hamlet, Dan Penyadaran" 624).

Postcolonial artists and critics have often looked to Shakespeare's disenfranchised Black men, Caliban and Othello, and their marginal realms as sites of anticolonial resistance. However, there is a more intimate disenfranchisement available in the figure of Hamlet and a complex site of resistance Elsinore. There is Elsinore as the *kasteel* and town of Jayakerta / Batavia / Jakarta, a palimpsest of loss poised ever between existential crisis and the imagination of a nation built on the ruins, reaching back to some enabling spectre from a nobler time. There is the disenfranchisement of a prince approached by his usurping uncle, who calls him "cousin" and "son."

Hamlet knows, as did Rendra, that he can never truly claim a place in a family built on such violence, on such suppression of the ghosts of his fathers. He has inherited a richness of cultural, political and intellectual traditions, which he wears in a clashing *gado-gado* (mixed salad) of styles. And yet, what power does he have in this endless "out of joint" postcolonial moment, to "set things right"? From the kings in Jakarta and London and elsewhere, he has been guaranteed equal human rights, but systematic limits on change and his own lack of stamina to fight for change ensure a comfortable stagnation. To those in power in Indonesia, the represented people remain "a little more than kin and less than kind."

Works Cited

Boleslavsky, Richard. *Enam Peladjaran Pertama Bagi Tjalon Aktor* (Six First Lessons for the Student Actor). Trans. Asrul Sani. Jakarta: PT Jaya Sakti, 1960.

Cohen, Matthew Isaac. "Timely Art: An Interview with Rendra." *International Institute for Asian Studies Newsletter* 19 (1999): 22-23.

Dahana, Radhar Panca. *Ideologi Politik Dan Teater Modern Indonesia* (Political Ideology and Modern Indonesian Theatre). Magelang: Indonesiatera, 2001.

Gillitt, Cobina Ruth. *Challenging Conventions and Crossing Boundaries: A New Tradition of Indonesian Theatre from 1968-1978*. Doctoral Diss. New York: New York U, 2001.

Java Government Gazette (16 August 1816).

Jonge, Johan Karel Jakob de, Marinus Lodewijk van Deventer, Leonard Wilhelm Gijsbert de Roo, Pieter Anton Tiele, J.E. Heeres, Johannes Jacobus Meinsma, J.W.G. Haarst. *De Opkomst Van Het Nederlandsch Gezag in Oost-Indie* (The Rise of Dutch Power in the East-Indies). Gravenhage: M. Nijhoff, 1862.

Kartanegara, E.H. "Hamlet 'Pribumi' Di Antara Dengkuran Penonton" (A 'Native' Hamlet Amongst Grunting Spectators). *Menonton Bengkel Teater Rendra* (Watching Rendra's Bengkel Theater). Ed. Edi Haryono. Yogyakarta: Kepel P, 2005. 630-32.

Machdan, Umar. "Nonton 'Hamlet'nya Rendra" ("Watching Rendra's *Hamlet*"). *Menonton Bengkel Teater Rendra*. Ed. Edi Haryono. Yogyakarta: Kepel P, 2005. 557-59.

Prasetyo, Hari. "*Hamlet*: Menonton Rendra Dan Perjalanannya" ("*Hamlet*: Watching Rendra and His Journey"). *Menonton Bengkel Teater Rendra.* Ed. Edi Haryono. Yogyakarta: Kepel P, 2005. 627-29.

"Rendra, Hamlet, Dan Penyadaran" ("Conversation with Muji Sutrisno"). *Menonton Bengkel Teater Rendra*. Ed. Edi Haryono. Yogyakarta: Kepel P, 2005. 623-26.

Ricklefs, M.C. *A History of Modern Indonesia since C. 1200*. Stanford: Stanford UP, 2001.

Saini, K.M. *Beberapa Gagasan Teater* (Some Theatrical Principles). Bandung: Nurcahaya, 1981.

Soemanto, Bakdi. *Jagat Teater* (The World of Theater). Yogyakarta: Media Presindo, 2001.

Taylor, Jean Gelman. *The Social World of Batavia: European and Eurasian in Dutch Asia*. Madison: U of Wisconsin P, 1983.

Van den Berg, N.P. "Het Tooneel Te Batavia in Vroegeren Tijd" ("The Theatre of Batavia in Former Times"). *Uit de Dagen Der Compagnie* (In the Days of the Company). Haarlem: H.D. Tjeenk Willink & Zoon, 1904. 97-191.

Winet, Evan Darwin. "Interpolations of American Method Acting in 1950s Indonesia." *Journal of Dramatic Theory and Criticism* 18.1 (2003): 89-106.

Worp, Jacob Adolf. *Geschiedenis Van Het Drama En Van Het Tooneel in Nederland* (History of Drama and Theatre in the Netherlands). Groningen: Wolters, 1904.

Remembering the Past in the Shanghai Jingju Company's *King Lear*

Elizabeth Wichmann-Walczak

In the wake of China's occupation by Western powers in the nineteenth century and defeat at the hands of her former vassal Japan, many Chinese intellectuals believed that only by learning from the West could China successfully stand up to the West. In the performing arts, this led to the study and performance of Western plays in Western styles. Plays based on Shakespearean plots were first given amateur productions by college students in the early twentieth century, and Chinese theater professionals began staging such plays in 1913 (Ruru Li, *Shashibiya* 18). These intellectual artists were dedicated to creating a new, "civilized theater" (*wenming xi*) that was based on Western dramatic and theatrical craft and could ultimately replace or at least stand in bold contrast to the more than 300 forms of China's own and primarily popular theater *xiqu*, a term often rendered in English as "Chinese opera" (it should be noted that opera, a separate concept in Chinese [Geju], is a misleading term for the range of theatrical techniques that distinguish these forms). Because these artists had very little exposure to any theater other than *xiqu*, their performances generally exhibited at least some of *xiqu*'s characteristics; nonetheless, they strove for modern, Western staging, and certainly did not want their productions to resemble *xiqu*, let alone intentionally represent a specific form of *xiqu*. As "civilized theater" developed into the more fully realistic *huaju* ("spoken drama," a major Chinese theater form today), Shakespearean production remained generally within its sphere; of the thirteen known professional productions of Shakespearean translations and adaptations in the 1930s and 40s, only two were mounted by *xiqu* companies, and those only at the very end of that period: a *yueju* (Yue or Shaoxing "opera") adaptation of *King Lear* in 1946 and a *jingju* (Beijing "opera") adaptation of *Romeo and Juliet* in 1948. But this circumstance changed after the Cultural Revolution. Between 1983 and 2003, eleven of Shakespeare's plays were adapted for twenty-three different productions in fifteen different forms of *xiqu,* with some productions restaged several times. *Macbeth* was adapted most often, with six separate productions. *Romeo and Juliet* and *The Merchant of Venice* were each adapted three times, and *Twelfth Night*, *The*

Merry Wives of Windsor, and *Lear* were each adapted twice. Three of these adaptations were for the *jingju* form: *Othello* (1983), *Macbeth* (1986), and *Lear* (1995) (Ruru Li, *Shashibiya* 234-40).

There are several reasons for the interest in adapting Shakespeare to *xiqu* during this twenty-year period. Beginning in the early 1980s, audiences for *xiqu* declined progressively as television, film, popular music, and other aspects of China's modernization became more widely available; at the same time, government support for the arts steadily decreased. This combination of circumstances created a crisis for *xiqu*, compelling artists and cultural officials to seek means of revitalizing the various forms and drawing new audiences for them (for a more detailed discussion of this, see Wichmann, "Tradition and Innovation"; Wichmann-Walczak). Shakespeare was recognized as a renowned Western author performed throughout much of the world; productions based on his plays offered prestige and an international cachet and were therefore a potential draw for both audiences and funding. Because some of the circumstances and actions found in Shakespeare's plays have no standard *xiqu* conventions for their portrayal, innovations in performance were needed and it was believed that such innovations also had the potential to draw new audiences. The possibility of invitations to tour abroad may also have influenced some theater companies to mount adaptations of Shakespeare. But the plays themselves were without question a major impetus. During the 1980s and 1990s, Shakespeare's plays were perceived in China as antifeudal and procapitalist. Since capitalism is seen as a necessary step on the way to socialism and then communism, the plays were considered politically neutral and thus "gave Chinese directors an opportunity to impose their own aesthetic and intellectual ideas" (Ruru Li, "The Bard" 75). And because in addition to his international renown, Shakespeare was regarded as "one of the favorite writers of both Marx and Engels," Chinese directors could act with "less risk of offending Marxist ideology as a whole" (Ruru Li, "The Bard" 75; for more on the purposes behind *xiqu* adaptations of Shakespeare in general and in several specific instances, as well as other aspects of Chinese Shakespeare productions in various *xiqu* forms, see also Diamond; Huang; Ruru Li, "Chinese Traditional;" Li and Jiang; Zhang).

The decision to stage a particular Shakespearean adaptation is generally based on at least some of the above reasons, as well as other considerations specific to the theater company staging the play. This is true of the Shanghai Jingju Company's early 1990s decision to mount an adaptation of *King Lear*. It was originally planned as the company's offering for the national celebration of the hundredth anniversary of the professional careers of Mei Lanfang, a renowned male performer of *dan* (young female) roles, and Zhou Xinfang, a renowned male performer of *laosheng* (older male) roles; the Lear role was to have been performed in Zhou's style and the Cordelia role in Mei's style. The stature of Shakespeare was felt appropriate to the statures of Mei and Zhou, and the company was very interested in pursuing innovations in performance. An initial script was written and explored in rehearsal, but this production did not materialize, reportedly because of the difficulty of applying the Zhou style to the performance of a character based on Lear (interview, Shang, 3 December 1995; translations of this and subsequent interview texts are mine). Later on, however, the Shanghai Jingju Company mounted and performed a version of *King Lear* using different approaches and conceptions. Throughout the 1990s, the Shanghai Jingju Company concerned itself with what its leaders termed "audience-ology" (*guanzhongxue*)—defining target audiences and creating new plays specifically for them. Company leaders felt that an innovative *jingju* play adapted from *King Lear* would appeal to the urban intellectual audience, which included cultural and educational officials and workers (such as writers, artists, university students, and faculty). They therefore did not want to drop the *Lear* project (interview, Li Zhongcheng, 8 May 1996). Company leaders were also concerned with convincing central government cultural officials to recognize their star performer, *hualian* ("painted-face" or bravura male role) actor Shang Changrong, as having created his own *liupai* (school or style of performance). The officials in Beijing had provided a list of conditions for that status, which included the creation of more than just a few leading roles in original plays that were retained in the permanent repertory of the company (*baoliu jumu*), the ultimate measure of success (interview, Li Zhongcheng, 7 December 1995). Shang already had created several such roles, including Cao Cao in the national-award-winning *Cao Cao and Yang Xiu* and it was felt that the Lear role in a *King Lear* adaptation, once rewritten and composed for a *hualian* rather than a *laosheng* lead, would make a compelling addition (interview, Li Zhongcheng, 8 May 1996). This new adaptation, known as *Qi Wang Meng* (*Dream of the King of Qi*), went through two separate creative processes: the first culminated in performances presented in Beijing in December 1995 as part of a five-production showcase of original works, and the second in performances at the Shanghai International Arts Festival in May 1996 (I was able to observe the last month of rehearsals for the former, the full six-weeks of rehearsals for the latter, and the performances of both).

With the aim of enriching the creative process through approaches and techniques from outside the company and *jingju* itself (interview, Li Zhongcheng, 7 May 1996), nationally known artists from other companies were invited to work on writing and staging *Qi Wang Meng*. The primary author was *huaju* playwright Wang Lian of Beijing and the chief director was initially *huaju*-based director Ouyang Ming of Wuhan, since *huaju* techniques and approaches were believed to have considerable modernizing potential for *jingju*. Wang Lian was assisted by company playwright Wang Yongshi and during the second creative process company director Ma Ke took over as director, assisted by Ouyang. Instrumental music outside the context of arias was composed by invited symphonic composer Gu Guanren of Shanghai, while the arias themselves were composed by company composer Gao Yiming working closely with Shang and the other leading singer-actors.

A few adaptations of Shakespeare to the *xiqu* stage have retained European settings, character names, and cultural behaviors, including the Beijing Experimental Jingju Company's *Othello* (initially staged in 1983 and restaged in 1986 and 1987), and the Shanghai Yueju Company's *Twelfth Night* (1986) (see Ruru Li, *Shashibiya*

161-96). But by far the most common method is to reset the play in an imaginary ancient Chinese kingdom. This approach, nonhistorical yet based on Chinese cultural norms, is believed to make productions more accessible to *xiqu* audiences, since playwrights and directors can modify cultural behaviors to prevent misunderstanding and create credibility. Additionally, designers can employ aspects of traditional *xiqu* costuming so that actors can use the full vocabulary of *xiqu* movement styles and techniques, many of which involve the manipulation of specific costume parts. This Sinicized approach was followed for Shanghai's *Qi Wang Meng*, set in the nonhistorical kingdom of Qi. As the written-character for "*qi*" means "fork, branch" as well as "divergent, different," the name has thematic connections to Shakespeare's *King Lear*, while also implying that the circumstances are not those of traditional Chinese culture.

It is widely accepted in China that Shakespearean plays are too long to be staged in their entirety in most forms of *xiqu*, including *jingju*. The arias, stylized speech and movement, and acrobatics of *jingju* require too much stage time to allow a full adaptation incorporating all the characters and subplots. Indeed, as Ruru Li points out, seventeenth-century playwright and theorist Li Yu "stressed the importance of 'trimming the threads' in [a] plot, and of focusing on 'one person and one thing throughout [a *xiqu*] play'" (*Shashibiya* 115). Having a single main character and a single-plot story line is not an absolute requirement. For instance, *Cao Cao and Yang Xiu* and some other new and traditional plays have two central characters and one or even two minor subplots. But this admonition is based in the traditional performance context and structure of most forms of *xiqu*. Historically, actor-managers were the main draw of commercial companies, so plays were created to feature them. And perhaps as a result, major scenes in most *xiqu* plays generally follow an emotional-progression structure (*cengcixing buju*) in which the major character experiences a series of emotional states in reaction to developments in the basic situation, and by way of expressing those states the actor playing that character can exhibit his or her mastery of *xiqu*'s four complex performance skills: song, speech, dance-acting, and combat (for more information on these performance skills, see Wichmann, *Listening to Theatre* 18-24). Plot structure and exposition in this traditional context can be compared to the chain of a necklace, with the arias, speeches, and movement sequences like a series of emotionally-expressive jewels suspended from it. The chain of exposition connecting them should be beautiful, but the jewels are clearly the main features. A streamlined plot, with focus on the main character, is therefore the structure most appropriate for the creative process and performance of *xiqu*.

In creating this characteristic *xiqu* structure for *Qi Wang Meng*, the characters and subplots of *King Lear* have been substantially reduced. Most significantly, two major characters, the earl of Gloucester and his son Edgar, have been cut entirely, along with all subplots connected with them. Edmund, now Shangguan Meng and no longer Gloucester's bastard, is an ambitious courtier in the Qi King's court; after the King divides his kingdom in two, Shangguan is more intent than Edmund on seducing the King's two elder daughters to achieve power. The Fool remains but is a young pre-teen boy played by a young woman. As in Shakespeare's original, the eldest daughter Chunying (spring child) is married to Kang Yong (the duke of Cornwall, now an incompetent alcoholic). Xiaying (summer child), the second daughter, is married to Ao Sheng (the duke of Albany), whom she regards as an "old book worm." The third daughter, Xueying (snow child; *xue* can also mean "to wipe out a humiliation" and "to right or avenge a wrong"), is claimed as wife by the good King of the non-historical kingdom of Bailize ("many *li* of abundant rivers and lakes"), who, unlike the King of France in the original, is killed by Shangguan when he attempts to rescue the King of Qi. As in Shakespeare's play, Kun Fu (Kent) is banished for supporting Xueying but continues to serve the King of Qi in disguise and the two older sisters refuse to house their father, then plot against and finally kill one another. Xueying arrives without her husband much earlier than in the original and accompanies the King into the wilderness. With Kun and the Fool she then witnesses the King's mock trial of his elder daughters.

Primarily because of perceived cultural clashes (interview, Wang, 11 November 1995), two more substantial changes were made in the basic story line, one at the very beginning and the other at the end of the play. It was widely believed by the playwrights, directors, and principal actors that for the King of Qi to disinherit his favorite daughter only because she refused to flatter him excessively was unbelievable, at least in the context of Confucian culture. Xueying therefore is not only mild in her sung statement of love for the King, but also expresses doubt about the appropriateness of the King giving up the throne in his own lifetime and dividing a nation that should be whole. The King is furious that she dares to give him advice in public, while Kun and the King of Bailize admire her wisdom and courage. The end of the play then stresses the King of Qi's willful disregard of good advice. Once he regains his senses, the King allows the devious Shangguan to convince him to return to court, believing that Shangguan will reinstate him as king in spite of Kun's urgent advice to the contrary. Shangguan then imprisons the King and kills Xueying in front of her father. Shangguan does not repent as Edmund does in Shakespeare's play and Xueying's death does not take place off stage. And the final moments of the play not only differ from but are essentially unrelated to Shakespeare's original. In chains, the King tells Shangguan that he cannot truly be king without the jade seal of office and speaks so softly about its whereabouts that Shangguan must lean over him to hear; the King then wraps his chains around Shangguan's neck and strangles him. At least in some measure, the King thereby rights the wrongs that have been done to him and avenges his daughter to expiate the wrong he did to her.

This story line is structured in seven scenes. 1) "Dividing the Nation" (*Fen Guo*) is set in the Qi court. 2) "Enduring Frustration" (*Shou Cuo*) is set in the palace of Chunying and Ao Sheng, which the King of Qi leaves in anger. 3) "Suffering Disgrace" (*Zao Ru*) takes place in the palace of Xiaying and Kang Yong, from which the King is expelled. 4) "Solitary Indignation" (*Gu Fen*) is set on a bleak plain during a thunderstorm; it features the King, who sings of his indignation and ultimately goes mad. 5) "Mad Trial" (*Feng Shen*) is set in the wilderness. 6) "Mutual Cruelty" (*Xiang Can*) is set in Xiaying and Ao Sheng's palace and concludes with the mutual murders of the two elder sisters. 7) "Dream Destroyed" (*Meng Hui*) takes place first in the wilderness and then in the Qi court dungeon.

Li Zhongcheng, an award-winning playwright and the executive director of the Shanghai Jingju Company, explains that in creating a new *jingju* production, it is critical to assure that the production will in fact be *jingju* ("Beijing opera"), and that this requires: 1) melodies that are composed in the musical language of *jingju*; 2) speech that has "musical flavor" (*yunwei*), even when it is not in the heightened "musical speech" (*yunbai*) style; and 3) many specific methods and techniques of performance (*shouduan*) from both *jingju* and other forms of *xiqu* (interview, 7 May 1996). He stresses that for the Shanghai company, aria music (*changqiang*) should be fundamentally traditional; that innovative changes and additions should be made only for special character expression and not just for show; and that even then they must not exceed the parameters of *jingju*. In his view, the more innovation carried out in other areas—such as subject matter, costumes, scenery, lighting, and orchestral instrumentation—the more traditional the aria music needs to be for a play to be acceptable to Shanghai audiences (interview, 7 May 1996).

Innovation in areas other than aria music was in fact a major part of the creative work on *Qi Wang Meng*. The stylized but essentially realistic set appeared sumptuous for the court and palace scenes, eerie and dangerous for the plains and the wilderness, and oppressive for the dungeon, in contrast to *jingju*'s traditional, nonrealistic stage. Nonetheless, it provided large, open playing spaces for every scene, distinguishing it from its realistic Huaju counterparts, as well as from the often cluttered, realistic sets in many new *jingju* productions of the period. In several instances, lighting was used in modern and nontraditional (for *jingju*) ways. It contributed substantially to the creation of atmosphere in all scenes and especially to the violence of the storm and the claustrophobic nature of the dungeon.

Director Ouyang Ming designed the costumes himself based on archeological discoveries from the Zhou Dynasty's Spring and Autumn period (BCE 770-476). In order to do so, he conducted research in thirteen separate museums over a period of several months (interview, 13 November 1995). His designs differed from traditional *jingju* costumes, although I think they were not particularly unusual for *huaju* costumes at the time, and gave an interesting historical feel to the visual production. They did not employ watersleeves, which meant that associated techniques could not be used. They did, however, provide kimono-like sleeves, cloaks, and other garment features that allowed for the use of many other types of costume-based traditional movement.

Shang Changrong designed his own *lianpu* (elaborate, "painted-face" makeup in which color and design have conventional significance) for the King of Qi, as is standard for leading *hualian* actors. His design consisted of a ruddy although not shiny-red face, an especially tall *tongtianpao* ("reaching heaven explosion," a tall, narrow triangle with its base between the eyes and its point at the top of the forehead) painted in matte white and outlined in gold and silver, and eyebrows of the same colors. The nontraditional eyebrows were each composed of three almost vertical strokes above the eye joined at the lower ends, with the tops leaning slightly toward the outside of the face, thus creating a crown-like brow and the effect of kingly wisdom and rash impetuosity. In *lianpu* designs, matte white indicates cruelty; red, loyalty and courage; and silver and gold, royalty or divinity. The *tongtianpao* represents masculine strength and when especially prominent like the one Shang designed, a martial nature. The face Shang created for the King suggested a martial hero of royal status with a tendency to rashness that harms others, expressed through the innovative use of traditional *lianpu* language.

Working with two *jidao* (technique directors), specialists in adapting and applying the physical techniques of *jingju* to productions of new plays, the directors and actors used their traditional combat skills in new martial interpretations in several specific scenes, and their traditional dance-acting skills in new contexts throughout the play (dance-acting, *zuo*, consists of all the visible results of acting in the Western sense, from facial expression to gesture to stylized dance-like movement through space). In doing so they created a number of innovative movement sequences for the production of *Qi Wang Meng*. One of the most difficult to develop was a wordless conversation between Shangguan and Xiaying in which the dynamics of hatching a plot—one talking while the other listens, one disagreeing and then being persuaded—were conveyed through the carefully controlled movements of their *lingzi*, the two yard-long feathers worn in the headdress of a military officer. While precise manipulation of individual *lingzi* through small head, neck, and torso movements is a technique used by *xiaosheng* (young male role) actors in traditional plays such *Lü Bu and Diaochan*, it is not part of the training for *daomadan* (a type of martial female role) or *laosheng* (older male role) actors; these two performers therefore underwent considerable special training for this *lingzi* conversation sequence.

The creation of the raging storm for scene four, "Solitary Indignation," involved considerable innovation of a different sort. A single large, light blue banner on a pole is traditionally waved by one performer as others leap around and over it to signify a battle in water. For this scene, multiple dark blue banners were swept about the Fool and the King amid traditional percussion, realistic sound effects, and sophisticated lighting. Moving vigorously around and under the banners, the Fool sometimes acrobatically "blown" into the air and then rescued by the King, these two characters seemed enveloped by the palpable fury of the elements, the result of a creative combination of traditional and modern techniques.

Along with song (*chang*), dance-acting (*zuo*) and combat (*da*), speech (*nian*) is one of the four major performance skills (*gong*) of *jingju* actors, yet it is not often employed in monologues of great length. In this play, however, two long monologues were written for the King to reflect the importance of the spoken word in the Shakespearean original (interview, Shang, 2 May 1996). The first is a bitter iteration of the King's own actions and those of his elder daughters and their supporters; it precedes and leads up to the major aria of scene four, in which his pain and indignation drive him mad. The second occurs in the final scene, "Dream Destroyed." In it, the King admits his own flaws, accepts those of the world, and begs Shangguan to spare his daughter Xueying so humanity will know that despite the flaws of the human world, a truly virtuous person is living in it. Shang believes that these two monologues are key to the play and especially to his character, with the first setting the stage for the second. He says that he was extremely moved by the second as soon as he read it, and skipped over it in rehearsals until he felt that he had fully developed his interpretation. The first time he actually performed it in rehearsal, he cried (interview, Shang 2 May 1996). Audience reactions were equally positive and strong, and in performances I saw, Shang's second speech was always greeted by an extended period of applause and enthusiastic cries of *hao* ("good," equivalent to "bravo" in English).

In view of Li Zhongcheng's belief that extensive innovations in other areas of performance should be accompanied by more traditional aria composition, it is intriguing that the company made significant innovations in this area as well. For instance, Shangguan and Chunying use harmony to indicate an apparent coming-together of thought and feeling parallel to the *lingzi* conversation between Shangguan and Xiaying, and the King and Xueying use it to express their transcendence of life and death (interview, Gao, 3 December 1995). Because harmony is completely absent from traditional *jingju*, Xia Huihua, the actress playing Xueying, had no training in it and in early rehearsals found it very difficult to sing. The problem was solved by having her part played by the main melodic instruments, the *jinghu* (principle spike-fiddle), *erhu* (secondary spike-fiddle), and *yueqin* (moon lute), while Shang Changrong sang his part alone. The combination worked (interview, You, 4 May 1996). Another innovation occurred because Ma believed that no traditional *hualian* arias conveyed the depth of thought that the King needed to express (interview, Ma, 26 April 1996). Gao and Shang therefore set out to create what they termed a "*huasheng*" approach to aria composition, combining the characteristics of *hualian* and *laosheng* singing (interview, Ma, 9 April 1996). In doing so they combined *ban* (metrical types) and brought in some extra-*jingju* musical material as well, because "deep and complicated feelings need to be expressed a number of ways" (interview, Gao, 3 December 1996).

Instrumental music outside the context of arias is very limited in traditional *jingju*. Since the Cultural Revolution, however, it has been common practice in Shanghai-style *jingju* to employ an expanded orchestra of *jingju* and Western instruments to perform atmospheric music and motifs for major characters in a score that is more akin to a film soundtrack than to traditional *jingju* music. This approach was followed for *Qi Wang Meng*, with one significant innovation: in addition to *jingju* and selected Western instruments, the orchestra included several ancient folk instruments (*minzu yueqi*) not usually found in standard "ethnic orchestras" (*minzu yuedui*). The featured instrument was the *xun*, an egg-shaped ceramic wind instrument that dates from at least the Zhou dynasty (eleventh to third centuries BCE) and has a soft, mellow sound. It was a solo instrument in several important passages of atmospheric music associated with the Qi King and his court, and was then played on stage by a minor character to help call the King back from madness, an interesting reversal of the enemy's use of tunes from his homeland to convince the Hegemon King that his kingdom had already fallen in the traditional *jingju* play *Farewell My Concubine* (*Bawang Bie Ji*, literally, "the hegemon king bids farewell to his favorite").

Ouyang and Ma had different directorial methods. In Ouyang's view, he himself took a Daoist approach, preferring to leave as much as possible to the actors throughout rehearsals and not to rehearse crowd scenes until the last week so that the actors, not yet comfortable with the action, would be nervous during opening night and therefore give a better performance. He regarded Ma as a Confucian instead, wanting to consider and set all details of performance (interview, Ouyang, 27 April 1996). Shang had another description of the difference between the two directors. In his view, Ouyang works with actors from the outside in—that is, he starts by establishing form and sound and lets the feelings and emotions of the character develop as a result of this outward performance—while Ma's approach is to begin on the inside and work outward to develop vocal and physical expression based upon inner psychology and emotions. Shang prefers Ma's approach: "*Xiqu* directors like Ma Ke have brought the best of *huaju* to *xiqu*, and start a rehearsal process with character analysis, with actors writing biographies of their characters, etc. This is in fact the contemporary embodiment of the traditional creative spirit of *jingju*" (interview, Shang, 3 December 1995). He Shu, the actor who played Shangguan Meng, had a similar view: "The time of just listening to theater is over. Audiences now also want to watch theater, and what they see must look good, must feature acting. With the focus on acting, actors must understand the full development of their characters" (interview, He, 30 November 1995).

Although Ma did not describe his directorial approach in detail, observation of his work in rehearsal substantiated Shang's description. Ma frequently discussed the psychology, thoughts, and feelings of a specific character with the actor playing that role, including those of the King of Qi with Shang Changrong. Ma started many rehearsals with exercises such as improvisations of waking up, washing the face, and brushing the teeth, explaining that this would help "stimulate the imagination, make the imaginary feel real" (spoken in rehearsal, Ma, 10 April 1996). When working with the actors playing attendants to the King at Chunying's palace, he told them that "you are characters, with thoughts and feelings," and helped them devise individual reactions to the actions of the major characters, as well as the reasons for those reactions (spoken in rehearsal, Ma, 15 April 1996).

While it was clear to me that Ma's approach was valued by and helpful for many of the actors involved, I did see evidence of the efficacy of Ouyang Ming's methods as well. For instance, one day after Ma had spent some time with the actress playing Chunying, trying to help her understand the complexity of her character's feelings, Ouyang performed a series of unspoken thoughts and reactions to them and when she then imitated him, her performance became much deeper and more multidimensional. It appeared to me that while the older performers who had more experience with outer form were benefiting the most from inner work, their younger colleagues, not as experienced in applying *jingju* 's outer forms to new circumstances, often felt lost when asked to work that way, and responded better to the more traditional demonstration and imitation teaching methods of *xiqu*. I found it ironic that the *huaju*-based director invited for his enriching new methods in fact made effective use of traditional *xiqu* approaches, while the experienced *xiqu* director enriched the performances of his more experienced actors with Stanislavsky-based methods from *huaju*—this was a remarkable binary instance of performative intertextuality.

Ouyang and Ma also had different views on the thematic import of *Qi Wang Meng*. For Ouyang, the play is about the results of human covetousness (*tantu*): "The Qi King covets flattery, his elder daughters and Shangguan Meng covet power. Initially all is well, but things happen by chance, people are covetous, individual problems arise, and people have to figure out what to do next. The main problem in contemporary society is too much covetousness, and maybe living standards will have to be raised before we can have less" (interview, Ouyang, 27 April 1996). For Ma, while he never stated his theme directly, the Qi King is a parallel of Mao Zedong. He destroys himself, his reputation, and his nation through the equivalent of the Cultural Revolution: "Giving the country to his daughters is a great mistake, because they don't know how to govern; and for them, with such a capricious, choleric old man still trying to wield power, life is difficult to endure" (interview, Ma, 9 April 1996); and "When it was outlawed, the Communist Party in China truly helped the average person. They were amazing heroes, but look at what [some of the leaders] became. Look at [other] authoritarian power systems, and you can find the same thing. That's why this play is so important" (spoken in rehearsal, Ma, 18 April 1996). Ma's thematic interpretation permeated his psychologically-based directing. He explained to the actors playing the two older sisters that "the Qi King has created a Cultural Revolution situation. You need to feel that having to protect yourself from your father, and to work against him, is awful—but that you truly have to. Also, you don't know whether or not your sister will take what you have said to the King—you need the sense of the Cultural Revolution" (spoken in rehearsal, Ma, 4 April 1996). Speaking with Shang about his character, Ma said that "the Qi King was a great hero and a good father, and rose to the top because of what he did himself. Then he destroyed it all, and fell to the bottom because of what he did himself. The tragedy is that a good person made such a mistake, and harmed so many people" (spoken in rehearsal, 25 April 1996). And with regard to the composition of aria music for the King's culminating aria in scene four, "Solitary Indignation," Ma stressed to Gao and Shang that "the main thing we need to hear here is not his madness, but his inner torment, so that in the end he can become aware that he did this to himself" (interview, 26 April 1996).

Ouyang's ultimate position was that "maybe people of different eras have different views. Ma Ke sees Lear as Mao, and the problem as arrogance. I see the covetousness of contemporary society, with everyone wanting to start companies and make money. And in many respects, these two ideas are not in fact contradictory" (interview, Ouyang, 27 April 1996). In the view of company leaders and government officials of culture, the application of these two possibly related themes to the production of *Qi Wang Meng* gave rise to a single difficulty: "The fundamental problem is that the play should be about a character flaw and it is now about political problems" (interview, Li Zhongcheng, 7 May 1996); and "Shakespeare's play should not be oversimplified. It is about how human nature can create tragedy, not simply politics or family relationships" (spoken in group meeting, Xu, 9 May 1996). These same company leaders and government cultural officials were extremely proud of *Cao Cao and Yang Xiu*, also directed by Ma, which paralleled these historical figures to Mao Zedong and Peng Dehuai respectively, as well as to Deng Xiaoping and Hu Yaobang respectively, and possibly to Deng Xiaoping and Zhaozi Yang (Peng urged Mao not to pursue policies that led to the catastrophic failure of the late 1950s Great Leap Forward, but was ignored and removed from office; Hu and Zhao lost official positions after remonstrating with Deng regarding his policies toward the democracy movement, which culminated in the killing of demonstrators at Tian'anmen Square in 1989). I therefore do not believe that their criticism arose from political concerns. Rather, I think it stemmed from the question of how to stay within the parameters of Shakespeare when creating a *jingju* adaptation, an issue similar to the challenge of staying within the parameters of *jingju* when creating a new play and production. In *Qi Wang Meng*, the language is no longer Shakespeare's. The characters are substantially recreated rather than simply resituated, and the plot has been cut to a single story line, which has itself been significantly changed from the original. Under these circumstances, is Shakespeare without his themes still Shakespeare?

Although *Qi Wang Meng* was well received by audiences in both Beijing and Shanghai, as I witnessed myself, it ultimately was not made a part of the Shanghai Jingju Company's permanent repertory. One of the main reasons for this was that although the script was revised many times, it never reached an acceptable condition for that important status. Li Zhongcheng felt that "the big problem is the logic of plot development. Important transitions and processes are missing, so that many actions are simply not believable" (interview, 8 May 1996). Gao felt that the lyrics were too far from the style of *jingju*, and he was never satisfied with his aria compositions for a number of them (interview, Gao, 3 December 1995). Unquestionably, however, the decision not to retain the play in the permanent repertory was also influenced by the plot simplifications and thematic choices. As Ouyang described it, "Shakespeare took a little folk story, enlarged it, and made it profoundly universal. We set out to make it small again, while keeping the meaning large. Instead, we've turned it into a new little folk story" (interview, 27 April 1996). Among the major questions that run through the discourse on the performance of Shakespeare in Asia, one in particular seems especially relevant here: "How is the past remembered in Asian Shakespeare performances?" For *Qi Wang Meng*, the simple answer is: for the purposes of the present. But a more complete answer must involve the numerous and sometimes conflicting purposes of the many artists and government officials involved in the project. In the creation and performance of *Qi Wang Meng*, at the very least remembering the past involved complex negotiations between multiple cultures, multiple forms of performance practice, and multiple distant and recent pasts and differing presents, with profound effects on creative process, content, and form. I very much wish that the result had been deemed a complete success and am thankful that some of the work involving Shang and his character was ultimately preserved in a one-act (*zhezixi*) solo performance piece, *Li'er Wang* (*King Lear*), now part of the permanent repertory of the Shanghai Jingju Company (interview, Shang, 28 February 2004).

Works Cited

Diamond, Catherine. "*Kingdom of Desire*: The Three Faces of *Macbeth*." *Asian Theatre Journal* 11.1 (1994): 114-33.

Gao, Yiming. Personal Interviews. Beijing: 3 December 1995; Shanghai: 3 May 1996.

He, Shu. Personal Interviews. Beijing: 30 November 1995; Shanghai: 6 May 1996.

Huang, Alexander C. Y. Huang. *Chinese Shakespeares: Two Centuries of Cultural Exchange*. New York: Columbia University Press, 2009.

Li, Ruru. "Chinese Traditional Theatre and Shakespeare." *Asian Theatre Journal* 5.1 (1988): 38-48.

Li, Ruru. "The Bard in the Middle Kingdom." *Asian Theatre Journal* 12.1 (1995): 50-84.

Li, Ruru. *Shashibiya: Staging Shakespeare in China.* Hong Kong: Hong Kong UP, 2003.

Li, Ruru and David Jiang. "The 1994 Shanghai International Shakespeare Festival: An Update on the Bard in Cathay." *Asian Theatre Journal* 14.1 (1997): 93-119.

Li, Zhongcheng. Personal Interviews. Beijing: 7 December 1995; Shanghai: 7 May 1996 and 8 May 1996.

Ma, Ke. Personal Interviews. Shanghai: 9 April 1996 and 26 April 1996. Spoken in Rehearsal. Shanghai: 4 April 1996, 10 April 1996, 15 April 1996, 18 April 1996, and 25 April 1996.

Ouyang, Ming. Personal Interviews. Shanghai: 13 November 1995 and 27 April 1996.

Shang, Changrong. Personal Interviews. Beijing: 3 December 1995; Shanghai: 2 May 1996; Tianjin: 28 February 2004.

Wang, Yongshi. Personal Interview. Shanghai: 11 November 1995.

Wichmann, Elizabeth. "Tradition and Innovation in Contemporary Beijing Opera Performance." *TDR: The Drama Review* 34.1 (1990): 146-78.

Wichmann, Elizabeth. *Listening to Theatre: The Aural Dimension of Beijing Opera*. Honolulu: U of Hawaii P, 1991.

Wichmann-Walczak, Elizabeth. "'Reform' at the Shanghai Jingju Company and Its Impact on Creative Authority and Repertory." *TDR: The Drama Review* 44.4 (2000): 96-119.

Xu, Kangsheng. Spoken in Group Meeting. Shanghai: 9 May 1996.

You, Jishun. Personal Interview. Shanghai: 4 May 1996.

Zhang, Xiao Yang. *Shakespeare in China: A Comparative Study of Two Traditions and Cultures.* Newark: U of Delaware P, 1996.

One Husband Too Many and the Problem of Postcolonial Hong Kong

Adele Lee

As recent scholarship suggests, one cannot confine an understanding of Shakespeare to that of a fixed and stable field of inquiry: "The position that a text occupies . . . at its originating moment of production is . . . no necessary indicator of the positions which it may subsequently come to occupy in different historical and political contexts" (Bennett 229). Therefore, how one reads Shakespeare depends on the specific cultural context one is located in, for instance, political affiliations, religious ties, social standing, race, ethnicity, and geographical locations all determine how one responds to and interprets Shakespeare's plays.

In the last two centuries, Anglophone scholarship constructed a Shakespeare as the best writer in the world, a Shakespeare who celebrated the superiority of the so-called civilized (Western) races, and a Shakespeare that colonial educationists and administrators could use to promote cultural and racial hierarchies thereby enforcing the vision from a single center of culture and generalizing it as a universal reality. The construction of the local as universal is a form of cultural imperialism, the exercise of intellectual supremacy over other competing or alternate ideas, or, in this case, over non-Western Shakespeares. British cultural hegemony in particular is often associated with empire building, as language itself is a tool of domination. Many canonical works of English literature, in particular Shakespeare's, created the cultural preconditions that enabled the work of empire by promoting certain beliefs and assumptions regarding other geographic regions and ethnic groups: "To have knowledge of a thing is to dominate it, to have authority over it" (Said 879). Thus, Shakespeare can be read not only as a colonial import, but also as an ideological tool in establishing the authority of the colonizer. In this context, Shakespeare's role in instilling the values, beliefs, and supposed greatness of British culture into the colonized subject made him an important component in the colonial education system, where both the topics that would be studied and how they were taught were determined by the colonizing power. In colonial India and Anglophone Africa knowledge of Shakespeare was made a compulsory prerequisite for those who wanted to advance to higher education including the education of the government elite. The institutionalization of Shakespeare, likewise, occurred in the former British colony of Hong Kong, where he was first performed in 1867 in a production that imitated Western staging. There, too, "the canonical status of Shakespeare was inscribed with all the colonial aggression of implanting a sense of the superiority of the colonizer's culture in the local Hong Kong people" (Wong 45).

In the second half of the twentieth century, the collapse of former empires precipitated anticolonial challenges to the way philosophy, history, culture, literature, and aesthetics have been written. For many postcolonial societies this has meant a return to a precolonial heritage (nativism), that is, a revival of nationalism which seeks to uproot all matters colonial. The supplanting of colonial icons such as Shakespeare with indigenous cultural icons can be traced to Ngugu wa Thiong'o's rejection of the supposed centrality and universality of the English tradition and the attempt to transform the University of Nairobi's Department of English into an Afro-centric department of literature. Instead of simply dropping Shakespeare from the English syllabus, however, some societies use Shakespeare as a politically charged site around which the counter discursive work of independence can be conducted. That is, the struggle for cultural autonomy involves the more complicated process of reordering and restructuring different ideological elements for a renegotiated identity in changing times (see Ku 343). In this struggle the formerly colonized write back to the center, making possible a new (and potentially exciting) kind of culture criticism and scholarship that challenges, disrupts, and contests the meaning of canonical texts such as Shakespeare's. Only through altering or redirecting, or indeed decolonizing, texts, can once-colonized societies create a Shakespeare, a Romeo, or a Juliet, relevant to their own circumstances and experiences.

After more than 150 years under British control, Hong Kong was handed over to the Chinese authorities on 1 July 1997. However, unlike the situation in India, Ireland, and other former colonies, the decolonization of Hong Kong was not the result of an indigenous liberation struggle, nor has the change in sovereignty prompted a backlash against everything colonial. While colonization is commonly regarded as an encroachment on the local indigenous culture, "few Hongkongers resent the infiltration of Western culture into the city" (Chan 281). In fact, the vast majority of the Hong Kong Chinese, prior to the scheduled handover, viewed the situation with trepidation and a sense of impending doom, rather than with hope for greater liberty. Their fear was that the People's Republic of China (PRC) would impose restrictive communist ideologies upon Hong Kong, trampling freedoms including freedom of the press, judicial freedom, academic freedom, and free elections (see, e.g., Hsiung). In other words, Hongkongers were afraid of being colonized again, this time by Mainland China. As a result many have been particularly anxious to assert their Britishness, as a sign of distinction from the mainland Chinese (Chan 272). Thus, far from wanting to supersede colonialism, either culturally or ideologically, many Hongkongers actively cling to their cultural inheritance.

This endeavour to stay British is evident in the Hongkonger's response to the Hong Kong Special Administrative Region government's decision, two months after Hong Kong's reunification with the PRC, that all public-sector secondary schools henceforth adopt Chinese (instead of English) as the medium of instruction for students in form 1 to form 3. The move provoked strong reactions from teachers, students, and their parents, and resulted in a series of public protests and appeals. It would seem that, for Hongkongers, the English language, the use of which will further one's chance of future success, is both symbolic and cultural capital: "If a person increases his/her cultural capital by acquiring the 'right' kind of knowledge at school, such capital can land the person a high-salaried job, thus converting cultural capital into economic capital" (Chan 272). The right kind of knowledge, according to many Hongkongers, is synonymous with Britishness. Thus the Hong Kong Chinese (unlike the nationalists in Ireland, for whom the Celtic language is a way of asserting their own cultural autonomy), by rejecting the mother tongue, continue to privilege the colonizer's culture. The failure of Hong Kong to interrogate or challenge Western culture is also reflected in their approach to Shakespeare after 1997. To many Hong Kong Chinese, in particular the aspiring middle-classes, the study of Shakespeare also represents "the 'right' kind of knowledge." This belief took root arguably in 1888, when, according to British colonial interests, knowledge of Shakespeare became a necessary prerequisite to those seeking employment in the Chinese Imperial Maritime Custom Service. Thus, the idea has been internalized by Hongkongers that one can acquire higher ranking social status through adopting and emulating the master's ideology, something which the Hong Kong Chinese are keen to hang onto, often without critical scrutiny. Read in this context, Shakespeare's role in Hong Kong is analogous to the adoption of other Western status symbols, like the Rolls Royce. Despite this ideological conundrum, Shakespeare is still one of Hong Kong's most popular and widely performed playwrights, often playing a prominent role in the annual Hong Kong Arts Festival. These productions have a tendency to pay uncritical reverence to received (Western) ideas (Ingham 30). The result is static, highly canonical, and moribund performances in which actors often wear Western-style dress, wigs, and prosthetic noses. Such performances do not break the grip of what John Gillies terms, "'canonic' doublet and hose style performances" (106). This style of performance emulates what is imagined as high British culture. Take for instance an article of 2000 by Daniel S.P. Yang, entitled "Shakespeare at the Hong Kong Repertory Theater": Yang calls for the need for a more "professional" approach to Shakespeare among Hong Kong theater companies, yet what he actually means is a more Western approach. His ideal is a show that "could compare favourably with major theater companies in the Western world" (76). In a similar vein, Murray J. Levith in his otherwise valuable *Shakespeare in China* claims that "Hong Kong stage Shakespeare seems poised to reflect the same professionalism and expertise as British or American Shakespeare in the new millennium" (105) without interrogating British or US-American preconceptions about Shakespeare's superiority.

Instead of challenging the Shakespeare one is accustomed to seeing performed by the likes of the Royal Shakespeare Company, all too often Hongkongers concur with the authority of colonial paradigms. One of the few attempts to appropriate Shakespeare to the Hong Kong context has been by a Japanese female theater troupe called Takarazuka. Their version of *The Tempest* and *The Tempest in Kowloon*, performed in 1999, can be read as a critique of British colonization of Hong Kong and a simultaneous effort to evade and erase the historical memory of Japanese colonial violence in Hong Kong from 1941 to 1945. Prospero is played as a Kowloon Mafia boss and an ex-British officer, while Sycorax and Caliban are Chinese rebels who seek their independence from Prospero. In the end Caliban shoots Prospero to death, cursing him in Chinese. The lack of experimentation in theater can also be seen in the Hong Kong educational system. Shakespeare's presence in the syllabus has not changed since 1997 and he is still to be found on the English Literature examination for university acceptance (Levith 95), nor has there been a significant revision of canonical ideas about Shakespeare's greatness, as indeed there has been in the West itself in recent decades. This can be seen in the module entitled "Shakespeare: An introduction to Genius" currently offered to students at the City University of Hong Kong's Department of English and Communication. The concept of genius is inseparable from the idea of universalism and in accepting the universality of Shakespeare, one is arguably accepting the specifically British values codified in Shakespeare as universal. The universality of Shakespeare advocated by such as US-American traditionalist Harold Bloom is also reflected in the University of Hong Kong's Shakespeare module: ENGL 2079. Limiting itself to the study of the formal elements of Shakespeare's texts (that is, the specific properties of literary material), this course, like the one currently available to undergraduates in English at the Chinese University of Hong Kong (ENG 4500), which exalts Shakespeare as "English literature's foremost dramatic poet" and focuses on Shakespeare's "modes of characterisation, and methods of creating dramatic situations," depoliticizes and hence by extension essentializes and universalizes the Shakespearean text.

The failure to decolonize Shakespeare is indicative of the larger issue of reforming the Hong Kong education system, which has been rooted in Western university models. Even in the present, postcolonial era, "most [Hong Kong] academics [100% of whom can read English] indicated that they must read books and journals published overseas in order to keep up with developments in their fields" (Postiglione 318). This reliance on (and reverence for) Western epistemologies exemplifies the difficulty facing the formerly colonized in undoing ideas about Shakespeare that have been ingrained over the course of decades. Of course, the irony is that postcolonialism itself, as a field of study, can be considered as yet another Western "ism," like psychoanalysis, which Andreas Bertoldi suspects is "founded on a Eurocentric, patriarchal and even racist theoretical foundation" (236). Indeed, the Western academy has been largely responsible for defining the terms and practices of postcolonial writing, much to the dismay of indigenous critics struggling to find their own critical voice and style, and, by extension, their own unique Shakespeare.

The need to break free from the colonial paradigm can be illustrated by the Hong Kong film, *One Husband Too Many* (1988), directed by and starring Anthony Chan. Unlike Hong Kong theater, which has not been celebrated for its experimental, avant garde proclivities in the past, Hong Kong cinema has never been heavily influenced by, or sought to emulate, Western cinematic practices. Indeed, in recent years Hong Kong cinema has acquired a global reputation and appeal and has influenced filmmakers such as Oliver Stone and Quentin Tarantino. As a medium film is, arguably, a more active site for the exploration of the Shakespearean dynamic per se, it gives us "our liberty in thinking and writing about Shakespeare" (Crowl 4). Hong Kong cinema, then, rather than theater, is the medium through which Hongkongers can challenge more effectively British cultural hegemony by means of the Shakespearean text. *One Husband Too Many* holds the possibility of an ideological critique of Western culture by showing the failure of *Romeo and Juliet* to engage the attention of rural audiences. It opens with an amateur actor called Hsin and his troupe giving a performance of *Romeo and Juliet* at a country fair. Hsin, played by Chan, aims to bring culture to the backwater. Prancing around the stage in traditional Renaissance garb, Hsin's Romeo and the film's Juliet (played by Hsin's on-screen wife Yuan Tung, actress Anita Mui Yim-Fong) both dress and posture in almost a parody of Zeffirelli's vision of the "star-crossed lovers." According to Robert Hapgood, Zeffirelli (who contends that Shakespeare's plays apply "to every human being on earth, no matter what cultural background") has achieved a compelling rapport with audiences "worldwide" through inviting identification with the young leading characters and their vulnerabilities (Hapgood 80-83). Hsin, however, does not find that his Zeffirelli-esque Romeo and Juliet strikes a chord with the Hong Kong Chinese audience. As the camera moves back and forth between the stage and the audience we catch the negative and highly vocal responses of the crowds. One woman refers to Hsin's Romeo as "tight pants" and another tells him to "Get on [with killing himself]." Male members of the audience are even more dissident than women. Hsin constructs the Hong Kong Chinese audience not as the passive or reverential consumers of Shakespeare but critical challengers of Western culture.

The contempt the audience shows for Hsin's production (aggressively biting off the sugar cane, standing on their feet, pointing and laughing, and shouting "Four eyes, finish her off!") in many respects mirrors Yun-Fat Chow's character's response to Shakespeare in *Now You See Love . . . Now You Don't!* (1992), directed by Alex Law and Mabel Cheung. In this film Chow plays a character called Shan-shui Ng, the reactionary head of a small rural village in the New Territories. This is a place where men drink in the yard and believe a woman's place is in the kitchen. In a later scene, however, by which time Ng's girlfriend, freshly returned from London, has left him, a city boy warns Ng that "Shakespeare said wine increases our desires in direct proportion to decreasing our potency," a challenge to Ng's masculinity that provokes his retort that "Shakespeare was a foreigner. They have more brains than balls." Ng's reaction creates here a dichotomy between the masculine Orient and the feminine (no balls) West. In doing so he turns the West's feminization of the

Orient on its head and rewrites the Occident as feminine as a way of devaluing its culture and the products of that culture such as Shakespeare. Ng's also refutes overtly Shakespeare's universality. Unable or unwilling to share in the West's empathy for the young lovers, the Hong Kong Chinese, who value filial piety and respect for elders, do not sympathize with the disobedient adolescents, Romeo and Juliet.

The audience's reaction signals the unsuccessful implementation of British cultural hegemony, at least up to a point. Driven backstage, the disillusioned Hsin and Yuan Tung sit in silence until three local councillors in European-style suits come to tempt them back out again: They are bad trouble makers, one of them states: "I can only hope they'll move one step forward." The Arnoldian idea that the ability to appreciate Shakespeare is somehow tantamount to the acquisition of culture, civility, and ultimately progress, is the effect of a colonial education system. The councillors' hope, however, is not realized, for when Hsin and Yuan Tung return onto the stage to perform the play's final scene several burly, half-clad men emerge to enforce order, warning one audience member who continues to shout "Finish her off!" that he will finish off whoever said that. The councillors then demand that the audience approve of the performance: "Applaud or you'll be beaten." Their display of authority suggests the way in which colonial regimes have attempted to coerce the Hong Kong population into appreciating Shakespeare. However, the silencing of the audience is only momentary and it is not before long that physical fighting breaks out. Hsin and Tung, the now literally persecuted lovers, are compelled to flee the fair pursued by a torch-bearing mob. At this point, it is as if Shakespeare's play has transcended the confines of the theater, broken free of its Anglo-centric bondage, and been transplanted into the world of twentieth-century Hong Kong cinema: "*Now* it's Romeo and Juliet" the beleaguered Hsin remarks while examining the stand off between the "bouncers" and the disruptive male members of the audience.

The film's message at this stage is ideologically mixed: is the audience's inability or refusal to appreciate a Western style production of Shakespeare to be commended or criticized? The ambiguity of audience response mirrors the more general problem of gauging the people of Hong Kong's attitude, both at the present moment and in the past, towards Shakespeare and the colonizer's culture of which he has become representative. This problem can be further illustrated by Michihko Obimori's *Young Lovers* (1978), an appropriation of *Romeo and Juliet* that stresses the social differences between the lovers. At one point the two teenagers, called Junming and Lanjin, sit with their fellow classmates during an English literature class, listening with vacant faces as their instructor, a middle-aged expatriate, recites monotonously Hamlet's "To be or not to be" speech. It is impossible to tell whether the students are either deeply stirred by the recitation or simply bored. Significantly, the class is interrupted by a messenger with the news of Jumning's brother's arrest for murder. Once again life in Hong Kong is depicted as at odds with the stale and moribund Anglicized Shakespeare. *One Husband Too Many*, however, is about more than the problem of introducing young—Chinese—minds to an English playwright. Rather, the film uses knowledge and appreciation of Shakespeare to distinguish the rural people of the New Territories from the more culturally refined and sophisticated people of Hong Kong city. The film privileges Shakespeare's role in determining class and social status in Hong Kong in a way that reproduces the Western prejudices inherent in the colonial education system. But the meaning of the film, I believe, ultimately pivots on whether we read it as offering a critique of Shakespeare for failing to appeal the Hong Kong people or as a critique of the Hong Kong people for failing to recognise the value of Shakespeare. By depicting the audience as rather lewd and impolite, the film would seem to be attributing their disruptiveness to ignorance alone rather than any failing on Shakespeare's part. Yet as the film progresses, and Chan eventually regroups his company of amateur actors, he says: "In retrospect, I feel that though we promote famous works only we've brought them out in a raw form. The dialogues are not in a live way. How can the viewers accept them? They're out of line with modern life. So I've decided to make the arts colloquial and vulgar. My first drama is *Modern Romeo and Juliet*."

Hsin articulates what his audience may have recognized but could not express, namely that the Shakespeare constructed and promoted by the West does not speak to and for the people of Hong Kong. Shakespeare needs to be colloquial and vulgar if his work is to have local appeal. Chan does not, however, as we might expect, advocate the need to appropriate Shakespeare's work to suit his geopolitical context. He thereby fails to acknowledge the role and importance of place in determining one's response to Shakespeare. This failure by Chan to realize that how we read is "inflected by our own positions on a particular cultural map" (Neill 174) illustrates again one of the problems that ails Hong Kong pedagogy. Hsin's desire to produce a modern *Romeo and Juliet* is never realized in the course of the film; instead, he forgets about Shakespeare as other events in his life take precedence, namely, his relationship with fellow actress Sogo (played by Cherie Cho-Hung Chung). When Hsin discovers that Sogo is also dating and prefers his best friend Hua Ah (Kenny Bee), he turns in his distress to the poetry, not of Shakespeare, but of Ch'ing-chao Li, a female poet of the Song Dynasty: "Searching, lonely, [and] sad," Hsin looks to and finds an indigenous writer with whom he can identify. This moment (and others) in *One Husband Too Many* is reminiscent of the Merchant-Ivory film *Shakespeare Wallah* (1965), which shows how Indian audiences lost interest in Shakespeare at the end of the British Raj. The scene in *Shakespeare Wallah* where India's Minister of mining and fuel quotes not Shakespeare but India's Sanskrit authors signals "a transitional stage in some post-colonial cultures when an enforced identification with the colonising power becomes displaced by the espousal of indigenous cultural icons" similar to Hsin's supplanting of Shakespeare with Li (Cartelli 106).

One Husband Too Many's role in highlighting and exposing the issue of Shakespeare reception in Hong Kong is much more complex than it would appear initially. The film alerts us to the wider ways in which the Hong Kong Chinese have refused to internalize passively the colonizer's ideology. Despite the manifold problems facing any attempt to break with Western epistemologies, especially when engaging with Shakespeare, a renewed sense of identity is evident in recent changes to the

English literature syllabus toward more postcolonial issues, and the growing critical interest in Hong Kong writing in English. Brian Hooper's 2003 *Voices in the Heart: Post-colonialism and Identity in Hong Kong Literature*, which gives "pride of place" to Hong Kong writing (15), illustrates this move to develop Hong Kong's cultural distinctiveness. According to Hooper "the vast majority of Hong Kong Chinese have never been fully Anglicised in any significant sense" (25). The drive toward asserting, and giving voice to Hongkongness is also evident in what Cecilia J. Pang identifies as the post-1997 "cultural resurgence" in Hong Kong theater. This resurgence includes productions that are performed in a new style of Cantonese opera, suggesting that Hongkongers are creating new forms of expression, not simply copying Chinese or Anglo models. It also signifies that creative energy is at work on the Hong Kong cultural scene. The post-1997 emergence of alternative (subcultural) bands, as well as the conspicuous rise of the Indie film scene, such as Fruit Chan's *Made in Hong Kong 1997*, which focuses on the crowded housing projects and pulsing streets of immigrants and the working class, also illustrate the push to recover an authentic Hong Kong-Chinese voice and a culture with which the ordinary people of Hong Kong can identify. Hongkongers are building an identity that does not simply define itself in opposition to the mainland Chinese or through a straightforward identification with the British. Indeed, many now are protesting against claims that Hongkongers internalize passively either colonizer's ideology: the refusal of the Hongkongers to mimic the colonizer's language, for instance, often "code-switching" or "code-mixing" both English and Cantonese and thus speaking a hybrid language sometimes termed "Cantonglish," illustrates that they are not willing to be molded into passive recipients of Western ideology, but are adept at a manipulative wordplay that refuses containment within any single ideological framework. As Elaine Chan puts it, Hong Kong equals Chineseness plus affluence, cosmopolitanism, capitalism; Chineseness plus Englishness, colonial education, colonialism; Chineseness plus democracy, human rights, and rule of law (281). Even a Hongkonger's Chinese and English names signify a cultural division between Chinese familialism and Western individualism, and thus an essentially hybrid identity. Thus the Hong Kong person really is "a bird of a different feather" (Abbas 2).

In conclusion, what impact will this hybridity have on Shakespeare post-1997? David Jiang's 2004 production of *Romeo and Juliet* that was "neither traditionally Chinese nor too close to Western cultural influences" (Li 45), is, I believe one of the ways in which Hongkongers can approach Shakespeare. Neither passively reproducing Western-style performances nor adopting Shakespeare to traditional Chinese theater practices, it marks a new, distinctively Cantonese appropriation.

Works Cited

Abbas, Ackber. *Hong Kong: Culture and the Politics of Disappearance*. Hong Kong: Hong Kong UP, 1997.

Bennett, Tony. "Text and History." *Re-Reading English*. Ed. Peter Widdowson. London: Methuen, 1982. 223-36.

Bertoldi, Andreas. "Shakespeare, Psychoanalysis and Coloniality." *Post-colonial Shakespeares*. Ed. Ania Loomba and Martin Orkin. London: Routledge, 1998. 233-58.

Cartelli, Thomas. *Repositioning Shakespeare: National Formations, Postcolonial Appropriations*. London: Routledge, 1999.

Chan, Elaine. "Beyond Pedagogy: Language and Identity in Post-Colonial Hong Kong." *British Journal of Sociology of Education* 23.2 (2002): 271-85.

Crowl, Samuel. *Shakespeare Observed: Studies in Performance on Stage and Screen*. Athens: Ohio UP, 1992.

Gillies, John. "Shakespeare Localized: An Australian Looks at Asian Practice." *Shakespeare Global/Local: The Hong Kong Imaginary in Transcultural Production*. Ed. Kwok-kan Tam, Andrew Parkin and Terry Siu-han Yip. Oxford: Peter Lang, 2002. 101-13.

Hapgood, Robert. "Popularising Shakespeare: The Artistry of Franco Zeffirelli." *Shakespeare, the Movie: Popularising the Plays on Film, TV, and Video*. Ed. Lynda E. Boose and Richard Burt. London and New York: Routledge, 1997. 80-94.

Hooper, Brain. *Voices in the Heart: Postcolonialism and Identity in Hong Kong Literature*. Oxford: Peter Lang, 2003.

Hsiung, James C. "Introduction." *Hong Kong the Super Paradox: Life After Return to China*. London: Macmillan, 2000.

Ingham, Mike. "Shakespeare in Asian English-Language Productions." *Shakespeare Global/ Local: The Hong Kong Imaginary in Transcultural Production.* Ed. Kwok-kan Tam, Andrew Parkin, and Terry Siu-han Yip. Bern: Peter Lang, 2002. 29-42.

Ku, Agnes S. "Postcolonial Cultural Trends in Hong Kong: Imagining the Local, the National, and the Global." *Crisis and Transformation in China's Hong Kong*. Ed. Ming K. Chan and Alvin Y. So. London: M.E. Sharpe, 2002. 343-62.

Law, Wing-Wah. "The Accommodation and Resistance to the Decolonisation, Neocolonisation and Recolonisation of Higher Education in Hong Kong." *Comparative Education* 33.2 (1997): 187-209.

Levith, Murray J. *Shakespeare in China*. London: Continuum, 2004.

Li, Ruru. "Negotiating Intercultural Spaces: *Much Ado About Nothing* and *Romeo and Juliet* on the Chinese Stage." *World-wide Shakespeares: Local Appropriations in Film and Performance.* Ed. Sonia Massai. London: Routledge, 2005. 40-46.

Neill, Michael, "Post-colonial Shakespeare? Writing away from the Centre." *Post-colonial Shakespeares*. Ed. Ania Loomba and Martin Orkin. London: Routledge, 1998. 164-85.

Now You See Love . . . Now You Don't! Dir. Alex Law Kai-Yui. Hong Kong: Golden Princess Film Production, 1992.

One Husband Too Many. Dir. Anthony (Yau) Chan. Hong Kong: Deltamac, 1988.

Pang, Celia J. Rev. of *The Story of Wu Zixu* and *Sweet and Sour Hong. Theater Journal* 56.3 (2004): 487-89.

Postiglione, Gerard A. "The Transformation of Academic Autonomy in Hong Kong." *Crisis and Transformation in China's Hong Kong*. Ed. Ming K. Chan and Alvin Y. So. London: M.E. Sharpe, 2002. 307-21.

Romeo and Juliet. Dir. Franco Zeffirelli. London: BHE Films, 1968.

Said, Edward. "Orientalism." *Literary Theory: An Anthology*. Ed. Julie Rivkin and Michael Ryan. Oxford: Blackwell, 2000. 873-86.

Shakespeare Wallah. Dir. James Ivory. London: Merchant Ivory Productions, 1965.

Wong, Dorothy. "'Domination by Consent': A Study of Shakespeare in Hong Kong." *Studies in Comparative Literature* 26.2 (2000): 43-56.

Yang, Daniel S.P. "Shakespeare at the Hong Kong Repertory Theater." *Shakespeare Global/ Local: The Hong Kong Imaginary in Transcultural Production*. Ed. Kwok-kan Tam, Andrew Parkin and Terry Siu-han Yip. Oxford: Peter Lang, 2002. 75-86.

Young Lovers. Dir. Michihiko Obimori. Hong Kong: Shaw Brothers, 1978.

Part Three

Shakespeare in Cyberspace

Aesthetics of Fragmentation in Taymor's *Titus*

Lucian Ghita

Julie Taymor's work as a theater maker and mixed media artist is an integral part of her cinematic vocabulary. As Peter Donaldson has shown, her 1999 film adaptation of Shakespeare's *Titus Andronicus* includes an ability to translate the circular eye movements of video games into camera work that centers on the young boy Lucius as he finds himself in the film's opening sequence transported from his kitchen table into a Roman arena (457-59). In *Titus*, Taymor experiments with a semiotics of fragmentation, which maps out the cultural roots and effects of violence onto the human body and at the same time reflects critically on the dismembering effects of new technologies and media. In deconstructing the Hollywoodian vocabulary of glamorized violence, she brings together aestheticized depictions of dismemberment in high-culture art and graphic imageries of rape and mutilation as found in popular media. By exploring the intersections between reel and real violence, Taymor's film throws into sharper focus the relationships between the aesthetics of cinematic representation and the ethics of spectatorship. Her emphasis on corporal iconographies, in turn, can be traced back to her interest in visual, nonlinguistic media of expressions, acquired through Jacques Lecoq's school of mime, Javanese wood-carving, and *bunraku* puppetry.

Lacking fluency in French and Indonesian languages during her work in Paris, central Java and Bali, Taymor took up miming, masked dance, and puppetry as means to challenge conventional language-centered protocols of Western theater. Her thematic recourse to madness and cultural transition, two of the issues she initially explored during her project with the Indonesian director W.S. Rendra, is therefore neither haphazard, nor extraneous to her stylistic treatment of intercultural violence in *Titus*. The film thematizes the nexus between violence and insanity within a wider cultural and aesthetic context, from visceral images (a Marat-like Titus sits in the tub writing revenge notes with the blood of his amputated arm) to elaborate, highly stylized representations (the surreal visions of violence captured by the five Penny Arcade Nightmares). Just as cyberspace will doubtlessly bring overlooked elements of Shakespeare to the attention of future generations, Taymor has found in Shakespeare's *Titus Andronicus* a way to represent an insatiable desire for revenge by exploring the anatomy of madness on the level of the protagonist's body. Madness brings with it not only the logic of masquerade and violent retaliation, but also the experience of physical and mental fragmentation, imagined as a slow descent into the dark recesses of human self. After Aaron chops off Titus's left hand in order to present it to Saturninus as ransom for the fault of Titus's two sons in Shakespeare's play, the emperor repays Titus by sending back to him his hand along with the heads of his two sons. In *Titus*, Taymor captures this intense moment in a grotesque freak show, echoing Fellini's absurd universe of riotous revelry. Against the backdrop of a crude carnival tune, a Clown lifts the metal side-door of the motorcycle wagon to reveal Titus's severed hand, flanked on each side by Martius and Quintus's heads floating in two specimen jars. In an image reminiscent of Renaissance anatomical blazons, the close-up shot of the heads conjures up the imagery of the masked heads from the opening sequence. The elaborate arrangement of body parts foreshadows the rampant cycle of violence, which culminates visually in the cannibalistic pastry stuffed with Chiron's and Demetrius's "shameful heads" (Taymor, *"Titus"* 162). At the same time, the image literalizes ironically the political urgency to "set a head on headless Rome," expressed by Marcus in the election scene (37). Taymor's camera movement and framing bring into play Shakespeare's semiotics of fragmentation and experiments with the possibilities of dismembering and reassembling the body into a fictional appendage of the spectator's *corps propre*. The cinematic *mise-en-scène*, which juxtaposes people, objects, and body parts, discloses the thin boundary between violence as atrocity and violence as consumerist entertainment. Throughout the film, bodies are literally severed, dismembered, and consumed. Their perilous materiality discloses the interstices between inanimate objects and animate subjects, which goes back to the roots of theater. Putting life into inanimate objects recalls the magic of puppetry.

Taymor's use of bodies and body parts as performing artifacts ties into her longstanding interest in Asian theater practices, from Japanese *Bunraku* to Indonesian masked dance drama (*topeng*). In her view, puppetry and masks reveal the interface between bodies and objects. The mixture of media—live actors next to puppets and other stage props—helps the viewer move through different levels of reality, from naturalistic scenes of suffering to grotesque scenes of over-the-top cruelty (Taymor, "Working with Puppets" 468). Taymor incorporates in her theater some of the earlier elements and techniques with which she experimented while working on Asian puppetry and masks during the 1970s. Her interest in avant-garde and visually oriented theater took her to East Europe, Indonesia, and Japan, where she studied theater, masked dance, and an extant pre-Bunraku style of puppetry. Among other formative influences in her career were Lecoq's school of mime and physical theater, in which she participated as a teenage student, and Herbert Blau's work on "ideographs," defined as pared-down forms that contain the essence of an action (Blumenthal and Taymor 12). The artistic cross-pollination and synthesis between Western theater and Asian theatrical forms has come to defined much of Taymor's work on stage and celluloid.

Borrowing technical and stylistic elements from her 1994 stage production of *Titus*, Taymor experiments with visual tropes of dismemberment throughout the film. She translates Shakespeare's imagery of bodily fragmentation into cinematic ideographs of violence, chiastically explored as consuming passions for revenge and as spectatorial obsessions with image consumption. According to the *Oxford English Dictionary*, the Latin *consūmere* means "to take up completely, make away with, eat up, devour, waste, destroy." The textual and visual iconography Taymor puts forth is visceral and symbolic, metaphoric and metamorphic at the same time. In the beginning of the film, Tamora's elder son Alarbus is ritually sacrificed in order to appease the Roman gods and his limbs are hewed upon a pile of wood "till they be clean consumed" (*"Titus"* 29). Ritual consumption by fire subsequently becomes sexual consummation. After Saturninus chooses Tamora as bride and Roman empress, the two lovers withdraw to their chamber to consummate their "spousal rites" (*"Titus"* 81). The film intercuts images of desire with scenes of sexual affliction. By revealing the ravished Lavinia to her father, Marcus brings "consuming sorrow" to Titus's eyes (98). Overwhelmed with gnawing pain, Titus concocts an elaborate revenge. The cycle of violence, inaugurated by the child's kitchen-table mayhem, reaches its apex in the final Thyestean banquet. The trope of consumption metamorphoses into a cannibalistic scene, in which Tamora daintily feeds on "the flesh that she herself hath bred" (66). The banquet erases the boundaries between eater and eaten. The hewing, the cooking, and the serving are part of the same fearful symmetry of bodily consumption. Taymor's camera captures this dialectic of fragmentation by interspersing slow-motion sequences with a series of medium and close-up shots. The juxtaposition of food, human bodies, and eating utensils, splashed in light and dark tones across the cinematic canvas, foregrounds the troubling relationship between bodies and objects. The fragmenting effect of the cinematic medium on the human body discloses the cinematic artifice. The viewer experiences the cinematic space in a state of double consciousness by being able to watch both the puppet and the puppeteer. "When you get rid of the masking," Taymor notes in an interview, "even though the mechanics are apparent, the whole effect is more magical" (qtd. in Schechner, "Julie Taymor" 42).

Taymor resists cinematic naturalism by constructing a multilayered symbolic space, which purposely exposes the viewer to the mechanics of cinematic artifice (see Snyder). Masks and puppets, both real and symbolic, feature prominently throughout the film and prompt desensitized audiences to reflect on the moral and communal effects of violence. The film's framing device recalls Adrian Noble's technique used in his 1996 film adaptation of *A Midsummer Night's Dream*. Real and surreal events are constantly filtered through the eyes of a ten-year-old child, identified in the credits with Titus's grandson Young Lucius (Osheen Jones). In the opening shot, a media-addicted boy wearing a brown paper bag over his face with holes cut out for the eyes and mouth watches cartoons on television as he bites into his hot dog. His blinking eyes peering through the mask are illuminated by the intermittent light of a television screen. The camera focuses on the boy's eyes and records the continual constricting and dilating of his pupils, which reproduce the movement of camera lenses. The cinematic *mise-en-abyme* captures the interplay between visual technology and the human body. The camera zooms out to reveal the interior of an urban kitchen where the child sits alone at a table littered with toys and food scraps. Incited by the sound of cartoon violence on the television, he stages a mock battle with his toy soldiers, dousing them with ketchup and salt. The masked boy marshals his plastic soldiers as a puppet master, turning the kitchen table into mayhem. His frantic war games conjure up a deafening explosion, which sets the kitchen on fire. A Clown figure bursts into the room, grabs the child from under the table, and carries him away through a corridor. As the smoke surrounding them clears, the boy finds himself inside an ancient coliseum, the spectral space of a distant past animated by his fantasy of violence and destruction. The pulsating drums of the Roman army entering the arena enlivens the plastic soldier that Young Lucius holds in his hand and transforms it into an army of Roman centurions. They march in highly choreographed formations, which evoke the mechanical movements of the boy's toy soldiers. Their bodies and limbs covered in layers of earth resemble the clay warriors of Emperor Qin's terracotta army.

In translating her mask work from stage to screen, Taymor is interested in the ways in which the body itself becomes a mask (Schechner, "Julie Taymor" 36). She achieves this effect in part by intercutting medium and close-up shots of Titus, Young Lucius, and the Roman soldiers. On screen, the mask slips into the skin of the actor as the camera explores the spatial interlayering between the human body and the creases of the mud mask. The iconic, hypnotic figure of Anthony Hopkins's Titus, caked in blue mud and wearing a helmet, is bound to stay with the viewer for a long time. The close-up shot of his face covered in clay reproduces analeptically the boy's paper mask. Although their material texture is different, both function as signifiers for the mediating space between camera and the body. The film explores in this way the materiality of the human body through the dialogue that takes place between the mask carrier and the mask itself (Schechner, "Julie Taymor" 36). Taymor experimented with a similar technique in her *bunraku*-inspired adaptation of *The Tempest* in 1986. In a convention borrowed from traditional Japanese puppetry, black-clad figures manipulated objects and characters over the sand-filled stage as a means to express Prospero's all-encompassing magic. The masks danced in the air echoing the relationship between performer and puppet in traditional *bunraku* (Woods 232). In the end of the play, Prospero frees a spellbound Ariel from his domination by removing the hood on the actor's face. In *Titus*, the unmasking effect translates the cinematic shift from the boy's plastic toys to the flesh-and-blood Roman soldiers marching into the coliseum, setting a face-to-face encounter between protagonists and viewers inside the Roman arena.

As Peter Donaldson suggests, in the very scene where the circular camerawork recalls the lines of sight of a computer game, the boy's mask also aligns him with tragic theater: "the kitchen table is a play space, play here is a form of cruel puppetry in which the boy takes the role of the unfeeling gods" (459). The space of the kitchen table blends into the space of the coliseum as the boy falls through an "Alice in Wonderland" time warp into the Roman arena. The boy shifts from the authority position of a puppeteer, manipulating and destroying his toy soldiers at will, to the role of a mere puppet, carried by the leather-clad strongman into the arena and lifted in the air as a war trophy. Captivated by the arrival of Titus's army, he watches from inside the coliseum the mechanical, toy-like movement of the Roman soldiers, bursting into elaborate maneuvers with their swords and spears. The boy's ambivalent journey into real-life violence and maturity discloses Taymor's fascination with ceremonies of initiation. As she recounts in an interview, while traveling on a Watson fellowship in a remote Indonesian village situated on the rim of a crater lake, she had the incredible privilege of witnessing a Balinese rite of passage, in which religion and art came together in a powerfully transformative experience (Taymor, "Interview"). Surrounded by darkness and with no audience around, she watched enthralled as several old men in full warrior costume performed a traditional initiation dance. Taymor's cinematic vision brings together within the space of the coliseum the choreographed movement of the Roman soldiers with the Balinese ritual dance that she witnessed during her formative years as a director.

The web of intercultural allusions is finally made transparent in the banquet sequence, in which the food items scattered on the kitchen table in the opening sequence become the gory ingredients of Titus's cannibalistic pie. In the absence of clear-cut boundaries between play and violence, the oval-shaped arena, which signals the cyclicity of revenge, becomes a silent receptacle for the shed blood. Titus's banquet ends in carnage, mirroring the mayhem at the boy's kitchen table. As the frame freezes on a pulp fiction tableau of the banquet slaughter, the camera zooms out and we are immediately transported back into the Roman coliseum. This time, a real crowd of Croatians witness the climactic scene of cruelty from the tiers of the Pula arena. The ideograph of the coliseum, shot on location in war-ravaged South Europe, draws attention precisely to the exchange of roles between civilized Romans and barbarians, victims and perpetrators. The image of the boy peering out of the paper-bag mask points metonymically to the viewer's scopic position, which oscillates between the benign universe of the suburban kitchen and the terrifying dreamscape of the Roman arena. Inspired by traditional *ningyō jōruri* (*Bunraku*) and Javanese *wayang golèk* theater (wooden hand puppets), Taymor believes that once we get rid of the mask and the mechanics of the show become apparent, the whole effect is more surreal, "not because it's an illusion and we don't know how it's done" but precisely because "we know *exactly* how it's done" (Schechner, "Julie Taymor" 42). Once the cinematic medium becomes transparent, the audience is exposed to a "heightened reality" (Johnson-Haddad 35). In order to render this cinematic effect, the camera focuses on the child's face as he picks up a plastic soldier from the smoking ruins of his house and magically breathes life into it. The camera immediately swoops across the ring-shaped arena and reveals a legion of flesh-and-blood soldiers.

The Roman baths sequence repositions the film action into a mode of reality, signified by the image of the naked warriors washing away the clay from their bodies and subtly transforming from "archaic sculptures into human beings" (Blumenthal and Taymor 225). Counterpoising the effects of graphic naturalism by the use of computer-generated imagery, Taymor creates a metaphorical world that can be grounded simultaneously in a sense of possibility and reality. As Jonathan Bate notes, there is a strong sense of ritual which underlies the film's treatment of violence (funeral rites, ritual slaying, sybaritic feasts) and contributes to the idea that the boy takes on an ambiguous object/subject position in his fantasy of aggression (8-10). Taymor creates this technical artifice in part with the aid of her production designer Dante Ferretti. By allowing time and space, civilization and barbarity to coexist and mingle, the film succeeds in creating a visual and stylistic extravaganza that blends a wide range of historical and cultural material, from ancient Rome to Mussolini's Italy and the present.

As well as capturing the inflections of modern media, Taymor and her cinematographer Luciano Tovoli experiment with camera movement techniques reminiscent of the theatrical devices employed by early filmmakers like Méliès and Murnau: "People think that when you say theater it's stilted. No. It just means that you're using the imagination and you're using the power of all these special effects to create a collage, a montage of imagery that can be like our dreamscapes" (Russell). A central component of Taymor's cinematic vocabulary of violence is a surreal, haiku-like sequence called Penny Arcade Nightmare (PAN). The five PAN sequences thematize bodily fragmentation and the collapse of boundaries between humanness and animality as means to catapult the viewer into visceral modes of perception: marble limbs bleed and fly through the air, a lamb-headed Mutius meekly awaits the sacrificial ceremony, a Venus of Milo-like Lavinia, stripped to her blood-stained petticoat and wearing the head of a doe, is beset by Demetrius and Chiron in a constantly transforming state of part human, part tiger (Blumenthal and Taymor 228). These surreal sequences intersperse rapid intercutting with striking tableaux vivants, delirious camera movement with frozen shots, foreshadowing the final scene of the bloody banquet.

The cinematic narrative is focalized through the eyes of Young Lucius, who shifts from disengaged spectator to active participant in Titus's revenge scenario. His metafictional position underscores Taymor's own view about the ways in which audience perceives the cinematic events. The sequence of ritualized killings and dismemberments is part of the boy's own theater of cruelty, which reveals the hallucinatory realm of cinematic experience. As Carol Rutter notes, the child simultaneously looks and is looked at, focalizing what is at stake: "My 'looking like a child' is of course a double entendre, not just what the child looks like to spectators, his image in performance, but what he's looking at, including how spectators look at him" (2). Throughout the sequence of Alarbus's sacrifice, the child's bright face stands out against the blood-spattered foreheads of Titus's sons, who bear the entrails of "the proudest prisoner of the Goths" (Taymor, *"Titus"* 25). His modern, casual attire (black T-shirt, shorts, black boots) reinforces his liminal position within the cinematic space, soliciting an engaged, self-reflexive perspective from the off-screen audience. Taymor's strategy of spectatorial engagement echoes her cinematic technique, according to which a story is more interesting if we, as spectators, are given the possibility to interpret or even question the particular style or viewpoint the artist introduces in his narrative or film. In other words, the audience is interested not so much in the object of the story itself, but, rather, in its telling, its representational modes, its nuances.

The boy's passage from innocent passivity to culpable agency in the cycle of revenge mirrors the spectator's *dédoublement*, resulting from a mixture of emphatic engagement and critical dissociation. This moral journey is not predetermined but rather unequal, with sudden outbursts of poignant compassion and startling aggression. Taymor assigns Young Lucius a more active role and makes him complicit in Titus's revenge plan. In a sequence reminiscent of Peter Brook's Royal Shakespeare company production of 1955, it is Young Lucius, not Marcus, who stabs the fly. Rebuked vehemently by Titus, the boy playfully reveals the rationale behind his "deed of death": "Pardon me, sir; it was a black ill-favour'd fly, / Like to the empress' Moor, therefore I kill'd him" (*"Titus"* 113). The stabbing of the fly reiterates the initial iconography of toy wrecking and cruel puppetry and foreshadows the film's climactic violence. The scene also brings forth the problematic of envisioning violence on screen, without recourse to its social glamour or taboos. The film thus intermingles stylized and visceral representations of violence as means to engage desensitized viewers. In doing so, Taymor places several violent events off-stage as the boy gradually takes on his Shakespearean persona. His scopic position challenges placid sensations or reassuring intimacy and operates directly upon the viewer's consciousness and emotions. Although the camera eye does not register a series of events, such as the ritual disembowelment of Alarbus or the rape and mutilation of Lavinia, the viewer is able to observe the boy's visceral reactions to the violent semiotic carved on the human body. The boy's viewpoint recontextualizes the acts of aggression for the viewers and, in doing so, shows them "how the lesson of violence is transmitted to, and thus perpetuated by, the younger generation" (Lindroth 111).

The open, oval-shaped arena underscores from the very beginning the relationship between viewers and performing space. Taymor's semiotics of violence crystallizes in her hybrid vision of Rome, which juxtaposes architectural elements of the ancient metropolis (the Baths of Caracalla, the ruins of Hadrian's villa) with twentieth-century iconic buildings, such as the Palazzo della Civiltà, a neoclassical, futuristic building built by Mussolini during the 1920s to celebrate the architecture of the Colosseum. The film's imagery of Rome is not that of the ancient marble pillars of the grandiose palaces, but a palimpsestic theater of cruelty, which triggers visual associations with Bosnia, Columbine, Rwanda, and other contemporary sites of violence (De Luca and Lindroth 29). The final banquet slaughter is notably shot inside the Pula amphitheater, one of the best-preserved Roman arenas in the world. Completed by Titus Flavius Vespasianus around 81 AD, it hosted gladiatorial combats and *venationes* (staged animal hunts). These gory spectacles, in which thousands of prisoners and animals were slaughtered, became the main ingredients for the lavish ceremonies arranged by the emperor to celebrate the construction of the coliseum. In the opening sequence, an absent crowd cheers and howls with delight as the strongman raises the child over his head like a war trophy. In the final banquet sequence, the empty bleachers are packed with a silent crowd of Croatians. The voyeuristic spectacle of violence becomes a site of specular reflection for both protagonists and off-screen viewers. Although inside the coliseum, the spectators remain silent, liminal witnesses to the violent dénouement of the play. As Taymor notes in her screenplay, they are of "many nationalities, races, ages," a testament to the cultural diversity of Pula's inhabitants themselves, living peacefully in conflict-ridden South Europe (166). They act as our own cinematic surrogates, standing in for us and watching with our eyes the climactic bloodshed. Drawing analogous effects with her puppetry work, the visible presence of the audience inside the story is part of Taymor's distinct directorial signature of keeping the magic effects of art apparent. As Young Lucius takes Aaron's baby in his arms and slowly proceeds towards the archway that leads out of the coliseum, the background gradually brightens up, suggesting the passage from darkness to daylight. Just as the Clown forcibly brought the child into the story, Young Lucius carries the baby outside the bloody arena, leaving the defamiliarized spectators in a liminal position, "reeling with the horror in their bellies and challenged with the dilemmas in their minds" (Blumenthal and Taymor 184).

The tropic image of "headless Rome," transformed by violence into a "wilderness of tigers," is literalized through a semiotics of corporal fragmentation (Taymor, *"Titus"* 98). The overlaying of play space and tragic space underscores the child's ambivalent role in his fantasy of revenge. His play is aggressive and aggregating, eliciting and resisting at the same time the violent act of communal dismemberment. His frantic war games gradually shift into a prosthetic form of re-membering Lavinia's mutilated body. After watching the Clown's freak show, we follow Young Lucius as he enters a woodcarver's shop, in which an old bearded man sands the chipped paint from two wooden hands. The camera zooms out and we realize he is surrounded by numerous wooden limbs, broken dolls, and puppets, reminiscent of the terracotta body parts from the ancient healing sanctuary of Asclepeion in Pergamum. The camera takes us behind the scenes into an actual set designer workshop at the Cinecittà studios in Rome. In a *mise-en-abyme* effect reminiscent of *Bunraku* puppetry, the film captures the "double event" of the artistic process, in which the conspicuous hand of the master puppeteer animates the puppet and brings theater to life. Taymor's directorial vision echoes her longstanding interest in Asian theatrical forms, a tribute to the Japanese and Indonesian way of looking at things: "I received from my experience in Japan an incredible sense of respect for the art of creating, not just the creative product. We're all about the product. To me, the process was also an incredibly important aspect of the total form. And in Indonesia even more so. So then I spent more time in Indonesia and watched these incredible ceremonies that would go on for nine hours that were completely—the separation between your function as a Hindu and your function as a puppeteer creating a puppet show in this Hindu (culture)—there is no separation" ("Interview").

By anatomizing the cultural and aesthetic roots of violence, Taymor seeks to capture the ritualized dimension of the work of art, whether theatrical or cinematic or cybereal. In her view, the act of watching violence on screen is fraught with voyeuristic implications, but bearing witness to it becomes a mode of collective responsibility. Drawing on ritualized action and imagery, Taymor's cinema explores the ambivalent role of violence as entertainment and ritual. In her view, the role of artistic production is to lay bare the social, cultural, and religious taboos of violence by foregrounding its processes of aesthetic production and reception. Titus and Lavinia's mutilated bodies dramatize the effects of cultural/communal dismemberment and evoke the fragmenting effects of film technology (close-ups, editing strategies). Similar to Balinese rites of passage, which enact a change in status for all participants, Taymor's theater and cinema attempt to relocate this transformation at the level of the viewer's consciousness. The film self-consciously foregrounds its own mechanisms for transformation by drawing actuality and representation into a common cinematic space, defined by the coliseum as the "archetypal theater of cruelty" (*"Titus"* 178). The trope of transformation is rendered semiotically at two levels: on a physical level, it is literalized through an imagery of bodily dismemberment; on a cinematic and aesthetic level, it draws the spectators into the amphitheater of Pula and compels a transformation of their "view of the world by rubbing their senses against enactments of extreme events, much more extreme than they would usually witness" (Schechner, *Performance* 193). This type of shamanic initiation—in which physical experiences and states of consciousness are tested by means of ritual mediation—defines, in Taymor's opinion, the essence of aesthetic production: "I'm not religious, but I believe in the ecstasy that art and religion can create in human beings, the ecstatic or the awe—as I like to call it, you know, 'a-w-e'—that it makes people feel in a way that isn't their banal, everyday feel" ("Interview"). The graceful and meticulous gestures with which the woodcarver lays out his tools and carves the wood evokes the figure of a *noh* mask carver, whom Taymor met during her theatrical apprenticeship in Japan ("Interview"). The woodcarver's shop becomes a corrective space, in which the boy's fantasy of violence and re-membering is played out. In this sense, the pair of wooden hands that Young Lucius offers Lavinia signifies the prosthetic energies of artwork. However, the reconfiguration of the body as an aesthetic artifact inevitably involves a lure. The fiction of wholeness remains a residual fantasy while the specter of fragmentation remains to haunt both protagonists and off-screen viewers.

Within the fictional space of the coliseum, the spectacle of dismemberment fragments the body into disposable stage props. Masquerade and puppetry function here as prosthetic forms of artistic production, inextricably tied to the materiality of the cinematic image and the viewer's own body. By foregrounding the artifices and mechanics of the cinematic medium, Taymor prompts viewers to reconsider their own unexamined assumptions about the nature, mediation, and effects of violence in art and real life. Synthesizing a vast body of Asian and Western theatrical forms, pointing the way to future development in computerized performance, Taymor's cinematic language for reworking and translating Shakespeare into contemporary idioms employs a poetics of fragmentation and defamiliarization. Her craft is a model for new media.

Works Cited

Bate, Jonathan. "Introduction to *Titus: The Illustrated Screenplay*." New York: Newmarket P, 2000. 8-13.

Blumenthal, Eileen, and Julie Taymor, eds. *Julie Taymor: Playing with Fire*. New York: Harry N. Abrams, 1999.

De Luca, Maria, and Mary Lindroth. "Mayhem, Madness, Method: An Interview with Julie Taymor." *Cineaste* 25 (2000): 28-31.

Donaldson, Peter S. "Game Space/Tragic Space: Julie Taymor's *Titus*." *A Companion to Shakespeare and Performance*. Ed. Barbara Hodgdon and W.B. Worthen. Malden: Blackwell, 2005. 457-77.

Jackson, Russel. "From Play-Script to Screenplay." *The Cambridge Companion to Shakespeare on Film*. Ed. Russell Jackson. Cambridge: Cambridge UP, 2000. 15-34.

Johnson-Haddad, Miranda. "A Time for *Titus:* An Interview with Julie Taymor." *Shakespeare Bulletin* 18 (2000): 33-37.

Lindroth, Mary. "'Some device of further misery': Taymor's *Titus* Brings Shakespeare to Film Audiences with a Twist." *Literature/Film Quarterly* 29.2 (2001): 106-15.

Marcus, Leah S. *Puzzling Shakespeare*. Berkeley: U of California P, 1990.

Russell, Paul. "*Titus*: A Classic Reborn." *DVD Angle* (16 August 2000): <http://dvdangle.com/fun_stuff/interviews/titus/print.html>.

Rutter, Carol Chillington. "Looking like a Child, or *Titus*: The Comedy." *Shakespeare Survey* 56 (2003): 1-26.

Schechner, Richard. "Julie Taymor, from Jacques Lecoq to *The Lion King*." *The Drama Review* 43 (1999): 36-55.

Schechner, Richard. *Performance Theory*. London: Routledge, 2003.

Snyder, Joel. "Sharing the Story within: An Interview with Julie Taymor." *National Endowment of the Arts* (31 August 1999): <http://www.uv.es/~fores/programa/snyder_taymor.html>.

Taymor, Julie. "Working with Puppets." *Conversations on Art and Performance*. Ed. Bonnie Marranca and Gautam Dasgupta. Baltimore: Johns Hopkins UP, 1999. 467-70.

Taymor, Julie. "Interview: Julie Taymor, Theater, Opera and Film Director." *Academy of Achievement* (3 June 2006): <http://www.achievement.org/autodoc/printmember/tay0int-1>.

Taymor, Julie. "*Titus*": *The Illustrated Screenplay, Adapted from the Play by William Shakespeare*. New York: Newmarket P, 2000.

Titus. Dir. Julie Taymor. Hollywood: Twentieth Century Fox Home Entertainment, 2000.

Walker, Elsie. "'Now is a Time to Storm': Julie Taymor's *Titus*." *Literature/Film Quarterly* 30 (2002): 194-207.

Woods, Alan. ""Bringing Together Man and Nature: The Theater of Julie Taymor." *American Puppetry: Collections, History and Performance*. Ed. Phyllis T. Dircks. Jefferson: McFarland & Company, 2004. 225-38.

Illustrations

The camera movement imitates the circular perspective of a video game in *Titus*, dir. Julie Taymor (Hollywood: Fox Searchlight Pictures, 1999).

Science Fiction, *Forbidden Planet*, and Shakespeare's *The Tempest*

Simone Caroti

The marriage between Shakespeare and Hollywood has produced some offbeat, fascinating, strange, and sometimes simply funny offspring. Virginia Vaughan and Alden T. Vaughan, while examining Freudian interpretations of Caliban's character in their introduction to the latest Arden edition of *The Tempest*, give in a nutshell the plot of *Forbidden Planet*, together with a hint or two about some of its themes. "Caliban as 'id,'" they write,

> became a palpable thread in twentieth-century psychoanalytic interpretations of *The Tempest*, a notion more dramatically presented in the 1956 science-fiction film, *Forbidden Planet*. Now a cult classic, this postwar film transports its Prospero figure to Altair-IV, a distant planet, where Professor Morbius (Walter Pidgeon) continues his scientific investigations, builds robots (Robby, the film's Ariel) and raises his daughter Altaira (the Miranda figure played by Anne Francis). When a spaceship from earth invades the planet, Altaira falls in love with its handsome captain (Leslie Nielsen), but their romance is threatened by an invisible force that nearly destroys the spaceship and kills several of its crew. The dramatic finale reveals that the mayhem is caused by the Professor's own inner psyche, projected on to an electromagnetic force (Caliban), which implements Morbius's repressed anger at the man who would take away his daughter and jealousy at her love for another man. Only with the destruction of Professor Morbius can the calibanic force be quelled. (Vaughan and Vaughan in Shakespeare 111-12)

When the film came out, reviewers reacted with enthusiasm to its strange blend of Shakespeare and 1950s science fiction (SF): "Shakespeare takes a journey into space," the headline above Alan Brien's review for London's *Evening Standard* proclaimed, and Brien went on to argue that Cyril Hume, the film's scriptwriter, had "produced the most rumbustiously enjoyable of all Hollywood planetary melodramas, apparently by dressing *The Tempest* in space suits" (qtd. in Rosenthal 150).

Today, watching *Forbidden Planet* represents an exercise in anachronistic nostalgia—an exploration of homesickness for a future that never was, for an advocacy of centuries to come that now feels more like decades gone by. It is a curious feeling, really; on the one hand the film constitutes, by the standards of 1950s cinematic special effects, a tour de force whose visual graces have stood the test of time better than the majority of contemporary science fiction productions, enriched as the story is by an intelligent use of several of *The Tempest*'s main themes. On the other hand, its vision of a technological future now exists only as history, eclipsed by events which the generation of SF practitioners that had made Robert Heinlein its spokesman had not—some say could not have—foreseen. In particular, these writers had not anticipated the developments in information technology that, only a few decades from their time, would usher in the age of the computer, an age which the SF field represented in the form of the heavily Balkanized, information-laden worlds of cyberpunk fiction. The term "cyberspace," introduced at the end of the 1970s by William Gibson's short story "Burning Chrome" and immortalized in his novel *Neuromancer* (1984), painted a vivid picture of an information-based future that has now become our present.

In his anthology *Age of Wonders*, science fiction editor David Hartwell provides us with an excellent expression of one of the genre's chief characteristics:

> A sense of wonder, awe at the vastness of space and time, is at the root of the excitement of science fiction. Any child who has looked up at the stars at night and thought about how far away they are, how there is no end or outer edge to this place, this universe—any child who has felt the thrill of fear and excitement at such thoughts stands a very good chance of becoming a science fiction reader. . . . To say that science fiction is in essence a religious literature is an overstatement, but one that contains truth. Science fiction is a uniquely modern incarnation of an ancient tradition: the tale of wonder. Tales of miracles, tales of great powers and consequences beyond the experience of people in your neighborhood, tales of the gods who inhabit other worlds and sometimes descend to visit ours, tales of humans traveling to the abode of the gods, tales of the uncanny: all exist now as science fiction. (Hartwell 42)

Of course, Hartwell is not saying that the mythological tale, the traveler's tale, medieval hagiography, and other ancient forms of storytelling are science fiction. He is simply suggesting that in their time they satisfied the same aesthetic and emotional needs SF satisfies today. The sense of wonder generated in the reader or viewer by the vicarious experience of extraordinary events, or by the perception of forces and time-scales far greater than those which can be commonly witnessed in the course of an individual's life, is the chief factor in science fiction's appeal, much in the same way it was for earlier literary forms. Perhaps the most interesting of those forms for our discussion is the traveler's tale, because with it we meet one of science fiction's most recurring features. It does not need to be overly emphasized that one of the best ways of generating the sense of wonder is to set a story in an exotic place, for the experiencing of unusual events will naturally stimulate this ability. Whether it is Ulysses walking in the garden of the Hesperides, Gulliver finding himself tied up in the country of the Lilliputians, David Bowman confronting the two-kilometer-long black monolith at the end of *2001: A Space Odyssey* or Stephano and Trinculo touring a strange island with Caliban, the sense of wonder is always there, ready to put us face to face with the marvels of the possible.

In a very material way, the trope of the fantastic voyage is one of the determining factors in the relationship between *The Tempest* and *Forbidden Planet.* Critics have argued for decades over whether Prospero's island, which the play locates somewhere in the Mediterranean between Tunis and Naples, was originally intended by Shakespeare as a representation of the New World or as a fictional counterpart of the African continent. All this critical back and forth, however, misses a more relevant point: "Caliban's/Prospero's island lies literally in the Mediterranean between Tunis and Naples, but its geographical location is less important than the fact that it is nameless, uncharted and largely unexplored. . . . Our sojourn on this enchanted island is akin to a trip to a distant planet, where we find a world dramatically unlike our own" (Vaughan and Vaughan 4-5). In other words, the placing of Prospero's island in the Mediterranean works very well as a conceptual basis for justifying its array of marvels, for peopling this virgin territory of the imagination with all the strange things that would not have been plausible in Stratford or London. Between the end of the sixteenth century and the beginning of the seventeenth, the New World and the African continent represented the site of England's sense of wonder.

If Shakespeare found in Africa and the New World the perfect fantastic landscape, it was to seventeenth-century Italy that he turned to in order to give us the perfect fantastic and adventurous plot. Renaissance Italy was, for the average English citizen, a place of danger and secret, a sophisticated, violent geo-political scene of constantly shifting alliances and endlessly renewing intrigue. From the point of view of a country that was still enjoying one of the most stable periods in its history, Italy must have looked as much like a dream of exoticism, power, and culture as a nightmare of anarchy and instability. Informed as it was by medieval notions of order and structure in all things, and used to thinking of Rome as the seat of religious corruption, the Elizabethan mind looked at Italy with a mixture of fear and fascination; fear for the utterly chaotic and often brutal nature of its political life, fraught with wars small and large into which major European powers were always more than willing to step, and fascination for the sophistication and depth of its cultural intercourse, both within and without its borders (such as they were). Seen from afar, and modified by the fantastic treatment of the fictional materials, it is small wonder that the characters of the *Tempest* should be Italian. Prospero, with his abrupt, violent mood swings and his books of arcane arts, always teetering on the brink between white and black magic, whose throne was usurped by his brother; Alonso, a king who is more than willing to do a bad turn to someone he does not happen to like very much; Antonio and Sebastian, cunning, corrupt, utterly immoral, and wholeheartedly devoted to the pursuit of power without consequences; these are only the most relevant examples, not of Renaissance Italy as it really was, but as it looked like from England at the beginning of the seventeenth century. It is, in other words, the imaginative translation of a cultural makeup, and from this point of view it is wholly identical to the fictional synthesis of a geographic nexus like Africa or America. Both operate using the same principles, and both provide the English imagination with locales, situations and opportunities that would have been far more difficult to justify on one's own doorstep. It is, indeed, a very interesting group of people, full of as yet untold potential, who remain stranded on Shakespeare's unnamed island.

The island is not simply unnamed, however. It is also unexplored and this is where the experiences of Prospero's unwilling guests come in. As the storm that brought their ship to the island subsides, the Neapolitans find themselves split into three separate groups: Ferdinand, Alonso with the rest of the court party, and Stephano with Trinculo and Caliban. For most of the play's duration, they all tour the mysterious territory in an attempt to find any survivors other than themselves, and in the process they discover the marvels the island has to offer. They all keep hearing strange sounds and unearthly music from invisible sources in the air. Ferdinand meets Prospero, falls in love with Miranda, is enslaved and freed again, and sees a wondrous masque acted by Prospero's spirits. Alonso, Sebastian, Antonio and Gonzalo are put to sleep by Ariel, in order to protect Alonso and Gonzalo from the others' murderous intentions; upon waking they are treated to a vanishing banquet, followed by a terrifying troupe of harpies who engender in them a state of guilty stupor from which only Prospero can free them. Stephano and Trinculo meet Caliban, who immediately proceeds to show the stupefied seamen the natural marvels surrounding them; they hatch with him a plot to kill Prospero and become lords of the island, are chased and stung by Ariel and the rest of the spirits, and are finally discovered by Prospero himself inside his house, wearing his robes. All this moving about and stumbling on incredible things institutes a twin process of exploration and discovery which, resulting as it does in a continuous stream of marvels parading in front of the characters'—and our—eyes, constitutes one of the chief attractions of Prospero's domain. The island is, in short, the perfect place to experience and exercise our sense of wonder, precisely because it has no name and has never really been explored. A hypothetical definitive answer to the America or Africa debate will therefore tell us nothing fundamental, for the same reasons that make it pointless to pinpoint the precise location of Trantor in Isaac Asimov's *Foundation* trilogy, or to find the exact inspiration for the sand-planet Arrakis in Frank Herbert's *Dune*.

The island is both Africa and America, at least as the Elizabethan and Jacobean imagination represented them. It is the territory of fantasy, and as such it is at the same time nowhere (except inside us) and everywhere (that is, anywhere our imagination sets up shop at any given time). At the end of the play Miranda and Gonzalo put the sense of wonder generated by this process of exploration into words. After Prospero has drawn the curtains that had been hiding Miranda and Ferdinand from the Neapolitans' eyes (itself an effective symbol of the play's celebration of the joys of discovery, since Alonso had thus far thought his son dead), Miranda exclaims "O wonder! / How many goodly creatures are there here! / How beauteous mankind is! O brave new world / That has such people in't" (5.1.181-84). An interesting aesthetic inversion is implied by what Miranda says, because her sense of the marvelous has been stimulated by the sight of Alonso, Sebastian, Gonzalo, Antonio and their retinue—in other words, people who for us are absolutely normal. For her, Caliban, Ariel and Prospero's powers are the norm, for the only place she really knows is the island. Her sense of what is strange and unknown represents the mirror opposite of everybody else's, and that includes the audience. *The Tempest* seems bent on providing everyone with a touch of the amazing. After a few lines, Miranda's words are echoed by a more experienced, conventional observer when Gonzalo attributes the happy ending of their tribulations to the gods "that have chalked forth the way / which brought us hither," and goes on to invite everyone to "rejoice / Beyond a common joy, and set it down / With gold on lasting pillars: in one voyage / Did Claribel her husband find at Tunis; / And Ferdinand, her brother, found a wife / Where he himself was lost; Prospero his dukedom / In a poor isle; and all of us ourselves, / When no man was his own" (5.1.203-04, 208-13).

Gonzalo's speech suggests that *The Tempest* configures the act of discovery as a morally positive factor in the characters' lives. Everyone leaves the island in some way enriched by their experiences, or at least, in the case of Caliban, Antonio, and Sebastian, not harmed by the logical consequences of their actions. Even the storm that brings Alonso and the rest of his group to the island, the fearful spectacle of the harpies at 3.3, and the spirits that chase Stephano, Trinculo and Caliban at 4.1, are subsequently revealed to be illusions, scarecrow spectacles produced chiefly for didactic purposes rather than an honest-to-god attempt at harming anyone. In Shakespeare's play, and in a relevant cross-section of SF texts as well, the contemplation of the wonderful and the miraculous seems to possess a special quality of kindness, of mercifulness towards our human failings. As when Ariel convinces Prospero to be lenient towards Alonso, Sebastian and Antonio, the play has the ability to bend our thoughts toward forgiveness rather than vengeance, and to make us willing to reexamine our personal convictions in the light of something greater than us.

Fast-forward four hundred or so years from the writing of *The Tempest*, and the world is a very different place. We have mapped every inch of our planet, explored every nook and cranny with survey ships, photo reconnaissance aircraft, submarines, satellites, microscopes. We have landed on the moon and watched our earth rotate with stately calmness on its moderately inclined axis, continents, oceans and cloud formations coming into view as it turned. As the pace of human discovery kept reducing the frontier of the unexplored, we gradually started losing interest in our planet. Enter outer space and faster-than-light travel. In the nineteenth century, Jules Verne decided it would be a nice idea to send men to the moon by having their spaceship shot from a really powerful cannon, and wrote a story about it. Forty years or so later, H.G. Wells did the same, this time using antigravity. Ever since then, science fiction writers have found several excuses to send their characters out there, but the most powerful boost for their imagination came in 1929, when the English astronomer Edwin Hubble looked at the sky with his telescope and discovered that Einstein's universe was not static, as Einstein himself had thought at the beginning, but was instead expanding at a speed that increased with distance. He also found out that it was much larger than had been assumed until then. When Hubble took a close look at the size of the universe as revealed by his calculations, he must have felt a little dizzy, for he had come up with a figure of about ten billion light-years. Later measurements would extend this figure to fifteen billion. After we had found the ideal playground for the sense of wonder (not only impossibly large, but expanding to boot), the only thing we needed was an imaginative expedient for getting there. There is thus little to be wondered at if it only took a small step for science fiction writers to imagine the construction of an engine that could kick the light-speed problem in the teeth. Whether one calls it warp engine, hyper-light thruster, dimensional jump capacitor, grid-deficient Heisenberg-Klapat thingamajig or Really Fast Way of Sauntering Along makes no difference. What the faster-than-light drive represents is the equivalent of Alice's rabbit hole and Dorothy's twister, or again of the storm that brings Alonso's ship to Prospero's island: an effective way of taking people to otherworldly realms of the imagination.

During the seventy years that followed Hubble's discovery, we have seen the universe. The *Mariner*, *Voyager*, and *Galileo* missions have brought back incredible images of our solar system, while ground-based telescopes have watched as far as they could and discovered a majestic dance of stars, nebulas and galaxies involving time-scales and the production of energies that we simply cannot make sense of. The Hubble Space Telescope has peered even further, and for every light-year it covers there is something unprecedented and wonderful that reveals itself to us. The promises of 1929 turned out to be even greater than we imagined. So now it is 1956, and even before the space probes and Hubble Space everyone knows that the universe is, in that immortal champion of all understatements, a pretty big place. Scriptwriter Hume and director Fred McLeod Wilcox want to make a film based on *The Tempest* that can preserve the play's sense of wonder, together with a few other themes the two happen to be keen on. What better way of doing so than placing Prospero's island in outer space and enlarging it a little bit? Instead of a lonely patch of earth in the middle of the Mediterranean we now have Altair IV, so called because it is the fourth nearest planet to its parent star, Altair, and instead of a wooden brig being tossed by the elements we have a saucer-shaped starship calmly traveling toward the planet at an appreciable multiple of the speed of light. Prospero is now Doctor Morbius, a philologist stranded on Altair IV with his daughter Altaira when the survey ship of which he was a member, the *Bellerophon*, is destroyed with all its crew by an invisible force of unknown nature. The Ferdinand character is now Commander Adams, captain of the "United Planets cruiser C-57-D, now more than a year out from Earth base on a special mission to the planetary system of the great main sequence star, Altair." The mission is, of course, to rescue the crew of the *Bellerophon*, from whom

Earth has not received a single transmission in nineteen years. We have the island and the characters. We have also retrieved our previously lost sense of wonder, and naturally there will be lots of incredible things happening on the planet.

Annoying as it seems, the question remains why Hume and Wilcox chose *The Tempest* and not, say, *A Midsummer Night's Dream*. After all, the night-time woods of the *Dream* harbor the same kind of wonders that people Prospero's island: elves and fairies, magical potion and strange transformations, Titania, Oberon, and Puck. The occurrences detailed in the play belong certainly to that category of larger-than-life events we have defined as the cornerstone of the sense of wonder, and thus of science fiction, and the act of stepping into the magical woods certainly feels like falling down the rabbit hole or being taken away by a twister. Why, then, did it have to be *The Tempest* and not the *Dream*? For that matter, why not *Macbeth* or even *Hamlet*? Let us assume that there really is a reason that explains the choice of this particular play for a science fiction film. If this is true, it must necessarily follow that the element of the sense of wonder is not enough to define the field of science fiction with sufficient accuracy. What else do we need? If we look at the kind of marvels featured in *A Midsummer Night's Dream*, we will discover that in their general outline they are almost identical to those portrayed in such modern-day works as J.R.R. Tolkien's *The Lord of the Rings*, Mervyn Peake's *Gormenghast* trilogy, Terry Brooks's *Shannara* series, and countless others. What all these works have in common, beyond obvious thematic similarities, is the umbrella label of the genre they belong to: fantasy. True, if we go to a bookstore and look for science fiction and fantasy, we will discover that these two categories are invariably put together on the shelves, since fans of the one have a passable chance of being interested in at least taking a look at the other. This, however, does not mean they are the same. What are the differences?

Possibly the most influential definition of science fiction of the last thirty years was given in 1979 by Darko Suvin (see also Wiemer). Mindful of the necessity of establishing once and for all a clearly defined critical identity for the genre, Suvin proceeded to the task of identifying a set of characteristics that would immediately include everything that was science fiction, while at the same time excluding anything that was not. The key factor in his separation of science fiction from other different but similar genres, like fantasy and horror, lies in his use of the twin elements of *estrangement* and *cognition*: "SF is a literary genre," Suvin writes, "whose necessary and sufficient conditions are the presence and interaction of estrangement and cognition, and whose main formal device is an imaginative alternative to the author's empirical experience" (7-8).

We have already encountered the first of the two terms. As defined by Suvin, estrangement (note also the concept's centrality in Russian Formalism) is an imaginative agent that excites the reader's sense of wonder by presenting him with a reality set that is radically different from the one he or she is used to. Depending on the work of fiction one reads or sees, the level of estrangement of this alternative reality set varies, ranging between two extremes: a single new element in an otherwise normal setting on the one hand, and a thoroughly altered environment—complete with a different timeline—on the other. Estranging factors are an indispensable element in all aspects of fantastic fiction and can therefore be found everywhere, from the great mythological cycles and *The Lord of the Rings* to Greg Bear's *Eon* and Gregory Benford's *Timescape*. As we have seen, however, this element alone is not sufficient to fully distinguish SF from fantasy or the mythological tale, and it needs the second term of the pair, cognition. Quoting from Suvin's work, Edward James writes: "Estrangement is offered by the fairy tale and other literary genres as well, but sf is distinguished also by *cognition*, the process of acquiring knowledge and of reason. 'It sees the norms of any age, including emphatically its own, as unique, changeable, and therefore subject to a cognitive view,' unlike, for instance, the myth or the fairy tale, which offer absolutes, not enquiry. 'Cognition' is, in fact, frequently the main subject of SF: the investigation, for instance, of possible social systems or new forms of science. A cognitive—in most cases strictly scientific—element becomes a measure of aesthetic quality, of the specific pleasure to be sought in SF" (James 108).

The crucial difference between science fiction and fantasy lies here. The act of cognition, of rationally making sense of—and coming to terms with—the estranging elements, increases the sense of wonder inherent in the former, whereas it destroys the pleasure of reading the latter. Magic as represented by writers like Tolkien is best left unexplained, because it belongs to the realm of the irrational. Like a fairy, it is a fragile thing, and trying to rationalize it or explain it away will kill it. On the other hand, a rationally constructed estranging element thrives on cognition, as will readily become apparent when a typical example of the genre is examined. Greg Bear's *Blood Music* (1985) is set in our times, and at the beginning of the novel no difference from the world we know is offered. However, estrangement soon rears its head in the form of a biologist's development of a new strain of sentient bacteria. When the private lab he is working for cuts his funds and fires him, deeming his experiment illegal and dangerous, this modern-day Victor Frankenstein injects himself with he latest batch of his creations and goes away. In only a few days, these bacteria spread from their original host to contaminate half the population of the planet. As the novel nears its completion, the world has indeed become estranged from what the reader is used to, but this is nothing compared to the discovery lying in wait at the very end, when the true nature of this biological agent is revealed. Far from being just another outlandish example of malevolent disease (like the monstrous alien virus in John Carpenter's 1982 film *The Thing*), these bacteria have evolved into a new life form inhabiting a different plane of existence, and have taken with them all the human beings who were thought dead. After we finish the last page, the sense of wonder is still with us, even stronger than before. The cognitive discovery of the new life form's true nature implies a series of revelations regarding our understanding of reality and our place in the universe. Far from diminishing our sense of wonder, these revelations greatly increase it, first of all by grounding its presence within a plausible rational framework, and then by extending the implications of this framework far beyond what we had at first imagined.

In my opinion, the reason Wilcox and Hume chose *The Tempest* as the basis for their film is that the play is a very fertile ground for a science-fictional treatment of Shakespearean themes. To suggest that the play *is* science fiction would probably be a little too much, but I do not think that describing it as a form of proto-SF would be too far-fetched. Consider the title, first of all: in Shakespeare's time, the term "tempest" represented "the alchemical term for the boiling of the alembic to remove impurities and transform the base metal into purest gold; if we see Prospero's goal as the transformation of fallen human nature—Caliban, Antonio, Sebastian and Alonso—from a condition of sinfulness to a higher level of morality, the play's episodes mirror the alchemical process" (Vaughan and Vaughan 64-65). When Prospero comments that "My charms crack not" (5.1.2) and later invites Alonso to "cure thy brains / (now useless) boiled within thy skull" (5.1.59-60), he is referring to the refining of his project of psychological and moral engineering, for which he had been preparing himself ever since he and his infant daughter were stranded on the island, twelve years before the events narrated in the play. Like every self-respecting mad scientist, Prospero has studied, planned and waited, and has not acted until the times were ripe and his powers were at their peak. We could therefore see *The Tempest* as a prototypical representation of a pseudo-scientific experiment, a process of cognition employing estranging factors with rationally conceived means for rationally conceived ends.

If *The Tempest* represents a proto-experiment, it necessarily follows that Prospero is a proto-scientist. First of all, the Folio edition of the play capitalizes the term "Art" when it refers to Prospero's powers. "Art" implies study, intellectual labor and hours of practice, not the association one would have in mind when thinking of magic (which is usually something one has either been given or just has), and moreover, Prospero's powers also derive from his books and his staff, in other words from his tools. A further layer of believability is provided while the former duke is reminding Ariel of his suffering at Sycorax's hands: "It was a torment / To lay upon the damned, which Sycorax / Could not again undo. It was mine art, / When I arrived and heard thee, / That made gape the pine and let thee out" (1.2.289-93). Here Prospero is not simply saying that his powers are stronger that Sycorax's. He is also referring to a series of treatises written by such neo-Platonic scholars as Plotinus, Porphyry and Iamblichus (translated by Marsilio Ficino) on the difference between the black arts and the white arts. Those works were certainly familiar to Shakespeare, who wove them into the texture of the play because he knew that his audience would have recognized them as well. The result is a clear definition of the abilities and limitations (admittedly very few) inherent in Prospero's powers, not so much to define them with respect to those of Sycorax (who after all has been dead for more than twelve years at the moment the play opens), but rather to clarify his abilities and moral stature before the arrival of the Neapolitans.

In *The Tempest*, irrationality (epitomized by Caliban, Sebastian, and Antonio) is evil; rationality (Prospero, Ariel, Gonzalo, Ferdinand) is good. The same kind of conflict between morally upright rational attitudes and the evils of an irrational behavior features prominently in *Forbidden Planet*, but as the Vaughans recognize in their introduction to *The Tempest*, Hume and Wilcox gave it a new twist. Linking the Suvinian twin elements of estrangement and cognition to Freud's theories, they used this strange hybrid as the carrier wave for a psychoanalytical treatment of the clash between the two conflicting sides in the Janus face of human nature: the Apollonian, rational world view of the conscious mind, and the Dionysian, rabidly-instinctual-and-proud-of-it irrationality of the unconscious. A brief look at the film's plot will quickly clarify the issue: *Forbidden Planet* is, for all intents and purposes, a multi-layered compendium of cognitively validated marvels. First of all, it is already set in the future, which of course is extraordinary for the audience but not for the characters. This situation, together with the matter-of-fact attitude the crew of the starship displays towards such exotic elements as faster-than-light drive, teleportation and beam weapons, further excites our sense of wonder. The perception of a plausible, rational environment is strengthened by the characters' use of well-structured twentieth-century terminology to indicate hierarchies within the command structure of the ship, engineering problems, physical principles and biological factors. The behavior of the starship's crew is exactly what one would expect from the crew of a vessel on a rescue mission, and their reactions to what happens on Altair IV is a more than an educated extrapolation of what a normal group of people would do in a similar situation. When Commander Adams tells Morbius that the cruiser is there to rescue him, he is warned by the doctor to avoid landing on the planet. Morbius appreciates their concern for his safety but claims he is all right, thank you very much. This modern Prospero prefers exile. Who will not be all right if they land on Altair IV, they are informed, are the Captain and his crew. As Adams and his two highest-ranking officers finally meet Morbius, they discover that the only living beings on the planet are he and his daughter. Everybody else is dead. The force that destroyed them is—in an interesting inversion of Ariel's power—invisible, incomprehensible, unstoppable, and soon begins to attack the starship, killing many of its crew. This force is something nobody is able to understand—not the audience, of course, but not the characters either.

The hunt for the truth is on, then, and in the way Adams and his men set about finding it *Forbidden Planet* reveals its fundamental nature. Footprints and energy signatures are examined, even the readings of the instruments connected with the cruiser's protective energy barrier at the time of the creature's attacks, while Adams engages in some old-fashioned pumping of witnesses for information. In the process, he falls in love with Altaira, who reciprocates his affection. Adams's tactics yield the best results. When he and his officers enter Morbius's inner sanctum, the doctor is finally forced to show them his discovery: a great number of planet-sized generators built by an unimaginably evolved alien race, the Krell. After a million years of continuous evolution, the Krell were annihilated in one single night, just as they were on the verge of an evolutionary breakthrough that would have allowed them to leave their baser instincts and physical bodies behind. By connecting their minds to the generators and tapping the well-nigh infinite energies these machines were able to muster, they would have become pure psychic energy, sheer quanta of unadulterated rationality free of the physical constraints of a messy, inefficient body as well as of the irrationality of the unconscious—the ultimate rationalist's dream. Predictably enough, their murderer is the same force that destroyed the *Bellerophon* and is now busy trying to slaughter Adams's crew. The final revelation comes as a result of yet another act of cognition: the ship's medical officer and Adams pool their mental efforts and discover that the Krell were annihilated by their own subconscious. As the monstrous generators were connected to the minds of every Krell individual, their "id" recognized the threat of annihilation they posed and protected itself, using the unimaginable energies produced by the machines to destroy everyone on the planet.

Of course, when all the Krell died their subconscious died with them, but now there is Morbius. During their first meeting, the doctor had told Adams that he was the only one of the *Bellerophon*'s crew who did not want to leave the planet, owing to his enthusiasm for the alien artifacts, an enthusiasm that the others did not share. The truth was a little different: the doctor had been the first to stumble on the discovery, and had been quick to connect his mind to the generators (still in perfect working order); what he had found was the combined power of a dozen stars at his disposal. The Krell were an entire population, numbering several billions, and their minds, Adams and his men are told, were immeasurably more advanced and capable than ours. Yet they were destroyed in one single night. What would happen if one mere human being were to receive all that power in one single gulp, without intermediaries or sharers? Morbius is conscious only of a chance for unprecedented scientific discovery. The doctor's "id," however, tells a different story, the refusal to share power that has affect tyrants throughout history. This refusal has nothing to do with rationality, of course, but it has everything to do with the Freudian irrational, the child-king that wants everything his way and is more than happy to annihilate any obstacle barring him from his goal. Fantasies of empowerment are extremely seductive, and once satisfied, practically impossible to let go of. Doctor Morbius faces this situation on Altair 4. When his companions decide to leave the planet to whatever fate awaits it, his subconscious is well aware that to agree to such a course of action would mean severing its connection to the machines that make it near-omnipotent, and the incalculable depowering that would result would equal death, or something even worse. It is simply unacceptable. Of course, Morbius constructs a series of rational arguments against leaving, but they are only a smoke-screen to cover the real reason: one does not share power, or let go of it. When the crew of the *Bellerophon* is ready to leave, safely tucked in their anti-g hammocks on board the ship, the doctor's "id" sucks power from the generators and defends itself, destroying everyone and everything.

Both *Forbidden Planet* and *The Tempest* represent an intelligent reflection on the uses and misuses of power, and every character has a role to play in it, from minor figures like the ship's boatswain (rather amusingly mirrored by Earl Holliman's perennially thirsty cook) to major players like Alonso or Antonio (who are without direct counterparts in *Forbidden Planet*). However, its cornerstone is once again represented by the twin character of Prospero/Morbius. In the play, this theme is introduced right at the beginning. When Gonzalo approaches the ship's boatswain to give him advice, the man answers back: "You are / a councilor; if you can command these elements to / silence and work the peace of the present, we will not / hand a rope more. Use your authority! If you cannot, / give thanks you have lived so long and make yourself / ready in your cabin for the mischance of the hour, if it / so hap.—Cheerly, good hearts—Out of our way, I say!" (1.1.20-23). The Neapolitans' arrogant assumption that they can give advice to experienced seamen during a storm is only the first in a long line of instances where the dangerous nature of power is examined. Not even the wise Gonzalo knows when it is time to let others do their job. In fact, it is Prospero himself who recognizes that his exile on the island was caused by his excessive dedication to his arcane arts: "those being all my study, / The government I cast upon my brother / And to my state grew stranger, being transported / And rapt in secret studies" (1.2.74-77).

It is fundamental to understand that those same powers that make Prospero so terrible on his island cost him his dukedom in the first place. He chose learning over politics. By contrast, Doctor Morbius must sacrifice his own life to get rid of his powers, and from this point of view the Freudian elements of *The Tempest* become a useful critical tool. Prospero is able to willingly give up his Arts because he has never repressed them; alternately gentle and raging, optimistic and morose, he is well aware of what he has let happen to himself and Miranda, and knows that his powers represent a danger for both. Painful as it was for him, his decision to let them go represents a substantial growing up on his part. His two Freudian alter-egos, his superego and his "id," are both outside, represented by Ariel and Caliban respectively, and his fondness for the former as well as his hostility towards the latter allow him to maintain a sane relationship with himself. When Prospero lets Ariel convince him that forgiveness is better than vengeance, he is listening to the better part of his nature, and he can do that because he can also see very well what his worst part looks like. Morbius, on the contrary, has been granted no such luxury. For someone who is supposed to be the very embodiment of rational enlightenment, he goes by a rather unsettling name: "Morbius" is a slight reconfiguration of the Latin *morbus* and the Italian *morbo*, both names meaning "disease," both of the body and of the mind, and the dangerous duality such a name implies is mirrored in the doctor's relationship towards the two aspects of his nature. Morbius has kept his Caliban inside, repressed and unrecognized for more than nineteen years. His apparently rational discourse conceals a seething, raging psyche over which he has no control. To further compound the problem, his Ariel is a robot, not a human being. It cannot help him. When he finds his life on Altair IV (his *powerful* life, with the energy output of a dozen suns at his command) threatened, and he learns that his daughter has found another man, he unleashes a force which he, lacking as he does Prospero's greater psychological awareness, will only be able to stop by killing himself. That Morbius does so, that he is finally able to make the ultimate unselfish decision and destroy himself in order to let others live, testifies to the basically good nature of the character.

At the beginning of *Science Fiction in the 20th Century*, James writes that SF stories are often at their most useful when we employ them as a critical look at today's world from a faraway time and place (vi). Under these terms, the experience of viewing *Forbidden Planet* and of considering the dialectic relationship it establishes with *The Tempest* is as fresh and useful today as it was the day the movie came out, and its achievements far outweigh its failure to foresee the actual course our all-too-human future would take. There is no cyberspace in Hume's movie (or in Shakespeare's play, for that matter), but there are a scientist, a ship, a doctor, a girl, and a problem to solve employing scientific and technological means. The props may have changed since the mid-1950s, but the basic concept remains valid: read the world, and understand its laws—then make things better, and move beyond your limitations. The relevance of this idea has not aged.

Works Cited

Hartwell, David G., ed. *Age of Wonders: Exploring the Worlds of Science Fiction*. New York: Walker, 1984.

James, Edward. *Science Fiction in the 20th Century*. London: Oxford UP, 1994.

Rosenthal, Daniel. *Shakespeare on Screen*. London: Hamlyn, 2000.

Suvin, Darko. *Metamorphoses of Science Fiction: On the Poetics and History of a Literary Genre*. New Haven: Yale UP, 1979.

Vaughan, Virginia Mason, and Alden T. Vaughan, ed. *The Tempest*. By William Shakespeare. London: Thomas Nelson and Sons, 2000.

Wiemer, Annegret. "Utopia and Science Fiction: A Contribution to Their Generic Description." *Canadian Review of Comparative Literature / Revue Canadienne de Littérature Comparée* 19.1-2 (1992): 171-200.

Mobilizing Foreign Shakespeares in Media

Richard Burt

When debating and theorizing the politics of Shakespeare adaptations, postcolonial and intercultural performance critics assume both the existence of a unified Shakespeare at the Western (or Westernized Indian) metropolitan centers and the existence of equally unified subversive, decolonizing Shakespeares, rewritings and translations that (ideally) leave colonial and imperial Shakespeare behind at the global margins (intercultural performance criticism comes out of anthropology: see Schechner; Schechner and Appel; Pavis; for a Shakespeare critic unself-consciously playing anthropologist with her "native informant" Mizo students, see Loomba). The more native and national, the more regional and the more local Shakespeare performances are said to be, the less recognizably Shakespearean, the more subversive they are said to be (see Singh; Loomba; De; Bhatia). Postcolonial critics in general and postcolonial critics of Shakespeare in particular tend to adopt a unidirectional model of cultural exchange whereby an originally unified, Western high culture text such as a Shakespeare play is imported, appropriated, and indigenized and thereby made possibly subversive. This anthropological model of culture opens up a corollary critique of the exporting and expropriation of the Indianized Shakespeare appropriation, which is said to either be recuperated and neutralized by Western entrepreneurs who want to take the local production on a global tour or poached by Western (Orientalist) theater directors (on touring Shakespeare, see Kennedy).

What happens to this cultural import and export model of indigenization and subversion when Shakespeare is mobilized in different media and framed across media? What happens to national cinemas when cinema and television have been transnationalized? These questions become particularly acute when we consider the way a film genre and narrative—in this case, a play or a film being produced within a film—cuts across even what are commonly regarded as national cinemas. Films with rehearsals and performances of *Othello* where a parallel is drawn between the plots of Shakespeare play and of the film, for example, cut across cinemas of Canada, France, Britain, the United States, Denmark, and India, to name a few such as *L'Histoire inventée, Les Enfants du Paradis, The Playboys, Men Are Not Gods, The Flesh and Blood Show, Paradise in Harlem, A Double Life, Alcatraz, Desdemona, Othello.* Focusing on foreign Shakespeares provides a more productive alternative to what I take to be self-defeating aspects of postcolonial criticism. That is, a strategic focus on Asian and American Pacific Rim Shakespeares might be leveraged against the notion of Eurocentrism were one to explore European films about a Shakespeare film or play being produced in a film (on Eurocentrism, see, e.g., Shoat and Stam). One would see another problem in postcolonial criticism, namely, its implicit mirroring of the authentic Shakespeare it wishes to oppose. Just as institutional Shakespeare is defined by its authenticity, so too are subversive, local (vanishing) Shakespeares defined by their authenticity (their locality, in contrast to their commodification for global, cosmopolitan consumption; on the authentic Shakespeare, see Orgel).

Our understanding of Asian drama and its cinema is conditioned by our understanding of Shakespearean and European drama and cinema. A proper contrast might begin, for example, with a selection of European films whose subplots involve theater productions of a Shakespeare play: *Paris Belongs to Us* (Jacques Rivette, 1960); *Le Rideau Rouge* (dir. Andre Barsacq, 1952), about a production of *Macbeth*; *Conte d'hiver* (dir. Eric Rohmer, 1992), a spin-off of *The Winter's Tale*; *L'Important c'est d'aimer* (dir. Andrej Zulawski, 1975), involving a production of *Richard III*, starring Klaus Kinski; *Rendez-vous* (dir. André Téchiné, 1985), involving a production of Romeo and Juliet; *Rosencrantz and Guildenstern are Dead* (dir. Tom Stoppard, 1990); *Ulysses' Gaze* (dir. Theodoros Angelopoulos, 1995) in which part of the balcony scene from *Romeo and Juliet* is performed in urban ruins; *San zimske noci* aka *Midwinter Night's Dream* (dir. Goran Paskaljevic, 2004), with a scene from a production of *A Midsummer Night's Dream* performed in a disabled children's hospital; *Les Amants de Verone* (dir. Andre Cayette, 1949), about a film production of *Romeo and Juliet*; and *Teatro di Guerra* aka *Rehearsal for War* (dir. Mario Martone, 1998), about an Italian stage production of *The Taming of the Shrew* performed in Sarajevo where theaters have remained open.

Obviously it would take a computer to sort through all the competing claims for cultural supremacy these films about theater are making: the task, one hopes, for a future cyberspace project. Its goal, I would like to suggest, would be to ask what we might do to consider "phoney" Shakespeare, that is, problems of reception, memory, and literary canonization related to recording media and that turn up in a number up in examples of the Shakespeare play on film. To that end, let us turn briefly to the work of Jacques Rivette. In *L'Amour par terre* (1984), Rivette references *Othello* (recited in English) and *Hamlet* (it is being translated into Finnish); and Rivette's "pirate film" *Noroît* (1976) is both a spin-off of Cyril Tourneur's *The Revenger's Tragedy* and involves the performance of scenes from the play (recited in English). But for our purposes the best example of this cultural interplay is *Paris nous appartient* (1960). The film involves two related plots, one about a production of *Pericles* (translated in French); the other about the mysterious death, possibly a murder, of a Spanish classical guitarist named Juan and a missing tape recording he made. In *Paris nous appartient*, we see that capitalism has replaced fascism as the center of European leftist resistance. The political conspiracy in the film, if there is one, comes from Franco's Spain and the McCarthy period in the United States where novelist and artist Philip Kaufman has gone into exile as a result of McCarthy's hearings; a US-American at a Paris bar is overheard talking about Nixon. The two plots intersect in relation to dislocation and recording. Gerard, who is directing the production of *Pericles*, tells the cast he too "feels like an exile." Furthermore, Gerard (Giani Esposito) tells Anne (Betty Schneider), a young student and actress he wants for the role of Marina, "the reason I want to stage [*Pericles*] is that it's 'unplayable.' It's shreds and patches, yet it all hangs together." When Anne asks when the production would begin, Gerard tells her he is waiting to find a tape of guitar music that Juan made and that has gone missing since his death. The choice of *Pericles* is apt here because its authorship too is a mystery in the fim. Anne's brother, Paul, tells her that Pericles "wasn't Shakespeare's work." Although Gerard's ex-girlfriend Françoise (Terry Jordan), an American ex-patriot, reveals near the end of the film that she has had Juan's tape all along, the production falls apart after Gerard and then Paul are murdered. In an astonishing montage, the film ends with a series of Anne's memories relating her pastoral location near a pond outside Paris and the production's auditions and rehearsals in different interior and exterior locations in Paris. The film ends by recalling the same line from *Pericles* recited variously in the audition and rehearsal scenes: "Is this wind westery that blows?" Repetitions of a fragment from the play undoes a narrative movement in the film from beginning to end: like the brief screening the cast watches of the Babel sequence in Fritz Lang's *Metropolis* (1924) that stops when the film projector breaks down and the briefly held shot of Juan in a Danish fashion model's apartment, the production of *Pericles* is stuck, frequently breaking down in rehearsal. Yet the production of *Pericles* is stuck in a groove that nevertheless keeps things going. The end of Rivette's film leaves open to question whether Juan was murdered and whether Anne will join the remaining few actors in continuing their production of *Pericles*. My brief examination of *Paris nous appartient* enables us to see Shakespeare's staying power has nothing to do with his staying in (one) place. Like the fragmented memories in the montage at the end of Rivette's *Paris nous appartient*, Shakespeare develops in the moment of his departing.

In what follows, I explore the Shakespeare in the context of film both in order to expand and call into question what counts as Shakespeare in performance. The first is a US documentary about a bi-cultural, bi-national, and bi-national Vietnamese and US-American theatrical production of *A Midsummer Night's Dream* that tours Vietnam, entitled *A Dream in Hanoi* (dir. Tom Weidlinger, 2001). The second is the Japanese film *Warai no daigaku* (University of Laughs) (dir. Mamoru Hosi, 2004). *A Dream in Hanoi* reveals itself to be a self-pitying, neo-imperialist apologia for a failed attempt to (re)colonize Vietnam. Similarly, *Warai no daigaku* is a vehicle for the melancholic and even nostalgic expressions of a felt loss of national identity.

Shakespeare's reception is always productive, I conclude, insofar as his reception is always more or less poor, more or less foreign, whether in Anglophone documentary or non-Anglophone period fiction film.

As if drawing for its narrative structure on the Hollywood musical *42nd Street* (dir. Lloyd Bacon, 1935, with Busby Berkeley's musical numbers), about a director who may literally die as he produces his last Broadway Show, *A Dream of Hanoi* documents a bi-national and bi-lingual US-American and Vietnamese coproduction of *A Midsummer Night's Dream* from its inception in Oregon to its traveling and touring in Hanoi. The idea for the coproduction came from one Lorelle Browning who teaches at an Oregon college not named in the film. Focusing less on the performance of the play than the efforts and tensions arising behind-the-scenes in the three months before the production premiered, this feel-good film takes as its ostensible subject the kinds of intercultural problems that arise from trying to integrate the two theaters. Although the subtitles at the film's beginning announce that the production "built a bridge" between US-Americans and Vietnamese, and sounds liberal minded and well-intentioned, the film is a disturbing exercise in latter-day US (cultural) imperialism arising from a failure to mourn the Vietnam war. What makes this film particularly appalling, in my view, is the way it does not acknowledge a disparity between the production of the play and the film. Unlike the bi-national theater production, the film is mono-national. It has only one director, a US-American, and the film uses an utterly conventional, male voice-over narrative in English, supplied by F. Murray Abraham. While Vietnamese used in the film is translated into English via subtitles, the English is not translated into Vietnamese via subtitles. The film is clearly directed, then, to a US audience; as well, it quickly becomes clear that the production *of A Midsummer Night's Dream* is tilted toward the US audience who will watch the film. Using the evasive passive tense, the narrator tells us that "it is agreed" the US director, Allen Nause, who has a Vietnamese woman translator present, will lay out the basic ideas, with the Vietnamese director, Doan Hoang Giang, taking a secondary role as the person who implements the US-American director's views. Somehow, this division of labor will produce a "uniquely Vietnamese interpretation."

In addition to the US-American and Vietnamese director having unequal billing, Browning's presence is explained in bizarrely custodial terms. She is there, the narrator says, "to defend Shakespeare's text against misinterpretation and mistranslation." No criteria are supplied to explain to us how Browning or anyone else in the film is deciding on what is interpretation and what is misinterpretation. Even more mystifying, the Vietnamese parts of the play are translated into contemporary US-American English subtitles, not back into Shakespeare's text. In stunningly reactionary fashion, Shakespeare is held up as a magic wand that the US-Americans can turn into a baton to brow beat the poor Vietnamese director, staff, and actors into doing the play the US-American way. When insisting on her view of the play, Browning tells the Vietnamese director that Shakespeare is a better director than he is or than she is or than the US-American director is. And Doug Miller, the actor who plays

Lysander and claims to bring a revolution to Vietnamese theater by openly kissing a Vietnamese actress on stage, says "We're going from zero to Shakespeare in three months." Destination Shakespeare is a given here, and one would never know from Miller's comment or from the film that the Vietnamese director had already done *King Lear* or that Shakespeare had been performed in Vietnam before Browning arrived. Despite the pretence of a coproduction, then, the traffic should move in one direction, as far as the Americans are concerned. They are not there to Vietnamese their US-American Shakespearean actors; they are there to colonize the Vietnamese actors and workers.

A Japanese film set just in 1940 as World War II looms, *University of Laughs* also involves delay but mourns Japan's wartime past through comedy. Americans are entirely missing from the film that focuses on Japan's mobilization due to the worsening situation with China. *Warai no daigaku* takes up Shakespeare in an almost entirely paratextual manner, locating a yet to be approved stage adaptation of *Romeo and Juliet* in the context of promoting Japanese nationalism and militarism, and in which casting is racially homogenous. Attention to this film will allow us to consider further how the use of Shakespeare to promote a particular vision of the nation, or ShakesPR, depends on relatively invisible para-Shakespeare material (on "ShakesPR," see Burt). The film makes visible a blindspot typical in films involving rehearsals and performances of a Shakespeare play, namely, preproduction negotiations between the state and the director; discussions about the politics of adaptations; script revision in light of censorship; and advertising posters. The film begins with the censor Mutsuo Sakisaka (Kôji Yakusho) frenetically stamping every manuscript that comes before him, and he makes it clear soon thereafter that he thinks there is no civic role from drama when war is impending. Sakisaka interviews a number of dramatists and either approves their plays when they agree to cuts or rejects them if the dramatist refuses. Eventually, Hajime Tsubaki (Goro Inagaki), a dramatist adapting *Romeo and Juliet* as a comedy entitled *Julio and Romiet*, is allowed to go forward with the play as the censor lightens up and acknowledges his own love of theater and even fantasizes about being a gag writer (he is actually pretty good) and an actor (playing a policeman, of course).

While the film sets up the censor and dramatist as good and bad guy, *Warai no daigaku* is of interest for opening up a dialogue about censorship as collaboration by making the film less of a play-within-a-film than a filmed play about the approval of a play (the film is in fact based on a 1996 stage play of the same title by the same writer, Koki Mitani). Nearly all the action takes place in the censor's office over a period of five days, and *Warai no daigaku* echoes *Waiting for Godot* in that it is very much like a play with two characters who go over and over the same ground without seeming to get anywhere. Initially, Sakisaka pounces immediately and absurdly on Tsubaki's script: the play has Westerners in it; the idea is not original, Sakisaka maintains. Furthermore, an English writer named William Shakespeare wrote a tragedy about similarly named characters. Changing the order of the first syllables and exchanging the second syllables of Romeo's and Juliet's names is part of the joke,

Tsubaki explains. It is not funny, counters Sakisaka. Tsubaki begins to act out the balcony scene to show how it is funny, explaining that the play is a play within the play, about an acting troupe putting on a production of *Romeo and Juliet*. Sakisaka does not laugh, however. "Why write a romance about the western barbarians with whom your country is at war?" he asks. Tsubaki says it is set in Italy and that Japan recently signed a treaty with Italy. But Sakisaka says that the author is English. "If Churchill made sushi, would you eat it?" he asks the dramatist. Tsubaki says no and adds that he would not eat sushi made by Hitler either, because nether Churchill nor Hitler would make it properly. Rather than reject the manuscript, however, the censor advises cuts: "Place the action in Japan. Get rid of the British influences." Tsubaki is at his wit's end, claiming that his play is a parody and that the genre of parody has its own rules.

As negotiations between the dramatist and censor continue over the next few days, it turns out that Sakisaka has a salutary effect on the dramatist. Political repression and aesthetic excellence are not necessarily at odds. On the second day, the dramatist concedes that by moving the play's action to Japan, his play is actually better, even funnier. Tsubaki eventually makes clear to Sakisaka that he struggles against the state's authority over the theater, which he regards as illegitimate, not by refusing to write or by staging a play without the censor's approval and risking arrest, but by taking the censor's demands, however unreasonable, and rewriting his play to improve it. At this, Sakisaka places one final demand on Tsubaki: revise his comedy by excising all humor in it. Tsubaki is drafted by the army and proceeds to make his play even funnier. In the epilogue, we see stills of the *Romeo and Juliet* play, staged after Tsubaki received the Sakisaka's approval, with the actress playing Julio wearing a blonde wig and the actor playing Romiet a brown wig. We also see the influence of Sakisaka in comic, successive shots of Churchill and Hitler making sushi. The closing credits end with the film screenplay getting the censor's stamp of approval. Tsubaki literally bows to the censor, repeatedly, in fact. Yet in the film's happy win-win outcome, both dramatist and censor serve the nation, the dramatist by leaving the stage for the war and the censor by taking over direction of the play and by acting all the parts in it, if necessary. Nevertheless, the conjunction of nationalism and Shakespeare depends on the play being censored in the film. We see Sakisaka laughing while reading the script but not reading aloud from the script. Similarly, we never see scenes from the play performed, only stills, unlike films like *To Be or Not to Be* (dir. Ernest Lubitsch, 1942), a wartime film unpopular with its audience because it appeared to make light of Hitler's invasion of Poland.

The film's closing credit sequences return us to the issue of performance promotion in functioning first as an epilogue and a kind of trailer for a play that was and never was performed and then in linking theater publicity to the film's credits. The closing credits begin with a shot the theater district, full of posters, advertisements, barkers, and so on, we have seen earlier in the film each time the dramatist begins his trek to the censor's office. A low angle medium long shot of the theater district tracks into a closeup of a theater poster with the screenwriter's credit written on it, and credits written in similar posters follow. The film ends with the title page of the film's script itself getting the censor's stamp of approval in the same manner the manuscript of Julio and Romiet was shot when censored. Stamped in red on the right are "Warning"; "The Metropolitan Police Department" (on the middle column); "Censored" (on the right column); and "Forbidden" (in the middle column). The black Japanese characters say: "It is forbidden by law to copy or change the contents of this video program. In order to show this program for commercial purposes, you must obtain the formal permission of the copy-right holder." The image suggests an analogue: the film, like a play script, has not been approved. Yet censorship serves as a model for the way making something nearly invisible also makes something else; paratextual materials displace performance. Two stamps shown next to each other in a number of shots figure a doubleness censorship, again an example of the uncanny.

Just as Shakespeare is not one thing in performance (film, theater, opera, and so on), so he is not one thing paratextually. The three-second gap of black film between the closing credits and this post-credits sequence of a stamp of approval is like the space between the paper and stamp when the censor suspends stamping at the last second. The same style of text and posters wittily link the title card of the film, as well as locations including, the theater, day, and the censor's office. Although *Warai no daigaku* is in some respects conservative in its sentimentality (endorsing collaboration by the dramatist with the censor and making poignant the dramatist's support of the dramatist when he is called up for military service at the end of the film) yet it is the very sentimentality that allows negotiations involving both resistance and surrender.

This analysis of *Warai no daigaku* may be extended to the DVD version of the film. The deluxe DVD version, in targeting the upscale Japanese market, extends the role of the censor to the DVD owner. As a figure for post-theatrical release film marketing, the deluxe DVD version of the film marks an extensive attachment of a blocked past to moments of suspension and delay. The DVD cleverly allows the collector the same options of the censor by allowing him jokingly to approve or censor not only the film itself but any other DVDs in his collection. It is unlikely, however, that collectors will actually ever use the stamps, since that would mean taking the joke too literally and also lower the value of the DVD should it be resold. It is such remains of the remains, from posters, film clips, ballets and so on in films to closing credits and DVDs, that allusions to Shakespeare may help us come to terms with globalization as it is allegorized and encrypted in increasingly transnational cinemas.

Works Cited

Bhatia, Nandi. "Shakespeare and the Codes of Empire in India." *Alif: A Journal of Comparative Poetics* 19 (1998): 96-126.

Bhatia, Nandi. "Imperialistic Representations and Spectatorial Reception in *Shakespeare Wallah*." *Modern Drama* 45 (2002): 61-75.

Burt, Richard. "Shakespeare in Asian and Post-Disaporic Cinemas: Spinoffs and Citations of the Plays from Bollywood to Hollywood." *Shakespeare the Movie: Popularizing the Plays on Film, TV, Video, and DVD*. Vol. 2. Ed. Richard Burt and Lynda E. Boose. London: Routledge, 2003. 265-302.

Burt, Richard. "Civic ShakesPR: Middlebrow Multiculturalism, White Television, and the Color Bind." *Colorblind Shakespeare: New Perspectives on Race and Performance*. Ed. Ayanna Thompson. London: Routledge, 2006. 157-85.

Burt, Richard. "Shakes(disap)pea . e. . r. . .s . . . in the Cinema: The Remains of the Play in 'Indian' Shakespeare Films." *Shakespeare in Asia: Contemporary Performance*. Ed. Yong Li Lan and Dennis Kennedy. Cambridge: Cambridge UP, 2009.

Burt, Richard. "Digital Film, Asianization, and the Transational Film Remake: Alluding to Shakespeare in *L'Appartement*, *The King is Alive*, and *Wicker Park*." *Shakespeare Yearbook XVII*. Ed. Yang Lingui and Douglas Brooks. Lewiston: Edwin Mellen, 2009.

De, Esha Nioyogi. "Modern Shakespeares in Popular Bombay Cinema: Translation, Subjectivity, and Community." *Screen* 43 (2002): 19-40.

Kennedy, Dennis. "Shakespeare and Cultural Tourism." *Theatre Journal* 50.2 (1998): 175-88.

Loomba, Ania. "Hamlet in Mizoram." *Cross-cultural Performances: Differences in Women's Re-Visions of Shakespeare*. Ed. Marianne Novy. Urbana: U of Illinois P, 1993. 257-70.

Loomba, Ania. "Shakespearian Transformations." *Shakespeare and National Culture*. Ed. John J. Joughin. London: Routledge, 1997. 83-108.

Loomba, Ania, and Orkin Martin, eds. *Post-Colonial Shakespeares*. London: Routledge, 1998. 143-63.

Pavis, Patrice, ed. *The Intercultural Performance Reader*. London: Routledge, 1996.

Schechner, Richard, ed. "Intercultural Performance." *The Drama Review* 26 (1982): 2-4.

Schechner, Richard, and Willa Appel, eds. *By Means of Performance: Intercultural Studies of Theatre and Ritual*. Cambridge: Cambridge UP, 1990.

Shoat, Ella, and Robert Stam, eds. *Unthinking Eurocentrism: Multiculturalism and the Media*. London: Routledge, 1994.

Singh, Joytsna. "Different Shakespeares: The Bard in Colonial / Postcolonial India." *Theatre Journal* 4 (1989): 445-58.

Singh, Joytsna. "Shakespeare and the 'Civilizing Mission.'" *Colonial Narratives / Cultural Dialogues: "Discoveries" of India in the Language of Colonialism*. London: Routledge, 1996. 121-52.

Appropriation and the Design of an Online Shakespeare Journal

Christy Desmet and Sujata Iyengar

In Shakespeare studies, online journals have been part of the landscape of new media scholarship for some time. *Early Modern Literary Studies*, for instance, launched its first issue in April 1995 and the first issue of *Renaissance Forum* appeared in March 1996. At least through the 1990s, however, scholars of early modernity envisioned the internet largely as a vehicle for creating and accessing electronic versions of familiar print artifacts such as refereed journals, scholarly editions, bibliographies or collection of resources, and repositories of syllabi. A survey by Ann Lancashire in 1998 revealed that scholarly users of online resources wanted electronic media primarily to speed up and simplify traditional reading tasks (see similar findings in Dorothy Marie Hett's annotated bibliography for secondary school teachers). Since then, Shakespeare online has ventured deeper into cyberspace. Although a keyword search on 21 July 2007 on "Shakespeare" and "cyberspace" in the online version of the International Bibliography of the Modern Language Association of America still yielded only five entries, Shakespeare has a robust second life, for instance, in the popular discourse spaces of the blogosphere (Presley). On a more theoretical level, Yong Li Lan has analyzed "Shakespeare as Virtual Event" in terms that help define Shakespeare's place in cyberspace: she discusses ancillary internet spaces (such as the National Theatre's Talkback website) that supplement theatrical events and thus extend their life in time and space and she examines the ways in which so-called live theater is itself re-mediated, both in a practical sense by the incorporation of digital media and, more philosophically, by blurring the boundary between "live" and "mediatized" performance. As Philip Auslander has argued, such a distinction proves to be historical and contingent rather than ontological or essential (Yong 57).

The term cyberspace entered the common vocabulary by way of William Gibson's *Neuromancer* (1984), which offers this allusive definition: "Cyberspace. A consensual hallucination experienced daily by billions of legitimate operators, in every nation, by children being taught mathematical concepts. A graphic representation of data abstracted from the banks of every computer in the human system. Unthinkable complexity. Lines of light ranged in the nonspace of the mind, clusters and constellations of data. Like city lights, receding" (51). Gibson's definition in his novel *Neuromancer* re-appears on the next page in a voice-over for an imagined "kids' show" (52). In this context, cyberspace is an unfenced playground, an infinite, "unthinkable . . . nonspace" of the mind. Perhaps the key to cyberspace's character lies in the optimistic, oxymoronic phrases, "consensual hallucination" and "unthinkable complexity." A shadowy hallucination and yet impossibly palpable in its complexity, cyberspace is both nowhere and everywhere, a disembodied space whose seeming reality is defined, maintained, and destroyed by human consensus. A Google search on "cyberspace," even today, yields predominantly sites that center on virtual worlds, both recreational and educational. And yet the root of the word imposes order upon this nonsensical, nonspecific "nonspace," and so builds a Foucauldian panopticon in the playground. The word "cyber" derives from the Greek word for a helmsman, which also gives us our English words "governor" and "gubernatorial." Norbert Wiener alluded to this sense of the word in 1948 when he defined the then-new science of cybernetics as "the entire field of control and communication theory, whether in the machine or in the animal" (*Oxford English Dictionary Online*). Communication and control go together, as do machine and animal. Going back even farther, James Clerk Maxwell employed implicitly the metaphor of the steersman sailing his vessel in his 1868 essay "On Governors," the first mathematical analysis of the theory of systems of continuous-control (see Mayr). Wiener cited Maxwell's paper as the first account of feedback mechanisms, returning to the term "cyber" in preference to the Latinized "governor" (Mayr 425; however, the *Oxford English Dictionary* and Mayr remind us that the Hellenized form "cyber" had existed in French, as *la cybernétique*, to refer to government since 1843; thus the new science "had not coined a new word" [Mayr 425] but revived an old one). This, then, is the genealogy of cyberspace: not

Figure 1. The page or web interface for *Borrowers and Lenders.*

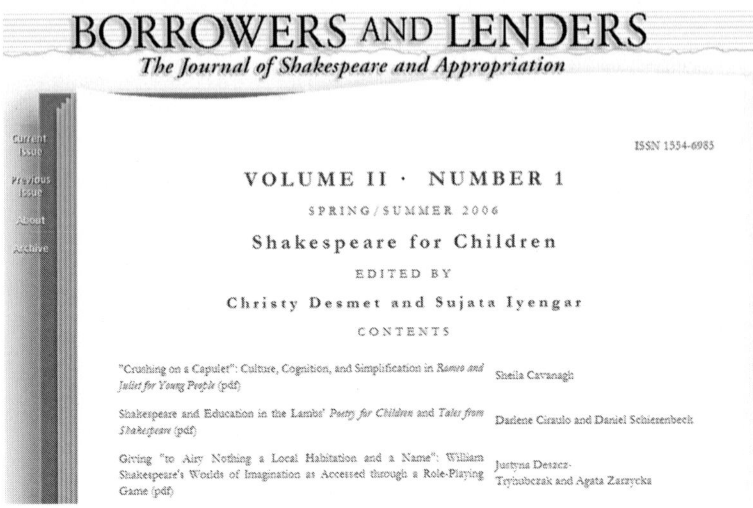

unfettered nonspace but communication governed by the continuous control of code and the mechanisms of feedback.

In this article, we consider the feedback (or we could say, the dialectic) between playground and panopticon in one example of digital Shakespeare that re-mediates the by-now familiar phenomenon of the online journal. *Borrowers and Lenders: The Journal of Shakespeare and Appropriation* (*B&L*) is a new, online, peer-reviewed journal that combines text delivered through XML (Extensible Markup Language) with multimedia. We explore tensions inherent in the journal's position between old and new media: first, its status as a publishing amphibology, one-half print artifact, one-half website and second, the way in which the combination of its underlying markup structure and use of the web as a display medium at once expand and restrict the reader's and writer's agency—hence, constructs a panopticon in the playground.

In the beginning was the page

Jay David Bolter and Richard Grusin have argued that new media begin by modeling both their *ethos* and *technē* on existing media. Not until practitioners discover different capabilities (or "affordances") of the new medium do they break out of existing paradigms for representation. *B&L*'s genealogy traces itself to both the printed book and the World Wide Web. Learned journals, of course, are an artifact of the print era, when, according to scholars and critics ranging from Walter Ong to Elizabeth Eisenstein, the move to regularize typography made printed text transparent, directing the reader's eye to "meaning" beneath the page's surface. Like many e-journals, *B&L* mimics the printed book self-consciously, even nostalgically, in the design of its web interface. There is, however, a touch of the hyperreal in designer Bill Reeves's cultivation of color and simulation of the material page's curving surface and even in the crispness of the journal's Garamond typeface (figure 1). The virtual page of *B&L* achieves its ostensible "reality" through a painterly illusion that, like cyberspace, reveals at the same time its status as an evanescent "constellation of data."

B&L's second structural paradigm, the World Wide Web, also works as "a graphic representation of data abstracted from the banks" of myriad computers. As theorizing about hypertext has emphasized repeatedly, the web's ability to move around and link data can liberate readers from the linear modes of reading encouraged by the printed book—making every act of reading a rewriting of the text, a perpetual demonstration of the contingent relation between signifier and signified. While the scholarly article remains *B&L*'s basic structural unit, we had originally planned to capitalize on the fluidity of electronic text by providing a dynamic Table of Contents for the journal, so that readers could move from one essay to another without returning to the home-page. Bolter and Grusin argue that new media can teach us to view anew how we in fact engage with existing ones, and surely enough, it turned out that this capability is latent in the print medium itself. As we developed *B&L*, we recognized that one of the pleasures of browsing a print journal is to flip from one article to another, without feeling compelled to return first to the Table of

Contents, perhaps without having made a conscious decision to read a particular article. Leah Price's assertion that novel readers are compilers perhaps comes into play here, too. Just as many fiction readers, especially when rereading, skip over or linger over certain parts of the text of a novel, not necessarily in order, so, perhaps, print journal readers compile mentally their own anthologies of scholarship as they browse a particular issue, pausing over certain pages, skimming others, annotating still more. This is a facility that, paradoxically, many online remediations of print articles (such as those housed by JSTOR or Project Muse) remove from readers and that we would like, eventually, to return to readers of *B&L*. But in the journal's present state, the Table of Contents still acts as a panopticon in the playground of unregulated reading, keeping in check the pleasure of clicking, the sensual diversions provoked by inserted media, hyperlinks, and the scroll bar.

The inclusion of multimedia content in *B&L* also works against the static, two-dimensional quality of the paradigmatic journal "page." In *B&L*, digitized versions of photographs, engravings, screen shots, cartoons, and other kinds of visual illustrations familiar from print publication are included. The ability to include sound and music clips, plus occasional video clips, however, dissolves the printed surface to give the journal a momentary illusion of virtual realism. In some cases (for example, in Yu Jin Ko's review of "Honolulu Theatre for Youth's Rap *Othello*"), the artists themselves provide the video footage and there are no copyright issues—and therefore no practical—restrictions on length. In the case of sound clips under copyright, by contrast, University of Georgia's legal advisors believe that fair use covers only thirty seconds of material. Thus, to include a sound clip to accompany a screen shot of Claire Danes in the balcony scene of Baz Luhrmann's *Romeo+Juliet*, we began with the bit of text quoted from an essay by Angela Keam: "What's in a name? That which we call a rose / By any other word would smell as sweet. / O Romeo would, were he not Romeo called / Retain that dear perfection which he owes / Without that title." Having seconds to spare, however, we continued recording beyond the printed excerpt, concluding the MP3 of Juliet's soliloquy with the splash and scream that signals Danes's plunge into the family swimming pool when Leonardo DiCaprio, playing Romeo, suddenly declares his presence (this aural moment anticipates the textual treatment of the swimming pool kiss in Keam's ensuing sentences, which is illustrated by yet another screen shot). The conjunction of static screen shots and brief sound clips therefore gestures toward, but does not quite achieve, the degree of immediacy familiar to viewers of DVDs on computer screen or of Quicktime films; what we get instead is a hybrid fashioned from two different media.

In the case of the previous example, cyberlaw functions as the panopticon constraining the virtual realism of *B&L*'s multimedia effects. Once again, however, the repression is not complete, as the slippage between static sight and dynamic sound foregrounds the medium through which the sensory experience of the moment is communicated. Even in the simplest examples of visual illustration, the relation between image and text moves in a continuum from denotative illustration to metonymic allusion. In the most striking example, the scientific illustrations of DNA strands and protein molecules that accompany Graham Holderness's essay in *B&L* 2.1 refer only allusively to his argument for a material continuity between Shakespeare and appropriations of Shakespeare:

> Protein may take many forms, but it's still protein. However broad the range of his permutations, Proteus remains Proteus. Like an elemental metal, the changes he undergoes are changes only of shape, not of identity or internal structure. If Shakespeare is like Proteus, then all his manifold and plural forms remain permutations of the same singular entity. All these permutations should, of course, carry, if this conceit holds, a DNA code that can be traced back to the biological parent. Just as the Human Genome Project has specified the sequence of amino acid beads along a protein chain, so it should be possible to identify even remote and dissimilar products of Shakespeare as nonetheless Shakespearean. (Holderness)

In this case, the visualizations of DNA dance symbolically with the author's rigorously logical argument, functioning as points of aesthetic wonder more than anything else. We have returned once again to the digital playground.

The DTD, or, code is law

In contrast to its lushly visible web displays, *B&L's* document structure is governed by unseen XML markup that tells the style sheet how to display textual data. XML identifies elements of a document according to *what they are*, not *how they should look*. Instead of a tag called <I>, for italics, for instance, we have a tag called <titleOfLongWork>. The browser is instructed to display <titleOfLongWork> in italics, but a different style sheet might call for a different display of book titles, for instance (eventually, this thick or dense tagging will allow *B&L* to construct a database of Shakespearean appropriations, searchable according to genre of appropriation, title of Shakespeare play, author, and so on). Because XML is human as well as machine legible, it puts the power of critical definition in the hands of the user—or more precisely, in this case, the software coder. Part of the editorial enterprise involves determining ahead of time what items in a document of the *B&L* genre can be marked (and therefore displayed). That list of items, which in turn conditions what is important and not important, visible and invisible, in the journal, is governed by the *B&L* DTD (Document Type Definition). The DTD determines what elements are "legal" for *B&L* documents and their logical relation to one another. XML tags, like those of the more familiar display language HTML, are hierarchical, with some tags nested within other, more general tags. For instance, the <titleOfLongWork> can be tagged within a <paragraph>, within a <worksCitedItem>, or an <essayTitle>. A <titleOfLongWork> cannot be tagged within, say, an <image> or even a <foreignWord> tag (figure 2).

In the fully free spirit of cyberspace, these forbidden relations might become real if the author of a particular DTD deemed it appropriate, but the sheer mental

Figure 2. The underlying XML code of a *Borrowers and Lenders* essay.

```
<paragraph>While scholars have long acknowledged the powerful influence of Shakespeare's
writings on Emily Dickinson, they have only recently discussed her appropriation of a specifically
Shakespearean vocabulary for the depiction of gender, sexuality, and eroticism (<inlineQuote
refid="r3"type="prose">Bennett 1990b</inlineQuote>; <inlineQuote refid="r26"type="prose">Farr
1992</inlineQuote>; <inlineQuote refid="r33" type="prose">Hart 1990</inlineQuote>; <in-
lineQuote refid="r27" type="prose">Finnerty 1998</inlineQuote>; <inlineQuote refid="r14"
type="prose">Comment 2001</inlineQuote>). This article considers Dickinson's appropriation of
the language of Shakespeare's Sonnets, a language that encourages "alternative and compet-
ing constructions of gender" and is especially useful to readers, such as Dickinson, who seek
to unsettle the normative limits of sexual desire (<inlineQuote refid="r4" type="prose">Bennett
1993, 95</inlineQuote>). Although Dickinson's edition of the Sonnets, now at the Houghton Li-
brary, Harvard suggests much use, this topic has been relatively unexplored by scholars (<inline-
Quote refid="r28" type="prose">Finnerty 2006, 118-19</inlineQuote>; <inlineQuote refid="r55"
type="prose">Richwell 1989, 22-31</inlineQuote>). Judith Farr notes the similarities between
the Sonnets and Dickinson's love poems that address both a male figure associated with <in-
lineQuote refid="r25" type="prose">"courtesy, loyalty, physical appreciation"</inlineQuote> and
an awe-inspiring female who is <inlineQuote refid="r25" type="prose">"false, feline, and distant"
(Farr 1990, 132, 182)</inlineQuote>. For Farr, the Sonnets are one of Dickinson's models of the
expressive lyric, a genre that offers <inlineQuote refid="r39" type="prose">"a personal encoun-
ter, a private moment publicized" (Jackson 2004, 10)</inlineQuote>. Yet it seems more likely
that Dickinson would have extended to Shakespeare her own disclaimer about the dangers of
reading lyric poetry as personal expression: <inlineQuote refid="r17" type="verse">"When I state
myself, as the Representative of the Verse &#8211; it does not mean &#8211; me &#8211; but a
supposed person" (L268)</inlineQuote>.<note>References to Dickinson's letters are to <inline-
Quote refid="r17" type="prose"><titleOfLongWork type="other">The Letters of Emily Dickinson</
titleOfLongWork>, edited by Thomas Johnson and Theodora Ward (1986)</inlineQuote>. All sub-
sequent references are to this edition, will be included in the body of the text, and will be indicated
by the abbreviation L, followed by the letter number.</note> From Dickinson's many references
to his plays, it seems that Shakespeare's importance to her lay in his powers of multiple identi-
```

labor of mapping out the conceptual territory of an entity such as *B&L* mitigates against such rogue associations; at the very least, any unusual mappings of tags then become "law" for the given DTD. In *Code: Version 2.0*, Lawrence Lessig makes the argument that in cyberspace, despite the attention paid to users' freedom and anonymity, "code is law" (1-8). While doubting the efficacy of conventional laws (such as those that protect intellectual property) within cyberspace, Lessig believes that on the Internet and in cyberspace, "there is regulation of behavior," but "that regulation is imposed primarily through code . . . In some places, life is fairly free; in other places, it is more controlled. And the difference between these spaces is simply a difference in the architectures of control—that is, a difference in code" (Lessig 24). Code regulates *B&L* in the following manner: we can point to the *B&L* DTD and say, "These—and no others—are the ingredients of an essay on Shakespeare and Appropriation for the journal *B&L*." Behind every document therefore lies the hidden DTD, a prison-house of code in our textual playground.

A governing DTD can be limiting in even the most mundane sense. It was virtually impossible, for instance, to imagine in advance every subspecies of visual image that would require tagging. To some extent, then, code is law in a broader intellectual sense because it defines the parameters of that species of critical endeavor called "Appropriation Studies." But as Lessig reminds us, "Cyberspace will present us with ambiguities over and over again" (25). To give one example, the *B&L* DTD contains a long list of subsidiary "attributes" nested within the element "image"—these include photograph, engraving, and drawing but the designers unfortunately had omitted from that list the term "screen shot," or "film still," and essays about film have been the most frequent submissions the journal has received so far. In this sense, *B&L*'s contributors, by virtue of their interpretation of the journal's mission and of the parameters of "Shakespearean Appropriation" as a field of critical endeavor, have exerted significant backpressure on the code. This is to be expected. Lessig says that when such ambiguities occur, "it will be a question of how best to go on. We have tools from real space that will help resolve the interpretive questions by pointing us in one direction or another" (25). In a more adventurous vein, as Willard McCarty reminds us, the computer fulfills its most important function as a "modeling machine," making failures as illuminating as success. The disorientation that ensues when coder, code, and user face off against one another or even collaborate in problem-solving—as when editors and software designer look for "work-arounds" to display particularly difficult eighteenth-century typeface or to deal with a font irregularity that shows up only in the Safari browser—is, in McCarty's view, healthy, and even progressive. Once again, the electronic playground makes its presence felt in the midst of the panopticon-of-code.

What allows code to become a "modeling machine" and therefore destabilize the regime of code as law is the status of modeling as "embodied action" (McCarty 38). N. Katherine Hayles critiques the earlier, more utopian visions of cyberspace in terms of their denial of the inextricable relation of body and mind. Hayles's own definition of a posthuman subjectivity is embodied; unlike the "liberal humanist subject" lurking behind the machine-as-man that she sees as dominating the thinking of early cyber-theorists, the "emergence of the posthuman as an informational-material entity is paralled and reinforced by a corresponding reinterpretation of the deep structures of the physical world" (11). In this way, our inevitably idiosyncratic tagging becomes evidence of what an earlier generation of Shakespeareans might have called the compositor's hand (we are thinking of Charlton Hinman and the so-called New Bibliography). We can also turn to Richard Lanham, whose interest in varieties of embodied subject/object encounters helps us to chart the rhetorical dynamics of a digital artifact/event such as *B&L*. Lanham's analysis of attention structures in digital rhetoric helps to explain the vitality of *B&L* as an online artifact and vehicle for scholarly communication.

Oscillating wildly at or through

While the page remains the basic unit of organization for *B&L*, its web interface allows for some interesting movement within that format. Lanham reminds us in his *The Economics of Attention* of the distinction between reading through an interface (typography, screen) and looking at an interface (seeing the frame of the picture, the buttons on the screen, the type of the print), a phenomenon that he calls "oscillation." In Lanham's exemplary matrix, this oscillation can occur along four parallel spectra: those of the signal, perceiver, motive, and life (figure 3).

If we look at *B&L* through Lanham's perceptual matrix, we can find encouraging fissures in the smooth page of print that remains the paradigm for scholarly

Figure 3. Adapted from Lanham, *The Economics of Attention*, p. 158.

Signal	**Through**	**A/T mixture**	**At**
Perceiver	Through		At
Motive	Game	Purpose	Play
Life	Life as Information	Life as Stuff	Life as Drama

journals. On the "signal" spectrum, our nostalgic page design paradoxically draws attention to the "at" polarity because of its incongruity in an online medium. Compare, for instance, the journal's emphasis on color and texture to the plainer interface of *Early Modern Literary Studies*, which strives to guide readers through the web interface to meaning and to keep them on track through a linear argument while scrolling down the web page with numbered paragraphs. In a more annoying fashion, perhaps, the author's and editor's inability to control absolutely the constellation of a web page in any given browser sometimes makes readers look at rather than through the page. In issue 1.2, Alexander C.Y. Huang worked to help us eliminate the variations on small caps that could occur with the browser Safari. Most difficult was the crisis surrounding Polish diacriticals for issue 2.1., in which the unicode identifiers for certain Polish letters worked perfectly in the web document, but came out as hash marks in the PDF (we eventually had to omit the diacriticals in the PDF version, to our great chagrin).

Activity on the perceiver spectrum has proven slightly more contentious. The ability to generate web pages and PDF documents as XSLT (Extensible Style Sheet) transformations from a single XML document is a benefit of the journal's medium, but in negotiating the tensions between reading *at* and reading *through* in these two formats, readers must engage with a new and unfamiliar hermeneutic. In *B&L*, images and multimedia are available only in the online view. The PDF indicates sign and sound either by absences (there are no images in the PDF) or the sign of absence (it denotes sound and film clips by a computer-generated message). The pragmatic reason for this decision is, once again, copyright (another trace of the panopticon); our image permissions permit online publication, but not print dissemination. The censored and sensorially deprived appearance of a PDF page also reflects our belief in using open-source software and our desire to use the online medium *qua* medium. Our style may be nostalgic for print, but our substance forces readers to engage in dialogic reading, maneuvering between printout and media-rich screen, or to adopt Lanham's term, "oscillating" between text and multimedia. To date, however, the majority of "perceivers" still inhabit the world of print text. Contributors routinely yearn for stability, transparency, and reproducibility: they want the PDF to contain everything available on the web page; they want the web interface to have the absolute regularity of print; and they want the two presentations to look exactly alike. On Lanham's spectrum of motive, then, we can see several attitudes in play. As editors, we strive mightily to achieve *sprezzatura*, in Lanham's terms a seemingly effortless collaboration of style and substance (255), and in the case of *B&L* the deliberate enrichment of the environment of "sensory denial" found in traditional print media (46). Such enrichment allows an "electronic text [to] liberate a shape and motion buried deep in a text designed to marmorealize fixity" (86).

We can now return to the images that accompany Holderness's theoretical paper on the term "appropriation," which refer allusively to his argument by calling on scientific discourse rather than illustrating either content or argument in a directly referential manner. We might say that the dominant motive here is *play;* the article can be read in the PDF version without significant loss of meaning. In some articles that rely heavily on images to make their argument, by contrast, the restriction of media to the web document proved problematic for both author and reader. Dan Juan Gil's article on asocial sex in Shakespeare and Welles employed necessarily over forty screen shots to argue for the perverse erotics of the shot/reverse shot. These images helped the essay transcend the tendency of much recent criticism of Shakespeare on film simply to narrativize or describe moments or scenes from films—the images made the argument—but the experience of reading the PDF lacks the immediacy and sense of innovation one gets from the web-page. Here, the perceiver's contribution is quite "purposeful." And in one of our favorite examples, Stephen Buhler's voice articulates Shakespeare's text (Sonnet 18) and Duke Ellington's music ("Sonnet to Hank Cinq") in a fusion of form and content that would be impossible in another medium. Play, competition with both the bard and duke, and purposeful illustration are present in equal proportions.

Turning to the fourth spectrum of Lanham's matrix, we see a new vector, from "Life as Information" (the genetic or mechanistic codes of DNA and neurochemistry) to "Life as Drama" (the *theatrum mundi*, or world-as-stage trope). In between is "Life as Stuff"—"stuff" being the term not just for the information that surrounds us, but also for how we organize and engage with it, at once grossly corporeal, Falstaffian matter and the metaphysical stuff that dreams are made on. The Life as Information/Life as Drama mix perhaps coheres most elegantly in an article that mingles critical approaches (ecocriticism, social science research on games, and pedagogy) with media (print, text, film, images, music) in an account of a project that introduces Shakespeare to Polish middle-school students through a Live-Action Role Playing Game (Deszcz-Tryhubczak and Zarzycka). The students received plenty of information in preliminary lectures, played their games, and turned Shakespeare into their own material. *B&L*'s readers also get a workout, oscillating along the Life spectrum as charming film clips of the students' playlets—sung and spoken in Polish and filmed sometimes with the uncertain focus of a home video—offered at once a look through the medium to the school life of fifteen-year-olds and a playful, dramatic look at the educational theories that undergird the essay's scholarly argument. The inability of many readers to understand literally the Polish dialogue adds a further opaque dimension to the interaction. We peek into an intimate environment where we understand the emotions and gestures of the Shakespeare being performed, but not the words.

"As the spiral grew"

Lanham's matrix of rhetorical motive for digital artifacts, like McCarty's notion of code as a modeling machine, depends on the manipulation of structures of attention (McCarty 18). Such structures function, as cyberspace and virtual reality do, by way of recursive feedback loops. In response to the aporia between the governing DTD and markup needs of accepted essays, *B&L* has adopted a spiral model of development. This model is particularly useful to a publication that documents the evolution of Shakespeare and Appropriation as a discipline. The journal's content—its substance, if you will—must respond to the scholarly "markup" just as its display options, or style, must respond to contributors' and readers' exigency. This whole mixed bag of motives and participants, from scholarly perspective to the fatally flawed panopticon at the heart of the XML playground, makes sense if we understand Lanham's perpetual oscillations along the rhetorical spectra as part of *B&L*'s developmental spiral. We imagined this spiral at first as a playground slide—perhaps like those that one sees in children's water parks—that would gleefully offer "the long slide / To happiness, endlessly" (Larkin, lines 8-9), away from the prison-house of code. But the slide hits the ground with a bump. The spiral model of development to which we aspire finally owes more to forms of nature than to the artificial (figure 4).

The Emperor Nautilus grows in a logarithmic or equiangular spiral. As the cephalopod inside grows and develops, it moves from its cramped quarters into successively larger chambers. Or, as Oliver Wendell Holmes put it: "as the spiral grew, / He left the past year's dwelling for the new, / Stole with soft step its shining archway through, / Built up its idle door, in his last-found home, and knew the old no more" ("The Chambered Nautilus," lines 17-21).

Figure 4. The Chambered Nautilus.

Kaz Chiba/Stockbyte/Getty Images

The nautilus's growth is subject both to mathematical certainty (the logarithm underpinning the spiral) and to environmental uncertainty (its growth rate varies considerably; this is one of the reasons why, contrary to popular accounts, the logarithmic spiral so often found in nature is rarely the so-called "golden ratio"). *B&L*'s spiral growth is also subject to the vagaries of funding, submissions, reviewers, and other external factors. Just as the shell of the Nautilus allows the cephalopod to remain "the same shape as it grows" (Vermeij 16), so *B&L* allows scholarly essays to retain the basic shape of traditional journal essays, even down to the appearance of the website, while including (and hiding, like the Nautilus's chambers) its growing database of Shakespearean appropriations and its ubiquitous tagging. When we become discouraged at our progress, we can think comfortingly of the mollusks again: "all evidence currently available suggests that Nautiluses take years to grow to full size" (Boyle and Rodhouse 59). Finally, the Chambered Nautilus seems a fitting metaphor not only for the process of editing in cyberspace or for the development of software, but also for the evolution of scholarship about Shakespeare and appropriation. "Increasing by accumulation from within itself, the logarithmic spiral grows wider, with the distance between its 'coils' increasing, as it moves away from the source, known as the pole" (Livio 117): we find that as we seem to move farther away from Shakespeare—the source or pole—with videos of Polish students, photographs of beehives and metals, and essays on Chinese state theater (Huang)—we nonetheless circle around him, drawn by some irresistible logarithm, "the great will that animates [the Nautilus] to sea" (Coleridge, line 39), or scholars to Shakespeare.

Works Cited

Auslander, Philip. *Liveness*. London: Routledge, 1999.

Bolter, Jay David, and Richard Grusin. *Remediation*. Cambridge: MIT P, 1999.

Borrowers and Lenders: The Journal of Shakespeare and Appropriation (*B&L*): < http://www.borrowers.uga.edu>.

Boyle, Peter, and Paul Rodhouse. *Cephalopods*. London: Blackwell, 2005.

Buhler, Stephen M. "Form and Character in Duke Ellington's and Billy Strayhorn's *Such Sweet Thunder*." *Borrowers and Lenders: The Journal of Shakespeare and Appropriation* 1.1 (2005): <http://www.borrowers.uga.edu/cocoon/borrowers/request?id=781406>.

Coleridge, Hartley. "To the Nautilus." *bartleby.com* (2007): <http://www.bartleby.com/246/>.

"Cybernetics." *Oxford English Dictionary Online*. 2nd ed. Oxford: Oxford University Press, 2008: <http://dictionary.oed.com/cgi/entry/50056595?single=1&query_type=word&queryword=cybernetics&first=1&max_to_show=10>.

Deszcz-Tryhubczak, Justyna, and Agata Zarzycka. "Giving 'to Airy Nothing a Local Habitation and a Name': William Shakespeare's Worlds of Imagination as Accessed through a Role-Playing Game." *Borrowers and Lenders: The Journal of Shakespeare and Appropriation* 2.1 (2006): <http://www.borrowers.uga.edu/cocoon/borrowers/request?id=781417>

Eisenstein, Elizabeth. *The Printing Press as an Agent of Change: Communications and Cultural Transformations in Early Modern Europe*. Cambridge: Cambridge UP, 1979.

Gibson, William. *Neuromancer: 20th Anniversary Edition*. New York: Ace Books, 2004.

Gil, Daniel Juan. "Avant-garde Technique and the Visual Grammar of Sexuality in Orson Welles's Shakespeare Films." *Borrowers and Lenders: The Journal of Shakespeare and Appropriation* 1.2 (2005): <http://www.borrowers.uga.edu/cocoon/borrowers/request?id=781447>.

Hayles, N. Katherine. *How We Became Posthuman: Virtual Bodies in Cybernetics, Literature, and Informatics*. Chicago: U of Chicago P, 1999.

Hett, Dorothy Marie. "Shakespeare is Alive and Well in Cyberspace: An Annotated Bibliography." *English Journal* 92.1 (2002): 94-97.

Hinman, Charlton. *The Printing and Proof-Reading of the First Folio of Shakespeare*. Oxford: Clarendon P, 1963.

Holderness, Graham. "'Dressing Old Words New': Shakespeare, Science, and Appropriation." *Borrowers and Lenders: The Journal of Shakespeare and Appropriation* 1.2 (2005): <http://www.borrowers.uga.edu/cocoon/borrowers/request?id=781442>.

Holmes, Oliver Wendell. "The Chambered Nautilus." *Representative Poetry Online*. Ed. Ian Lancashire. (2005): <http://rpo.library.utoronto.ca/poem/1025.html>.

Huang, Alexander C. Y. "The Politics of an 'Apolitical' Shakespeare: A Chinese-Soviet Joint Venture, 1950-1979." *Borrowers & Lenders: The Journal of Shakespeare and Appropriation* 1.2 (2005): <http://www.borrowers.uga.edu/cocoon/borrowers/request?id=781450>.

Keam, Angela. "The 'Shakesteen' Genre: Claire Danes's Star-Body, Teen Female Fans, and the Pluralization of Authorship." *Borrowers and Lenders: The Journal of Shakespeare and Appropriation* 2.1 (2006): <http://www.borrowers.uga.edu/cocoon/borrowers/request?id=781413>.

Ko, Yu Jin. Rev. of Honolulu Theatre for Youth's Rap *Othello*. *Borrowers and Lenders: The Journal of Shakespeare and Appropriation* 2.1 (2006): <http://www.borrowers.uga.edu/cocoon/borrowers/request?id=781427>.

Lancashire, Anne. "What Do the Users Really Want?" *Early Modern Literary Studies* 3.3 (1998): <http://purl.oclc.org/emls/03-3/alanshak.html>.

Lanham, Richard. *The Economics of Attention: Style and Substance in the Age of Information*. Chicago: U of Chicago P, 2006.

Larkin, Philip. *High Windows*. London: Faber, 1974.

Livio, Mario. *Golden Ratio: The Story of Phi, the World's Most Astonishing Number*. New York: Broadway, 2002.

Lessig, Lawrence. *Code: Version 2.0*. New York: Basic Books, 2006.

Maxwell, James C. "On Governors." *Proceedings of the Royal Society* 16 (1867-1868): 270-83.

Mayr, Otto. "Maxwell and the Origins of Cybernetics." *Isis* 62.4 (1971): 424-44.

McCarty, Willard. "Modelling." *Humanities Computing*. Ed. Willard McCarty. New York: Palgrave MacMillan, 2005. 20-72.

"Number Symbolism." *Encyclopaedia Britannica Online* (2007): <http://search.eb.com/eb/article-248180>.

Ong, Walter. *Orality and Literacy*. Oxford: Oxford UP, 1982.

Presley, Erin. "'Ol Billy Shakes': Shakespeare in the Blogosphere." *Borrowers and Lenders: The Journal of Shakespeare and Appropriation* 2.2 (2006): <http://www.borrowers.uga.edu/cocoon/borrowers/request?id=781466 >.

Price, Leah. *The Anthology and the Rise of the Novel: From Richardson to George Eliot*. Cambridge: Cambridge UP, 2000.

Vermeij, Geerat J. *A Natural History of Shells*. Princeton: Princeton UP, 1995.

Wiener, Norbert. *Cybernetics; Or, Control and Communication in the Animal and the Machine*. Cambridge: Technology P, 1948.

Yong, Li Lan. "Shakespeare as Virtual Event." *Theatre Research International* 28.1 (2003): 46-60.

Performing Shakespeare for the Web Community

Peter Holland

For a while in 2008 one could not only buy Arden Shakespeare editions but also enter *Arden: The World of William Shakespeare* on the internet. Not an extension of the marketing of excellent textual scholarship but, instead, an extension of the Shakespeare brand-name into the virtual world of online quest gaming and an extension of the creative workshops for the development of online games into academe, *Arden: The World of William Shakespeare* is the creation of Ted Castronova who teaches at Indiana University Bloomington and is the creator of the Indiana University Synthetic Worlds Initiative. The project was in part funded by a MacArthur Foundation grant of a quarter of million dollars and has Linda Charnes as its Shakespeare consultant. At root parasitic on a well-known, if now rather old-fashioned, Atari game called *Neverwinter Nights*—you need the *Diamond Edition* before you can even start to download the online patches and add-ons for the Arden game—Castronova's version is a familiar form of gaming with quests, adventures, and other such new media interactivity/intermediality, built around a war game that follows the narrative of *Richard III*.

Such online quest-games or MMOGs (Massive Multiplayer Online Games) are a form of theatrical experience in which the player becomes transforming performer, engaging not only with the ingenuity of the platform's creators in setting tasks, and providing screen effects sufficient to engage and maintain interest, curiosity and a determination to reach the next level, to continue playing, but also the opportunity for connection with other gamers, to become part of a community, to share the experience in real as well as in virtual time, though not real space. The playgoer becomes actor and the space for the performance of Shakespeare and the ways in which such performances are commodified, bought and consumed becomes radically different from the previous four hundred years of Shakespeare play-going.

To enter such virtual worlds one needs to create an avatar and my virtual alter ego was Peter Leonsbane, a good cleric avatar (because there was not one of a Shakespeare professor). The trope for questing in this Arden is that it is a world dreamed by Shakespeare. One's first encounter at the entrance to the Arden world is with Peaseblossom who will answer questions. If you want to know what to do in Arden, Peaseblossom tells you: "Once you are in the Eastcheap Tavern, talk to

Falstaff to start a quest line involving Mistress Quickly. Another quest in the Tavern, from the Nurse's Servingman Peter, involves talking to rude mechanicals and thieves. Outside, there's a fool in town who gives you Shakespeare trivia . . . In the School, talk to Goodman Dull at the right time to see a scene from Love's Labour's Lost . . . Outside the Tavern, Mr. Cates will start you on a quest that mimics the plot of Richard III" (dialogue box).

By now, thoroughly confused by the simultaneity of existence of many plays at once and the lack of even fake Elizabethan diction, I went through the portal and talked to Falstaff whose first reply goes: "First time in the Eastcheap Tavern in Ilminster, eh? Ah, ill place indeed. I have been struck down by Fortune, landing here to be ministered by ill companions and worse ale. Had the golden Harry done his part, we'd all be well." This at least has a decent quasi-Shakespearean pun in it, although I am still confused by the fact that the Boar's Head Tavern in Eastcheap seems to have metamorphosed into the Eastcheap Tavern in the county of Somerset where the action lies. There were no other gamers there and so I could not play board games with Nym. It took me twenty minutes to find the torch that I needed to hold in order to walk out of the tavern's front door. Then I ran around looking for people for a while and got a quest from Mr. Cates and that is as far as I got on my first visit. Ah, the joys of online gaming!

It is a relief to read the answers to the FAQs on this Arden website posted in 2006, long before the game was developed, let alone released: "16. If I play this game can I skip my Shakespeare class? No. No game can replace detailed, intellectual analysis of the texts under the guidance of a trained mentor. That's what you do in class. . . . 19. If I play this game, can I skip reading Shakespeare plays? No. No game can replace the experience of reading and pondering the texts on your own," and so on down to question "41. To be or not to be? That is the question" (*Arden*: FAQ Version 1.2, 2006). No, I am not making this up. For someone unused to gaming, all this is novel but quite tiresome. For my computer support person, Ben, moonlighting from his graduate studies in church history, my interest and my incompetence have been a source of endless amusement. Charnes spoke eloquently at the Shakespeare Association of America meeting in February 2008 about the moment early in the quest when, to enter Arden, you have to abandon all the equipment you have chosen, to go through the moment of commitment in order to be reborn in the virtual world. Ben was amused by my fascination with this event when I talked to him about it: "But that's what happens in all games."

But what is most intriguing about this online Shakespeare game is that it has proved to be a disaster, a total flop. If you go to the link-site you will find that Arden 1 is unavailable while they develop Arden 2 (this starts to sound uncannily like a succession of Shakespeare editions), subtitled "London's Burning." In *Wired Magazine*, a, perhaps the, major online journal for gaming, Castronova explained why Arden 1 failed in his "5 Tips for Making Games that Don't Suck." I quote here tips 3 and 5: "Think About Your Audience. We put Arden in front of Shakespeare experts and they loved it. We put it in front of play testers and they yawned. . . . Too much reading, not enough fighting. *Arden II* will be more of a hack-and-slash Dungeons and Dragons type of game. Concede Screwups. You face a moment where you can admit something isn't working or you can lie about it. It's like in Shakespeare's plays: The tragic heroes keep making new mistakes that compound their original mistakes. The comic heroes muddle around and find themselves in ridiculous circumstances, but in the end they accept their own humanity, and the audience respects them for it." It is good to know that Shakespeare plays can teach game designers a thing or two and that the principle of the reversion to the mean operates in game design. I will probably not be playing Arden 2.

Castronova's failure to create a good Shakespeare game showed most especially why a university professor and his team of graduate students could not possibly compete with the millions of dollars and huge teams of designers who create the most successful games—one needs to remember that the cost of creating a game can be significantly larger than the cost of creating a large-budget feature film. But it was also evidence of the ways in which the Shakespeare tag, attached to an improbable mode of performance, was sufficient to unlock the purse strings of a major foundation. Without the name Shakespeare, as one of Castronova's graduate students admitted to me, it would have been highly unlikely that their gaming project would have got as much as $250,000 from the MacArthur Foundation, a large sum for a humanities scholar but a trivial amount even for computer research, let alone for game development. But what may mark a change more significant, at least in the minds of its creators, than the Shakespeare MMOG is the development of Shakespeare production on *Second Life,* that overpopulated virtual world, where, apart from other events, seventy US universities and equal numbers from elsewhere have bought virtual land for research and recruitment, classrooms, international collaboration, and self-marketing. The Second Life Shakespeare Company, the *soi-disant* "premier professional Shakespeare performance troupe in the virtual world of Second Life" (see Centaur)—and I wonder what the competition is like—performs in what they describe as "a meticulously accurate replica of the Globe Theatre," but which I might describe as a tourist vision of a possible form rendered in half-timbered kitsch. The company, in its publicity, claims it "integrates technology with professional rich content": "Each play will be performed in a way that should excite both the zealous Shakespeare fan and the die-hard technologist," a binary taxonomy of performance-goers that must be unprecedented (see their description at Tech page). Since the end of February 2008, the company has been slowly putting together a performance of *Hamlet*, performed by *Second Life* avatars, directed by Enniv Zarf (these are *Second Life* names), with Ina Centaur as Visual Director and Hastur Pierterson as Accoustic Alchemist, and others as Animations and Technical Directors. From 20 June 2008 for five weeks, they interrupted their *Hamlet* progress or process in order to offer a staged reading of *Twelfth Night*, one act per week, finishing in July. This production, suggests Zarf, is "an experimental way of performing Shakespeare. But hey we are in Second Life. If we can't try it here, where else could we possibly try this [?]" (Centaur).

What is not clear is what constitutes the experiment. It clearly is not in the exploration of meaning in the play—at no point in any of the documentation about the company's work is there the slightest sign that the Shakespeare text has meaning at all, let alone shifting and multiple and needing to be determined meanings. Text here becomes nothing other than technological challenge and narrative, reduced to a combination of *fabula* and lip-synch. Nor can it be in the fact of the staged reading itself, even when performed in "outfits" that are "grayscale." It may instead possibly be in the mode of casting for the production is being "performed by a moving cast, and audience members from the last week who wish to enlist would have the possible chance to make the cast" (Centaur). Playgoers become performers and the community of participation in the performance is redefined.

But the experimentation the creators trumpet is most likely to be located in the dual nature of the Second Life performers themselves, the closest approximation I have seen to Edward Gordon Craig's desire for the actor as Übermarionette. The forms of the performers' representation are as Second Life avatars, CGI forms. Like the actor-sharer/hireling division in early modern theater—although unacknowledged as such—the *bots* that perform are primarily split between "*Infobots*, which are autonomous and feed directly on encoded data, and *Avabots*, which require real time live input from actors to function" (Tech page). Like Shakespeare's Globe in London now, the company is obsessed by the possibility of audience interaction and are threatening to provide "attachments that would allow the audience to launch various temporary objects and particles onstage" while, conversely, "in scenes where blood is involved, quite a bit of gore may be flung onto the audience" (Tech page). The manifest concern throughout the company's self-representation is with the technology of creation. The desire is to meet the audience by encouraging their passing through to the sphere of making theater and away from a passive consumption, creating a new community of play-goers, interactive participants in the experience of performance.

Elsewhere on the web, one can type in the word "shakespeare" on *YouTube.com* and find 27,000 hits. YouTube is a compelling and compulsive space where people upload pirated clips from films and television, where mini-companies (theater or film or both, whether professional or amateur, good or bad, coming from high school shows and college classrooms as well as those who work in their backyards and bedrooms) show off their wares, and where the games of parody, transformative adaptation and endless imitation lead to, say, the ten currently available versions of *Macbeth* acted out by Lego figures, including the really very funny "My Name is Macbeth," a Lego rap version, taking off from Eminem's "My Name Is"—or so my daughter tells me. Among the other Lego versions of *Macbeth*, I recommend "Macbeth Act V" by Pirate Monkey Productions and Logan Stromberg's "Lego MacBeth" (see also Desmet, "Paying Attention in Shakespeare Parody").

On YouTube viewers are also performers and creators (i.e., as posters of their own chosen clips, whatever their sources). For scholars interested in the construction of an aesthetics of reception YouTube helps by encouraging its viewers to comment on what they are watching. Shakespeare clips on YouTube attract some intelligent comment (e.g., on Toby Stephens as Coriolanus, clipped from the 1995 Royal Shakespeare Company's "Great Performances" video, "onemagnolia" praises his "easy physicality") and some less so (e.g., "My Name is Macbeth," the rap version acted out by Lego figures, is, for "funkerdelik," "hahaha awsum ands its all true lol" [sic]), while some clips defy or prohibit comment altogether: Lucy Pinder's performance of Volumnia's speeches in *Coriolanus* 3.2 as part of her "Book at Bedtime" series while she poses sprawling on a bed in a negligee has had its comments facility "disabled." Of course, "lol" means "laughing out loud."

In the state of mystification in which I view much of the Shakespeare YouTube material, I cannot begin to fathom why Ms. Pinder chose that section of text, although the playlist of 23 videos from her "Book at Bedtime" series for NUTS television station includes eight extracts from Shakespeare, including pieces from *Henry VIII* and *All's Well*, as well as chunks of *War and Peace* and *The War of the Worlds*. YouTube induces in the naïve spectator (like me) a kind of wondering at what wandering through its links makes visible, awestruck at the range and, by turns, the brilliance or awfulness of the materials others post. This community of people indecipherably to be designated producers and receivers (for, at the very least, the comments turn viewers into producers of an ongoing text of reception reaction) requires a reformulation of what it means to watch or to share watching Shakespeare on screen as well as redefining what Shakespeare on screen might include. The lonely activity of viewing is redefined as shared experience in the moment of communicating or of reading others' communications. Alone in the theaters of our studies—or is that too academic a location for the domestic placing of the home computer?—or hiding in our offices, YouTube viewers both recognize and attempt to deny our isolation. We share in other ways too: sending friends e-mails with links to clips we want them to know about, moving the exchange discourse from one kind of web location to another, passing on URLs excitedly. The desire to share the experience of watching, either at the moment of consumption or through the other's enjoyment of the identical object is paramount to the experience. We mistake this mode of watching if we see it solely as solitary.

Just as the conceptualization of spectatorship needs altering in the context of webcasts, so too does the extent of watching, the unit of viewing consumption. YouTube is by definition a collection of clips. Everything is reduced to a tightly limited extent (less than ten minutes) and longer materials have to be reassembled. Certain kinds of materials guarantee rapid posting and hence, for instance, the episode of *Dr. Who*, "The Shakespeare Code," in which the Doctor met Shakespeare was rapidly posted on YouTube in segments. The entire episode is available there in five chunks, posted by "doctorwhofanatic," a British youth aged 14, who has posted 41 videos in all and watched 4,907.

But YouTube Shakespeare, often exhilaratingly witty, can also engage in its own sense of the clipped, fragmented world of trailers and teases, those texts that so fascinatingly allude to the as yet unseen text. As well as the trailers for "The Shakespeare Code" there is a new teaser: in anticipation of the Royal Shakespeare

Company's 2008 production of *Hamlet* starring David Tennant who plays Dr Who, Garry Watkinson and Lisa Watkinson posted a 24-second video of "The Doctor Does Shakespeare" with "There is nothing either good or bad but thinking makes it so" (2.2.249-50) spoken by Tennant as Dr. Who, entirely made up of clips of each word in turn taken from different moments in the series, created with a kind of obsessive perseverance reminiscent of that staple of detective fiction, the letter constructed out of words clipped from newspapers. If Tennant for a moment imagines that his Stratford performances can somehow be divorced from his television success and only exist as reconnections to his earlier time with the Royal Shakespeare Company, the Wilkinsons offer a different, clever and witty comment on the inseparability of the one from the other. Analyzing the trailers for screen Shakespeare is a fascinating project (the lengthy voiceover commentary in the one for Branagh's *Henry V* managed never to mention the word "Shakespeare" at all) but YouTube retrieves for us television's cultural markings of its anticipations and temptations.

Shakespeare's place on the YouTube realms of the internet is, then, clipped into fragments to share, parasitic rather more often than performed, primarily existing as adaptation and derivative, comic in manner, irrespective of the originating genre, Shakespeare as sketch and moment more than action and extent. But it can also allude to more conventional performance, invite connection with live theater, suggest the possibilities of different and more traditional communities of consumption. Among the many organizations that post clips on YouTube is the National Theatre which, in September 2008, had posted 67 clips, ranging from trailers and performance extracts to talks and interviews. As revolutionary for British theater as its announcement in the same month that it would perform on Sundays, the National Theatre's willingness to engage the web intelligently and even energetically is striking. It was, for instance, the prime mover behind the development of the Stagework site, supported by government funding as an educational outreach possibility, a space which other companies have now joined (see also Flood-Page.)

As I wrote an earlier version of this article in November 2007, I was reading week by week the accumulating rehearsal diary for Nicholas Hytner's production of *Much Ado About Nothing*, with Simon Russell Beale and Zoe Wanamaker as Benedick and Beatrice, that opened the following month, in December 2007. I could see how, at least in the eyes of the diarist, Annette Vieusseux, Hytner explored possibilities, tried ideas, allowed the actors to find character and meaning, from the director's speech at the first rehearsal, the first read-through and the designers' showing of set models and costume designs onwards. Observed but not directly visible, mediated both by the author's perception (and the limits of her perceptiveness) and by what is appropriate to be made public—for I take it that, say, major and disturbing creative tensions and shouting matches would not make it into the web diary—the account was, as I finished that version of this article, up to the end of week five and I could enjoy seeing (by reading this controlled account) how the opening exchanges were turning into testing out of character and relationship, how familial and social structures that Hytner had described early in rehearsal were now becoming blocking and business, how the remarkable choice of historical setting (early modern) and geography (Sicily)— that is, unusually in contemporary production, both the time of the play's writing and the place in which its fiction is set (rather than, say, nineteenth-century Hungary)—were enabling the play to be uncovered, mined or whatever other metaphor is appropriate to the "journey" of rehearsal and creation.

Rehearsal, in Western theater practice, has completely blocked the spectator's direct access. Rehearsals are closed spaces of exploration, weeks of work that leave the participating creators vulnerable and open. Hence, in most theater traditions, few if any people outside the creative team have access. There may occasionally be an observer in the rehearsal room, either as dramaturg or as permitted outsider, and the outsider may silently watch, record and, eventually, write up what happened. The rehearsal log, whether recorded by a performer or an observer, was a fascinating but distinctly infrequent document. We cherish and return to, say, David Selbourne's incisive account of the rehearsals for Peter Brook's production of *A Midsummer Night's Dream*, or even Kristina Bedford's distinctly less incisive one for Peter Hall's 1984 *Coriolanus*, or the wonderful twinning of William Redfield and Richard Sterne on Gielgud directing Burton in *Hamlet*, two actors working in the same production but with diametrically opposed views of the worth of the experience (see Selbourne; Bedford; Redfield; Sterne). We value these accounts precisely because of their rarity, their privileged access to the long and fraught process of making Shakespeare performance. Even in the many cases of the substantial absence of the documentation of the eventual product, the performance itself, for the visual records of the first two of these, for example, are fragmentary, they serve as striking and transgressive acts, denials of the borders between preparation and production, between what the theater-goers have paid to see and what has preceded or accompanied that commercial fact, entertainment as the object that has been bought.

In the last few years, the National Theatre in London has developed a practice of documenting rehearsal in the form of a diary account that, unlike the substantial, often scholarly versions that take some time to produce, can be on sale in the theater very soon after the show has opened. Hence, it becomes possible for the audience members to buy as souvenir a slim book that recounts the process through which the production was created that they are about to see, have just seen or are in the middle of seeing (for I suspect that interval sales are strong). Jonathan Croall's diary of John Caird's production of *Hamlet* with Simon Russell Beale or Bella Merlin's of Hytner's production of the two parts of *Henry IV* are good Shakespearean exemplars of the genre (see Croall; Merlin; also Butler for Hytner's production of Jonson's *The Alchemist*; and the numerous others published in the "National Theatre at Work" series as a collaboration between NT Publications and Oberon Books). But even these rapid transitions from journal to print pale beside the web's versions.

The rehearsal diaries for *Much Ado About Nothing* are purely verbal but they are accompanied on the website by the kinds of other documentation that *Stagework* often provides. For the production of *Richard III*, directed by Barrie Rutter for Northern Broadsides with the West Yorkshire Playhouse, for instance, I can watch (and have enjoyed watching) interviews with the designer and director, numerous interviews with many of the members of the cast, footage of the materials of construction sites out of which the set design concept emerged, or a description of how clogging, the rhythmic dancing in heavy industrial clogs that have been a part of Northern Broadsides' work since its inception (and which derive from Rutter's experience of working with Tony Harrison on his *Trackers of Oxyrhynchus*), functions both as a way of making battles work on stage and as a means of unifying the company in physical activity in the early stages of the rehearsal weeks. For the play's opening speech I can watch Conrad Nelson speaking it in rehearsal and in performance and giving his own glossed commentary of what he is processing it as meaning. The list of video and audio extracts and the complex and structured interrelationships between them would take ages to describe.

Stagework is designed for school students and schoolteachers, for the general public, and for scholars, and it is a remarkably successful achievement. The theater companies have clearly committed themselves fully to the enterprise and the willingness of the cast and production team to work so hard to create materials specifically for the site is exceptional. Not attached to a theater company's marketing department—nor really to their education/outreach department either—the *Stagework* documentation achieves, in its series of fragments and glimpses, a kind of perception of creation. But it is only a kind of perception. A clip offers a rehearsal glimpse of Richard's opening speech: it is certainly filmed in the rehearsal room with director and assistant at a desk watching Nelson. Suspicious I am, I do not see this as staged for the camera. But all the clip contains is Nelson running the speech through; there is no comment from director or actor about what has been achieved in that run nor how it might develop. I can, of course, compare it with the same speech "in performance": here is Nelson in costume standing on the set but it is not a live performance (for his speaking out of the frame straight to camera is not the same as looking at the theater audience and there is no hint of a live audience presence). The performance is staged for the camera, moved from its liveliness to a mediated presentation that implicitly gestures towards the actuality of theater while actually simultaneously denying itself as theater at all (not least since the camera angle is not one that represents the point of view of any member of the audience). The POV (point of view) is an artifice and the performance is, in volume, scale, gestural range and focus, designed for watching on the computer screen through the *Stagework* site, rather than being the end-product of the rehearsal process which can be (implicitly) seen within the other clip of the speech.

At such times what is available goes beyond anything that theater performance makes possible through its need to find a mode of recording that mediatizes and hence transforms that which it ostensibly documents. The viewer has both passed through to the rehearsal room and yet is ironically denied access both to what happens in rehearsal (since we do not see anything other than an early stage of performance, none of the interaction that is the primary activity of rehearsal) and to what happens/will happen in performance itself. Of course there are numerous other pieces whose relationship to performance is much more exact. Unsurprisingly it is Hytner's National Theatre production of *Henry V* that is most fully available (that is, the production is less subject to the transformations through its recording and webcasting), unsurprising since the production made extensive use of video materials, turning the play's public visibility into analogies to the forms of television representation of the movement to war and the actuality (as it were, implicitly, the French word *actualité*) of the Iraq invasion. Watching on a computer screen Adrian Lester as Henry in smart suit speaking direct to camera as he gives the rationale for the invasion both is the performance itself (for the video is exactly what was used onstage at the National) and, through its being displaced onto my computer, becomes a representation of that performance, the object and its mediatization. The "home video" quality of the filmed sequence of Prince Henry with Falstaff and his crew, the memory of the past that in the production the mourners at the wake after Falstaff's funeral watch before switching off the video player and switching on the snooker channel, becomes on the computer a fully achieved YouTube clip, complete with time-coding, moving from the pub television screen of the stage set to the domestic space of consumption of such clips that are our online experience.

If such data of performance change in their transition to the web-site, redefining their place and their parameters, the boundaries and contexts of our assimilation and consumption of them as part of performance, the *Stagework* presentation of Richard agreeing to accept the crown (*Richard III*, 3.7) in the Northern Broadsides' production shows a different redefining of the limits of theater. Part of the scene is available in a complex hierarchy of clips with the possibility of stopping the scene to view interview segments with actors commenting on their character's perception of the scene's principal action. But it can also be watched from four different perspectives (i.e., from four camera-angles taken from more than one performance) representing the POVs of Buckingham, Richard and the Mayor of London as well as the audience. This is a kind of web-delivered version of the spectographic technique for workshopping, in which the scene is redirected by a sequence of different characters to represent their view of the action: imagine, say, the division of the kingdom in *King Lear* 1.1 from the perspective of, in turn, Lear, Kent, Cordelia, and Regan. Since the *Richard III* material was all taped for the purpose of placing on the web-site, even the perspective of the audience is a manufactured construction rather than an access to live consumption of the object. Fascinating as is this exploration of positioning and viewpoint, especially given the vertical layering that the blocking of the scene necessitates with Richard and the "two right reverend fathers" (3.7.60) above the rest of the actors looking vertiginously down on the others, the digitized experience is a form of representation of performance that also denies the singleness of our perspective from the bounded constriction of our view that marks our theater seat (except, say, in promenade performance or moving around the yard at the Globe).

But for all the quantity of the segments of the site, for all the imaginative and successful ways in which the data has been accumulated and presented, for all the perspectives it offers, *Stagework* still offers only fragments and reformulations, inadequate glimmerings of process and consequence, of preparation and performance. *Stagework* is a remarkable site, a space in which inventively the designers have achieved conjunctions of different materials, only rarely tricksy for their own sake (like the distinctly camp "interactive" exploration of a speech created with Ian McKellen, stopping to ask us questions that we must answer before he continues). Informative for the theatrically naïve (what exactly does a director do?), rich in its documentation of the thoughts of those involved in a production, engaging in its web-designs, *Stagework* teases us with having passed through to the space in which productions are created; yet it always redefines the boundaries of that creativity, allowing us access only through the eyes of our guides (the camera, the writer of the rehearsal log, the webmaster), never the kind of unmediated access to the event of theatrical creativity and the preservation of performance for which we yearn. Exciting and frustrating in equal measure, it stands both as an enticing advance on anything previously widely available and as the limit of what the web has achieved – at least at the moment of my writing this and no doubt superseded by the time this reaches print. Eschewing the lure of the quickly palling pleasures of the novelty of transforming playgoers into actors, *Stagework* mediates backstage creativity not as a denial of live non-virtual performance but as a space between the theater and the web in which new communities can be forged.

Works Cited

Arden: The World of William Shakespeare (2008). MMOG. <http://swi.indiana.edu/ardenworld.htm>.

Bedford, Kristina. Coriolanus *at the National: "Th'Interpretation of the Time."* Selinsgrove: Susquehanna UP, 1992.

Butler, Robert. *The Alchemist Exposed.* London: Oberon Books, 2006.

Castranova, Ted. "5 Tips for Making Games that Don't Suck." *Wired Magazine:* <http://www.wired.com/print/gaming/gamingreviews/magazine/16-04/pl_games>.

Centaur, Ina. Post on SHAKSPER listserv SHK 19.0362. 24 June 2008.

Coriolanus. Great Performances. With Toby Stephens as Coriolanus. YouTube. <http://www.youtube.com/watch?v=NWOhcWmmqJs>.

Coriolanus. Book at Bedtime. With Lucy Pinder as Volumnia. You Tube. <http://www.youtube.com/watch?v=xHzl-Q9El6Y&feature=related>.

Croall, Jonathan. *Hamlet Observed: The National Theatre at Work.* London: NT Publications, 2001.

Desmet, Christy. "Paying Attention in Shakespeare Parody: From Tom Stoppard to YouTube." *Shakespeare Survey* 61 (2008): 227-38.

"The Doctor Does Shakespeare." YouTube. With David Tennant as Doctor Who. <http://www.youtube.com/watch?v=uFDS4Rp7HRs>.

Flood-Page, Michael. "Shakespeare and Theatre on New Media Platforms." *A Guide to Shakespeare on Film, Television and Radio.* Ed. Olwen Terris. London: BUFVC, forthcoming.

"Macbeth Act V." Pirate Monkey Productions. YouTube. <http://www.youtube.com/watch?v=osk_jqQ0-Kc&feature=related>

Merlin, Bella. *With the Rogue's Company: "Henry IV" at the National Theatre.* London: Oberon Books, 2005.

"My Name is Macbeth." YouTube. <http://www.youtube.com/watch?v=xHzl-Q9El6Y&feature=related>.

Pinder, Lucy. Playlist. *Book at Bedtime* series. YouTube. <http://www.youtube.com/view_play_list?p=BF2ABE71380F18CE>.

Redfield, William. *Letters from an Actor.* New York: Viking, 1967.

Selbourne, David. *The Making of* A Midsummer Night's Dream. London: Methuen, 1982.

The National Theatre. *Stagework.* <http://www.stagework.org.uk>.

Sterne, Richard L. *John Gielgud Directs Richard Burton in "Hamlet."* New York: Random House, 1967.

Stromberg, Logan. "Lego MacBeth." YouTube. <http://www.youtube.com/watch?v=4QEgH-sTW9c&feature=related>.

Tech page. *The SL Shakespeare Company.* <http://slshakespeare.com/pages/tech>.

Part Four

Chronology and Selected Bibliography

A Chronology of Shakespeare in Hollywood, Asia, and Cyberspace

Alexander C.Y. Huang

Year	Historical Events	Worldwide & Hollywood Shakespeares	Asian Shakespeares
1596		English players tour extensively in Germany, France, Austria, the Netherlands, Sweden, and elsewhere in Europe in the 1590s	Transmission of Renaissance culture begins in China and East Asia
1602	*Hamlet* entered in the Stationer's Registry on 26 July		
1604	Coronation of King James I in England	*Romeo and Juliet* performed in Nördlingen	
1607	John Smith founds colony of Virginia at Jamestown		*Hamlet* performed on board the Red Dragon, anchored near Sierra Leone
1609	Dutch East India Company imports first tea from China		*Hamlet* performed in Socotra, Gulf of Aden (Arab Republic of Yemen) in 1608
1619			*Hamlet* performed by employees of the Dutch East Indies Company in Jayakerta, Indonesia
1624	Taiwan colonized by the Dutch, 1624-1662		
1807		Charles and Mary Lamb publish *Tales from Shakespeare*, which has a great influence on the initial reception of Shakespeare in East Asia	

Year	Historical Events	Worldwide & Hollywood Shakespeares	Asian Shakespeares
1839	Opium Wars begin (1839-1842); Lin Zexu publishes *Annals of the Four Continents* in China	*Twelfth Night*, dir. Karl Immermann, Düsseldorffer Künstler; Thomas Carlyle publishes *On Heroes, Hero Worship, and the Heroic in History* in 1840	First mention of Shakespeare in Chinese by Lin Zexu, who attempts to stop the opium trade
1842	China cedes Hong Kong to Britain for 150 years (Treaty of Tianjin)	Ludwig Tieck collaborates with Felix Mendelssohn on their 1843 production of *A Midsummer Night's Dream*	First mention of Shakespeare in Japanese (1841 translation of a Dutch translation of an English grammar book)
1859			Birth of Tsubouchi Shoyo, pioneer of Shakespeare studies and translation in Japan
1864	China's self-strengthening movement begins	Deutsche Shakespeare-Gesellschaft founded	
1867			Hong Kong Amateur Dramatic Club stages Francis Talfourd's *Shylock, or the Merchant of Venice Preserved,* revived in 1871
1868	Meiji reform begins in Japan		Public reading of excerpts from *A Midsummer Night's Dream* and *Romeo and Juliet* in Yokohama, in 1866 and 1869
1875			Katagaki Robun's *kabuki Hamlet*
1879		Scenes from *The Taming of the Shrew* performed in English in the Gaiety Theatre in Yokohama	Guo Songtao, China's first Minister to England, attends Henry Irving's *Hamlet*
1882		*Romeo and Juliet*, dir. Henry Irving, Lyceum Theatre, London	Shakespeare introduced into Hong Kong's school curriculum
1894	First Sino-Japanese War; China cedes Taiwan to Japan in 1895	Karl Marx's *Das Kapital* 2nd and 3rd vols., unfinished by Marx, edited and published by Engels	Katsu Genzô's *kabuki* adaptation of *The Merchant of Venice* staged in Osaka
1899	Boer War begins	First cinematic Shakespeare: *Sir Herbert Beerbohm Tree's King John*, dir. William Dickson, a silent film	Shakespearean scenes with Juliet, Beatrice, Rosalind and others staged in English by the Janet Waldorf Company in Yokohama in 1899

Year	Historical Events	Worldwide & Hollywood Shakespeares	Asian Shakespeares
1903			Kawakami Otojiro's *Othello* recasts Taiwan as the outpost of the colonial Japanese empire
1904			Lin Shu and Wei Yi, trans. Charles and Mary Lambs' *Tales from Shakespeare* into Chinese
1909			Kawakami Otojiro's *Hamlet* performed in Korea by a Japanese shinpa theater company
1911	Republic of China established Colonization of Korea by Japan, 1910-1945	*Hamlet*, dir. E. G. Craig and K. S. Stanislavsky, Moscow	Tsubouchi Shoyo's *Hamlet* produced by the Bungei Kyokai (Literary Arts Society) at the Imperial Theatre in Tokyo
1913		*Twelfth Night*, dir. Harley Granville-Barker, London, 1912 Max Reinhardt stages ten Shakespearean plays at Deutsches Theater, Berlin	*Hamlet Rajah of Denmark*, The Straits Opera Company, Malaysia, 1912 Hong Kong Mummers stages *Twelfth Night*
1914			First Chinese opera performance of Shakespeare: Ya'an *chuanju* Theatre's *Hamlet* *Romeo and Juliet*, Geijutsu Club, trans. Tsubouchi Shôyô, Japan
1919	Treaty of Versailles ends World War I; May Fourth movement begins		*The Tempest* from the Lambs' *Tales from Shakespeare* translated into Korean
1921		Asta Nielsen's *Hamlet: The Drama of Vengeance* (1920), a silent film	*Hamlet,* dir. Nobuchi Akira, produced by Elan Vital, a *shingeki* theater company (Kyoto)
1922	Singapore becomes a major British naval base		
1925			First Korean production of Shakespeare (*Julius Caesar*, by Kyungsong vocational school)

Year	Historical Events	Worldwide & Hollywood Shakespeares	Asian Shakespeares
1927	Chinese civil war begins		*Macbeth*, trans. Mori Ôgai, dir. Osanai Kaoru and Aoyama Sugisaku, produced by Tsukiji Shôgekijô, Japan
1928			Tsubouchi Shoyo completes his translation of the *Complete Works* into Japanese Novelist Mori Ogai's translation of *Macbeth* produced at Tsukiji Little Theatre
1931	Japan takes Manchuria	*Romeo and Juliet*, dir. Arnold Szyfman, Warsaw	Bu Wancang's silent film adaptation of *The Two Gentlemen from Verona*
1933	Hitler named chancellor of Germany		
1935		*Romeo and Juliet*, dir. John Gielgud, London *A Midsummer Night's Dream*, dir. Max Reinhardt and William Dieterle	*Khoon Ka Khoon* (*Hamlet*), dir. Sohrab Modi (black-and-white film with sound, India)
1937	China's War of Anti-Japanese Invasion begins; World War II begins; The Rape of Nanjing; colonial Japanization campaign begins in Taiwan (1937-1945)	*Julius Caesar*, dir. Orson Welles, New York	
1941	Pearl Harbor		Novelist Dazai Osamu's anti-militarist rewriting of *Hamlet* (*Shin Hamuretto*)
1942	Mao Zedong, "Talk at the Yan'an Forum on Literature and Arts" The British surrender and the Japanese Occupation of Singapore begins		*Hamlet*, dir. Jiao Juyin, is staged in a Confucian Temple in Jiang'an
1944		Laurence Olivier's *Henry V*	Li Jianwu publishes *Wang Deming*, an adaptation of *Macbeth*
1945	Atomic bomb dropped on Hiroshima; Japan surrenders to the Allied Forces End of Japanese colonization of Taiwan	*Strange Illusion*, dir. Edgar G. Ulmer (*film noir Hamlet*, USA)	*The Hero of a Tumultuous Time*, dir. Huang Zuolin, Shanghai, based on Li's *Wang Deming*

Year	Historical Events	Worldwide & Hollywood Shakespeares	Asian Shakespeares
1947	Republic of India established	*Romeo and Juliet*, dir. Peter Brook, Stratford; *Richard II*, dir. Jean Vilar, Avignon	
1948	Republic of Korea established	Laurence Olivier's *Hamlet* *Macbeth*, dir. Ingmar Bergman, Gothenburg; *Macbeth*, dir. Orson Welles (USA; film)	
1949	The People's Republic of China founded The nationalists, led by Chiang Kai-shek, retreat to Taiwan		Sol Jun-Sik publishes the first Korean translation of *Hamlet* directly from the English text
1950	Korean War begins (1950-1953)		
1954	Deng Xiaoping is appointed Secretary General of the Communist Party Mutual Defense Treaty between the USA and Taiwan	*Hamlet*, dir. Nikolai Okhlopkov, Moscow *The Taming of the Shrew*, dir. Tyrone Guthrie, Stratford, Ontario	Shakespeare festival in Hong Kong, April 23
1957		*Coriolanus*, dir. Giorgio Strehler, Milan	*Throne of Blood* (*Macbeth*), dir. Akira Kurosawa
1958	Mao Zedong launches the Great Leap Forward	*Kiss Me Kate* (*Taming of the Shrew*), dir. George Schaefer (black-and-white TV, USA)	Laurence Olivier's *Hamlet* screened in China (dubbed in Chinese by Sun Daolin) and exerts great influence on subsequent Chinese performances
1961	The Chinese Communist Party temporarily loosens control over art and literature Showa Genroku--period of rapid economic growth in Japan	Jan Kott, *Szkice o Szekspirze* (Warszawa: Panstwowy Instytut Wydawniczy)	Shakespeare Society of Japan established
1963			The Shakespeare Association of Korea established
1964	The Olympics held in Tokyo		Shakespeare Theatre Festival, Seoul
1966	Ten-year Cultural Revolution begins War in Vietnam	*Chimes at Midnight* (*Henry IV*), dir. Orson Welles (film, Spain / Switzerland)	Shakespeare and all foreign writers banned in China
1967		Tom Stoppard's *Rosencrantz and Guildenstern Are Dead* produced by the Royal National Theatre	

Year	Historical Events	Worldwide & Hollywood Shakespeares	Asian Shakespeares
1968	Yasunari Kawabata wins Nobel Prize in Literature		
1970			Royal Shakespeare Company tours to Tokyo for the first time with *The Merry Wives of Windsor* and *The Winter's Tale*
1974			Ninagawa Yukio's debut Shakespeare production, *Romeo and Juliet* Hyokyung Kim's *The Marowitz Hamlet*
1976	Mao Zedong dies	*Othello,* dir. Peter Zadek, Hamburg *Macbeth*, dir. Trevor Nunn, Stratford	
1977		*Intikam Melegi - Kadin Hamlet* (*Female Hamlet*), dir. Metin Erksan (Ugur Film, Turkey)	*The Revenge of the Prince* (*Hamlet*), dir. Ho Man Wui, Hong Kong Repertory Theatre
1978	Deng Xiaoping announces the open door policy		
1981	The Chinese Communist Party formally condemns Mao for his role in the Cultural Revolution	*Richard II*, dir. Ariane Mnouchkine, Cartoucherie de Vincennes, France; Japan's Shakespeare Theatre Company finishes staging all of Shakespeare's plays (1975-1981); monthly productions in an underground theater called Jean Jean in central Tokyo (artistic director, Deguchi Norio)	*Measure for Measure*, dir. Tolby Robertson, Beijing People's Art Theatre
1983	Arthur Miller visits China	*Noh Hamlet*, dir. Munakata Kuniyoshi, Noh Shakespeare Kenkyûkai, Japan	*Othello*, dir. Ma Yong'an, Beijing Experimental *Jingju* Theatre Mandarin-English bilingual *A Midsummer Night's Dream*, dir. Tisa Chang, Pan Asian Repertory Theater, New York
1984	Sino-British Joint Declaration, Hong Kong	*King Lear*, dir. Ingmar Bergman, Stockholm *1 Henry IV*, dir. Ariane Mnouchkine, Paris	Shakespeare festival in Hong Kong
1985	Mikhail Gorbachev becomes the general secretary of the Communist Party of the Soviet Union		*Ran* (*King Lear*), dir. Kurosawa (film, Japan) Noda Higeki directs *Twelfth Night* for Toho

Year	Historical Events	Worldwide & Hollywood Shakespeares	Asian Shakespeares
1986	Nuclear disaster at Chernobyl	*The Winter's Tale*, dir. Anzai Tetsuo, Engeki Shûdan En, Japan *Romeo and Juliet*, dir. Michael Bogdanov, Stratford	First Shakespeare festival in mainland China (Beijing and Shanghai, April 10-23) *Kingdom of Desire* (*Macbeth*), a Beijing opera adaptation by Wu Hsing-kuo and Taiwan's Contemporary Legend Theatre
1987	Taiwan's martial law is lifted	Ninagawa Yukio's *kabuki Macbeth*, London (seen at the Edinburgh Festival in 1985) *Shakespeare Wallah*, dir. James Ivory (film, India)	*Kunju Macbeth* (*Story of Bloody Hands*), dir. Huang Zuolin, tours Edinburgh, London, and other European cities
1988	The Olympics held in Seoul	Tokyo Globe opens	*One Husband Too Many* (*Romeo and Juliet*), dir. Anthony Chan (film, Hong Kong) Sergei Yutkevich's *Othello* (USSR, 1956), dubbed in Mandarin, screened in Qufu, Shandong province, China
1989	Tiananmen Square massacre Fall of the Berlin Wall	*Kathakali King Lear*, dir. David McRuvie and Annette Leday *Is Shakespeare Still Our Contemporary?* Ed. John Elsom	*Richard III*, dir. Peng Liqi, trans. Zhu Shenghao, Shanghai Theatre Academy
1990	Nelson Mandela released from prison and becomes deputy president of the African National Congress	*Hamlet*, dir. Heiner Müller, Berlin *The Tempest*, dir. Peter Brook, Paris *Hamlet*, dir. Franco Zeffirelli	Neo-*kabuki Romeo and Juliet*, dir. Kanô Yukikazu (Hanagumi *Shibai* Company) *Hamlet*, dir. Watanabe Moriaki (Tokyo Globe Theatre production)
1991	Collapse of the Communist bloc in Europe	*Prospero's Books*, dir. Peter Greenaway; World Congress of the International Shakespeare Association (ISA) in Tokyo	

Year	Historical Events	Worldwide & Hollywood Shakespeares	Asian Shakespeares
1992		A Midsummer Night's Dream, dir. Robert Lepage, London	*King Lear*, dir. Suzuki Tadashi (SCOT) *A Midsummer Night's Dream*, dir. Hideki Noda, Tokyo Tsutsumi Harue's *Kanadehon Hamlet*, a satire on Meiji *kabuki* actors *Shamlet*, dir. Lee Kuo-hsiu, Pingfeng Acting Workshop, Taipei (a parody of *Hamlet*), revived in 1995, tours Shanghai in 1994 and Toronto in 1996, and re-staged in Taipei in 2000, 2006, 2007
1993		*Much Ado About Nothing*, dir. Kenneth Branagh (UK, Italy; film)	*The Comedy of Errors*, dir. Ian Judge, Royal Shakespeare Company, Taipei International Drama Festival *Hamletmachine*, dir. Seon-geun Chae
1994	Kenzaburo Oe wins Nobel Prize for Literature China's GDP grows at an average annual rate of 10 %		Second Shakespeare festival in mainland China (Shanghai) *A Midsummer Night's Dream*, dir. Ninagawa Yukio, Tokyo
1996		*Hamlet*, dir. Kenneth Branagh *William Shakespeare's Romeo+Juliet*, dir. Baz Luhrmann *Looking for Richard*, dir. Al Pacino *A Midsummer Night's Dream*, dir. Adrian Noble	Qin Zhongying and Luo Jiaying's *Hero Betrays His Country* (*Macbeth*), Jin Ying Hua Cantonese Opera Troupe, Hong Kong
1997	Britain returns Hong Kong to Chinese jurisdiction Globe Theatre opens in London Jiang Zemin legalizes private enterprise in China	Welcome Msomi's *uMabatha* (1972) is one of the six productions chosen to open the Globe Theatre in London	*Kiss Me Nana*, dir. Liang Chi-min, Godot Theatre, Taipei; revived in 1999 Pan-Asian multilingual *Lear*, dir. Ong Keng Sen (Singapore, Hong Kong, Tokyo)

Year	Historical Events	Worldwide & Hollywood Shakespeares	Asian Shakespeares
1998		*Shakespeare in Love*, dir. John Madden *Macbeth*, dir. Michael Bogdanov	*Othello, bleeding but not to be dead* by Keunhyung Park Conference on Shakespeare and India organized by the Shakespeare Society of India Conference on Shakespeare in Asia (September, Shanghai) organized by the Shakespeare Society of China, Hong Kong Shakespeare Society, and Shanghai Theatre Academy *Lady Macbeth* by Taesuk Han
1999	Shakespeare voted Writer of the Millennium, BBC News	*Titus*, dir. Julie Taymor	*King Lear*, dir. Ninagawa Yukio, Tokyo, London, Stratford Bilingual *Othello: A Play in Black and White*, dir. Royston Abel, Edinburgh Festival
2000	Chinese-French playwright, painter, and novelist Gao Xingjian awarded the Nobel Prize of Literature	*Hamlet,* dir. Michael Almereyda (film) *Hamlet*, dir. Peter Brook, Paris	Hong Kong Experimental Shakespeare festival *Chicken Rice War* [*Jiyuan qiaohe*], dir. Cheah Chee Kong (Singaporean film)
2001	"9/11" attacks	*Scotland, PA*, dir. Billy Morrissette	*Richard III*, dir. Lin Zhaohua (Beijing People's Art Theatre), Berlin Asia Pacific Cultural Festival *Romeo and Juliet*, dir. Taesuk Oh, Bremen *Ang Pagpapaamo sa Maldita* (*Taming of the Shrew*), dir. Ricardo Abad (Philippines) *King Uru* by Myunggon Kim (*King Lear*), Korean National Theatre
2002	Massive demonstration in Hong Kong against the legislation of the Hong Kong Basic Law Article 23 which erodes the freedom of speech	Sulayman Al-Bassam's *The Al-Hamlet Summit* wins the Fringe First award at the Edinburgh International Fringe Festival	*Search: Hamlet*, dir. Ong Keng Sen, Kronborg Castle, Denmark *A Dream in Hanoi*, dir. Tom Weidlinger, documentary film Shakespeare Performance in New Asias Conference held in Singapore

Year	Historical Events	Worldwide & Hollywood Shakespeares	Asian Shakespeares
2003	SARS outbreak	*In Search of Shakespeare*, dir. Michael Wood (BBC)	Shakespeare in Taipei Festival *Kyogen* actor Nomura Mansai stars in *Hamlet* in new translation by Kawai Shoichiro
2004	Tsunami in South and Southeast Asia	*Huapango* (*Othello*), dir. Ivan Lipkies (Vlady Realizadores, Mexico) *The Merchant of Venice*, dir. Michael Radford (film; Al Pacino as Shylock)	Shakespeare in Asia, international conference and festival, held at Stanford University; http://sia.stanford.edu *Mian Maqbool*, dir. Vishal Bharadwaj (film, India)
2005	Beijing's National Grand Theatre of China opens (designed by Paul Andreu)	*The Merchant of Venice*, dir. Michael Radford	*Wheel Performance: Romeo and Juliet*, dir. Kim Jin-man (Korea), features extreme sports stunts Shanghai *Jingju* Company's *Hamlet* performed at Denmark's Hamlet Sommer festival
2006		*Ur-Hamlet*, dir. Eugenio Barba, Hamlet Sommer festival, Kronborg Castle, Denmark, with a cast of *Noh*, Balinese, Indian, Afro-Brazilian, and European performers	*The Banquet* (*Hamlet*), dir. Feng Xiaogang (feature film in Mandarin) *Prince of the Himalayas* (*Hamlet*), dir. Hu Xuehua (feature film in Tibetan) *Romeo and Juliet*, dir. Oh Tae-suk, Mokhwa Repertory Company (Korea), London
2007		*As You Like It*, dir. Kenneth Branagh (HBO film), set in Japan Shakespeare in Washington (January - June), "a landmark festival of theater, music, dance, film, art, and more throughout the nation's capital"	Wu Hsing-kuo's *Lear Is Here* staged at the Lincoln Center Festival and in San Jose, California *The Witches' Sonata--Poetic Macbeth*, dir. Lü Po-shen, Tainan Jen Ensemble of Taiwan, staged at the Festival d'Avignon OFF
2008	The Olympic Games held in Beijing		

Bibliography of *Shakespeare in Hollywood, Asia, and Cyberspace*

Lucian Ghita and Alexander C.Y. Huang

Given the vast scholarship on Shakespeare, the scope of this bibliography is limited to provide a useful and informed starting point for Shakespeare scholars who work in the field of Shakespeare in Hollywood, Asia, and cyberspace. The bibliography includes selected books, articles, and other printed and online sources on Shakespeare in intercultural and multimedia environments 1970-2009. For work on Shakespeare in Hollywood, focus is on titles published in the last fifteen years while for Asian stage and screen adaptations of Shakespeare, works from a broader period are listed.

Abdullah, Nurul Farhana Low bt. "Bangsawan Shakespeare in Colonial Malaya." *Shakespeare in Hollywood, Asia, and Cyberspace*. Ed. Alexander C.Y. Huang and Charles S. Ross. West Lafayette: Purdue UP, 2009. 139-51.

Aebischer, Pascale, Edward J. Esche and Nigel Wheale, eds. *Remaking Shakespeare: Performance across Media, Genres and Cultures*. Basingstoke: Palgrave Macmillan, 2003.

Albanese, Denise. "The Shakespeare Film and the Americanization of Culture." *Marxist Shakespeares*. Ed. Jean E. Howard and Scott Cutler Shershow. New York: Routledge, 2001. 206-26.

Alter, Iska."'To See or Not to See': Interpolations, Extended Scenes, and Musical Accompaniment in Kenneth Branagh's *Hamlet*." *Stage Directions in Hamlet: New Essays and New Directions*. Ed. Hardin Aasand. Madison: Fairleigh Dickinson UP, 2003. 161-9.

Anderegg, Michael A. *Cinematic Shakespeare*. Lanham: Rowman & Littlefield, 2004.

Anderegg, Michael A. *Orson Welles, Shakespeare, and Popular Culture*. New York: Columbia UP, 1999.

Ashizu, Kaori. "Kurosawa's *Hamlet*?" *Shakespeare Studies* 33 (1995): 71-99.

Associaton of Asian Performance Streaming Video Library (2008): <http://www.yavanika.org/video/ >.

Auslander, Philip. *Liveness: Performance in a Mediatized Culture*. London: Routledge, 2008.

Barnet, Sylvan. "*Macbeth* on Stage and Screen." *Macbeth*. Ed. Sylvan Barnet. New York: Penguin, 1998.

Bate, Jonathan. "Introduction." *Titus: The Illustrated Screenplay*. New York: Newmarket P, 2000. 8-13.

Belsey, Catherine. "Shakespeare and Film: A Question of Perspective." *Literature /Film Quarterly* 11.3 (1983): 152-58.

Bertoldi, Andreas. "Shakespeare, Psychoanalysis and Coloniality." *Post-colonial Shakespeares*. Ed. Ania Loomba and Martin Orkin. London: Routledge, 1998. 233-58.

Bevington, David. "Shakespeare's Asia and Imagining the East." *Shakespeare in Hollywood, Asia, and Cyberspace*. Ed. Alexander C.Y. Huang and Charles S. Ross. West Lafayette: Purdue UP, 2009. 67-77.

Bevington, David. *This Wide and Universal Theater: Shakespeare in Performance, Then and Now*. Chicago: U of Chicago P, 2007.

Bevington David, Anne Marie Welsh, and Michael Greenwald. *Shakespeare: Script, Stage, Screen*. London: Longman, 2005.

Bharucha, Rustom. "Foreign Asia/Foreign Shakespeare: Dissenting Notes on New Asian Interculturality, Postcoloniality, and Recolonization." *Theatre Journal* 56.1 (2004): 1-28.

Bharucha, Rustom. *Theatre and the World: Essays on Performance and Politics of Culture*. New Delhi: Manohar, 1990.

Billings, Timothy. "Caterwauling Cataians: The Genealogy of a Gloss." *Shakespeare Quarterly* 54.1 (2003): 1-28.

Blumenthal, Eileen. *Julie Taymor: Playing with Fire: Theater, Opera, Film*. New York: Harry N. Adams, 1999.

Bock, Audie. *Japanese Film Directors*. Tokyo: Kodansha International Ltd., 1978.

Boose, Lynda E. and Richard Burt, eds. *Shakespeare, the Movie I: Popularizing the Plays on Film, TV, and Video*. New York: Routledge, 1997.

Boose, Lynda E. and Richard Burt, eds. *Shakespeare, the Movie II: Popularizing the Plays on Film, TV, and Video*. New York: Routledge, 2003.

Bourus, Terri. "The First Quarto of *Hamlet* in Film: The Revenge Tragedies of Tony Richardson and Franco Zeffirelli." *Entertext* 1.2 (2001): 180-91.

Brandon, James R. "Some Shakespeare(s) in Some Asia(s)." *Asian Studies Review* 20 (1997): 1-26.

Brode, Douglas. *Shakespeare in the Movies*. Oxford: Oxford UP, 2000.

Brook, Peter, Peter Hall, and Richard Loncraine. "Shakespeare in the Cinema: A Film Directors' Symposium." *Cineaste* 24 (1998): 48-55.

Brown, John Russell. "Asian Theatres and European Shakespeares." *Shakespeare-Jahrbuch* 138 (2002): 11-22.

Brown, John Russell. *New Sites for Shakespeare: Theatre, the Audience, and Asia*. London: Routledge, 1999.

Buchanan, Judith. *Shakespeare on Film*. London: Longman, 2005.

Buhler, Stephen M. *Shakespeare in the Cinema: Ocular Proof.* Albany: State U of New York P, 2002.

Bulman, James C., ed. *Shakespeare, Theory, and Performance*. London: Routledge, 1995.

Burch, Noël. *To the Distant Observer: Form and Meaning in the Japanese Cinema.* Berkeley: U of California P, 1979.

Burnett, Mark Thornton. *Filming Shakespeare in the Global Marketplace*. New York: Palgrave Macmillan, 2007.

Burnett, Mark Thornton. "'To Hear and See the Matter': Communicating Technology in Michael Almereyda's *Hamlet* (2000)." *Cinema Journal* 42 (2003): 48-69.

Burnett, Mark Thornton. "The 'Very Cunning of the Scene': Kenneth Branagh's *Hamlet*." *Literature/Film Quarterly* 25.2 (1997): 78-82.

Burnett, Mark T., and Ramona Wray, eds. *Shakespeare, Film, fin de siècle*. New York: Palgrave, 2000.

Burt, Richard. "Mobilizing Foreign Shakespeares in Media." *Shakespeare in Hollywood, Asia, and Cyberspace*. Ed. Alexander C.Y. Huang and Charles S. Ross. West Lafayette: Purdue UP, 2009. 231-38.

Burt, Richard. *Shakespeare after Mass-Media*. New York: Palgrave, 2002.

Burt, Richard. "Shakespeare and Asia in Postdiasporic Cinemas: Spin-offs and Citations of the Plays from Bollywood to Hollywood." *Shakespeare, the Movie II: Popularizing the Plays on Film, TV, and Video*. Ed. Richard Burt and Lynda Boose. New York: Routledge, 2003. 265-303.

Burt, Richard. "Shakespeare and the Holocaust: Julie Taymor's *Titus* is Beautiful, or, Shakesploi Meets (the) Camp." *Colby Quarterly* 37.1 (2001): 78-106.

Burt, Richard, ed. *Medieval and Early Modern Film and Media*. New York: Palgrave Macmillan, 2008.

Burt, Richard, ed. *Shakespeares after Shakespeare: An Encyclopedia of the Bard in Mass Media and Popular Culture*. Westport: Greenwood, 2007.

Butler, Martin. "Prospero in Cyberspace." *Re-Constructing the Book: Literary Texts in Transmission*. Ed. Maureen Bell, Shirley Chew, Simon Eliot, Lynette Hunter, and James L.W. West. Aldershot: Ashgate, 2001. 184-96.

Campbell, Kathleen. "Zeffirelli's *Hamlet*: Q1 in Performance." *Shakespeare on Film Newsletter* 16.1 (1991): 7-8.

Cardullo, Bert. "One Dramatic Character, Two Artistic Media: Shakespeare's *Falstaff* in Drama and Film." *Lamar Journal of the Humanities* 31.2 (2006): 43-68.

Caroti, Simone. "Science Fiction, *Forbidden Planet*, and *The Tempest*." *Shakespeare in Hollywood, Asia, and Cyberspace*. Ed. Alexander C.Y. Huang and Charles S. Ross. West Lafayette: Purdue UP, 2009. 218-30.

Cartelli, Thomas. *Repositioning Shakespeare: National Formations, Postcolonial Appropriations*. London: Routledge, 1999.

Cartelli, Thomas, and Katherine Rowe. *New Wave Shakespeare on Screen*. Cambridge: Polity, 2007.

Cartmell, Deborah, and Michael Scott, eds. *Talking Shakespeare: Shakespeare into the Millennium*. New York: Palgrave, 2001.

Cartmell, Deborah. *Interpreting Shakespeare on Screen*. New York: St. Martin's P, 2000.

CBEL Shakespeare (2008): <http://www.cbel.com/shakespeare/>.

Chaudhuri, Sukanta, and Chee Seng Lim, eds. *Shakespeare without English: The Reception of Shakespeare in Non-Anglophone Countries*. Delhi: Pearson/ Longman, 2006.

Coe, Jonathan. Rev. of Branagh's *Hamlet*. *New Statesman* (14 February 1997): 41.

Collick, John. *Shakespeare, Cinema and Society*. Manchester: Manchester UP, 1989.

Cook, Hardy M. "Jane Howell's BBC First Tetralogy: Theatrical and Televisual Manipulation." *Literature/Film Quarterly* 20 (1992): 326-31.

Coursen, Herb. *Teaching Shakespeare with Film and Television: A Guide*. Westport: Greenwood, 1997.

Crowdus, Gary. "Recent Shakespeare Films." *Cineaste* 23.4 (1998): 13-19.

Crowl, Samuel. "The Bow is Bent and Drawn: Kurosawa's *Ran* and the Shakespearean Arrow of Desire." *Film /Literature Quarterly* 22 (1994): 109-16.

Crowl, Samuel. "Communicating Shakespeare: An Interview with Kenneth Branagh." *Shakespeare Bulletin* 20.3 (2002): 24-28.

Crowl, Samuel. *The Films of Kenneth Branagh*. Westport: Praeger Publishers, 2006.

Crowl, Samuel. "Julie Taymor's Film of *Titus*." *Shakespeare Bulletin* 18 (2000): 46-47.

Crowl, Samuel. "The Marriage of Shakespeare and Hollywood: Kenneth Branagh's *Much Ado About Nothing*." *Spectacular Shakespeare: Critical Theory and Popular Cinema*. Ed. Courtney Lehmann and Lisa S. Starks. Madison: Fairleigh Dickinson UP, 2002. 111-24.

Crowl, Samuel. *Shakespeare and Film: A Norton Guide*. New York: Norton, 2007.

Crowl, Samuel. *Shakespeare at the Cineplex: The Kenneth Branagh Era*. Athens: Ohio UP, 2003.

Crowl, Samuel. *Shakespeare Observed: Studies in Performance on Stage and Screen*. Athens: Ohio UP, 1992.

Davies, Anthony, and Stanley Wells. *Shakespeare and the Moving Image: The Plays on Film and Television*. Cambridge: Cambridge UP, 1994.

Davies, Anthony. *Filming Shakespeare's Plays: The Adaptations of Laurence Olivier, Orson Welles, Peter Brook and Akira Kurosawa*. Cambridge: Cambridge UP, 1988.

Dawson, Anthony B. *Hamlet: Shakespeare in Performance*. Manchester: Manchester UP, 1995.

DeLuca, Maria, and Mary Lindroth. "Mayhem, Madness, Method: An Interview with Julie Taymor." *Cineaste* 25 (2000): 28-31.

Designing Shakespeare: An Audio Visual Archive, 1960-2000. Ed. Christie Carson. <http://ahds.ac.uk/performingarts/collections/designing-shakespeare.htm>.

Desmet, Christy, and Sujata Iyengar. "Appropriation and the Design of an Online Shakespeare Journal." *Shakespeare in Hollywood, Asia, and Cyberspace*. Ed. Alexander C.Y. Huang and Charles S. Ross. West Lafayette: Purdue UP, 2009. 239-51.

Desmet, Christy, and Robert Sawyer. *Shakespeare and Appropriation*. Ed. Christy Desmet and Robert Sawyer. London: Routledge, 1999.

Díaz-Fernández, José Ramón. "Shakespeare on Television: A Bibliography of Criticism." *Early Modern Literary Studies* 6.1 (2000): <http://purl.oclc.org/emls/06-1/diazbibl.htm>.

Dionne, Craig and Parmita Kapadia, eds. *Native Shakespeares: Indigenous Appropriations on a Global Stage*. Aldershot: Ashgate, 2008.

Donaldson, Peter. *Shakespearean Films / Shakespearean Directors*. Boston: Unwin Hyman, 1990.

Donaldson, Peter. "'All Which It Inherit': Shakespeare, Globes and Global Media." *Shakespeare Survey: An Annual Survey of Shakespeare Studies and Production*. 52 (1999): 183-200.

Donaldson, Peter. "Cinema and the Kingdom of Death: Loncraine's *Richard III*." *Shakespeare Quarterly* 53.2 (2002): 241-59.

Donaldson, Peter. "Digital Archive as Expanded Text: Shakespeare and Electronic Textuality." *Electronic Text: Investigations in Method and Theory*. Ed. Kathryn Sutherland. Oxford: Clarendon, 1997. 173-97.

Donaldson, Peter. "Game Space/Tragic Space: Julie Taymor's Titus." *A Companion to Shakespeare and Performance*. Ed. Barbara Hodgdon and W.B. Worthen. Oxford: Blackwell, 2005. 457-77.

Donaldson, Peter. "Taking on Shakespeare: Kenneth Branagh's *Henry V*." *Shakespeare Quarterly* 41 (1991): 60-71.

Edgerton, Ellen. "'Your Answer, Sir, Is Cinematical': Kenneth Branagh's *Much Ado About Nothing*." *Shakespeare Bulletin* 12.1 (1994): 42-44.

Esche, Edward J., ed. *Shakespeare and His Contemporaries in Performance*. Aldershot: Ashgate Publishing, 2002.

Fernie, Ewan, Ramona Wray, Mark Thornton Burnett and Clare McManus, eds. *Reconceiving the Renaissance: A Critical Reader*. Oxford: Oxford UP, 2005.

Fischer-Lichte, Erika, Josephine Riley, and Michael Gissenwehrer, eds. *The Dramatic Touch of Difference*. Tübingen: Gunter Narr, 1990.

Fotheringham, Richard, Christa Jansohn, and R.S. White, eds. *Shakespeare's World / World Shakespeares*. Newark: U of Delaware P, 2008.

French, Emma. *Selling Shakespeare to Hollywood: The Marketing of Filmed Shakespeare Adaptations from 1989 into the New Millennium*. Hatfield: U of Hertfordshire P, 2006.

Fujita, Minoru, and Michael Shapiro, eds. *Transvestism and the Onnagata Traditions in Shakespeare and Kabuki*. Folkestone: Global Oriental, 2006.

Fujita, Minoru, and Leonard C. Pronko. *Shakespeare East and West*. Richmond: Japan Library, 1996.

Gallimore, Daniel. "Shakespeare in Contemporary Japan." *Shakespeare in Hollywood, Asia, and Cyberspace*. Ed. Alexander C.Y. Huang and Charles S. Ross. West Lafayette: Purdue UP, 2009. 109-20.

Gallimore, Daniel. "Measuring Distance: Tsubouchi Shoyo and the Myth of Shakespeare Translation." *Translating Others*. Vol. 2. Ed. Theo Hermans. Manchester: St Jerome, 2006. 438-92.

Gerlach, John. "Shakespeare, Kurosawa and Macbeth: A Response to J. Blumenthal." *Literature/Film Quarterly* 1.4 (1973): 352-59.

Ghita, Lucian. "Aesthetics of Fragmentation in Taymor's *Titus*." *Shakespeare in Hollywood, Asia, and Cyberspace*. Ed. Alexander C.Y. Huang and Charles S. Ross. West Lafayette: Purdue UP, 2009. 207-17.

Ghita, Lucian and Alexander C.Y. Huang. "Bibliography of *Shakespeare in Hollywood, Asia, and Cyberspace*." *Shakespeare in Hollywood, Asia, and Cyberspace*. Ed. Alexander C.Y. Huang and Charles S. Ross. West Lafayette: Purdue UP, 2009. 275-287.

Gillies, John, Ryuta Minami, Ruru Li, and Poonam Trivedi. "Shakespeare on the Stages of Asia." *Cambridge Companion to Shakespeare on Stage*. Ed. Stanley Wells and Sarah Stanton. Cambridge: Cambridge UP, 2002. 259-83.

Green, William. "Falstaff the Braggart Samurai." *Shakespeare Bulletin* 12.1 (1994): 41.

Grehan, Helena. "Performed Promiscuities: Interpreting Interculturalism in the Japan Foundation Asia Centre's LEAR." *Intersections: Gender, History, and Culture in the Asian Context* 3 (2000): <http://wwwsshe.murdoch.edu.au/intersections/issue3/grehan.html>.

Halio, Jay. "Dreaming in Chinese." *Shakespeare in Performance: A Midsummer Night's Dream*. Manchester: Manchester UP, 2003. 173-83.

Halpern, Richard. *Shakespeare Among the Moderns*. Ithaca: Cornell UP, 1997.

Hamlet on the Ramparts. Ed. Peter S. Donaldson. (2008): <http://shea.mit.edu/ramparts/>.

HamletWorks. Ed. Bernice W. Kliman, Frank Nicholas Clary, Hardin Aasand, and Eric Rasmussen. (2008): <http://hamletworks.org/>.

Hapgood, Rovert. "Kurosawa's Shakespeare Films: *Throne of Blood*, *The Bad Sleep Well*, and *Ran*." *Shakespeare and the Moving Image: The Plays on Film and Television*. Ed. Anthony Davies and Stanley Wells. Cambridge: Cambridge UP, 1994.

Harner, James L., ed. *World Shakespeare Bibliography Online* (2008): <http://www.worldshakesbib.org>.

Harvey, Paul A.S. "Bunraku *Hamlet*." *Shakespeare Studies* 39 (2001): 59-79.

Hatchuel, Sarah. *Shakespeare: From Stage to Screen*. Cambridge: Cambridge UP, 2004.

Hatchuel, Sarah. *A Companion to the Shakespearean Films of Kenneth Branagh*. Winnipeg: Blizzard Publishing, 2000.

Hatchuel, Sarah. "Leading the Gaze: From Showing to Telling in Kenneth Branagh's *Henry V* and *Hamlet*." *Early Modern Literary Studies* 6.1 (2000): <http://www.shu.ac.uk/emls/06-1/hatchbra.htm>.

Henderson, Diana E., ed. *A Concise Companion to Shakespeare on Screen*. Oxford: Blackwell, 2006.

Henderson, Diana E. *Collaborations with the Past: Reshaping Shakespeare across Time and Media*. Ithaca: Cornell UP, 2006.

Hodgdon, Barbara. *The Shakespeare Trade: Performances and Appropriations.* Philadelphia: U of Philadelphia P, 1999.

Hodgdon, Barbara, and W.B. Worthen, eds. *A Companion to Shakespeare and Performance.* Oxford: Blackwell, 2005.

Holderness, Graham. *Visual Shakespeare: Essays in Film and Television.* Hatfield: U of Hertfordshire P, 2002.

Holderness, Graham, and Christopher McCullough. "A Selective Filmography." *Shakespeare and the Moving Image.* Ed. Anthony Davies and Stanley Wells. Cambridge: Cambridge UP, 1994. 18-49.

Holland, Peter. *English Shakespeares: Shakespeare on the English Stage in the 1990s.* Cambridge: Cambridge UP, 1997.

Holland, Peter. "Performing Shakespeare for the Web Community." *Shakespeare in Hollywood, Asia, and Cyberspace.* Ed. Alexander C.Y. Huang and Charles S. Ross. West Lafayette: Purdue UP, 2009. 252-62.

Holland, Peter, ed. *Shakespeare, Memory and Performance.* Cambridge: Cambridge UP, 2006.

Holste, Gayle. "Branagh's Labour's Lost: Too Much, Too Little, Too Late." *Literature / Film Quarterly* 30.3 (2002): 228-30.

Hopkins, Lisa. "'Denmark's a Prison': Branagh's *Hamlet* and the Paradoxes of Intimacy." *Entertext* 1.2 (2001): 226-46.

Hopkins, Lisa. "'A Tiger's Heart Wrapped in a Player's Hide': Julie Taymor's War Dances." *Shakespeare Bulletin: A Journal of Performance Criticism & Scholarship* 21 (2003): 61-69.

Howard, Tony. *Women as Hamlet: Performance and Interpretation in Theatre, Film and Fiction.* Cambridge: Cambridge UP, 2007.

Howlett, Kathy M. *Framing Shakespeare on Film.* Columbus: Ohio UP, 2000.

Hsiung, Yuwen. "Kurosawa's *Throne of Blood* and East Asia's *Macbeth.*" *Shakespeare in Hollywood, Asia, and Cyberspace.* Ed. Alexander C.Y. Huang and Charles S. Ross. West Lafayette: Purdue UP, 2009. 78-87.

Huang, Alexander C.Y. "Asian Shakespeares in Europe: From the Unfamiliar to the Defamiliarized." *The Shakespearean International Yearbook* 8 (2008): 51-70.

Huang, Alexander C.Y. *Chinese Shakespeares: Two Centuries of Cultural Exchange.* New York: Columbia UP, 2009.

Huang, Alexander C.Y. "A Chronology of Shakespeare in Hollywood, Asia, and Cyberspace." *Shakespeare in Hollywood, Asia, and Cyberspace.* Ed. Alexander C.Y. Huang and Charles S. Ross. West Lafayette: Purdue UP, 2009. 265-74.

Huang, Alexander C.Y. "Shakespeare, Performance, and Autobiographical Interventions." *Shakespeare Bulletin: A Journal of Performance Criticism and Scholarship* 24.2 (2006): 31-47.

Huang, Alexander C.Y. "Shakespearean Localities and the Localities of Shakespeare Studies." *Shakespeare Studies* 35 (2007): 186-204.

Huang, Alexander C.Y. "Site-Specific Hamlets and Reconfigured Localities: Jiang'an, Singapore, Elsinore." *The Shakespearean International Yearbook* 7 (2007): 22-48.

Huang, Alexander C.Y. "Shakespeare bunt geschminkt. Die chinesische Shakespeare-Werkstatt." *Lebendige Erinnerung—Xiqu. Zeitgenössische Entwicklungen im chinesischen Musiktheater*. Ed. Tian Mansha and Johannes Odenthal. Berlin: Verlag Theater der Zeit, 2006. 156-65.

Huang, Alexander C.Y. "*Shamlet*: Shakespeare as a Palimpsest." *Shakespeare Without English: The Reception of Shakespeare in Non-anglophone Countries*. Ed. Sukanta Chaudhuri and Chee Seng Lim. Delhi: Pearson/Longman, 2006. 21-45.

Huang, Alexander C.Y. "The Visualization of Metaphor in Two Chinese Versions of *Macbeth*." *Shakespeare in Hollywood, Asia, and Cyberspace*. Ed. Alexander C.Y. Huang and Charles S. Ross. West Lafayette: Purdue UP, 2009. 98-108.

Huang, Alexander C.Y. "Where is Shakespeare? Locality and Performative Translation." *Ilha do Desterro: A Journal of Language and Literature* 49 (2005): 255-64.

Internet Shakespeare (2008): <http://internetshakespeare.uvic.ca/index.html>.

Jackson, Russell, ed. *The Cambridge Companion to Shakespeare on Film*. Cambridge: Cambridge UP, 2000.

Jackson, Russell. *Shakespeare Films in the Making: Preparation, Production and Reception*. Cambridge: Cambridge UP, 2007.

Jin, Lei. "Silence and Sound in Kurosawa's *Throne of Blood*." *Shakespeare in Hollywood, Asia, and Cyberspace*. Ed. Alexander C.Y. Huang and Charles S. Ross. West Lafayette: Purdue UP, 2009. 88-97.

Johnson-Haddad, Miranda. "A Time for *Titus*: An Interview with Julie Taymor." *Shakespeare Bulletin* 18 (2000): 33-37.

Jorgens, Jack J. "Kurosawa's *Throne of Blood*: Washizu and Miki Meet the Forest Spirit." *Literature-Film Quarterly* 66 (1983): 167-73.

Jorgens, Jack J. *Shakespeare on Film*. Bloomington: Indiana UP, 1977.

Keller, James, and Leslie Stratyner, eds. *Almost Shakespeare: Reinventing His Works for Cinema and Television*. Jefferson: McFarland & Co., 2004.

Kennedy, Dennis. *Foreign Shakespeare: Contemporary Performance*. Cambridge: Cambridge UP, 1993.

Kennedy, Dennis. *Looking at Shakespeare: A Visual History of Twentieth-Century Performance*. Cambridge: Cambridge UP, 1993.

Kishi, Tetsuo, and Graham Bradshaw, eds. *Shakespeare in Japan*. London: Continuum, 2005.

Kishi, Tetsuo, Roger Pringle, and Stanley Wells, eds. *Shakespeare and Cultural Traditions*. Newark: U of Delaware P, 1994.

Klein, Holger, and Dimiter Daphinoff, eds. *Hamlet on Screen. Shakespeare Yearbook* 8 (1997).

Kobayashi, Kaori. "Touring in Asia: The Miln Company's Shakespearean Productions in Japan." *Shakespeare and His Contemporaries in Performance*. Ed. Edward J. Esche. Aldershot: Ashgate, 2000. 53-72.

Krontiris, Tina, and Jyotsna Singh, eds. *Shakespeare Worldwide and the Idea of an Audience*. Special issue *Journal of Theory and Criticism* 15 (2007).

Kurosawa, Akira. *Something Like an Autobiography*. Trans. Audie Bock. New York: Vintage, 1983.

Lee, Adele. "*One Husband Too Many* and the Problem of Postcolonial Hong Kong." *Shakespeare in Hollywood, Asia, and Cyberspace*. Ed. Alexander C.Y. Huang and Charles S. Ross. West Lafayette: Purdue UP, 2009. 195-202.

Lee, Meewon. "*Hamlet* in Korea." *Shakespeare in Hollywood, Asia, and Cyberspace*. Ed. Alexander C.Y. Huang and Charles S. Ross. West Lafayette: Purdue UP, 2009. 129-38.

Lehmann, Courtney. "Dancing in a (Cyber) Net: 'Renaissance Women,' Systems Theory, and the War of the Cinemas." *Renaissance Drama* 34 (2005): 121-61.

Lehmann, Courtney, and Lisa. S. Starks, eds. *Spectacular Shakespeare: Critical Theory and Popular Cinema*. Madison: Fairleigh Dickinson UP, 2001.

Levith, Murray J. *Shakespeare in China*. London: Continuum, 2004.

Li, Ruru. *Shashibiya: Staging Shakespeare in China*. Hong Kong: Hong Kong UP, 2003.

Li, Ruru: "Shakespeare on the Chinese Stage in the 1990s." *Shakespeare Quarterly* 50.3 (1999): 355-67.

Li, Ruru: "The Bard in the Middle Kingdom." *Asian Theatre Journal* 12.1 (1995): 50-84.

Library of Congress. *Shakespeare on Film and Television* (2002): <http://www.loc.gov/rr/mopic/findaid/willfilm.html>.

Lindroth, Mary. "'Some device of further misery': Taymor's *Titus* Brings Shakespeare to Film Audiences with a Twist." *Literature/Film Quarterly* 29.2 (2001): 106-15.

Manheim, Michael. "The Function of Battle Imagery in Kurosawa's Histories and the *Henry V* Film." *Film /Literature Quarterly* 22 (1994): 129-35.

Maori Merchant of Venice (2008): <http://homepages.ihug.co.nz/~hetaonga/merchant/>.

Massai, Sonia, ed. *World-Wide Shakespeares: Local Appropriations in Film and Performance*. London: Routledge, 2006.

McCandless, David. "A Tale of Two *Titus*es: Julie Taymor's Vision on Stage and Screen." *Shakespeare Quarterly* 53 (2002): 487-511.

McClain, Bill. *Shakespeare on Film and Video* (2003): <http://home.salamander.com/~wmcclain/ws-movies.html>.

McCombe, John P. "Toward an Objective Correlative: The Problem of Desire in Franco Zeffirelli's *Hamlet*." *Literature-Film Quarterly* 25.2 (1997): 125-31.

Minami, Ryuta, Ian Carruthers, and John Gillies, eds. *Performing Shakespeare in Japan*. Cambridge: Cambridge UP, 2001.

Mou, Xianfeng. "Cultural Anxiety and the Female Body in Zeffirelli's *Hamlet*." *Shakespeare in Hollywood, Asia, and Cyberspace*. Ed. Alexander C.Y. Huang and Charles S. Ross. West Lafayette: Purdue UP, 2009. 54-63.

Niki, Hisae. "Kurosawa's *Kumonosujo*: A Japanese *Macbeth*." *Shakespeare Studies* 7 (1968-69): 33-60.

No Sweat Shakespeare (2008): <http://www.nosweatshakespeare.com/>.

Orkin, Martin. *Local Shakespeares: Proximations and Power*. London: Routlegde, 2005.

Osborne, Laurie. "Clip Art: Theorizing the Shakespeare Film Clip." *Shakespeare Quarterly* 53 (2002): 227-40.

Palmer, Chris. "'What Tongue Shall Smooth Thy Name?' Recent Films of *Romeo and Juliet*." *The Cambridge Quarterly*. 32.1 (2003): 61-76.

Parker, Barry M. *The Folger Shakespeare Filmography*. Washington: Folger Books, 1979.

Petersen, Robert S. *MATA: Modern Asian Theatre Archive* (2002): <http://www.ux1.eiu.edu/~cfrp1/MATA/index.html>.

Peterson, William. "Consuming the Asian Other in Singapore: Interculturalism in TheatreWorks' Desdemona." *Theatre Research International* 28:1 (2003): 79-95.

Phelan, Peggy. *Unmarked: The Politics of Performance*. London: Routledge, 1993.

Pilkington, Ace. *Screening Shakespeare from Richard II to Henry V*. Newark: U Delaware P, 1991.

The Poor Yorick Shakespeare Multimedia Catalogue (2004): <http://www.bardcentral.com>.

Prince, Stephen. *The Warrior's Camera: The Cinema of Akira Kurosawa*. Princeton: Princeton UP, 1991.

Pun, Tzoh Wah. "Shakespeare and the Function of Art." *Southeast Asia Review of English* 14 (1987): 68-84.

Quigley, Daniel. "'Double Exposure': The Semiotic Ramifications of Mel Gibson in Zeffirelli's *Hamlet*." *Shakespeare Bulletin* 11.1 (1993): 38-39.

Quinn, Edward. "Zeffirelli's *Hamlet*." *Shakespeare on Film Newsletter* 15.2 (1990): 1-2, 12.

Reeves, Geoffrey. "Finding Shakespeare on Film: From an Interview with Peter Brook." *Film Theory and Criticism: Introductory Readings*. Ed. Gerald Mast and Marshall Cohen. New York: Oxford UP, 1974. 234-49.

Reuck, Jenny de. "The Mirror Shattered into Tiny Pieces': Reading Gender and Culture in the Japan Foundation Asia Centre's LEAR." *Intersections: Gender, History, and Culture in the Asian Context* 3 (2000): <http://wwwsshe.murdoch.edu.au/intersections/issue3/jenny3.html>.

Richie, Donald. *The Films of Akira Kurosawa*. Berkeley: U California P, 1984.

Richie, Donald. *A Hundred Years of Japanese Film*. Tokyo: Kodansha International, 2002.

Ross, Charles S. "Underwater Women in Shakespeare on Film." *Shakespeare in Hollywood, Asia, and Cyberspace*. Ed. Alexander C.Y. Huang and Charles S. Ross. West Lafayette: Purdue UP, 2009. 36-53.

Rothwell, Kenneth S., and Annabelle H. Melzer. *Shakespeare on Screen: An International Filmography and Videography*. New York: Neal Schuman, 1991.

Royal Shakespeare Company Exploring Shakespeare (2008): <http://www.rsc.org.uk/learning/Learning.aspx>.

Rowe, Katherine. "Medium-Specificity and Other Critical Scripts for Screen Shakespeare." *Alternative Shakespeare 3*. Ed. Diana E. Henderson. London: Routledge, 2008. 34-53.

Rutter, Carol Chillington. "Watching Ourselves Watching Shakespeare-Or-How Am I Supposed to Look?" *Shakespeare Bulletin: A Journal of Performance Criticism and Scholarship* 25.4 (2007): 47-68.

Rutter, Carol Chillington. "Looking Like a Child, or, *Titus*: The Comedy." *Shakespeare Survey: An Annual Survey of Shakespeare Studies and Production* 56 (2003): 1-26.

Rutter, Carol Chillington. "Snatched Bodies: Ophelia in the Grave." *Shakespeare Quarterly* 49.3 (1998): 299-319.

Sammons, Eddie. *Shakespeare: A Hundred Years on Film*. London: Shepheard-Walwyn, 2000.

Sasayama, Takahashi, J.R. Mulryne, and Margaret Shrewing, eds. *Shakespeare and the Japanese Stage*. Cambridge: Cambridge UP, 1998.

Senda, Akihiko. *The Voyage of Japanese Theatre*. Trans. Thomas Rimer. Hawaii: U of Hawaii P, 1997.

Schechner, Richard. "Julie Taymor, from Jacques Lecoq to *The Lion King*." *TDR: The Drama Review* 43 (1999): 36-55.

Bibliography Shakespeare on Film & Video. (2008): <http://www.lib.berkeley.edu/MRC/ShakespeareBib.html>.

Shakespeare Performance in Asia. (2008): <http://web.mit.edu/shakespeare/asia/>.

SHAKSPER's Selected Guide to Shakespeare on the Internet (2008): <http://www.shaksper.net/archives/files/internet.sites.html>.

Sh:in:E—Shakespeare in Europe (2008): <http://pages.unibas.ch/shine/>.

Shaughnessy, Robert. *The Shakespeare Effect: A History of Twentieth-Century Performance*. New York: Palgrave, 2002.

Shaughnessy, Robert. *Shakespeare on Film: Contemporary Critical Essays*. New York: St. Martin's P, 1998.

Sheppard, Philippa. "The Castle of Elsinore: Gothic Aspects of Kenneth Branagh's *Hamlet*." *Shakespeare Bulletin* 19.3 (2001): 36-39.

Shin, Jungok. *Shakespeare Came to Korea*. Seoul: Baeksin Publisher, 1998.

Stanford University. *Shakespeare in Asia* (2008): <http://sia.stanford.edu>.

Starks, Lisa S., and Courtney Lehmann. *The Reel Shakespeare: Alternative Cinema and Theory*. Madison: Fairleigh Dickinson UP, 2002.

Stokes, Lisa Odham, and Michael Hoover. *City on Fire: Hong Kong Cinema*. London: Verso, 1999.

Stone, James W. "Black and White as Technique in Orson Welles' *Othello*." *Literature/Film Quarterly* 30.2 (2002): 189-93.

Su, Periui. "Method Acting and Pacino's *Looking for Richard*." *Shakespeare in Hollywood, Asia, and Cyberspace*. Ed. Alexander C.Y. Huang and Charles S. Ross. West Lafayette: Purdue UP, 2009. 26-53.

Suematsu, Michiko. "The Tokyo Globe Years 1988-2002." *Shakespeare in Hollywood, Asia, and Cyberspace*. Ed. Alexander C.Y. Huang and Charles S. Ross. West Lafayette: Purdue UP, 2009. 121-28.

Suzuki, Masae. "*Noh, Kyōgen*, and *Okinawa Shibai*." *Shakespeare in Hollywood, Asia, and Cyberspace*. Ed. Alexander C.Y. Huang and Charles S. Ross. West Lafayette: Purdue UP, 2009. 152-65.

Tam, Kwok-kan, Andrew Parkin, and Terry Siu-han Yip, eds. *Shakespeare Global/ Local: The Hong Kong Imaginary in Transcultural Production*. Frankfurt: Peter Lang, 2002.

Tatlow, Antony. *Shakespeare, Brecht, and the Intercultural Sign*. Durham: Duke UP, 2001.

Taymor, Julie. "Interview: Julie Taymor, Theater, Opera and Film Director." *Academy of Achievement* (3 June 2006): <http://www.achievement.org/autodoc/printmember/tay0int-1>.

Taymor, Julie. *Titus*: *The Illustrated Screenplay, Adapted from the Play by William Shakespeare*. New York: Newmarket P, 2000.

Taymor, Julie. "Working with Puppets." *Conversations on Art and Performance*. Ed. Bonnie Marranca and Gautam Dasgupta. Baltimore: Johns Hopkins UP, 1999. 467-70.

Thompson, Ann. "Kurosawa's *Ran*: Reception and Interpretation." *East-West Film Journal* 3 (1989): 5.

Tibbetts, John. "Breaking the Classical Barrier: Franco Zeffirelli Interviewed by John Tibbetts." *Film /Literature Quarterly* 22 (1994): 136-40.

Trivedi, Harish. "The Anglophone Shakespeare: The Non-Anglophone Shakespeare." *Shakespeare without English: The Reception of Shakespeare in Non-Anglophone Countries*. Ed. Sukanta Chaudhuri and Chee Seng Lim. Delhi: Longman Pearson, 2006. 192-208.

Ueno, Yoshiko, ed. *Hamlet and Japan*. New York: AMS P, 1995.

Vaughan, Virginia Mason. "Looking at the 'Other' in Julie Taymor's *Titus*." *Shakespeare Bulletin: A Journal of Performance Criticism & Scholarship* 21 (2003): 71-80.

Walker, Elsie. "'Now Is a Time to Storm': Julie Taymor's *Titus*." *Literature/Film Quarterly* 30 (2002): 194-207.

Weller, Philip. "Freud's Footprints in Films of *Hamlet*." *Literature/Film Quarterly* 25 (1997): 119-24.

Wells, Stanley, and Sarah Stanton, eds. *The Cambridge Companion to Shakespeare on Stage*. Cambridge: Cambridge UP, 2002.

Welsh, James M., and Peter Lev, eds. *The Literature/Film Reader: Issues of Adaptation*. Lanham: Scarecrow P, 2007.

Welsh, James M. *Shakespeare into Film*. New York: Checkmark Books-Facts on File, 2002.

Wetmore, Kevin J. Jr. "Samritechak and Intercultural Shakespeare in Cambodia." *Shakespeare in Hollywood, Asia, and Cyberspace*. Ed. Alexander C.Y. Huang and Charles S. Ross. West Lafayette: Purdue UP, 2009. 166-71.

Wichmann, Elizabeth. *Listening to Theater: The Aural Dimension of Beijing Opera*. Honolulu: U of Hawaii P, 1991.

Wichmann, Elizabeth. "'Reform' at the Shanghai Jingju Company and Its Impact on Creative Authority and Repertory." *The Drama Review* 44.4 (2000): 96-119.

Wichmann-Walczak, Elizabeth. "Remembering the Past in the Shanghai Jingju Company's *King Lear*" *Shakespeare in Hollywood, Asia, and Cyberspace*. Ed. Alexander C.Y. Huang and Charles S. Ross. West Lafayette: Purdue UP, 2009. 183-94.

Willson, Robert F., Jr. "Kenneth Branagh's *Hamlet*; Or, the Revenge of Fortinbras." *The Shakespeare Newsletter* 47 (1997): 7-9.

Winet, Evan Darwin. "Spectres of *Hamlet* in Colonial and Postcolonial Indonesia." *Shakespeare in Hollywood, Asia, and Cyberspace*. Ed. Alexander C.Y. Huang and Charles S. Ross. West Lafayette: Purdue UP, 2009. 172-82.

Wong, Dorothy. "'Domination by Consent': A Study of Shakespeare in Hong Kong." *Studies in Comparative Literature* 26.2 (2000): 43-56.

Worthen, W.B. "Shakespeare 3.0: Or Text versus Performance, the Remix." *Alternative Shakespeare 3*. Ed. Diana E. Henderson. London: Routledge, 2008. 54-77.

Worthen, W.B. *Shakespeare and the Force of Modern Performance*. Cambridge: Cambridge UP, 2003.

Yang, Daniel S.P. "Shakespeare at the Hong Kong Repertory Theater." *Shakespeare Global/Local: The Hong Kong Imaginary in Transcultural Production*. Ed. Kwok-kan Tam, Andrew Parkin, and Terry Siu-han Yip. Bern: Peter Lang, 2002. 75-86.

Yau, Esther C.M., ed. *At Full Speed: Hong Kong Cinema in a Borderless World*. Minneapolis: U Minnesota P, 2001.

Yong, Li Lan. "Ong Keng Sen's *Desdemona*, Ugliness, and the Intercultural Performative." *Theatre Journal* 56.2 (2004): 251-73.

Yong, Li Lan. "Shakespeare as Virtual Event." *Theatre Research International* 28.1 (2003): 46-60.

Yoshimoto, Mitsuhiro. *Kurosawa: Film Studies and Japanese Cinema*. Durham: Duke UP, 2000.

Zambrano, Ana Laura. "*Throne of Blood*: Kurosawa's *Macbeth*." *Literature/Film Quarterly* 2.3 (1974): 262-74.

Zarilli, Philip B. "For Whom is the King a King: Issues of Intercultural Production, Perception, and Reception in a *Kathakali King Lear*." *Critical Theory and Performance*. Ed. Janelle G. Reinelt and Joseph R. Roach. Ann Arbor: U of Michigan P, 1992. 16-40.

Zhu, Mei. "Shakespeare's *Taming of the Shrew* and Screwball Comedy." *Shakespeare in Hollywood, Asia, and Cyberspace*. Ed. Alexander C.Y. Huang and Charles S. Ross. West Lafayette: Purdue UP, 2009. 17-25.

Contributors' Profiles

Nurul Farhana Low bt Abdullah is completing her Ph.D. literature at the University of Malaya. Abdullah was an ASEAN Research Fellow at the National University of Singapore in 2004 and she is a fellow with the Academic Staff Training Program of the University of Science Malaysia in Penang.

David Bevington has written or edited more than thirty volumes on Shakespeare and his contemporaries. His books include *From "Mankind" to Marlowe: Growth of Structure in the Popular Drama of Tudor England* (1962), *Tudor Drama and Politics: A Critical Approach to Topical Meaning* (1968), *Action Is Eloquence: Shakespeare's Language of Gesture* (1984), *Shakespeare: The Seven Ages of Human Experience* (2002), *This Wide and Universal Theater: Shakespeare in Performance, Then and Now* (2007). He has edited *Medieval Drama* (1975), *Bantam Shakespeare*, in 29 paperback volumes (1988), and *The Complete Works of Shakespeare* (1992).

Richard Burt teaches English literature and film and media studies at the University of Florida. His books include *Medieval and Early Modern Film and Media* (2008), *Unspeakable ShaXXXspeares: Queer Theory and American Kiddie Culture* (1998, 1999), and *Licensed by Authority: Ben Jonson and the Discourses of Censorship* (1993), and he is editor or co-editor of *Shakespeares After Shakespeare: An Encyclopedia of the Bard in Mass Media and Popular Culture* (2006), *Shakespeare After Mass Media* (2002), *The Administration of Aesthetics: Censorship, Political Criticism, and the Public Sphere* (1994), *Enclosure Acts: Sexuality, Property, and Culture in Early Modern England* (1994), *Shakespeare the Movie: Popularizing the Plays on Film, TV, and Video* (1997), and *Shakespeare the Movie, II: Popularizing the Plays on Film, TV, Video, and DVD* (2003). He is currently writing a book on *Macbeth* film adaptations and another book entitled *Alluding to Shakespeare: The Remains of the Plays in Transnational Cinema and Media.*

Simone Caroti teaches in the English Department at Purdue University. He graduated in Anglo-American literature at the University of Trieste in 2002 with a thesis on H.P. Lovecraft's geography of the fantastic and recently completed his dissertation, *The Generation Starship in Science Fiction, 1934-1977.*

Christy Desmet teaches English literature at the University of Georgia. Her book publications include *Reading Shakespeare's Characters: Rhetoric, Ethics, and Identity* (1992) and its online version with netLibrary (2000). Desmet co-edited with Robert Sawyer two books, *Shakespeare and Appropriation* (1999) and *Harold Bloom's Shakespeare* (2001). She is founding co-editor with Sujata Iyengar of *Borrowers and Lenders: The Journal of Shakespeare and Appropriation* <http://www.borrowers.uga.edu>.

Daniel Gallimore teaches English literature at Nihon Joshi Daigaku (Women's University). He writes in English and Japanese on various aspects of the reception of Shakespeare in Japan and his recent publications include translations of modern Japanese drama. He is currently researching the work of Tsubouchi Shōyō, the pioneer of Shakespeare studies and translation in early twentieth-century Japan.

Lucian Ghita is working towards his Ph.D. in comparative literature at Yale University. In his research, Ghita focuses on the drama of Shakespeare and his contemporaries, French avant-garde theater, critical theory and performance, early modern cross-cultural encounters, and Shakespeare on stage and screen. He has published articles in *CLCWeb: Comparative Literature and Culture*, *Literature Compass*, *Prose Studies*, and the *Shakespeare Yearbook*.

Peter Holland teaches in the Department of Film, Television, and Theatre at the University of Notre Dame. He is editor of *Shakespeare Survey*, co-editor with Stanley Wells of *Oxford Shakespeare Topics*, and co-editor with Adrian Poole of *Great Shakespeareans*. Among recent books, he edited *Shakespeare, Memory and Performance* (2006) and a five-volume series for Palgrave, *Redefining British Theatre History* (2003-07). He is currently completing his edition of *Coriolanus* for the Arden Shakespeare series. He was Director of the Shakespeare Institute and Professor of Shakespeare Studies at the University of Birmingham (1997-2002).

Yuwen Hsiung teaches in the Department of Modern Languages and Literatures at Swarthmore College. She received her Ph.D.in comparative literature from Purdue University in 2007 with a dissertation entitled *Expressionism and Its Deformation in Contemporary Chinese Theatre*. Her recent publication is on contemporary Chinese theater published in *Asian Theatre Journal.*

Alexander C.Y. Huang teaches comparative literature at the Pennsylvania State University. He is Research Affiliate in Literature at the Massachusetts Institute of Technology. He is the author of *Chinese Shakespeares: Two Centuries of Cultural Exchange* (2009), co-editor of *Class, Boundary, and Social Discourse in the Renaissance* (2007), guest editor of a film review cluster for *Borrowers and Lenders: The Journal of Shakespeare and Appropriation* <http://www.borrowers.uga.edu>, video curator for an exhibition at the Folger Shakespeare Library (2009), and core collaborator of *Shakespeare Performance in Asia*, an online video archive < http://web.mit.edu/shakespeare/asia/ >. He has contributed to *MLQ: Modern Language Quarterly, Shakespeare Bulletin, The Shakespearean International Yearbook, Shakespeare Studies, Asian Theatre Journal, Archiv für das Studium der neueren Sprachen und Literaturen*, and other journals and collections.

Sujata Iyengar teaches English literature of the Renaissance at the University of Georgia. She is founding co-editor with Christy Desmet of *Borrowers and Lenders:*

The Journal of Shakespeare and Appropriation <http://www.borrowers.uga.edu>. Her publications include *Shades of Difference: Mythologies of Skin Color in Early Modern England* (2005) and her articles on early modern race, sexuality, and embodiment appeared in *ELH* (2002), *Literature/Film Quarterly* (2001), and *MaRDiE* (2007). She has also published articles in the collected volumes *Senses of Touch* (2003), *Othello: New Critical Essays* (2001), *Color-blind Shakespeare* (2006), and in the Folger Shakespeare Library's exhibition catalogue, *Voices for Tolerance in an Age of Persecution* (2004). Currently, she conducts research at the Folger Shakespeare Library for a new book, *Shakespeare's Medical Language*.

Lei Jin recently completed her Ph.D. in comparative literature at Purdue University. Her interests include eighteen-century Chinese, US-American, and Japanese supernatural stories, and translation. She teaches Chinese at the University of Charleston.

Adele Lee is working towards her Ph.D. in English at the Queen's University Belfast. In her research, Lee's interests include the early modern encounter between England and the Far East and the reception of Shakespeare in contemporary China and Japan. Lee has published book reviews in *Theatre Research International* and *The Modern Language Review* and is currently working for an online database as part of an AHRC funded project entitled *Filming and Performing Renaissance History, 1500-1660*.

Meewon Lee received her Ph.D at the University of Pittsburgh in 1983 and teaches theater studies and drama at Korean National University of the Arts. She is Vice President of Korean Theatre Studies Association (since 2005). Lee has published books and articles in Korean on playwrights and theaters in Korea.

Xianfeng Mou is completing her Ph.D. in comparative literature at Purdue University with a dissertation entitled *One Hundred Years' of Solitary Light: Rites of Passage for Modern American and Modern Chinese Women Writers (1899-1996)*. Her areas of interest include Modern American Literature, Modern Chinese Literature, Aesthetics, and Women's Studies. Prior to her graduate work at Purdue, Mou was an editor at the China International Publishing Group.

Charles S. Ross teaches comparative literature at Purdue University. His books include the first translation of Boiardo's *Orlando Innamorato* (1989), *The Custom of the Castle from Malory to Macbeth* (1997), *Elizabethan Literature and the Law of Fraudulent Conveyance: Sidney, Spenser, Shakespeare* (2003), and a verse translation of Statius's *Thebaid* (2004). Ross is co-editor of *Fortune and Romance: Boiardo 1994 in America* (1998), *Lectura Dantis: Inferno* (1998), and *Purgatorio* (2008). He has published articles in *Modern Philology*, *MLN*, *Italica*, *Philological Quarterly*, *Prose Studies*, *Comparative Literature and Culture*, and other journals and edited collections, including *Milton in Italy* (1991) and *The Law in Shakespeare* (2007). Ross has lectured on *The Taming of the Shrew* at universities in Shanghai and Wuhan, and he gave the first introduction to Boiardo ever heard in Taipei, R.C. His article on Boiardo and Marco Polo, read as a paper at Ningbo Da Xue, P.R. China, is forthcoming.

Peirui Su is completing her Ph.D. in comparative literature at Purdue University with a dissertation entitled *Epiphany in Joyce and Fei Ming*. Her areas of research include Shakespeare, Joyce, film studies, and modern Chinese literature.

Michiko Suematsu teaches English literature at Gunma University. Her recent publications include "Shakespeare à la Carte: Shakespearian Themes in Films, Adaptations, Fine Arts and Music," *On the Way to Shakespeare* (1998), "The Remarkable Licence: Shakespeare on the Recent Japanese Stage," *Shakespeare Yearbook* (1999), and "Innovation and Continuity: Two Decades of Deguchi Norio's Shakespeare Theatre Company," *Performing Shakespeare in Japan* (2001).

Masae Suzuki teaches English at Kyoto Sangyo University. She is also a member of the "Noh Macbeth" project of the Research Institute of Japanese Culture at Hagoromo International University, Osaka. Her papers on Asian reception of Shakespeare include "The Rose and the Bamboo: Noda Hideki' s *Sandaime Richaado*," *Performing Shakespeare in Japan* (2001), "Three Japanese Othellos," *Shakespeare Global/ Local The Hong Kong Imaginary in Transcultural Production* (2002) and a report to the Japanese Ministry of Education for the Grant-in-Aid Research Project for Scientific Research entitled "The Reception and Production of Shakespeare in Asia: Focusing on Mainland Japan and Okinawa" (2004).

Elizabeth Wichmann-Walczak teaches theater at the University of Hawaii where she also directs the Asian Theatre Program. She has published extensively on the performance structure and aesthetics of Chinese theater and has translated and directed one modern, one "newly-written historical" and four classical *jingju* plays at the University of Hawaii. Her book publications include *Listening to Theatre: The Aural Dimension of Beijing Opera* (1991) and *The Phoenix Returns to Its Nest* (1986). Her articles have been published in various journals such as *The Drama Review* and in books including *Three Kingdoms and Chinese Culture* (2007), *Diasporas and Interculturalism in Asian Performing Arts* (2005), and *Chinese Aesthetics and Literature* (2004). She is a founding editor and the current China editor of the *Asian Theatre Journal.*

Evan Darwin Winet is an independent scholar based in Berkeley, California. His book, *Indonesian Postcolonial Theatre: Spectral Genealogies and Absent Faces* (2009), is a critical history of that country's modern theater and drama. He has also published articles in *Staging Nationalism* (2005) and *Writing and Rewriting National Theatre Histories* (2004). His translations of several modern Indonesian plays into English are forthcoming in the *Lontar Anthology of Indonesian Drama*. Winet is contributing editor on Asian drama to the *Norton Anthology of Drama* and to the *Encyclopedia of Asian Theatre*.

Mei Zhu teaches British and US-American literature at Huaqiao University. Most of her research centers around literary theory, comparative literature, and US-American literature. Zhu has published a number of articles on Toni Morrison and Don DeLillo in Chinese journals such as *Foreign Literature Review*.

Index